Solarizing the Moon

Solarizing the Moon

Essays in honour of Lionel Sims

Edited by

Fabio Silva and Liz Henty

ARCHAEOPRESS ARCHAEOLOGY

ARCHAEOPRESS PUBLISHING LTD
Summertown Pavilion
18-24 Middle Way
Summertown
Oxford OX2 7LG
www.archaeopress.com

ISBN 978-1-80327-112-5
ISBN 978-1-80327-113-2 (e-Pdf)

Contents

Part III: Theory

Contributors

Nicholas Campion
Associate Professor in Cosmology and Culture
Director, Sophia Centre for the Study of Cosmology in Culture
University of Wales Trinity Saint David, United Kingdom
n.campion@uwtsd.ac.uk

David Fisher
Independent Scholar
docfishers@gmail.com

A. César González-García
Institute of Heritage Sciences INCIPIT-CSIC
Santiago de Compostela, Spain
a.cesar.gonzalez-garcia@incipit.csic.es

John Grigsby
Independent Scholar
grigsby_john@hotmail.com

Liz Henty
Honorary Research Fellow
Sophia Centre for the Study of Cosmology in Culture
University of Wales Trinity Saint David, United Kingdom
lizhenty2@gmail.com

Chris Knight
Emeritus Professor of Anthropology
Department of Anthropology
University College London, United Kingdom
chris.knight@live.com

J. McKim Malville
Emeritus Professor
Department of Astrophysical and Planetary Science
University of Colorado, United States of America
kim.malville@colorado.edu

Estelle Orrelle
University of East London, United Kingdom
estelleorrelle@gmail.com

Emília Pásztor
Türr István Museum
Baja, Hungary
pasztoremilia@tolna.net

Camilla Power
Honorary Research Fellow
Department of Anthropology
University College London, United Kingdom
camilla.power@gmail.com

Michael A. Rappenglück
Adult Education Centre and Observatory
Gilching, Germany
mr@infis.org

Fabio Silva
Department of Archaeology & Anthropology
Bournemouth University, United Kingdom
fsilva@bournemouth.ac.uk

Ian Watts
Independent scholar
ochrewatts@hotmail.com

Introduction: Lionel's Legacy

Fabio Silva and Liz Henty

The study of prehistoric monuments has long been the domain of archaeologists who excavate, measure, date, record and interpret them. Archaeoastronomers, on the other hand, have provided a different picture based on their belief that the builders understood celestial movements and consequently enshrined astronomical alignments into their monuments. This picture was hotly contested by most archaeologists in the 1960s and 1970s and the two fields, archaeology and archaeoastronomy, largely went their separate ways in the 1980s (Henty 2020; Hutton 2013). One of the scholars who broke this stalemate was Lionel Sims who, as an anthropologist, had a wealth of ethnographic material to draw from, allowing him to re-envision archaeoastronomy from an interdisciplinary perspective.

Lionel Sims, Professor Emeritus of Anthropology at the University of East London, produced an influential body of work which has challenged both existing narratives about British prehistoric monuments and, equally importantly, the way archaeoastronomy has been done in the past. His work was not without controversy, but his unique approaches and thought-provoking conclusions have had an impact on the thinking of students and colleagues. To celebrate his achievements and legacy, this *festschrift* publishes contributions from colleagues that extend and contextualise his research and theoretical advancements. This introduction presents a summary of what we perceive to be Lionel's most enduring contributions to the field of archaeoastronomy, namely his concept of the solarisation of the Moon, his theoretical advancements and his commitment to education.

Solarization of the Moon

Our first meeting with Lionel was at the seventh annual Sophia Conference at Bath, 'Cosmologies', 6th – 7th June, 2009 at the Bath Royal Literary and Scientific Institute. As the programme advertised, presentations were centred around answering the question, 'how do we human beings relate to the cosmos?' (Campion 2009: 2). Given the wide nature of the question, subjects discussed included 'Calendars and Divination in the Dead Sea Scrolls', 'The Beltane Fire Festival', 'Cyberspace and the Sacred Sky' and 'Northern European Cosmologies of the Tree and the Well'. As part of this eclectic mix Lionel's talk was 'Stonehenge decoded: the conflation of winter solstice with the southern minor standstill moonsets'. You couldn't have heard a pin drop, partly because of the nature of the material which favoured a new interpretation of Britain's most iconic monument, suggesting that there was an emphasis on winter over summer, settings over risings and Dark Moon over Full Moon, and partly because he was such a charismatic speaker. The content of his talk was controversial for two reasons: firstly, it countered the 'official' version relating to summer solstice sunrise at Stonehenge – 'At Stonehenge on the summer solstice, the sun rises behind the Heel Stone in the north-east part of the horizon and its first rays shine into the heart of Stonehenge' (English Heritage, 2020), where the winter solstice takes second place. Secondly, few in the audience would have been aware of the significance of the Dark Moon in anthropology unless they were familiar with the sex-strike theory of Chris Knight ([1991] 1995) that underpinned Lionel's model of Stonehenge.

Liz: Shocked into silence we broke for lunch. The conference ended with a panel discussion hosted by the Sophia Centre's director of studies, Nicholas Campion, and other panel members including Patrick Curry, Ronald Hutton and Lionel Sims. This was my first academic conference and I certainly wasn't prepared for the combative nature of the panel discussion, nor the rudeness (in my mind) that was extended to Lionel. I was so shocked that I sought him out at the end of the day to apologise or at least extend my sympathies. He just laughed and said that the level of criticism directed at his ideas was normal. Of course, this was because he was ahead of the times and his work in archaeoastronomy had yet to be appreciated. We got talking and it turned out that we had both been at the London School of Economics around the same time. I had taken anthropology as part of my sociology degree and we laughed at some of the reading material we had shared, even remembering the quote from Wittfogel's *Oriental Despotism* (1957), 'absolute power corrupts absolutely'. A friendship was formed.

In his talk Lionel discussed what was to become the concept that he was most famous for, and that from which this volume takes its title, the '*solarization of the Moon*' (Sims 2006). In his paper on Stonehenge, where he first developed this idea, Lionel summarised it as the 'religious substitution to mimic and estrange Palaeolithic hunters' lunar motifs into an emerging Mesolithic and Neolithic solar cosmology' (Sims 2006: 204). Essentially Lionel saw Neolithisation not as a revolution, as per Gordon Childe (1936), but as a counter-revolution, that is a revolution that opposes or attempts to reverse the results of the original revolution – that which separated humans from their primate ancestors. His thesis was built on the anthropological work of Knight, Power and Watts (Knight [1991] 1995; Knight *et al.* 1995; Power 2009) who, through a combination of social anthropology, biological anthropology and archaeology, have suggested how and why human symbolic culture emerged, through female-led sex strike action. This revolution – *the* human revolution – would have given rise to a hunter-gatherer society whose economic and cultural activities were timed by the phases of the Moon which were symbolically related to other aspects of culture, such as Dark Moon being associated with blood and Full Moon with fire.

The sex-strike, or Female Cosmetics Coalition, model – as it came to be known – is paradoxically simple yet complex. It is simple in its conception, but complex in its derivation and the sheer amount of interdisciplinary evidence which it is built upon. Due to this complexity, it is difficult to argue for an interpretation of megalithic monumentality based around it, without having the necessary space to fully explain the nuances. We feel that many have misunderstood or dismissed Lionel's ideas because they failed to understand or engage with the anthropological minutiae which underpinned Lionel's thinking. As a way to remedy this, we have invited Chris Knight, Camilla Power and Ian Watts, the three anthropologists who fleshed out this theory, to contribute chapters detailing different aspects of the model and the evidence in favour of it. These anthropological chapters, in Part I of this volume, *Anthropology and Human Origins*, not only illustrate the strong link between the celestial objects, especially the Moon, within different societies but also provide the necessary anthropological context to understand Lionel's archaeoastronomical work.

While these anthropologists focused on the question of human origins in the Palaeolithic period, Lionel was focused on the Neolithic. He posited that if some variation of the Female Cosmetics Coalition model was present in hunter-gatherer Mesolithic Britain, then the introduction of cattle-herding and horticulturalism in the Neolithic would have amounted to nothing short of a counter-revolution whereby such concepts as ownership (whether of land, animals or people) and patriarchy would have been introduced (Sims 2015). This ontological shift would have equally encompassed a cosmological shift, from an early emphasis on the Moon to the solar cults known to be a key feature of the religions of the Bronze and Iron Ages throughout Europe. From this perspective, Stonehenge and the megalithic monuments of western Europe, would be testament to the period of transition.

Such a transition would not have happened haphazardly, but would have followed the structural rules first observed by Lévi-Strauss in his intense studies of mythology (e.g. 1969, 1973, 1978, 1981). The core idea is that the original human state became a 'transformational template' which the powers that be, in this instance those of the Neolithic and Early Bronze Ages of southern Britain, abused and modified to suit their needs (Sims 2010a: 6-7). A proposed male-led cult had to reference the earlier matriarchal source of power – the Moon – by reversing and transferring its power to the new cosmic symbol of the patriarchy – the Sun. Monuments, such as Stonehenge, were devices built to either effect or mark that transformation and this is evidenced by their double alignments to both Sun and Moon. The transformational rules of Lévi-Strauss invariably involve what has been called a 'double twist' (Maranda 2001): they mirror and reverse the template they are based on – and it is exactly this combination of factors that Lionel observed within the alignments of Stonehenge. This transformation is done by, firstly, showing how the annual cycle of the Sun mirrors the monthly cycle of the Moon and, secondly, by reversing the cycle of lunar phases visible at these key moments of time. According to Lionel, this is only achievable on specific years when the Moon is said to be at a lunar standstill by looking at specific directions where the Dark Moon combines with winter solstice and the Full Moon with the summer solstice (see Sims 2016 for a lengthier discussion). By doing this, Lionel explained and considerably expanded the many examples of megalithic alignments to the lunar standstills that Thom (1971), and later Ruggles (1999), had identified. This emphasis on the Moon, in particular, has drawn attention from his peers, as can be seen in Part II of this volume, *Prehistory and Megalithic Monuments*, which comprises chapters by David Fisher, A. César González-García, John Grigsby, J. McKim Malville, Estelle Orrelle and Emília Pásztor.

Theoretical Contributions

Lionel's contributions have extended well beyond his interpretation of prehistoric monumentality in southern Britain, they have directly addressed the way archaeoastronomy had been done in the past in order to provide new ways to approach it. Lionel's first printed forays into this revolved around his observation that 'European archaeoastronomy has settled into a narrow routine seemingly in an effort to gain wider acceptance' (Sims 2010b). This routine generally involved the application of statistical reasoning, as epitomised by the works of Ruggles (e.g. 1999) and Hoskin (2001), which could not be deployed for unique monuments such as Stonehenge, Avebury or Newgrange (Sims 2010a: 10). This, Lionel believed, was due to archaeology's disfavour with archaeoastronomy, which led archaeoastronomers to accumulate 'aggregated data sets' and apply statistical testing to reject the null hypothesis that prehistoric monuments were orientated at random. However, as he put it, 'A discipline that stands still waiting for others to accept it is a discipline in danger' (2010a: 11).

Lionel's critique was not so much an attack on the statistical method per se, but rather on two flaws which arose from it. Firstly was the fact that archaeoastronomers tended to stop their work at the level of identifying statistically significant celestial alignments, with 'very little development in the cultural interpretation of the alignments that have been found' (Sims 2010a: 11). An anthropologist by training, Lionel conceived archaeoastronomy as having the potential to bridge the four fields that comprise anthropology, namely archaeology, social anthropology, linguistics and biological anthropology (Sims 2010b). To achieve this, the archaeoastronomer must attempt to interpret celestial alignments, thereby not only relating them to social anthropology but making archaeoastronomy itself relevant for anthropologists. Secondly, Lionel critiqued the over-emphasis on statistics to the exclusion of other methods that can be used to interrogate individual monuments (Sims 2010b). On this note, he highlighted four methods, namely Monte Carlo modelling, landscape phenomenology, emergence through consideration of embodied experience and virtual 3D modelling. Together with the more traditional statistical approach, these five methods 'constitute a significant battery of techniques to test the null hypothesis for intentional alignments for *both* regional groups and individual monuments' (Sims 2010b). From these early reflections on the state of archaeoastronomy, Lionel developed and continued to evolve his own approaches to the study of, largely, the Stonehenge and Avebury complexes (see, more recently, Sims 2021). These contributions have been largely unrecognised, which has motivated us to highlight three theoretical trends that demonstrate Lionel's unconventional, but ahead of his time, stance.

Attention to Archaeological Detail and Context

Lionel always paid a degree of attention to the archaeological detail and context of the monument being studied that went well above the norm within archaeoastronomy. His works included detailed archaeological plans and delved deep into excavation details or the minutiae of the interpretive models of other scholars. The most illustrative examples of this include his work on the Avebury coves (Sims 2010a), on West Kennet Avenue (Sims 2010b) and on the Stonehenge palisades (Sims and Fisher 2020) where he systematically assembled the wider archaeological evidence for each of these architectural features before deploying them for interpretive purposes. Such attention to detail is not widespread within archaeoastronomy which still relies almost exclusively on orientation data.

Testing of Interpretive Models

A second constant in Lionel's works was his emphasis on the testing of interpretive models. In several works (Sims 2010a, 2016; Sims and Fisher 2020), Lionel painstakingly trawled through the literature and listed all interpretive models for a given monument, including their key predictions. He then listed features of the monuments in question which he used to put the models to the test by interrogating whether they are capable of explaining all features. For this task, the role played by 'evidence anomalous to theory' (2009a: 340) is key, and Lionel's eyes were second to none in spotting such anomalies – no doubt fuelled by the attention to detail and archaeological context just discussed. From this interrogation process, new interpretive models emerge, often combining elements of the previous models, which feature previously dismissed or ignored archaeoastronomical alignments and focus on the embodied experience of the monument. Lionel's approach was innovative not only within archaeoastronomy which, as mentioned above, lacks engagement with interpretation, but also within archaeology. Interpretive, hermeneutic or postprocessual models abound in archaeology, but the processual idea of formally testing them is not as ubiquitous (see Eve and Crema 2014 for a rare example).

Emphasis on Embodied Experience

Lionel's engagement with cultural interpretation and symbolic meaning emerges from the embodied experience of the monument, as reconstructed from his methodology of combining archaeoastronomy, landscape phenomenology and the testing of interpretive models. The actual lived experience of prehistoric people both determines the possibilities for alignments and limits the scope of their interpretation – facts that are hardly ever considered in archaeoastronomy. No doubt fuelled by phenomenology, Lionel always placed such embodied experiences above any potential geometrical or mathematical relationships which led to more vivid depictions and understandings of the experience of the alignments – as it did when he repeated North's (1996) observation that walking into Stonehenge from the Heel stone, the 'observer's rising eye would have counter-balanced the motion of the setting winter solstice sun to create the illusion of '"time" standing still' (Sims 2009b: 398). In all of his works, he made sure to consider the average height of the Neolithic person and its impact on eye height, and hence on the altitude of any observed celestial alignments (e.g. Sims 2015: 203). This approach often led him to realise why certain architectural choices were made by the prehistoric builders, as he did when he wrote:

> A route that loses height to then require immediately regaining it is not what we would expect of Mesolithic foragers, just as tourists today seem to agree by taking the modern shortcut! However, such a strategy is perfect for lowering the eye of the observer processing along the Avenue (Sims 2010b).

Fabio: I distinctly remember one of my first conversations with Lionel, at the SEAC 2009 meeting in Alexandria, Egypt. After a busy day of talks, a group of us ventured into the hotel bar to continue the discussions. Around the table was Nicholas Campion, Kim Malville, Lionel, his student John Macdonald and me. Somehow, the conversation moved to Avebury and Silbury Hill. Summarising the findings of a then recently published paper (Sims 2009b), Lionel challenged me to place myself in the shoes of a prehistoric visitor to Avebury. His descriptions were exciting and vivid, almost as if he had been there himself. He told me that I would have been able to see the Moon rise, transit the sky, and then set over Silbury Hill – whose glistening white chalk terrace was a symbolic representation of the Moon, as he had argued before. Lionel then said: 'The Moon has already set, yet you can still see it [referring to the chalk terrace]. Where are you then?'. I puzzled at this question which, at the time, made no sense to me. Lionel provided the answer, which came as an example of ontological tension: 'You are in the underworld!'. For a society whose Moon goes into the underworld when it sets, the answer would have been obvious. This revelation was foundational to my current reasoning that archaeoastronomy in particular, and archaeology more broadly, should be about thinking differently. The entire conversation was also representative of Lionel as a public speaker, with his passionate delivery that pulls the listener in to the puzzle he was trying to solve while, at the same time, forcing him or her to think like a prehistoric person.

Lionel may not have explicitly presented the above three points as paradigmatic or as exemplars to be followed. Nor did he feel the need to justify or otherwise demonstrate the validity of his approaches – rather they were presented as intuitive steps following a logical sequence. His critique of past and current approaches was always done through case studies rather than through extended theoretical exposition. From this perspective, Lionel was not a theorist, but he actively engaged with and developed theoretical points in archaeoastronomy. The present authors and volume editors, believe that, perhaps more than his contributions to the understanding of megalithic skyscapes in southern Britain, these largely unrecognised theoretical and methodological contributions, applicable as they are to any archaeoastronomy project anywhere in the world, are likely to be Lionel's most enduring legacy. This is reflected in Part III of this volume, *Theory*, in the chapters by Nicholas Campion, Liz Henty, Michael Rappenglück and Fabio Silva, all of which pick up and expand upon elements of theory in Lionel's body of work.

Commitment to Education

Lionel was an innovative educator. As former Head of Anthropology at the University of East London, he designed a course entitled 'Decoding Stonehenge' for his students to teach them archaeoastronomy. This ran from 1993 until 2011 as an optional choice on a BSc (Hons) anthropology degree programme. The course was, as its title suggests, a new examination of Britain's iconic monument, though it included Avebury and monuments at Bru na Boinne and Loughcrew in Ireland. Unlike Gerald Hawkins' (1965) work from which the course title derived, Lionel's course did not focus solely on astronomical alignments but attempted to examine how archaeoastronomy could deal with cultural complexity. It was more focused on understanding the needs which drove a culture to enshrine alignments in their monuments rather than on the methods of finding alignments. Lionel approached the material from an interdisciplinary perspective, combining a number of methodologies and approaches, as a way of mining all avenues. This revolved around an anthropological critique of five disciplines; archaeoastronomy; archaeology; behavioural ecology (socio-biology); Indo-European poetics and cultural anthropology; key texts from these were part of the reading material. He drew on theories from those disciplines 'to model the likely scenarios for late Neolithic monument building cultures' and to argue for a new approach to prehistoric monuments which could shed light on similar sites of the period. As he explained to Liz in 2015, his practice 'included archaeoastronomy as part of the American definition of anthropology which integrates biological, social, cultural anthropology with archaeology, linguistics, myth and folk lore'. He was keen to describe his methodology as 'emergence - the product of integrating all of the extant methodologies' which came about as a result of his being 'struck by the lack of integration between anthropology and archaeology into the origins of social complexity'. He believed that one 'subdiscipline' in particular 'stood at the centre of this intersection yet itself was in disarray – archaeoastronomy' (Sims, 2013: 8). His integrated methodology approach required not just a new way of conducting field work, but also a new interpretive method (Sims 2013: 11). A further rationale for his point of view was that other disciplines which specialise in prehistory only have access to 'fragments' which reveal some aspects of the culture so that no one discipline 'possesses a rich enough set of data to independently interpret a prehistoric culture as a whole' (Sims, 2013, 22). Lionel continued to believe that by exploring single sites such as Stonehenge, which was the main focus of the course, new insights could be found. Overall, the content of not just his course but his work in general, enables the humanitarian, societal analysis missing from so much archaeoastronomical work.

In a small field like archaeoastronomy and cultural astronomy, there aren't many professional bodies that can steer the ship to a good port. One such organisation is the European Society for Astronomy in Culture (SEAC), where Lionel chaired the Educational Sub-Committee from 2015 to 2020. One of its key outputs during this time, and something Lionel strongly spearheaded, was the development of an educational strategy 'to assist in enhancing our discipline's significance, reputation and performance'. The proposals included: (a) the creation of a registry of cultural astronomy courses, (b) the development of benchmarking statements for the field, (c) the implementation of a SEAC 'kite mark' for archaeoastronomy courses validated by the Sub-Committee, (d) the development of innovative postgraduate curricula targeting archaeologists and anthropologists, and (e) an outreach programme. Although this document was a collective effort, it was symbolic of Lionel's commitment to education, outreach and cross-disciplinary fertilisation.

Generally, archaeoastronomy has been sidelined by most archaeologists so it was a characteristically brave move for Lionel to organise two sessions at the Theoretical Archaeology Group (TAG) conferences in 2005 and 2007 respectively. The first session in Sheffield in 2005 stemmed from his interest in using anthropology to explore the cultural relevance of the Sun,

Moon and stars. Consequently, the session was entitled 'The Anthropology and Archaeology of Moonshine' and aimed to provide an explanatory framework for the appearance of lunar motifs stretching back to the Palaeolithic (TAG 2005, 50-52). The individual presentations were focused either on the reassessment of Lévi Strauss or on discoveries of the importance of the Moon in indigenous cultures such as the Hazda in Tanzania and the Curripaco of the Northwest Amazon. In his talk Lionel put forward an early version of his theories about the solarisation of the Moon at Stonehenge, drawing together archaeological interpretations of burial practices and recent anthropological modelling of hunter-gather communities. His second session entitled, 'Reconstructing the underworld: the anthropology and archaeology of other-worlds' (TAG 2007, 35-37) came in 2007 at York and aimed to find out how concepts of the underworld could aid the interpretation of prehistoric cosmologies. Looking back at the abstracts for the session it is surprising that there was so much adverse criticism from the archaeologists present on the day, though the presentations on Silbury Hill and Avebury were certainly treading on their toes.

Lionel's Legacy

By 2012, which marked the first of a series of 'skyscape' sessions at TAG, times had changed and archaeologists were more in favour of welcoming skyscape archaeology (Henty 2020). Lionel was a key contributor to this changing of the tide, having participated in these TAG sessions as well as joining the editorial board of the *Journal of Skyscape Archaeology* which we co-founded in 2015. Moreover, he enabled us to think differently about monuments, to reconceptualise celestial bodies, not merely in connection to their rising and setting points on the horizon, but as part of an embodied skyscape that was lived by the prehistoric users of these monuments. Through his relentless research and vision for creating a better and interdisciplinary archaeoastronomy, he was a true inspiration to his students and colleagues. No more is this evident than in this volume, where in its three separate parts, colleagues have written chapters which provide new thought-provoking directions and underline the importance of interdisciplinarity. Sadly, Lionel died in October 2021 but before that we sent him this volume in pre-publication form. In what was to become his last email to us he wrote: 'I think it [the volume] will hopefully become a useful stimulus to our discipline'. These chapters show how Lionel's influence lives on in lively debate, whether this be about theory, anthropology or prehistoric monumentality.

References

Campion, N. 2009. Programme. Ceredigion, Wales: The Sophia Centre, University of Wales, Lampeter.

Childe, V.G. 1936. *Man Makes Himself.* London: Watts & Company.

English Heritage, 2020. Things to See and Do, Solstice, viewed December 2020, <https://www.english-heritage.org.uk/visit/places/stonehenge/things-to-do/solstice/>.

Eve, S. and E. Crema 2014. A house with a view? Multi-model inference, visibility fields, and point process analysis of a Bronze Age settlement on Leskernick Hill (Cornwall, UK). *Journal of Archaeological Science* 43: 267-277. DOI: 10.1016/j.jas.2013.12.019

Hawkins, G.S. 1965. *Stonehenge Decoded*. New York: Doubleday.

Henty, L. 2020. Skyscape archaeology: the place of the sky in the academy. In L. Henty and D. Brown (eds) *Visualising Skyscapes: Material Forms of Cultural Engagement with the Heavens*: 13-34. Oxon: Routledge.

Hoskin, M. 2001. *Tombs, Temples and their Orientation*. UK: Ocarina Books.

Hutton, R. 2013. The Strange History of Archaeoastronomy. *Journal for the Study of Religion, Nature and Culture* 7(4): 376-396.

Knight, C. [1991] 1995. *Blood Relations: Menstruation and the Origins of Culture*. Newhaven, USA: Yale University Press.

Knight, C., C. Power and I. Watts 1995. The Human Symbolic Revolution: A Darwinian Account. *Cambridge Archaeological Journal* 5(1): 75-114.

Lévi-Strauss, C. 1969. *The Raw and the Cooked, vol. 1 of* Mythologiques. New York: Harper and Row.

Lévi-Strauss, C. 1973. *From Honey to Ashes, vol. 2 of* Mythologiques. New York: Harper and Row.

Lévi-Strauss, C. 1978. *The Origins of Table Manners, vol. 3 of* Mythologiques. New York: Harper and Row.

Lévi-Strauss, C. 1981. *The Naked Man, vol. 4 of* Mythologiques. New York: Harper and Row.

Maranda, P. (ed.) 2001. *The Double Twist: From Ethnography to Morphodynamics*. Toronto: University of Toronto Press.

North, J. 1996. *Stonehenge: Neolithic Man and the Cosmos*. London: Harper Collins.

Power, C. 2009. Sexual selection models for the emergence of symbolic communication: why they should be reversed. In Rudolf Botha and Chris Knight (eds) *The Cradle of Language*: 257-280. Oxford: Oxford University Press.

Ruggles, C. 1999. *Astronomy in Prehistoric Britain and Ireland*. New Haven and London: Yale University Press.

Sims, L. 2006. The 'Solarization' of the Moon: Manipulated Knowledge at Stonehenge. *Cambridge Archaeological Journal* 16(2): 191-207. DOI: 10.1017/S0959774306000114

Sims, L. 2009a. The Logic of Empirical Proof: A Note on the Course of the Beckhampton Avenue. *Time & Mind* 2(3): 333-345. DOI: 10.2752/175169609X12464529903218

Sims, L. 2009b. Entering, and returning from, the underworld: reconstituting Silbury Hill by combining a quantified landscape phenomenology with archaeoastronomy. *Journal of the Royal Anthropological Institute* 15: 386-408.

Sims, L. 2010a. Which Way Forward for Archaeoastronomy? West Kennet Avenue as a Test Case. *Journal of Cosmology* 9: 2160-2171. URL: http://journalofcosmology.com/AncientAstronomy107.html

Sims, L. 2010b. Coves, Cosmology and Cultural Astronomy. In Nicholas Campion (ed) *Cosmologies: Proceedings of the Seventh Annual Sophia Centre Conference 2009*: 4-28. Lampeter: Sophia Centre Press.

Sims, L. 2013. Interpretation through emergence: reconstituting the lost complexity of the late Neolithic/Early Bronze Age cosmovision by multi-disciplinary method. PhD thesis, University of East London.

Sims, L. 2015. Out of Africa: The Solarization of the Moon. In F. Pimenta *et al.* (eds) *SEAC 2011 Stars and Stones: Voyages in Archaeoastronomy and Cultural Astronomy*: 200-206. BAR International Series 2720. Oxford: Archaeopress.

Sims, L. 2016 What is the Minor Standstill of the Moon? *Journal of Skyscape Archaeology* 2(1): 67-76. DOI: 10.1558/jsa.v2i1.30212

Sims, L. 2021. Returning from the Underworld: The West Kennet Palisades in the Avebury Monument Complex. *Proceedings of the Prehistoric Society*, First View: 1-23. DOI: 10.1017/ppr.2021.7

Sims, L. and D. Fisher 2020. Through the Dark Vale: Interpreting the Stonehenge Palisade through Interdisciplinary Convergence. *Journal of Skyscape Archaeology* 6(1): 5-29. DOI: 10.1558/jsa.38690

TAG 2005, Session and Paper Abstracts, viewed December, 2020. <https://antiquity.ac.uk/tag?>.

TAG 2007, Programme, viewed December, 2020. <https://antiquity.ac.uk/tag?>.

Thom, A. 1971. *Megalithic Lunar Observatories*. Oxford: Clarendon Press.

Wittfogel, K.A. 1957. *Oriental Despotism: A Comparative Study of Total Power*. Newhaven, USA: Yale University Press.

Part I:

Anthropology and Human Origins

Lunarchy: The Original Human Economics of Time

Camilla Power

The Moon doesn't like the boys, just the girls, Nharo saying in Guenther (1989: 52).

Women's biggest husband is the moon, BaMbendjele saying in Lewis (2008: 299).

In the final analysis, all forms of economics can be reduced to an economics of time Marx (1971: 76).

Lionel Sims makes his boldest and most original claims by applying anthropological understanding of religious structures and their transformation to the archaeology of megalithic sites. In decoding Stonehenge, Avebury and other lunar/solar aligned monuments, he has shown that they are complex machines 'designed to entrain winter sunset with dark moon' (Sims 2006: 204). Further, they endow the winter setting Sun with ritual characteristics of Dark Moon, enabling a 'religious logic of estrangement' (Sims 2006: 204). The ritual potency accorded Dark Moon by Palaeolithic hunting cultures was transformed and conferred onto a solar annual cycle. In this process of 'solarization', the Sun was invested with the former religious significance of the Moon.

The phenomenological experience of processing uphill in the final Avenue approach at Stonehenge towards a descending winter sun has the effect of momentarily freezing the sunset. Such ritual prolongation demonstrated the power to 'stop time' (Sims 2006: 203). While that experience may have been shared among initiates, more esoteric, and probably kept secret among elite, insider groups, the appearance of the Moon 'within the upper window, over a minor standstill year', formed a 'reversed set of lunar phases culminating at winter solstice with dark moon' (Sims 2006: 204). Time is controlled and sent into reverse.

Sims proposes 'specialist knowledge of the lunistice moon' as the preserve of a 'high-ranking group', with solar symbolism now invested with concepts of male power (2006: 204). If Sims is right, this is the symbolic hallmark of a process of counter-revolution, shifting the balance of gender power towards masculinisation of ritual and new forms of hierarchy: patriarchy. It took huge costs of time and energy invested in the construction of Stonehenge, and other megalithic monuments, to effect this shift. This implies it was no simple matter to annex the ancient syntax of ritual power organised by the Moon.

But where did the 'time-resistant' lunar syntax come from? It is unlikely that patriarchal Neolithic societies invented this form of time-keeping. Yet it persists even in modern patriarchal 'world' religions. All world religions are organised on lunar calendars. In fact, it may be a defining feature of religion to work with the Moon – the source of magic, transformation and the other world, the fundamental metaphor of life, death and resurrection.

One telling marker of a shift in gender relations around the onset of the Neolithic is the bottleneck of male-transmitted Y-chromosomes detected within the last 10,000 years (Karmin *et al.* 2015). This rapid reduction in diversity of male lineages corresponds to a change in the archaeological record characterised by the spread of Neolithic cultures. These demographic, social and cultural changes radically affected the degree of variance in male reproductive success. Among egalitarian African hunter-gatherers, the opposite genetic signature of high Y-chromosome diversity is found (Tishkoff *et al.* 2007), implying more equal fitness, as a result of equal distribution and access to resources (see e.g. Stibbard-Hawkes *et al.* 2020 on Hadza generalised sharing). One hypothesis proposes warfare among patrilineal clans to explain the collapse of Y diversity (Zeng, Aw and Feldman 2018).

I do not intend to investigate the question of changing Neolithic gender relations here, but to argue that Palaeolithic hunting cultures were both more gender fluid and egalitarian from their African origins (Power and Watts 1997, 1999; Power 2019). In the first part of the chapter, I will set out the main reasons for inferring an original gender egalitarianism, particularly among African hunter-gatherer ancestors during our speciation. Then I will consider how female strategies for maintaining egalitarian gender relations generated a specifically lunar ritual syntax. Lastly I will examine East, Central and Southern African hunter-gatherer lunar cosmology and its impact on gender politics.

How gender egalitarianism made us human

There are several indicators in our species biology, our life history and our evolved psychology – the evidence of our bodies and minds – of an increasing egalitarian tendency in human evolution. This necessarily had a dimension of gender (Power 2019).

Egalitarian features

The egalitarian features of our anatomy, life history and psychology include:-

1. *Our eyes* – Alone of over 200 primate species, we have evolved eyes with an elongated shape and a bright white sclera background to a dark iris (Kobayashi and Kohshima 2001). Known as 'cooperative eyes' (Tomasello *et al.* 2007), they invite anyone we interact with to see easily what we are looking at. By contrast, great apes have round, dark eyes, making it very difficult to judge their gaze direction.
2. *Intersubjectivity* – Our eyes are adapted for mutual mindreading, also called intersubjectivity; our closest primate relatives block this off. To look into each other's eyes, asking 'can you see what I see?' and 'are you thinking what I am thinking?' is completely natural to us from an early age (Tomasello and Rakoczy 2003).
3. *Mothers and others* – the most convincing account of how, when and why intersubjectivity and cooperative eyes evolved is given by Sarah Hrdy in her landmark book *Mothers and others* (2009). We do babysitting in all human societies, mothers being happy to hand over their offspring for others to look after temporarily. African hunter-gatherers deploy this collective form of childcare (Hewlett and Lamb 2005), indicating that it was routine in our heritage. In stark contrast, 'hyperpossessive' great ape mothers – chimpanzees, bonobos, gorillas and orangutans – do not dare to let their babies go.
4. *Grandmothers, menopause and childhood* – Monkeys behave differently from apes, being prepared to leave a baby with a trusted relative. The key factor involved is exactly how closely related individuals are. Old World monkey mothers usually live with female

relatives; great ape mothers rarely do. So, ape mothers have no one nearby whom they can trust sufficiently. This indicates something significant about the social conditions in which we evolved. Our foremothers must have been living close to trusted female relatives, the most reliable in the first place being a young mother's own mother. This 'grandmother hypothesis' has been used to explain our long postreproductive lifespans – the evolution of menopause (Hawkes, O'Connell, Blurton Jones, Alvarez, and Charnov 1998; Hawkes and Paine 2006; Voland, Chasiotis and Schiefenhövel, 2005).

Coevolving with grandmothers were children. Childhood is defined as the period after an infant is weaned and before the child has any permanent teeth (Bogin 2006). During that time, children need help with finding a diet they can process. This is where grandmother steps in, since she is able to assist the newly weaned child, while the mother can begin the cycle of having her next baby (Sear 2018; Sear and Mace 2008). In this way, in evolution mother's mother would have had a big impact on a child's survival and/or increased her daughter's fertility. This has resulted in the special characteristic of 'stacked' families among humans, where a mother has several dependent offspring at once (Hawkes and Paine 2006). With no one to help, other great ape mothers need very long intervals between births and breastfeeding until each offspring can become an independent juvenile. Apes have no supportive transition period of childhood, and juveniles suffer high mortality.

Hrdy (2009) argues multi-parental care shaped the evolution of our species' unique psychological nature. Cooperative childcare has to start with the mother-daughter relationship because it requires trust, enabling the mother to hand over her baby to a closely related female (as in the case of monkeys). But such bonding with grandchildren could quickly lead to the involvement of aunts, sisters, older daughters and other trusted relatives. Males as brothers may be involved in female childcare coalitions earlier than male mates (putative fathers). There are two reasons why grandmother strategies are unlikely to involve mother's sons in early stages. Firstly, sons will not necessarily have certainty of paternity (so their mothers will not have certainty); and secondly, males tend to have first reproduction at a later age than females, requiring a son's mother to live longer to have an effect.

From the moment when mothers allow others to hold their babies, says Hrdy, selection pressures for new kinds of mindreading are established. These give rise to novel responses – mutual gazing, babbling, kissfeeding and so forth – which enable this variegated triad of mum, baby and new helper to consolidate bonds while monitoring one another's intentions.

5. *Our huge brain volumes* – While a human and chimp mother have a fairly similar body weight, adult humans today have upwards of three times the brain volume of a chimp (Isler and Van Schaik 2012). Brain tissue is very expensive in terms of energy requirements (Aiello and Key 2002; Aiello and Wheeler 1995; Foley and Lee 1991; Power and Aiello 1997). Doing the whole job by themselves, great ape mothers are constrained in the amount of energy they can provide to offspring and so apes cannot expand brains above what is known as a 'gray ceiling' at 600cc (Isler and Van Schaik 2012). Our ancestors smashed through this ceiling some 1.5-2 million years ago with

the emergence of *Homo erectus*, who had brains more than twice the volume of chimps today. This tells us that cooperative childcare was already part of *Homo erectus* society, with concomitant features of evolving cooperative eyes and emergent intersubjectivity.

We can track the degree of egalitarianism among descendants of *Homo erectus*, by measuring brain sizes in these early humans, using the fossil record. Materially more energy was channelled to females and their offspring. This implies an inevitable gendering of the strategies that enabled this to happen. Male dominance and strategic control of females (cf. Foley and Gamble 2009) would have obstructed such unprecedented increases of brain size. Those populations where male dominance, sexual conflict and infanticide risks remained high were not our ancestors. Our forebears solved the problem of great ape male dominance, instead harnessing males into routine support of these extraordinarily large-brained offspring.

The few African fossils from 800–600,000 years ago have cranial capacities in the range of 1,200–1,300cc; that is, in the modern range, three times a chimpanzee volume. However, the steepest increase in cranial capacities occurs later – from ~300,000 years ago (de Miguel and Henneberg 2001: Figure 1). African fossils suggest that this last phase coincided with our speciation (see Hublin *et al.* 2017; Power, Sommer and Watts 2013: 42, Table 1; Watts 2014). It also appears consequent on a suite of behavioral changes in the period ~500–300,000 years ago, incorporating regular fire use/camp fire social organization, new technologies in lithics, meat procurement, and shelter (Brooks *et al.* 2018; Watts, Chazan and Wilkins 2016).

In sum, these aspects of our biology, life history, and evolved psychology – our intersubjectivity, our cooperative eyes, large brain size, and life history stages of grandmothering and childhood – could only have been favoured in social conditions of greater egalitarianism and reduced tendency to dominance.

Increasing Machiavellian intelligence produces egalitarian relations

Large increases of brain size are vanishingly rare in evolution because of the expense. What are these large brains for? One major hypothesis is the Social Brain theory. This relates brain size, specifically the size of the neocortex, across primate species, to the degree of social complexity, the network of relationships that any individual needs to deal with (Dunbar 1998). Originally, 'social brain' was called Machiavellian intelligence (Byrne and Whiten 1988). This subtle idea sees animals in complex social groups competing in evolutionary terms by becoming more adept at cooperation and more capable of negotiating alliances. In this theoretical perspective, then, the significant increases of brain size in the primate order, from monkeys to apes, and then from apes to hominins, result from increasing political complexity and ability to create alliances.

Egalitarianism is difficult to explain using Darwinian theory premised on competition. Andrew Whiten, one of the inventors of Machiavellian intelligence theory and his student David Erdal saw that Machiavellian intelligence could generate the difference between primate-style dominance hierarchies and typical hunter-gatherer egalitarianism (Erdal and Whiten 1994, 1996; Whiten and Erdal 2012). At a certain point, the ability to operate within alliances exceeds the ability of any single individual, no matter how strong, to dominate others. If the dominant tries, he (assuming 'he' for the moment) will meet an alliance in resistance who together can deal with him. Once that point is reached, the sensible strategy becomes not to try to dominate others, but to use alliances to resist being dominated oneself. This was termed 'counterdominance' by Erdal and Whiten (1994, 1996; Whiten and Erdal 2012), and they used it to describe what is found regularly in African hunter-gatherer societies, so-called demand-sharing, an attitude of 'don't mess with me' humour as a levelling device, with the impossibility of coercion since no particular individual is in charge.

Whiten and Erdal saw counterdominance as fundamental to the evolution of human psychology, with competing tendencies for individuals to try to get away with bigger shares where opportunity presents, but, faced with demands from others, to give in and settle for equal shares. They focused on food-sharing as the most visible aspect of hunter-gatherer egalitarianism. But how does sex fit into this model? From an evolutionary perspective, equality in reproductive fitness is most significant. Without concomitant reduction of reproductive variance, counterdominance could not be a stable strategy. Pawlowski and colleagues (1998: 361, Fig.1) show that increasing Machiavellian intelligence in monkeys and apes does indeed result in reproductive counterdominance. Bowles (2006) points to reproductive levelling among predominantly monogamous hunter-gatherers as critical to egalitarianism. Whiten and Erdal noted the hunter-gatherer tendency for monogamy, or serial monogamy, which contrasts with polygyny among propertied farmers and herders (cf. the Y-chromosome diversity collapse with onset of farming). Again our biology shows underlying features of reproductive physiology that lead to reproductive egalitarianism.

This suggests a further 'egalitarian' feature of our anatomy:

6. *Women's sexual physiology* – If a hominin female needs extra energy for her hungry offspring, better to give reproductive rewards to males who will hang around and do something useful for those offspring. Our reproductive signals make life hard for males who want to identify fertile females, monopolise the fertile moment and then move on to the next one – a classic strategy for dominant male apes (Power, Sommer and Watts 2013). We have concealed and unpredictable ovulation. A man cannot reliably tell when his partner is ovulating. Also, women are sexually receptive, potentially, for virtually all of their cycle, a much larger proportion than any other primate (Gangestad and Thornhill 2008). The combined effect is to scramble the information for males about exactly when a female is fertile. For a dominant male controlling a harem of females this is disastrous. While he is guessing about the possible fertility of one cycling female, he has to stay with her, and is missing other opportunities. Meanwhile, other males will be attending to those other sexually receptive females. Continuous sexual receptivity spreads the reproductive opportunities around many males, hence is levelling from an evolutionary perspective (Marlowe and Berbesque 2012).

BaYaka women of the Congo forest have a chorus perfectly expressing their resistance to male philandering: 'One woman, one penis!' (Knight and Lewis 2017a: 440) This serves as their ritual rallying cry against any attempt by a man to form a harem. Basically, hunter-gatherer women demand one man each to support their energy requirements and investment in costly offspring.

Symbolic resistance to 'alpha' males

Women's bodies evolved over a million years to favour the 'one woman, one penis' principle, rewarding males who were willing to share and invest over those who competed for extra females, at the expense of investment. But as we became more Machiavellian in our strategies, so did would-be alpha males. The final steep rise in brain size up to the emergence of modern humans likely reflects an arms race of Machiavellian strategies between the sexes.

As brain sizes increased, mothers needed more regular and reliable contributions from male partners. In African hunter-gatherers this has become a fixed pattern known by anthropologists as 'bride-service' (Collier and Rosaldo 1981; Lee 1979; Woodburn 1968). A man's sexual access depends on his success in provisioning and surrendering on demand any game or honey he gets to the family of his bride – mainly his mother-in-law who is effectively his boss. Where women are living with their mothers, this makes it almost impossible for a man to dominate by controlling distribution of food (*contra* Foley and Gamble 2009; Seabright 2012).

The problem for early modern human females as they came under the maximum stress of increased brain size would be with males who tried to get away with sex without bride-service. To deal with this threat, mothers of costly offspring extended their alliances to include just about everyone against the potential alpha. Men who were relatives of mothers (brothers or mother's brothers) would support those females. In addition, men who willingly invested in offspring would have interests directly opposed to the would-be alpha, who undermined their reproductive efforts. This pits a whole community as a coalition against a would-be dominant individual. Evolutionary anthropologist Christopher Boehm describes this as 'reverse-dominance', a political dynamic that for the first time established a morally regulated community (Boehm 1999).

So the occasion for reverse-dominant, collective – *moral* – action happened whenever a prospective alpha male tried to abduct a potentially fertile female. Can we describe this in more detail in terms of actual behaviour? The alpha male strategy is to find and mate with a fertile female, before moving on to the next one. But how does a male identify fertile females, considering that in human evolution ovulation became progressively concealed? One cue to the human reproductive cycle could not be so easily hidden: menstruation. With no sign for ovulation, menstruation became a highly salient cue to males that a female was near fertility.

For an alpha male, a menstruating female is the obvious target. Guard her and have sex with her until she is pregnant. Then, look for the next one. In nomadic hunter-gatherer camps, women of reproductive age are pregnant or nursing much of the time, making menstruation a relatively rare event. Undermining cooperative childcare, menstruation threatens to trigger male competition for access to an imminently fertile female, and also competition among females, because a pregnant or nursing mother risks losing male support to a cycling female.

Mothers have two possible responses to this problem. Following the logic of concealed ovulation, they might try to hide the menstruant's condition so that males would not know. But because the signal has potential economic value by attracting male attention, females are predicted to do the opposite: make a big display advertising imminent fertility. Whenever a coalition member menstruated, the whole coalition would join that female in amplifying her signal to attract males. Females within coalitions would begin to use blood-coloured substances as cosmetics to augment their signals. This is the Female Cosmetic Coalitions model of the origins of art and symbolic culture (Power 2009; Power, Sommer and Watts 2013).

In creating a cosmetic coalition in resistance, females deter alpha males by surrounding a menstrual female and refusing to let anyone near. They are creating the world's first taboo, on menstrual blood collectively imagined, speaking the world's first word: NO! To reinforce this message of refusal they would act out and perform through pantomime 'Wrong sex, wrong species' (Knight, Power and Watts 1995; Power and Watts 1997, 1999; Knight and Lewis 2017b).

But even as a negative, this cosmetic display encourages investor males who are willing to go hunting and bring back supplies to the whole female coalition. Cosmetically decorated females who create a show of solidarity against alpha males ensure that investor males will get the fitness rewards. It is fully in the interests of investor males to sexually select females belonging to ritual cosmetic coalitions, because they then eliminate competition from the would-be alphas.

The Female Cosmetic Coalitions (FCC) model shows us the prototype of a moral order, upheld through those puberty rituals, taboos, and prohibitions that surround menstruation in so many ethnographic accounts (Knight 1991). The FCC strategy is also the prototype symbolic action, with collective performative agreement that fake or imaginary 'blood' stands for real blood. While it is revolutionary at the level of morality, symbolism and economics, the strategy emerges as an *evolutionary* adaptation, driven by male sexual selection of female ritual participants. On this basis, through *reverse gender dominance*, the hunter-gatherer institution of bride-service emerges, with roughly equal chances of reproductive success for all hunters.

Finally, the FCC model explains what we find as the earliest symbolic material in the archaeological record. When the theory was first advanced in the mid-1990s (Knight, Power and Watts 1995), it predicted that the world's earliest symbolic media would consist of blood-red cosmetics. It predicted where and when we should find them: in Africa, preceding and during our speciation, in relation to the increases of brain size. This points to a pigment record no earlier than 6-700,000 years ago and especially coinciding with rapid growth of brains in the last 300,000 years.

These theoretical predictions have been strikingly confirmed. Pervading the record of the African Middle Stone Age are blood-red iron oxides: red ochres. These pigments are the first durable materials to be mined, processed, curated and used in design. They date back at least 300,000 years in the East (Brooks *et al.* 2018) and southern African record (Watts, Chazan and Wilkins 2016), possibly as old as half a million years. From the time of modern humans they are found in every southern African site and rock shelter. They become the hallmark of modern humans as they move out of Africa around the world, found in copious quantities in both the Upper Palaeolithic of Europe and in Australia from the first entry of modern humans to those continents.

Synchrony and the Moon

The model makes several predictions about the cosmology that emerged among early human hunter-gatherer communities deriving from the original ritual strategy. It expects that cosmology measures time through lunar and menstrual cyclicity.

There is a widespread 'myth' of menstrual synchrony that both Western and Indigenous women tenaciously cultivate as an expression of solidarity (Fahs 2016). Science remains skeptical of the phenomenon. Women have variable cycle lengths, both between individuals and as experienced by any one woman throughout her reproductive life. Today data is being gathered in large quantity through menstrual apps. Although this comes predominantly from women leading western lifestyles, it is still revealing. The more cycles that are averaged, the more that these are ovulatory cycles (hence fertile), the more the mean falls into the 29-30 day range. If women in their 20s, at peak fertility, are sampled, at the lower end of BMI range (better representative of women in evolutionary time), the closer the mean gets to 29.5 days – the length of the synodic lunar cycle (Bull *et al.* 2019). Pregnancy may also show a mean length nine times this (Jukic *et al.* 2013; Martin 1992: 263-64, 2013: 82, 95; Power and Aiello 1997: 160). In a recent analysis of over 4100 menstrual onsets among rural German women with longterm menstrual records, Helfrich-Förster and colleagues (2021) showed a 29.4 day mean cycle length for women under 35 years and a significant clustering of menstrual onset at either New or Full Moon, compared with 1st and 3rd quarters.

The excellent night-vision of big cats and other carnivores suggests moonlight periodicity would have had important impacts on hominin evolutionary ecology, stretching back millions of years in Africa before any symbolic culture. Lions hunt at night when there is no visible Moon, giving them night-vision advantage (Joubert and Joubert 1997). Still today, in Tanzania, the record of humans being eaten by lions is lunar-phased (Packer *et al.* 2011). So there are material reasons for an ancient lunar-phase effect on human social and reproductive life.

If the evolutionary effect of synchronising menstruation is understood in terms of synchronising ovulation, then we find a further mechanism for reproductive egalitarianism. Where a coalition of women synchronise ovulation, it is difficult for any single male to monopolise fertile matings. Synchrony operates to undermine philanderer strategies by males; it reinforces 'one woman, one penis'.

In a traditional bush camp of nomadic Ju/'hoansi or Hadza hunter-gatherers of perhaps 30 individuals, only two or three women or girls (depending how many local young women) are likely to be cycling at any time. So, it is remarkable that evidence in ethnography (Buckley 1988), myth (Knight 1983), rock art (Garlake 1995, Knight 1991: 446), games (Knight 1991: 445) and ritual practice (Power 2015) points to the same finding – women use idioms of bleeding together to express connection and belonging.

Science may not be able to demonstrate the existence of physiological menstrual synchrony. But ritualised or cultural menstrual synchrony certainly exists in societies whose lifeways most resemble those of our ancestors. And it is an expression of power. Ancient rock art in Africa, Australia and Europe portrays pairs of females linked by epic menstrual flows (Garlake 1995; Knight 1991; Power 2004); mythology of these hunter-gatherers obsesses over the taboo powers and cosmic creativity of girls in menstrual seclusion (Power and Watts 1997). Ritual practices enact dramas of a Dreaming or First Creation where women bleed together (Keeney and Keeney 2013), using red pigmented cosmetics (Power 2004; Watts 1999) to simulate it. Women's menstrual observances govern success in hunting (Lewis 2008).

The original sex-strike model outlined in Chris Knight's *Blood Relations* (1991) argues that human culture was born in a revolution when women went on strike. Women with their kin, sons and brothers, would celebrate ritually at Dark Moon, signalled by menstrual blood (real or fake); as the Moon waxed and the night sky brightened, men would go hunting for large game, bringing back kills to their wives' camp for the Full Moon feast, when all taboos on marital sex and meat were relaxed. At the next Dark Moon, women would go on sex-strike again to keep the cosmos turning. This syntax – waxing vs. waning, raw vs. cooked, fast vs. feast, blood vs. fire, kinship vs. marriage – persists at the core of all magical myths, fairytales and ritually derived narrative dramas (Cardigos 1996; Knight 1987, 1997; Power 2011; Power and Watts 1997; Watts 2005).

Men were not the first to imagine menstruation as a symbol of solidarity and ritual power; myths themselves repeatedly claim that men 'stole the secrets' from women. Knight (1991: 374-416) realised that menstruation must have been the original signal of 'sex-strike' and taboo. In a strike, everyone needs to strike together, and the obvious clock to use would be the Moon. Add to this that hunters require moonlight to hunt or travel overnight and the initial waxing Moon/waning Moon model alternating kinship with marital relations fits together (Knight 1991: 414-415).

African hunter-gatherer lunar cosmology

How a society organises time reveals what it truly values. The earliest human economy operated on an alternation of women's availability and non-availability, in line with the Moon and menstruation. African hunter-gatherer cosmology takes the lunar cycle as the crucial timeframe for ritual, sex and economic activities. The shared sources of this cosmology carry us back to earliest human symbolic culture, the very origins of art and ritual itself, over 100,000 years ago (Power 2017).

The special emphasis on African foragers arises because these peoples bear the oldest and most genetically diverse lineages of humanity (Chan *et al.* 2015; Power 2017 and see refs). The model specifies a 'time-resistant' signature of ritual power. It delineates an initial situation of ritual, art and religion: what 'God' or sacred power first looked like. From that point over 100,000 years ago among proto-Khoesan big-game hunters, there have been many historic changes in modes of subsistence as modern human populations moved around the world. Even among foragers, hunting strategies have changed to become more privatised than collective (e.g. use of bows and arrow poison where previously a group of men might cooperate with spears, d'Errico *et al.* 2012; Lombard 2020). Therefore, we may not see in real economic life of people today the exact lunar periodic hunting cycle in relation to female menstrual cycles. But what we expect is that there should be remnant beliefs and taboos relating women's cycles to the Moon, and to men's hunting success. We also expect that ritual practice in relation to boys' and girls' initiation will echo the ancient signal (bloodflow plus wrong sex/species reversal).

Hunting, menstruation and the Moon: the Hadza

Besides critical effects on prey-predator interactions, the Moon and its phases underpin symbolism. For example, a Kalahari Ju/'hoan metaphor for a lion is 'moonless night' (Biesele 1993: 24). Hadza hunters of the Tanzanian rift valley also pay careful attention to the Moon (Power 2015). A Hadza man will *not* go hunting, but lions will go hunting at the time of *Epeme*, when no Moon is in the sky. Hadza cosmology envisions an alternating shift between lion and human hunters.

Taboo structures among the Hadza suggest an ideal template of the relationship of hunting, menstruation and the Moon, mitigated by arrow poison (Power 2015). A wife's menstruation prevents her husband from hunting – because her blood is believed to destroy arrow poison (Peterson 2013: 148; Woodburn 1982a: 188; cf. Biesele 1993: 93, 196 for Ju/'hoansi). In addition, she and her husband cannot have sex and she should not gather berries, in case they all fall down and spoil, nor gather honey (or it would dry). Woodburn (1964: 274-276) describes the regular observance of restrictions relating a wife's menses/pregnancy to a man's hunting as the 'confirmation of their marital status'. Skaanes (2017a) records an idea that if weapons are touched by a menstrual girl, their 'thirst' for blood will be assuaged and they will not work on animals. Women's blood is hence equated with animal blood (cf. Knight and Lewis 2017b).

Hadza adults will agree or assert women have a relationship to the Moon (Power 2015). But there are differing answers to 'when do women menstruate in the Moon?' Two seniors – a man and a woman – independently argued that women would menstruate together and named the dark of the Moon. Women still having menstrual cycles dispute that, probably reflecting their own variable experience. But they reconcile these different views by agreeing 'it used to be like that in the old days'. Both Dorothea Bleek (1930: 700) and James Woodburn (pers. comm. 1993) heard this belief in women's synchronisation of menstruation at Dark/New Moon.

In recent research, Katherine Fitzpatrick (2018: 129) found that 'Hadza women appear to constantly monitor the waxing and waning of the moon as well as its position in the sky'. One informant told her: 'I look at the moon every day. The moon says if I am going to or not going to menstruate'. Some women mentioned 'after the moonlight disappeared' in reference to timing. This now gives us a fourth independent ethnographer documenting Hadza women's association of menses to the Moon and specifically to Dark Moon: Bleek in 1930, Woodburn from the 1960s, Power in 2003-2004 and Fitzpatrick most recently, covering the best part of a century.

A senior *epeme* man also spelled out in digital on/off terms how the Moon itself affected arrow poison (Power 2015; cf. Bleek and Lloyd 1911: 67, 77, for the /Xam; Power and Watts 1999: 112-3). He related this to the topography of a camp in Yaeda Valley that has a rock wall horizon behind which the young Moon sets. He calibrated the efficacy of arrow poison in terms of the hour at which the Moon set: very early in the evening, when the Moon was small, the poison would not work; later, as the Moon waxed and set after nine o'clock, it would be fine.

If women really did synchronise their cycles, this would give a template (Figure 1) with three different idioms ruling out effective hunting in the early new Moon: because women themselves affect arrow poison; because the Moon does; or because of the danger of lions.

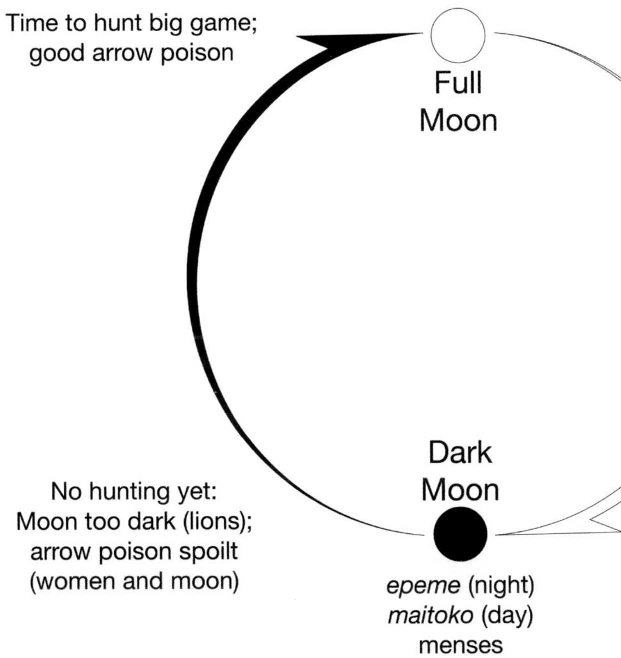

Figure 1. Lunar template framing *Epeme*, hunting and menstruation.

A man who went hunting when his wife was menstrual would likely be eaten by those lions which can see so well. At waxing to Full Moon, good moonlight favours hunting, in particular the successful waterhole ambush technique in late dry season (Bunn *et al.* 1988: 424; Hawkes *et al.* 1991: Table 2; Marlowe 2010: 118–119; Peterson 2013: 35; Woodburn 1964: 49; and see Watts this volume).

The lunar template

Hadza society in traditional bush camps is powerfully organised by moonlight and darkness. The major ritual celebration of the Hadza is the *Epeme* dance, held in pitch darkness for two or three nights every month around the time of Dark Moon (Power 2015). Traditionally, most camps hold an *Epeme*, the period of dry-season aggregation being most favourable for the ceremony. But even in the wet season, an *Epeme* would be danced each Dark Moon somewhere in Hadza country. The ritual requires several adult women providing the accompaniment of special polyphonic *epeme* songs. I have been in *Epeme* ceremonies ranging from three to four women singers, up to 15 or more, each with its own special atmosphere. The key feature is gender segregation with women and older girls comprising one group, sitting apart from and out of sight of the group of initiated *epeme* men.

The lunar phase of darkness is emphasized by the extinguishing of fires; everybody complies, raising a hue and cry if any light shows. Initiated men dance, one after another, embodying the 'spirit' *Epeme* or as the 'shadow' of *Epeme*, with a costume of dark cloth, shining ostrich-feather head-dresses (*kembako*), leg-bells (*!ingiribe*) and a gourd rattle (*sengeno*). As the singing grows strong, moved by joy and emotion, women get up to dance around the shadowy figure who stamps down with a special step on his right foot, the bells jingling in time with his rattle. Skaanes (2017b: 209, 212) relates this sound to the tendon-clicking of heavy eland antelope bulls as they trot.

With spirited singing, the mood under the panoply of the Milky Way is ethereal and uplifting. Failure to hold the dance, says Woodburn 'is believed to be dangerous' (1982a: 190). *Epeme* promotes and maintains 'general well-being, above all good health and successful hunting'. Peterson (2013: 162) describes the aspect of community harmony, uniting men as a group with women as a group: 'harmony-breaking illness can be cured at the *epeme* dance'. This refers especially to illness arising from *epeme* violations.

The *Epeme* dance, says Woodburn, 'stresses kinship and joint parentage, and seeks to reconcile the opposed interests of men and women which are so manifest in other contexts' (Woodburn 1982a: 190). A man may dance in the guise of *Epeme* two or three times, each dance being for someone. First, he may dance for himself; then, most commonly for one of his children – either an actual child or an object owned by his wife that stands for a child. This may be a decorated gourd in which fat is kept, or a stone or clay decorated 'doll'. A man may also dance for other close kin or affines. At each dance, a dialogue is held between the *epeme* dancer and

Figure 2. Hadza dances in the dry river at Sekobe by full moonlight (photo by author).

the women. The dancer uses a ritual 'whistling' language special to the context, the women answering with greetings, using the kinship term applicable to the person for whom that dance has been held (Woodburn 1982a: 190).

At the Full Moon, Hadza men and women, youths and girls will join a joyful party of songs and dances, with no restrictions on who sings or dances together, held in some clear space like a dry sandy riverbed (Figure 2). While *Epeme* is sacred, intense and emotional, at the Full Moon people really relax and enjoy themselves. Oscillation through the lunar cycle between relations structured by kinship (Dark Moon) and then relaxation of restrictions or taboos (Full Moon) corresponds to the model of ritual lunar periodicity (Knight 1991: 414, 1997: 135-6; Knight, Power and Watts 1995: 83, 91) here described as a 'time-resistant syntax'.

Bushman and Forest hunter-gatherer traditions

Lunar cosmology is widespread in Khoesan traditions from southern Africa (Barnard 1988; Guenther 1999; Hahn 1881; Schapera 1930; Watts 2005). A story found among almost all Khoesan groups, the *Moon and Hare,* relates the origins of death (Barnard 1992: 83; Guenther 1999); among several Bushman groups, the waning Moon is linked to spirits of the dead, the New Moon to new life (Barnard 1992: 56; Guenther 1999: 65; Hewitt 1986: 42; Watts 2005). Such potent entities as Trickster and Eland are identifiably lunar – they grow large, fade away, come back alive (Power and Watts 1997). Moon phases – notably the appearance of New Moon – schedule menarcheal ritual and prayers for hunting luck and have the power of cooling arrow poison, just as with the Hadza. While the New/waxing Moon is associated with hunger and hunting, the fat Full Moon signifies repletion and feasting (Watts 2005). The time of hunger is linked among the !Xũ to menarche at Dark Moon when camp fires are extinguished (Watts 2017: 259, citing Viegas Guerreiro).

For the Hadza, the 'Moon is brother to all women'. This compares to Nharo Bushman lore: 'he doesn't like the boys, just the girls' (Guenther 1989: 52). For the Western Pygmy BaYaka, 'women's biggest husband is the moon' (Lewis 2008: 299). When the *Malobe* ritual is called on a night of no Moon, it leads to a special intense and aesthetic experience (Lewis 2002: 150–151). Just as at *Epeme*, campfires are extinguished so the singing group, again largely women, sit in complete moonless dark; they may hold 'mystical conversations' with the Moon; their singing lures luminescent forest spirits to dance around them. These spiritis, as at *Epeme*, are secretly engendered by male initiates. Recurrently among these African hunting cultures we find links between Dark Moon, menstruation, hunger and extinction of cooking fire (Power 2017). Again this conforms to Knight's time-resistant syntax.

Lunarchy in action

Contrary to presumed Neolithic gender relations, these hunter-gatherer societies are among the most gender egalitarian on earth (Finnegan 2013, 2017; Power 2015). But how does such egalitarianism work? Initiation ritual is vital to cultural transmission among hunter-gatherers: it is the means by which culture is passed down the generations and maintains continuity. Initiation is therefore expected to be extraordinarily conservative, preserving with fidelity archaic signals of ritual power. Myth and ritual of initiation (for both girls and boys) among Khoesan (southern Africa) groups, can be compared with those among the Hadza

(Tanzania) revealing 'wrong sex/species' reversal motifs in connection to menstruation and the Moon. The dynamic of initiation, as recapitulation of early ritual strategies, should be of *reverse gender dominance.*

The ethnography of immediate-return African hunter-gatherers, including Khoesan, Pygmies and Hadza, provides many examples of women defying potentially dominant males by forming intergenerational ritual coalitions. These foster intense female solidarity, both for resisting harassment and actively motivating male hunting (Bombjaková 2018; Finnegan 2013; Knight 1991; Lewis 2002, 2008; Power 2015; Power and Watts 1997, 1999).

When hunter-gatherer women mobilise their community, their reverse dominance performances apply leverage by temporarily withdrawing from sex, but at the same time performing collectively, publicly and erotically. Morna Finnegan (2013) describes this as the 'politics of eros'. Women's body language as a public group actively disrupts sex presently while motivating men with the prospect of future reward.

A girl's first menstruation ritual among various northern, central and southern Khoesan groups, known as the Eland Bull dance, is so widespread that it is likely to be very ancient (Lewis-Williams 1981; Power and Watts 1997). The girl herself is conceived as constantly transforming, changing her identity from female to male, human to animal (Keeney and Keeney 2013), and the ritual observances, including sharing of haematite (a form of red ochre), must control and distribute this potency (Power and Watts 1997). Metamorphosed into the Eland Bull, while under stringent taboos and seclusion, the girl is now clearly unavailable to any man – she is of the wrong sex, species, and time. The women's community celebrates by dancing around the metamorphosing girl, playfully – and erotically – mimicking behavior of mating elands. This gives a clear signal they are not available for sex with their human husbands.

A lunar schedule is implicated in this ritual. The Ju/'hoansi speak of menstruation as a sickness, sometimes called 'eland sickness', but often attributed to the Moon. 'The Moon torments me' is to have menstrual cramps (Biesele 1993: 93). Among the Nharo, 'Moon medicine' is used to treat menstrual discomfort (Barnard 1979). Significantly, among widespread groups, the /Xam, the !Xu and the G/wi and G//ana, the menarcheal girl was released from seclusion at the appearance of New Moon (Bleek 1928: 122; Lloyd n.d: 4001-4002; Valiente Noailles 1993: 94-97). The maiden in her 'sickness' and emergence dies and is reborn to wax fat with the Moon. Maiden, eland bull and the Moon fatten together.

While elder male healers and grandfathers may be involved as eland dancers (e.g. among Ju/'hoansi or Nharo), women alone may hold the horns in the Eland dance, as witnessed by Valiente-Noailles (1993) with the 'Kua' (G/wi or G//ana). There women dance around the menstrual seclusion hut using sticks as horns to keep men at a respectful distance. This picture of disarmed or immobilised hunters on the receiving end of sticks wielded by women compares with the pattern among Hadza *Maitoko* girls or Mbuti *Elima* girls.

Among the East African Hadza, the girls' initiation ritual *Maitoko* involves similar sexual defiance (Power 2015). Dressed as hunters and armed with sticks, *Maitoko* initiates chase

Figure 3. Reverse dominance in action: Hadza *Maitoko* girls battle older boys at Omboi camp (photo by author).

young men in a dramatic reversal of gender roles. Much joking, teasing, provocative flirting and taunting ensues as the disarmed boys try to disarm the girls of their weapons (Figure 3).

In the Central African forests, gender reversal plays a key role in maintaining gender egalitarianism. Among the Mbuti in the east, the girls' initiation *Elima* involves girls becoming 'hunters' and chasing young men with sticks in a manner extremely similar to the Hadza (Turnbull 1960). At first menstruation, 'blessed by the moon', girls would enter the *elima* house residing for one or two Moons in 'seclusion' with their friends and older women who taught them songs. Periodically, the *elima* girls would march, painted, out of the house to chase the boys in the forest, armed with long, thin *fito* whips (Turnbull 1960: 183, 1984: 171). Aggressive targeting of the boyfriends they fancied increased towards the end of the seclusion period and climaxed in an all-out battle between *Elima*, the female initiation group, and *Molimo*, the male initiation group (Turnbull 1957: 208). Again, the Hadza have a similar climactic battle of youths and girls over a pot of food, representing the original *epeme* meat.

Mbuti youths who had been hit on by the girls were meant to fight their way to a date in the *elima* house, running the gauntlet of a vigilant guard of women grouped around it and a defence force of 'between fifteen and twenty girls armed with long whips' (Turnbull 1960: 188). If the women had any objections to a candidate they were more than able to stop him: 'I have known them to throw a brave but unwanted suitor into the river after beating him soundly' (Turnbull 1960: 188). Turnbull (1960: 185) also records public performance of 'a number of swearing and sex songs, and erotic dances' by *elima* girls.

This erotic license recalls the obscene songs of the Western Yaka *ngoku* groups (Finnegan 2013; Lewis 2002). During *Ngoku*, women initiates of all ages storm into the central area of the camp and assume riotous control. They sing beautifully but rudely and defiantly, taunting men for their sexual ineptitude. *Ngoku*, conceptualised as women's communal spirit, acts out the mythic theme of a primordial time when women lived without men and possessed the spirit *Ejengi*. Older women and demure young girls adopt mock penises and aggressive male postures, imitating male misbehaviour in sexual intercourse.

Ngoku teaches young women how to control men by acting together in solidarity, periodically refusing sex while simultaneously arousing desire. Women's reverse dominance displays are answered by men in a corresponding ritual show of strength, known as *Ejengi*. Accepting that the potential for male violence is real, Finnegan argues that this very fact explains why 'the perpetual motion against dominance must be continually reinvented' (Finnegan 2008: 137). BaYaka men use *Ejengi* to remind all of their greater physical strength. Women's countervailing solidarity is mobilised by this provocation. So effectively do women inhibit male aggression using *Ngoku* that the community collapses into song, ribald laughter and erotic play. The

Figure 4. Reverse dominance: Hadza *Maitoko* girls, armed and ready for action at Kideru (photo by Chris Knight, with permission).

outcome is what Finnegan (2008: 218) terms 'communism in motion' – a swing between gendered poles of power and their celebratory overturn; between brute force on the one hand and female collectivised seductiveness (while mimicking male anatomy) on the other. Crucially, these maxima and minima of reverse gender dominance during ritual generate time outside ritual with relatively relaxed gender egalitarianism and counterdominance between men and women (Lewis 2014). Again, this resembles the waxing/waning logic of the Knight model. Finnegan (2013: 699) stresses the 'fizzing' of women's singing and dancing, as a vital alert flow, able to launch into action at any moment necessary, 'visceral, kinetic, erotic, live'.

Women especially assert power through collective bodily performance to resist any threat of male exploitation. We see here the gender aspect of the assertive egalitarianism as understood by James Woodburn (1982b). Equality is never taken for granted but vigilantly guarded: 'actions speak loudly: equality is repeatedly acted out, publicly demonstrated, in opposition to possible inequality' (Woodburn 1982b: 432). The ritual dramas of initiation for both sexes propel the swing of a 'pendulum of power' now with one sex, now with the other, as visualised by Finnegan (2013, 2015; and see Lewis 2002, Lewis 2014: 237). Only by maintaining this movement can any fixity of hierarchy be resisted.

Both collective ritual performances of Hadza women in their different ways, *Maitoko* and *Epeme,* are examples of this 'bodily counter-power', as Finnegan (2008: 228) calls it, in response to the threat of male control or dominance, because 'absence of hierarchy in this moment is no guarantee of its absence in the next' (Figure 4). While referring to Mbendjele situations, Finnegan's remarks apply strongly to the Hadza: 'it is the possibility of concerted male violence in any inter-sexual negotiation that makes women's collective responses so profoundly serious'. (Finnegan 2008: 141)

As the Moon waxes and wanes, the dynamic of power switches in more or less playful battles between the sexes. The Moon provides the concrete timeframe for women's ritual expression of menstrual solidarity. Rather than patriarchy or matriarchy, we observe lunarchy – rule by the Moon.

This pulse of waxing and waning, ritual power ON, ritual power OFF, is expressed in very ancient concepts of hunter-gatherer religion. The Khoesan trickster, in his – or rather 'their' since a gender fluid pronoun is decidedly appropriate – multifarious guises (Guenther 1999), can be seen as an embodiment of this oscillatory logic of lunarchy. In certain narratives we find a strong periodic function of gender antagonism and egalitarianism, for example, in the comic trick/counter-trick story of Kaoxa from the Ju/'hoansi (Biesele 1993: 171-185). There is stark contrast between trickster's awesome powers as guardian of menstrual maidens or game animals, seen in ritual practice, as against the mean, cheating, deceiving comedy fool of story. This reflects the structural opposition of ritual taboo during waxing Moon, giving way to lifting of taboos during waning Moon, as people relaxed and told tales.

A retelling of the story of /Xam trickster /Kaggen's creation of both the eland and the Moon from an old shoe (Bennun 2004: 57-65) reveals two typical aspects of trickster lore. First a motif of reversal: /Kaggen fights the meerkats who have killed his beautiful eland, by trying to fire off arrows, but they stop, turn around and come straight back at him. Motion goes into reverse. Second, /Kaggen escapes his tormentors when, finding an eland's gall bladder, he pierces it to create total darkness bringing the day to an end. Not able to see, he throws the old shoe up into the sky to become the New Moon, giving light to the hunt. The trickster's lunarchic powers control time itself, sending it into reverse, stopping and starting at each switch of lunar phase.

The remarkable ethnography of the Keeneys (2013) working with Nyae Nyae Ju/'hoan healers has revealed the recursive frame of healing, girl's first menstruation and boy's first-kill as seeking re-entry to First Creation – original time 'before time and place' when nothing was named or fixed in form, everything kept changing, there was no death or sickness, and people had 'eland heads'. Trickster, inhabiting the western sky (as the New Moon and spirits of the dead), is gatekeeper of this inchoate world in perpetual flux, 'central denizen of the First Order of existence' according to Guenther (1999: 96).

Trickster is this oscillation switching energy between First and Second creation; from anti-structure to structure; reverse gender to biological sex; waxing to waning; blood taboo to lifting of taboo. As people come back out of the rapid, emotional transformations of ritual experiences where trickster is intense, powerful and cosmic, they laugh with relief, chatter and tell each other what happened in the weird, fantastical world. Now, trickster becomes the butt of all jokes.

Conclusion

Lionel Sims (2006) has argued that Stonehenge was a stage for a shifting balance of gender power towards masculinisation of ritual and new forms of esoteric knowledge. He demonstrates in great detail how the winter setting Sun annexed the former religious significance of the Dark Moon. This chapter has explored how that lunar syntax of ritual power first emerged.

The human symbolic revolution was the culmination of an evolutionary process of increasing tendency to gender egalitarianism among African modern human ancestors. The first symbolically structured division of labour emerged through reverse gender dominance. Female cosmetic coalitions resisted alpha males who refused to do bride-service by periodic ritual performance signaling sexual refusal through collective menstrual bloodflow. A lunar/menstrual cosmology organised the first human 'economics of time', with oscillation between waxing phase of ritual taboo and production followed by waning phase of taboos relaxed and consumption of flesh (of both women and animals). A lunar syntax of ritual power has persisted to this day in patriarchal religion, mythology, narrative and drama.

When no one rules but the Moon, it instills balance of power and time. As humans evolved under the sway of the Moon, our ancestors created the revolution which worked – the symbolic revolution, a realm of trickery and deception where everyone entered equally into the fantasy. It worked because no one held power forever; it kept ebbing and flowing, between the phases of the Moon, between the sexes and genders, between parents and children, between kin and in laws. The trick was to shed blood together in time with the Moon and the animals while being simultaneously female AND male. Initiation ritual of African hunter-gatherers preserves this logic of reverse gender dominance under auspices of the trickster.

References

Aiello, L.C. and C.A. Key 2002. Energetic consequences of being a *Homo erectus* female. *American Journal of Human Biology* 14: 551–565.

Aiello, L.C. and P. Wheeler 1995. The expensive tissue hypothesis: the brain and the digestive system in human and primate evolution. *Current Anthropology* 36: 199–221.

Barnard, A. 1979. Nharo Bushmen medicine and medicine men. *Africa* 49: 68-80.

Barnard A. 1988. Structure and fluidity in Khoisan religious ideas. *Journal of Religion in Africa* 18: 216–236.

Barnard, A. 1992. *Hunters and Herders of Southern Africa.* Cambridge: Cambridge University Press.

Bennun, N. 2004. *The Broken String. The Last Words of an Extinct People.* London: Viking.

Biesele, M. 1993. *Women Like Meat. The Folklore and Foraging Ideology of the Kalahari Ju/'hoan.* Johannesburg and Indiana: Witwatersrand University.

Bleek, D.F. 1928. Bushmen of Central Angola. *Bantu Studies* 3: 105-125.

Bleek, D.F. 1930. Unpublished Hadza notebooks. African Studies Library, University of Cape Town.

Bleek, W.H.I. and L.C. Lloyd 1911. *Specimens of Bushman Folklore.* London: George Allen.

Boehm, C. 1999. *Hierarchy in the Forest: The Evolution of Egalitarian Behavior.* Cambridge, MA: Harvard University Press.

Bogin, B. 2006. Modern human life history: the evolution of human childhood and adult fertility, in K. Hawkes and R. Paine (eds) *The Evolution of Human Life History*: 197–230. Santa Fe, New Mexico: SAR Press.

Bombjaková, D. 2018. The Role of Institutions of Public Speaking, Ridicule, and Play in Cultural Transmission among Mbendjele BaYaka Forest Hunter-gatherers. Unpublished PhD dissertation. University of London.

Bowles, S. 2006. Group competition, reproductive leveling, and the evolution of altruism. *Science* 314: 1569–1572.

Brooks, A.S. *et al.* 2018. Long-distance stone transport and pigment use in the earliest MSA. *Science* 360: 90-94. DOI: 10.1126/science.aao2646

Buckley, T. 1988. Menstruation and the power of Yurok women, in T. Buckley and A. Gottlieb (eds) *Blood Magic. The Anthropology of Menstruation*: 187-209. Berkeley, CA and London: University of California Press.

Bull, J.R. *et al.* 2019. Real-world Menstrual Cycle Characteristics of More than 600,000 Menstrual Cycles. *npj Digital Medicine* 2:83 https://doi.org/10.1038/s41746-019-0152-7

Bunn, H.T., L.E. Bartram and E.M. Kroll 1988. Variability in bone assemblage formation from Hadza hunting, scavenging and carcass processing. *Journal of Anthropological Archaeology* 7: 412–457.

Byrne, R.W. and A. Whiten (eds) 1988. *Machiavellian Intelligence: Social Expertise and the Evolution of Intellect in Monkeys, Apes and Humans.* Oxford: Clarendon Press.

Cardigos, I. 1996. *In and Out of Enchantment. Blood Symbolism and Gender in Portuguese Fairytales.* Helsinki: Academia Scientiarum Fennica.

Chan, E. *et al.* 2015. Revised timeline and distribution of the earliest diverged human maternal lineages in southern Africa. *PLoS ONE* 10(3): e0121223.

Collier, J. and M. Rosaldo 1981. Politics and gender in simple societies, in S. Ortner and H. Whitehead (eds) *Sexual Meanings: The Cultural Construction of Gender and Sexuality*: 279–325. Cambridge: Cambridge University Press.

de Miguel, C. and M. Henneberg 2001. Variation in hominid brain size: How much is due to method? *Homo* 52: 3–58.

D'Errico, F. *et al.* 2012. Early evidence of San material culture represented by organic artifacts from Border Cave, South Africa. *Proceedings of the National Academy of Sciences* 109: 13214-13219. https://doi.org/10.1073/pnas.1204213109

Dunbar, R.I.M. 1998. The social brain hypothesis. *Evolutionary Anthropology* 6:178-189.

Erdal, D. and A. Whiten 1994. On human egalitarianism: an evolutionary product of Machiavellian status escalation? *Current Anthropology* 35: 175–183.

Erdal, D. and A. Whiten 1996. Egalitarianism and Machiavellian intelligence in human evolution, in P. Mellars and K. Gibson (eds) *Modelling the Early Human Mind*: 139-150. Cambridge: McDonald Institute Monographs.

Fahs, B. 2016. Demystifying menstrual synchrony: women's subjective beliefs about bleeding in tandem with other women. *Women's Reproductive Health* 3: 1-15. DOI: 10.1080/23293691.2016.1150132

Finnegan, M. 2008. The Personal is Political: Eros, Ritual Dialogue and the Speaking Body in Central African Hunter-gatherer Society. Unpublished PhD dissertation, Edinburgh University.

Finnegan, M. 2013. The politics of Eros: ritual dialogue and egalitarianism in three Central African hunter-gatherer societies. *Journal of the Royal Anthropological Institute* 19: 697-715.

Finnegan, M. 2015. Dance, play, laugh: what capitalism can't do. *Hunter Gatherer Research* 1: 85–105.

Finnegan, M. 2017. Who sees the elephant? Sexual egalitarianism in social anthropology's room, in C. Power, M. Finnegan and H. Callan (eds) *Human Origins. Contributions from Social Anthropology*: 130-152. New York and Oxford: Berghahn Books.

Fitzpatrick, K.K. 2018. Foraging and Menstruation in the Hadza of Tanzania. Unpublished PhD dissertation, University of Cambridge.

Foley, R.A. and C. Gamble. 2009. The ecology of social transitions in human evolution. *Philosophical Transactions of the Royal Society*, Series B 364: 3267–3279.

Foley, R.A. and P.C. Lee 1991. Ecology and energetics of encephalization in hominid evolution. *Philosophical Transactions of the Royal Society, London* 334: 223–232.

Gangestad, S.W. and R. Thornhill 2008. Human oestrus. *Proceedings of the Royal Society*, Series B 275: 991–1000.

Garlake, P. 1995. *The Hunter's Vision. The Prehistoric Art of Zimbabwe.* New Haven and London: Yale University Press.

Guenther, M. 1989. *Bushman Folktales: Oral Traditions of the Nharo of Botswana and the /Xam of the Eastern Cape.* Stuttgart: Franz Steiner Verlag Wiesbaden.

Guenther, M. 1999. *Tricksters and Trancers.* Bloomington: Indiana University Press.

Hahn, T. 1881. *Tsuni//goam: the Supreme Being of the Khoikhoi.* London: Trubner and Co.

Hawkes, K., J.F. O'Connell and N.G. Blurton Jones 1991. Hunting income patterns among the Hadza. *Philosophical Transactions of the Royal Society*, Series B 334: 243–251.

Hawkes, K., J.F. O'Connell, N.G. Blurton Jones, H. Alvarez, and E. Charnov 1998. Grandmothering, menopause, and the evolution of human life histories. *Proceedings of the National Academy of Sciences* 95: 1336–1339.

Hawkes, K. and R. Paine (eds) 2006. *The Evolution of Human Life History*. Santa Fe, New Mexico: SAR Press.

Helfrich-Förster, C. *et al.* 2021. Women temporarily synchronize their menstrual cycles with the luminance and gravimetric cycles of the Moon. *Sciences Advances* 7: eabe1358 DOI: 10.1126/sciadv.abe1358

Hewitt, R.L. 1986. *Structure, Meaning and Ritual in the Narratives of the Southern San.* Hamburg: Helmut Buske Verlag (Quellen zur Khoisan-Forschung 2).

Hewlett, B.S. and M. E. Lamb (eds) 2005. *Hunter-gatherer Childhoods.* New Brunswick, New Jersey: Transaction.

Hrdy, S.B. 2009. *Mothers and Others.* Cambridge, MA: Harvard University Press.

Hublin, J.J. *et al.* 2017. New fossils from Jebel Irhoud, Morocco and the pan-African origin of *Homo sapiens. Nature* 546: 289-305. DOI:10.1038/nature22336

Isler, K. and C.P. van Schaik. 2012. How our ancestors broke through the gray ceiling: comparative evidence for cooperative breeding in early *Homo. Current Anthropology* 53 (S6): S453–S465.

Joubert, D. and B. Joubert 1997. *The Lions of Savuti: Hunting with the Moon.* Washington: National Geographic Society.

Jukic, A.M. *et al.* 2013. Length of human pregnancy and contributors to its natural variation. *Human Reproduction* 28: 2848–2855. doi: 10.1093/humrep/det297

Karmin, M. *et al.* 2015. A recent bottleneck of Y chromosome diversity coincides with a global change in culture. *Genome Research* 25: 1-8. DOI:10.1101/gr.186684.114

Keeney, B. and H. Keeney 2013. Reentry into First Creation: a contextual frame for the Ju/'hoan Bushman performance of puberty rites, storytelling, and healing dance. *Journal of Anthropological Research* 69:65-86.

Knight, C. 1983. Lévi-Strauss and the dragon: *Mythologiques* reconsidered in the light of an Australian Aboriginal myth. *Man* (N.S) 18: 21-50.

Knight, C. 1987. Menstruation and the Origins of Culture. A Reconsideration of Lévi-Strauss's Work on Symbolism and Myth. Unpublished PhD. dissertation. University of London.

Knight, C. 1991. *Blood Relations: Menstruation and the Origins of Culture.* London and New Haven: Yale University Press.

Knight, C. 1997. The wives of the sun and moon. *Journal of the Royal Anthropological Institute* 3: 133-153.

Knight, C. and J. Lewis 2017a. Wild voices: mimicry, reversal, metaphor, and the emergence of language. *Current Anthropology* 58: 435–453.

Knight, C. and J. Lewis 2017b. Towards a theory of everything, in C. Power, M. Finnegan and H. Callan (eds) *Human Origins: Contributions from Social Anthropology*: 84–102. New York & Oxford: Berghahn.

Knight, C., C. Power and I. Watts 1995. The human symbolic revolution: a Darwinian account. *Cambridge Archaeological Journal* 5: 75–114.

Kobayashi, H. and S. Kohshima. 2001. Unique morphology of the human eye and its adaptive meaning. *Journal of Human Evolution* 40: 419–435.

Lee, R.B. 1979. *The !Kung San: Men, Women, and Work in a Foraging Society.* Cambridge: Cambridge University Press.

Lewis, J. 2002. Forest Hunter-gatherers and their World. Unpublished PhD dissertation. University of London.

Lewis, J. 2008. *Ekila*: Blood, bodies, and egalitarian societies. *Journal of the Royal Anthropological Institute* (N. S.) 14: 297–315.

Lewis, J. 2014. Egalitarian social organization: the case of the Mbendjele BaYaka. In B. S. Hewlett (ed.) *Hunter-gatherers of the Congo Basin. Cultures, Histories and Biology of African Pygmies*: 219-243. New Brunswick and London: Transaction Publishers.

Lewis-Williams, J.D. 1981. *Believing and Seeing*. London: Academic Press.

Lloyd, L. n.d. Unpublished notebooks from the Bleek and Lloyd Collection, Vol. VI. Jagger Library, University of Cape Town.

Lombard, M. 2020. The tip cross-sectional areas of poisoned bone arrowheads from southern Africa. *Journal of Archaeological Science: Reports* 33: 102477. https://doi.org/10.1016/j.jasrep.2020.102477

Marlowe, F.W. 2010. *The Hadza hunter-gatherers of Tanzania*. Berkeley, CA and London: University of California Press.

Marlowe, F.W. and J.C. Berbesque. 2012. The human operational sex ratio: Effects of marriage, concealed ovulation, and menopause on mate competition. *Journal of Human Evolution* 63: 834-842. http://dx.doi.org/10.1016/j.jhevol.2012.09.004

Martin, R.D. 1992. Female cycles in relation to paternity in primates, in R. D. Martin, A.F. Dixson and E.J. Wickings (eds) *Paternity in primates: Genetic Tests and Theories*: 238-274. Basel: Karger.

Martin, R.D. 2013. *How we do it*. New York: Basic Books.

Marx, K. 1971 [1857-1858]. *Grundrisse*, trans D. McLellan. London: Macmillan.

Packer, C., A. Swanson, D. Ikanda and H. Kushnir 2011. Fear of darkness, the full moon and the nocturnal ecology of African lions. *PLoS ONE* 6:e22285.

Pawlowski, B., C.B. Lowen and R.I.M. Dunbar. 1998. Neocortex size, social skills and mating success in primates. *Behaviour* 135: 357–368.

Peterson, D. 2013. *Hadzabe. By the Light of a Million Fires* (with R. Baalow and J. Cox). Dar es Salaam: Mkuki na Nyota.

Power, C. 2004. Women in prehistoric art, in G. Berghaus (ed.) *New Perspectives on Prehistoric Art*: 75-103. Westport, CT/London: Praeger.

Power, C. 2009. Sexual selection models for the emergence of symbolic communication: why they should be reversed, in. R. Botha and C. Knight (eds) *The Cradle of Language:* 257–280. Oxford: Oxford University Press.

Power, C. 2011. Lunarchy in the Kingdom of England. *Radical Anthropology* 5: 18-26.

Power, C. 2015. Hadza gender rituals – *Epeme* and *Maitoko* – considered as counterparts. *Hunter Gatherer Research* 1:333-358.

Power, C. 2017. Reconstructing a source cosmology for African hunter-gatherers, in C. Power, M. Finnegan and H. Callan (eds) *Human Origins. Contributions from Social Anthropology*: 180-203. New York and Oxford: Berghahn Books.

Power, C. 2019. The role of egalitarianism and gender ritual in the evolution of symbolic cognition, in T.B. Henley, M.J. Rossano and E.P. Kardas (eds) *Handbook of Cognitive Archaeology. Psychology in Prehistory*: 354-374. New York & London: Routledge.

Power, C. and L.C. Aiello. 1997. Female proto-symbolic strategies, in L. D. Hager (ed.) *Women in human evolution*: 153–171. London: Routledge.

Power, C., V. Sommer and I. Watts 2013. The seasonality thermostat: female reproductive synchrony and male behaviour in monkeys, Neanderthals and modern humans. *Paleoanthropology* 2013: 33-60. doi:10.4207/PA.2013.ART79

Power, C. and I. Watts 1997. The woman with the zebra's penis. Gender, mutability and performance. *Journal of the Royal Anthropological Institute* (N. S.) 3: 537–560.

Power, C. and I. Watts. 1999. First gender, wrong Sex, in H.L. Moore, T. Sanders and B. Kaare (eds) *Those who Play with Fire: Gender, Fertility and Transformation in East and Southern Africa*: 101-132. London: Athlone Press.

Schapera, I. 1930. *The Khoisan Peoples of South Africa: Bushmen and Hottentots.* London: George Routledge and Sons.

Seabright, P. 2012. *The War of the Sexes.* Princeton and Oxford: Princeton University Press.

Sear, R. 2018. Family and fertility: does kin help influence women's fertility, and how does this vary worldwide? *Population Horizons* 14: 18-34. doi: https://doi.org/10.1515/pophzn-2017-0006

Sear, R. and R. Mace 2008. Who keeps children alive? A review of the effects of kin on child survival. *Evolution and Human Behavior* 29: 1–18.

Sims, L. 2006. The 'solarization' of the Moon: manipulated knowledge at Stonehenge. *Cambridge Archaeological Journal* 16: 191-207.

Skaanes, T. 2017a. Cosmology Matters - Power Objects, Rituals, and Meat-sharing among the Hadza of Tanzania. Unpublished PhD dissertation: Aarhus University.

Skaanes, T. 2017b. Sounds in the night. Ritual bells, therianthropes and eland relations among the Hadza, in C. Power, M. Finnegan and H. Callan (eds) *Human origins. Contributions from Social Anthropology*: 204-223. New York and Oxford: Berghahn Books.

Stibbard-Hawkes D.N.E., R.D. Attenborough, I.A. Mabulla, and F.W. Marlowe. 2020. To the hunter go the spoils? No evidence of nutritional benefit to being or marrying a well-reputed Hadza hunter. *American Journal of Physical Anthropology* 173: 1–19. https://doi.org/10.1002/ajpa.24027

Tishkoff, S.A. *et al.* 2007. History of click-speaking populations of Africa inferred from mtDNA and Y chromosome genetic variation. *Molecular Biology and Evolution* 24: 2180–2195.

Tomasello, M., B. Hare, H. Lehmann and J. Call. 2007. Reliance on head versus eyes in the gaze following of great apes and human infants: the cooperative eye hypothesis. *Journal of Human Evolution* 52: 314–320.

Tomasello, M. and H. Rakoczy 2003.What makes human cognition unique? From individual to shared to collective intentionality. *Mind and Language* 18: 121–147.

Turnbull, C. 1957. Initiation among the Bambuti Pygmies of the Central Ituri. *Journal of the Royal Anthropological Institute* 87: 191-216.

Turnbull, C. 1960. The *Elima*: a premarital festival among the Bambuti Pygmies. *Zaïre* 14: 175-192.

Valiente Noailles, C. 1993. *The Kua: Life and soul of the Central Kalahari Bushman.* Rotterdam, Brookfield: A. A. Balkema.

Voland, E., A. Chasiotis and W. Schiefenhövel (eds) 2005. *Grandmotherhood.* Princeton, New Jersey: Rutgers University Press.

Watts, I. 1999. The origin of symbolic culture, in R.I.M. Dunbar, C. Knight and C. Power (eds) *The Evolution of culture*: 113-146. Edinburgh: Edinburgh University Press.

Watts, I. 2005 Time, too, grows on the moon, In W. James and D. Mills (eds) *The Qualities of Time: Anthropological Approaches*: 95-118. Oxford and New York: Berg.

Watts, I. 2014. The red thread: pigment use and the evolution of collective ritual, in D. Dor, C. Knight and J. Lewis (eds) *The Social Origins of* Language: 208–227. Oxford: Oxford University Press.

Watts, I. 2017. Rain serpents in Northern Australia and Southern Africa, in C. Power, M. Finnegan and H. Callan (eds) *Human Origins. Contributions from Social Anthropology*: 248-271. New York and Oxford: Berghahn Books.

Watts, I., M. Chazan and J. Wilkins 2016. Early evidence for brilliant ritualized display: specularite use in the Northern Cape (South Africa) between ~500 ka and ~300 ka. *Current Anthropology* 57: 287-310.

Whiten, A. and D. Erdal. 2012. The human socio-cognitive niche and its evolutionary origins. *Philosophical Transactions of the Royal Society*, Series B 367: 2119–2129.

Woodburn, J. 1964. The Social Organization of the Hadza of North Tanganyika. Unpublished PhD dissertation. University of Cambridge.

Woodburn, J. 1968. Stability and flexibility in Hadza residential groups, In R.B. Lee and I. DeVore (eds) *Man the Hunter:* 103–110. Chicago: Aldine.

Woodburn, J. 1982a. Social dimensions of death in four African hunting and gathering societies, In M. Bloch and J. Parry (eds) *Death and the Regeneration of Life*: 187–210. Cambridge: Cambridge University Press.

Woodburn, J. 1982b. Egalitarian societies. *Man* 17: 431–451.

Zeng, T.C., A.J. Aw and M.W. Feldman 2018. Cultural hitchhiking and competition between patrilineal kin groups explain the post-Neolithic Y-chromosome bottleneck. *Nature Communications* 9: 2077. https://doi.org/10.1038/s41467-018-04375-6

Hunting by the Moon in Human Evolution

Ian Watts

Introduction

Currently there are understood to be two stages in the emergence of modern humans: first, evolution of a flatter face from c. 320,000 years (Hublin *et al.* 2017); second, globularisation of the skull, from c. 230,000 years (Neubauer *et al.* 2018; Vidal *et al.* 2022). With a globular vault more widely established by c. 150,000 (Bergstrom *et al.* 2021), it appears that brain-size only reached maximum values during this second stage (Watts 2014: tbl.16.1). This paper proposes that during this second stage a critical role was played by a novel, highly productive hunting strategy – dry season ambush hunting close to water holes on moonlit nights. Any brain-size increase placed additional costs on maternal energy budgets. Dry seasons were inherently calorically challenging, a problem exacerbated by the persistently dry climates prevailing from 195-145,000 years ago. This new productive strategy enabled our ancestors to afford slightly larger brains under unfavourable conditions.

The germ of the proposal came from hearing a conference presentation by Kristen Hawkes in 1991, where data was presented showing dry season nocturnal ambush hunting to be the most productive form of hunting among the Hadzabe of the Eyasi Basin in northern Tanzania (Hawkes *et al.* 1991), using bows and poisoned arrows. Hawkes did not mention lunar periodicity, but this had already been reported by other scholars (Bunn *et al.* 1988: 425). In the audience were Lionel Sims, Chris Knight, Camilla Power, and myself. There were three reasons this aspect of Hawkes' findings, which was not her main focus, struck us as having potential evolutionary significance. First, the close ranges involved in nocturnal ambush hunting (Bunn *et al.* 1988) suggested that it would have been even more important before the invention of the bow and arrow or of poisons. Second, there was also evidence that the technique, with similar seasonal and lunar constraints, was shared by Kalahari Bushmen (Crowell and Hitchcock 1978), suggesting a widespread adaptation to African seasonality. Third, we were theoretically engaged with an abstract model of the origin of symbolic culture that posited the successful return of hunters to a home-base around Full Moon as part of its initial conditions (Knight 1991).

The potential significance of night ambush hunting to our understanding of human evolution was touched on in a revision to Knight's 'sex-strike' model (Knight, Power and Watts 1995: 90; see also Watts 2005: 105-106), but it has never been developed. In Knight's original model, men are motivated to go hunting by women's ritual action. A successful hunt will bring sexual rewards but failure will not. With the limitations of Middle and earlier Late Pleistocene hunting technology, a greater role for collective hunting was assumed relative to later periods. For logistically organised collective hunting of medium to large game, hunters needed to optimise available natural light – to allow for overnight stays away from a home-base. The optimal time would, therefore, be when moonlight took over from sunlight, the Moon's second quarter – the Waxing Gibbous phase. This constraint led to a monthly peak of hunting activity in the period of sexual abstinence building up to Full Moon, with men then returning home to inaugurate a period of cooking, feasting and sexual availability, formally coming to an end at Dark Moon. Knight simply argued that evolving hominins should have had the flexibility to exploit extended natural light during the Waxing Gibbous Moon, whether to 'travel overnight or extend the hunt into the twilight hours' (Knight 1991: 345). No ethnographic predictions were made about hunting techniques or timing, only that if lunar periodicity figured at all in *normative beliefs* about hunting, it should be consistent with this logic.

Recent updating of Crowell and Hitchcock's ethnoarchaeological case study (Hitchcock *et al.* 2019) and this festschrift for Lionel Sims provide the opportunity to begin to develop an evolutionary perspective on moonlit ambush hunting and to consider how – informed by the 'sex-strike' or 'Female Cosmetic Coalitions' model – it might mediate between two previously unrelated fields: the energetics of our African speciation in the late Middle Pleistocene and aspects of Hadza and Bushman symbolic practices and beliefs.

Hadza lunar ambush hunting

One reason the Hadzabe attracted the attention of behavioural ecologists was because they are the only surviving low-latitude hunter-gatherers whose hunting is focused on medium to large game, similar to the focus of both our immediate ancestors and Neanderthals. Among the research topics addressed by Hawkes' team was *why* men preferentially hunt medium to large game, questioning the standard assumption that it was to feed themselves and their immediate family (Hawkes *et al.* 1991). They compared the return rates for the different kinds of meat/fat procurement actually practised against an experimentally-based return rate for focusing on small game, concluding that the latter would be optimal for nuclear family provisioning.

The three main techniques for obtaining medium to large game were scavenging (primarily dry season, accounting for 15-20% of carcass acquisition), daytime pursuit hunting (all seasons) and nocturnal ambush hunting from blinds by waterholes in the late dry season. Nocturnal ambush hunting was more than three times as successful as the combination of scavenging and pursuit hunting over the same season, more than twice as productive as scavenging/pursuit hunting over all seasons and about 50% more productive than wet season scavenging/pursuit hunting (Hawkes *et al.* 1991: tbl.2). It was estimated that almost half of the animals >40kg annually killed or scavenged by the Hadza were obtained in the three months of the late dry season (O'Connell *et al.* 1992: 320 and tbl.1). Game tend to approach waterholes by well-trodden trails. Search time is eliminated; concealed behind blinds, hunters wait for the animals to come to them, with a good chance of being within close range. Henry Bunn and colleagues reached a similar conclusion about the seasonal productivity of night ambush hunting, adding that it typically occurred on moonlit nights (Bunn *et al.* 1988). Combining the results from both research teams, the species most frequently taken this way were zebra and impala, followed by wildebeest and hartebeest; warthog and giraffe were hardly ever killed this way (O'Connell *et al.* 1992: tbl.3). With only two elands in the samples (both encounter hunted), no inference can be drawn about their vulnerability to ambush hunting.

Bunn and colleagues provided the following summary of the technique:

> hunters, either singly or in pairs, spend moonlit nights at these localities in anticipation of getting a relatively easy, close range (i.e. 20m or less) shot at a large animal, including zebra, impala, or hartebeest. The hunters wait in ambush in recurrently used spots including trees above game trails, rocky ledges overlooking swampy water holes, and artificially constructed blinds. ... A fire is built in the firepit and allowed to die down to embers, ... Then there may be a long period during which the hunter waits for the moon to rise and listens for the sound of approaching animals. The hunter may fall asleep, but the sound of the clattering hooves ... is usually sufficient to wake him in time to prepare for a shot. ... At dawn, the hunter leaves the blind to track any wounded animal or to walk back to the base camp (Bunn *et al.* 1988: 425).

A Hadza bow is accurate up to about 50 metres (Cooper 1949; Pontzer *et al.* 2017), more than twice the typical maximum range involved in ambush hunting. To the range of natural features sometimes used for ambushing, Stephenson (2000: 23-27) adds the simple expedient of flattening tall grass, leaving a standing periphery adjacent to a game trail.

Bunn's quantitative data, with dates of acquisition, spanned the period from the beginning of October to mid-December 1986, with the first rains falling at the very end of October. Of the 26 medium-to-large herbivores obtained, half were obtained in October (1988: tbl.3). Seven of these were obtained by night ambush hunting (4 impala, 2 zebra and a buffalo), four by daytime encounter hunting (2 warthog, a baboon and a buffalo), and two where the technique was unspecified (a kudu and a hartebeest). Surprisingly, only four of the successful nocturnal ambush hunts were during moonlit nights (from 2nd and 3rd quarters); three of the four impala were killed on moonless nights. This might be explained by twilight (crepuscular) rather than nocturnal hunting, with the hunter needing to be in position well before evening or morning drinking (Marlowe 2010: 119; Mouriki fieldnotes, 7th June 2005). No night ambush hunting occurred after October. The late Frank Marlowe's considerably larger body of unpublished data would have to be analysed to establish conclusively whether ambush hunting was disproportionately around Full Moon. This is assumed here on the basis of all general characterisations (Bunn *et al.* 1988: 425; Stephenson 2000: 88; Marlowe 2010: 118).

I spent time with the Hadzabe in the dry seasons of 2004 and 2005. In the middle of the 2004 dry season, two nights after the Full Moon of 31st July (96% illumination), I joined two Hadza for ambush hunting and can add some observations to Bunn's descriptive summary. The location was very similar to that described and illustrated by O'Connell and colleagues (1992: fig.1), with three or four blinds in the tree-line adjacent to a spring-fed marsh; their location meant that a man standing up to take a shot offered no clear silhouette. A fire was not lit in the blind, but a few metres back in the bushes (where there was a heavily curated whetstone for arrowheads); live coals were transferred to small fire-pits in the two blinds to be occupied and tamped down with soil to eliminate smoke and flame. The blind I co-occupied was semi-circular, about 1.5m in diameter and partially cut into the soil at the base of a tree (with lithic artefacts in the profile); this reduced the above-ground height of the blind by about 20 centimetres.

There is a small body of earlier Hadza literature providing complementary and/or additional insights (Rech 1914: 14, citing Obst 1912; Bagshawe 1924-5: 123-4; Bleek 1930: 190-193; Kohl-Larsen 1958: 63, 162 [fieldwork in 1934-35]; Woodburn 1968: 51). Obst and Kohl Larsen reported that ambush hunting was done from blinds partially cut into the earth. Bagshawe described it as 'One of their favourite methods of hunting', adding that they camped away from waterholes so as not to disturb game coming to drink and that, following the construction of a blind, it was left for a period to allow the game to become accustomed to it. The blinds were occupied without fire, which Bagshawe considered a contributory factor to 'many of the best hunters' having been taken by lions (Bagshawe 1924: 124). That fire is not a prerequisite is corroborated by Stephenson (2000: 23), but the threat from lions is real enough (Petersen, Barlowe and Cox 2011: 63).

Bushman lunar ambush hunting

Unremarked in the behavioural ecologists' initial reporting of Hadza night ambush hunting was that similar findings had been made a decade earlier by Aron Crowell and Bob Hitchcock, working with informants from two Kalahari Bushman groups, the Ju|'hoansi (!Kung) of the northwestern Kalahari and the Tyua (|Kaicwa), a Tshwa speaking group living along the Nata River in the eastern Kalahari (Crowell and Hitchcock 1978). Night ambush hunting had seemed of minor importance among the Ju|'hoansi (J. Marshall 1958: 378; L. Marshall 1960: 342; Lee 1979: 211). John Marshall mistakenly thought it was restricted to the rainy season. Lorna Marshall thought it was 'extremely rare', believing that eland and gemsbok 'seldom come to water-holes'. Richard Lee first mentioned the technique fifteen years after starting fieldwork, reporting it as crepuscular rather than nocturnal. Among other intensively studied Bushman groups, it had gone entirely unreported (Tanaka 1980; Silberbauer 1965, 1981). Prior to 1978, one of the few reported details was that unspecified Namibian Bushmen burnt special herbs and pieces of wood in the blind: 'to absorb the human odour. Even elephants pass close to the hunter without smelling him' (Castell-Rudenhausen 1966: 133).

Crowell and Hitchcock's work came about through archaeological investigations at ≠Gi pan, where Ju|'hoan explained the former use of the numerous circular stone structures, recounting details of ambush hunting at this and other pans and salt licks in the Dobe area. All the larger pans in Dobe and areas immediately to the west and east provide evidence for hunting blinds and/or pit traps (Brooks and Yellen 1987: 75; Hitchcock *et al.* 2019: tbl.1; see also Müller 2005: 200; Gaerdes 1966-67: fig.4). Crowell and Hitchcock's informants reported that ambush hunting was restricted to moonlit nights (1978: 38). A fire was lit in the blind, allowed to burn down and the coals carefully banked. Compared to the Eyasi Basin, the benefits of fire are greater, as freezing temperatures are common in the early dry season (Silberbauer 1981: fig.2); its use for protection from lions was not mentioned (but see Peters and Vogelsang 2009: 150).

While the ≠Gi blinds were on the surface, those at several nearby sites were pit-blinds, dug 20 to 30cm into the ground. An important factor in the placement of blinds in relation to game-trails was the seasonally prevailing wind direction (see also Peters and Vogelsang 2009: 150). In common with most Bushman groups, the primary weapon was the bow and poisoned arrows. However, Bushman bows are much smaller than Hadza counterparts, only accurate to a range of between 20-30 metres (Tanaka 1996: 15; Marshall 1999: 145; Silberbauer 1981: 206). For medium sized prey, they do not cause a serious wound; consequently, metal-tipped spears were also brought along for killing wounded prey (likely to occur the following day) and for protection from lions whilst in the blind (Crowell and Hitchcock 1978: 38).

The 14 blinds around ≠Gi had a mean distance to game trails of 6.6 metres (Hitchcock et al. 2019: tbl.5 [closest trails have a mean distance of 3.3m]). Informants recalled getting roan (a large antelope in the *Hippotragus* genus), kudu, wildebeest, and numerous duiker (a small antelope). Roan were said to be almost exclusively taken this way hunting (Hitchcock *et al.* 2019: 139-140; see also Müller 2005: 200). The mean distance of successful bow shots was 26m (1978: 49). Based on informants' recollections of the number of nights spent in blinds and the species and number of animals killed, a rough calculation of productivity (kg per man hour) was derived and compared to that of diurnal pursuit hunting: Ju|'hoan night ambush hunting in the Dobe area 'was approximately two and a half times' more productive than diurnal pursuit hunting in the same season (Hitchcock *et al.* 2019: 129; see Brooks and Yellen 1987: 76 for an even larger differential).

Crowell and Hitchcock noted that diurnal pursuit hunting of large game was 'minimally productive' during the dry season (1978: 43, citing Wilmsen 1976; see Wilmsen 1989: fig.6.11), on which basis they suggested – as a historical rather than evolutionary assessment – that night ambush hunting 'may formerly have provided the easiest method of obtaining large game during that time of year'. By contrast, among the Kua of the Western Sandveld, nocturnal ambush hunting was poorly productive compared to all other techniques (Hitchcock and Bleed 1997: 357-9), probably attributable to exceptionally low game densities in a region long-dominated by pastoralism (Campbell *et al.* 2006: 197).

Tyua use of blinds was similarly restricted to moonlit nights and typically involved 2-3 men occupying different blinds. Trees along the Nata River meant that some were elevated platforms (hunting stands), providing protection from lions (Hitchcock 1982: 249), but most were chest-deep, log-roofed pit-blinds and sometimes just a reed screen (Crowell and Hitchcock 1978: 44). Guns or spears were the weapons used, buffalo being exclusively killed with guns. Night ambush hunting was more productive than among the Ju|'hoan, not only because of guns, but the larger number of animals coming to drink and the much shorter average range at which kills were made (around 10 metres). It was less seasonally restricted, but dry season hunting of (formerly) large herds of wildebeest and small herds of buffalo coming to drink at remaining pools in the river was so productive that the meat was traded with neighbouring groups. As wildebeest and buffalo approached the river pools in groups, hunters could select the fattest individuals (Crowell and Hitchcock 1978: 44). A subsequent analysis of 43 Tyua spear hunts found that nocturnal ambush hunting greatly predominated over three kinds of diurnal pursuit hunting (stalking, with dogs, on horseback) and was the only technique to be 100% successful when game was encountered (Hitchcock and Bleed 1997: fig.3).

In the updated presentation of Dobe Ju|'hoan data (Hitchcock *et al.* 2019: tbl.1), we learn that there had been a resurgence of ambush hunting between the 1970s and 1990s, followed by a subsequent decline, both in response to increasingly harsh state policies curtailing hunting. Across the Kalahari, the authors report more than 180 blinds from 30 pans. As in the original paper, attention is drawn to the slightly more collective nature of ambush hunting compared to pursuit hunting. However, among the paper's conclusions was the following statement: 'They use blinds mainly on non-moonlit nights in the winter so the prey animals and other predators (e.g., lions) would not see them' (2019: 139). That this directly contradicted the original research passed without comment. I asked Bob Hitchcock about this and he kindly replied:

> I would change my conclusions in light of additional interviews in June 2019 in Nyae Nyae [neighbouring Dobe, on the Namibian side of the border]; the hunters there (n=16) say that they *do* hunt on Full Moon nights so they can see the animals. They also say that they worry about lions, even though they realise that lions are mainly Dark Moon hunters. They say that they have seen them on both Full Moon and Dark Moon nights. Their preference is for Full Moon hunting in Nyae Nyae. (pers. comm. 3.12.20, square parentheses and emphasis added).

To the already-mentioned Ju|'hoansi, Kua, and Tyua/Tshwa accounts, several other Kalahari Bushmen groups can be added: the Hei||om around Etosha pan in Namibia (Cippriani 1931: 21-22; Gordon 1997: 155 and photograph BA22; Peters and Vogelsang 2009: 124, 148, 150); the Nharo in Botswana's Ghanzi District (Bleek 1928: 16, regarding salt licks; see also Baines 1864: 199, 205 for blinds in the Ghanzi area); the !Xóõ of the southwestern Kalahari (Hitchcock 2017: 18; Hitchcock and Bleed 1997: 354); and the G|wi and G||ana of the Central District (Valiente-Noailles 1993: 63). In short, almost all Bushman groups in the Kalahari practised ambush hunting by waterholes.

All indications are that this was overwhelmingly a nocturnal technique, largely restricted to the dry season. Productivity was presumably lowest in areas lacking surface water at this time, but it was clearly still worthwhile, presumably because salt licks typically associate with pans. Gemsbok for example, accounting for 38% of total game weight procured by the G|wi (Tanaka 1996: 15), primarily visited pans for salt (Knight *et al.* 1988: 278; Passarge 1997 [1907]: 165). Nocturnal ambush hunting was most productive in the better watered eastern Kalahari, where it could produce a surplus to be traded. Elsewhere, the late dry season associates with minimum hunting returns and in these contexts the technique considerably improved otherwise dismal prospects – as among the Ju|'hoansi. The only caveat is when game has become *so* scarce that diurnal pursuit hunting remains the best option, as among the Kua. Notwithstanding the stark contrast in dry season hunting productivity between the Hadza and most Bushman groups, nocturnal ambush hunting plays a critical role in both environments.

Historical records

Soon after Dutch settlement at Cape Town, it was being reported that the Khoikhoi pastoralists would kill a wide range of wild game that came to drink at the few remaining waterholes in the dry season (Schreyer 1668; Raven-Hart 1971: 123). Perhaps the earliest account of moonlit hunting was that that of Hendrik Wikar in 1779, describing Khoikhoi along the Orange River collectively hunting grazing hippopotamus with spears (Wikar [1779] 1935: 103). Contemporaneously, Robert Jacob Gordon repeatedly reported stone hunting blinds in the Karroo, the interior plateau immediately beyond the Cape fold-belt mountains, inhabited by both Khoikhoi pastoralists and Bushmen (Raper and Boucher 1988: 88, 118, 121, 122; see also Sparrman 1975 [1785-86]: 195). Immediately north of the Vaal River, Hodgson reported that Bushmen 'conceal themselves in the grass by the side of a river or watering place to which the animals resort and then kill them with their assegais' (Hodgson 1977: 139, entry from 1823). In 1836, Harris (1952: 35-6) made a similar general observation about Bushmen on the Ghaap Plateau in the northern Cape, adding that this was a reason Bushmen did not camp by the waterholes. At a spring near the confluence of the Vaal with the Orange, Backhouse (1844: 445) reported several hunting blinds. Recalling observations from the 1870s, Dunn

(1931: 33) reported that Bushmen of the Karroo would block springs to force animals to drink at an ambush site. At Stink Fontein in the Eastern Cape, Gordon Cumming (1850: 147-8) was informed by a Bushman that the wildebeest would come to drink once the Moon had risen.

Most of these accounts would have concerned the |Xam, whose principal prey were springbok, a dependence doubtless exacerbated by the impact of colonialism from the late eighteenth through to the mid-nineteenth century, which took a heavy toll on larger antelope (Farini 1886: 114). There are numerous references in the Bleek and Lloyd archive to springbok being hunted nocturnally, including mention of earth and brush blinds and a hunter's return at Full Moon (Bleek and Lloyd 1911: 53-5, 283; see also Watts 2005: 105 and endnote 27). That they were particularly susceptible to dry season ambush hunting by water holes was noted by Holub (1881: 34; see also Chapman 1971a: 141, 1971b: 43).

While the evidence from the Cape is scrappy, ambush hunting by waterholes was evidently widespread; by analogy with the Kalahari data, the likelihood is that it was predominantly restricted to the dry season, nocturnal, and reliant on moonlight. From the mid-nineteenth century, the corpus of literature rapidly expands in quantity, detail and geographic extent (embracing Namaqualand, the entire Kalahari Basin, Matabeland [eastern Zimbabwe] and the headwaters of the Zambesi), largely due to the boom in demand for ivory following the invention and industrialised manufacture of upright pianos (Gordon 1992: 33-40). Moonlit ambush hunting by waterholes became a prime contributor to the decimation of elephant and rhino populations across southern Africa (Selous 1888: 191, see also Galton 1853: 274-6; Andersson 1856: 397; 409; Tindall 1856: 22).

Aside from all the Bushman groups mentioned above, most other Kalahari peoples also practised night ambush hunting – Damara, Nama, Tjimba, Tswana, Bakalahadi (Tindall 1959: 59; Galton 1853: 271, 276; Holub 1881: 32; Hodson 1912: 22). While many were drawn into the ivory trade (often using Bushman as serfs for this purpose), night ambush hunting had been an integral part of subsistence economies, underscoring the productivity of the technique. Europeans primarily considered it a Bushmen technique (Livingstone 1857: 161); Chapman reused Bushman blinds (1971b: 50), Baines (1864: 205) described circular stone blinds in Ghanzi district identical to the Ju|'hoan examples at ≠Gi and Gautscha Pans, and, as noted above, a Bushman told Gordon Cumming that the wildebeest would come to drink once the Moon had risen. The adoption of the technique by Europeans was so thorough that by the early twentieth century, a German settler-farmer in Namibia believed that the cultural transfer had been in the reverse direction, from Boer to Bushmen (Willhelm 1958: 124).

A wealth of detail is available, concerning seasonality, the animals that came to drink, their numbers, the use of salt-licks, the importance of lunar phase, the construction of blinds and the danger from lions. One of the most valuable accounts is James Chapman's (1971a, 1971b), with at least 62 dated mentions of nocturnal ambush hunts and/or of nocturnal drinking, spanning all seasons and all lunar phases over periods between 1852 and1864. At least 15 nights were spent nocturnal ambush hunting during the rainy season months of January-March of 1862, of which only five had potential lunar visibility equal to or greater than 50% (probably reduced by cloud-cover). Nothing came to drink on seven of these nights and only elephant and rhino in the remainder, with no patterning by lunar phase. Irrespective of season or lunar phase, these were the most habitual nocturnal drinkers. In better watered regions, the next most frequently reported species was buffalo, with most visits being when there was more than 50% illumination. Zebra and wildebeest were probably numerically predominant, often coming in large herds, overwhelmingly in the dry season. Of the six wildebeest reports, only one was when illumination was lower than 40%, whereas three of the seven zebra reports were on nights with less than 15% illumination, suggesting a difference in visual acuity between the two species, consistent with indigenous knowledge regarding wildebeest (Metzger 1995: 16).

There are fewer accounts of other species, nearly all from the dry season. Giraffe and eland appear to have been unconcerned with illumination, but visits by springbok, sable, roan, waterbuck and steenbok were all on nights with 75% illumination or more. At a pan in the eastern Kalahari at the height of the 1852 dry season, just after a Full Moon, Chapman estimated that approximately 12,000 animals came to drink (1971a: 141). A few years later, at Mutomabye pan, in the same region, during a Full Moon at the beginning of the dry season, he reported 'thousands of thirsty game' (1971b: 50). Springbok came within two yards of his blind (1971a: 141). While such proximity was not the norm, it was not rare either; Chapman's companion Thomas Baines (1864: 319, 361, 394) reported proximities of five feet, three yards and six yards, for elephant, rhino and hyena respectively. One of the main reasons given for building blinds was for protection, both from large, wounded game, and from lions (Baines 1864: 356; Clifford 1930: 20; Schultze 1907: 290).

In the wider historical literature, other species were also reported as nocturnal drinkers (tsessebe, blesbok, kudu [Cumming 1850], impala [Selous 1888]). Selous's account of eland drinking habits and ecological adaptability is worth quoting:

> Along the Chobe [northern Botswana], the elands drink regularly in the river, usually during the night or just at daybreak, and then feed away through the forest-clad sand-belts, ... In other parts of the country, however, where for several months of the year there is absolutely no water, elands, in common with gemsbuck and giraffe, live and thrive, ... (Selous 1888: 206-7).

The historical literature is consistent with numerous scientific censuses in different regions where – after elephant and rhino – the most habitual dry season nocturnal drinkers are buffalo, giraffe and eland (Weir and Davidson 1965; Ayeni 1975; du Preez and Grobler 1977; Hayward and Hayward 2012; Kasiringua *et al.* 2017). Under conditions of no lion predation risk, eland were predominantly nocturnal drinkers (Kasirungua *et al.* 2017); even where lions might be present, it was noted that 'Eland was the only herbivore that regularly used waterholes at night' (Hayward and Hayward 2012: 120). The historical accounts have one advantage over the censuses, most of which were conducted at Full Moon; they indicate that while there was more drinking around Full Moon, it was not restricted to this phase, suggesting that the human preference had as much to do with our poor night vision as herbivore behaviour. Most hunters bemoaned missing their mark on moonless nights (Cumming 1850: 83; Chapman 1971a: 63; Holub 1888: 269-73; Hodson 1912: 23-4). However, as noted, it was very large animals that were more likely to drink under poor illumination, generally the ones that would have been hardest and most dangerous to try and kill without firearms, with eland being the relative exception (Lewis-Williams 1981).

The reason most medium sized game preferred moonlit nights was presumably the threat from lions, a consideration even for Europeans with guns. Lion predation is mostly nocturnal (Crosmary *et al.* 2012; Valeix *et al.* 2009), disproportionately during Dark Moon (Funston *et al.* 2001; Packer *et al.* 2011; but see Cozzi *et al.* 2012), when lions are most active (Traill *et al.* 2016: fig. S1). This extends to lion predation on humans, with the most dangerous nights being immediately after Full Moon – with the successively longer intervals of darkness between sunset and moonrise (Packer *et al.* 2011). Galton, travelling in what is now eastern Namibia during the height of the 1851 dry season, reported that two native hunters (possibly Nama) had recently been killed by lions while sitting in their hunting blinds (Galton 1853: 259). It was believed that the threat was greater on dark nights (e.g. Tindall 1959: 60; Cumming 1850: 198), with some evidence supporting the belief (Chapman 1971a: 140, 1971b: 42). Cumming (1850) believed that lions preferentially drank when there was no Moon. On the other hand, from Chapman's diaries, of the seven mentions of nocturnal presence of lions at pans, only two were on Dark Moon nights; five were on nights with greater than 50% visibility – although on at least two of these occasions lion activity preceded Moon rise.

A range of historical factors contributed to a reduced importance of nocturnal ambush hunting from the late nineteenth century onwards, to the point where anthropologists in the third quarter of the twentieth century considered it insignificant. These factors ranged from European overkill (Farini 1886: 114; Gordon 1992: 39), habitat degradation through pastoralist expansion enabled by boreholes – typically at pans (Campbell 1981; Gordon 1992), fencing (Campbell 1981), government prohibitions (Gordon 1992: 540) – including two Bechuanaland decrees outlawing ambush hunting (Hitchcock *et al.* 1996: 185; Hitchcock and Bleed 1997: 360), and a long-term trend of reduced surface water over much of the Kalahari (Raseroka 1975; Campbell 1981).

Archaeological evidence likely to bear on nocturnal ambush hunting

Stone-tipped spear technology

The transition from the Acheulean to Middle Palaeolithic industries (Middle Stone Age [MSA] and loosely analogous Mousterian) is when points and/or blades were added to the million-year-old tradition of hand axes and cleavers. In southern Africa, this transition is known as the Fauresmith, between around 500 thousand years ago (500 ka, for short) and 300 ka (Porrat *et al.* 2010; Wilkins and Chazan 2012; Chazan *et al.* 2013). One aspect of this major technological transition concerns the appearance of archaeologically recognisable hunting technology. On the basis of impact fractures, basal modification and edge damage, some Fauresmith points from Kathu Pan are interpreted as hafted spear armatures, probably used as thrusting rather than thrown weapons (Wilkins *et al.* 2012; Wilkins *et al.* 2015; Wilkins and Schoville 2016). Wooden spears do not require composite armatures to be effective, particularly if the point is fire-hardened (Waguespack *et al.* 2009), but a stone point creates a significantly larger inner wound cavity, a critical variable in the stopping or killing power of a penetrative weapon (Wilkins *et al.* 2014), more likely to cause haemorrhage. For medium sized game and predator-defence, this would be especially important for a thrust weapon, where the mass of the armature contributes to the high kinetic energy required for a severe wound (Churchill *et al.* 2009).

Two complementary strategies are used to investigate the development of stone point hunting technology: assemblage-scale, probabilistic analyses and individual artefact analysis (Wilkins *et al.* 2015). Lombard and Churchill (2022) has presented a southern African, multi-site analysis of the 'tip cross-sectional areas' (TCSA) of stone points from the Fauresmith through the MSA. This suggests a gradual shift from reliance on thrusting spears that could also be thrown effectively over short distances, to increased use of lightweight javelins, accurate up to 30 m (ibid: 7). The latter were habitually used by c. 80 ka (alongside heavier predecessors), with their initial development tentatively identified from c. 190 ka (Lombard 2021). A global survey of ethnographic literature suggested the effective distance of a hand-cast spear is about 10m (Churchill 1993). Subsequent experimental data combined with re-evaluation of ethnographic sources suggests a range of 15-20m, although the experimental data with trained throwers showed that accuracy declined from 58% at 5m, to 33% at 10m (Milks *et al.* 2019: 7).

Turning to individual artefact analysis, one of the earliest claims for thrown ('projectile') stone-tipped spears is from Ethiopia at round 300 ka (Sahle *et al.* 2013; but see Douze and Delange 2016). Currently, the most compelling early evidence for stone spear points interpreted as projectiles comes from use-wear analysis at Misliya (Levant), dating between about 212 ka and 166 ka (Groman-Yaroslavski *et al.* 2021). At Pinnacle Point (southern Cape), it is inferred that projectiles capable of being thrown more than 5m were probably being used from around 100 ka, possibly as far back as 170 ka (O'Driscoll and Thompson 2018). In Natal, a compelling case for specialised, serrated bifacial projectile points has been made for the basal layers at Sibudu (>77 ka), with spear-thrower or bow delivery proposed (Rots *et al.* 2017). However, Lombard (2021; Lombard and Churchill 2022) has concluded that all proposed spear-thrower darts –including Brooks *et al*'s (2006) proposal for Gi Pan points at c. 77 ka and Sahle and Brooks' (2019) proposal for c. 80 ka points at Aduma– are better interpreted as occupying the lighter end of the 'javelin' distribution of tip cross-sections. Also, at Sibudu, a circumstantial case has been made for bow and arrow technology going back to the Howiesons Poort sub-stage of the MSA, at about 64 ka (Lombard and Phillipson 2010). The earliest direct evidence for use of poisons is around 24 ka (d'Errico *et al.* 2012), with possible circumstantial evidence at little over 77 ka (Rots *et al.* 2017).

The increased range and penetrative power of these Late Pleistocene hand-cast spears would have assisted ambush hunting, but they were probably primarily developed as an aid to diurnal pursuit hunting. A stalking bow-hunter can rarely get within 20m of prey in open habitats (Tanaka 1978: 202), a 10m range being exceptional (Tanaka 1996: 15). This non-technological constraint suggests that nocturnal ambush hunting, with relatively short (<10m) ranges to game-trails, was established prior to these early Late Pleistocene improvements in spear-tip design. Lombard's analyses indicate that the earliest potential stone-tipped javelins do not predate c. 190 ka; a plausible implication is that by that date, thrusting spears could accurately be cast distances of 5-10m, adequate to the requirements of nocturnal ambush hunting.

MSA hunting blinds?

Decades ago, drawing on Crowell and Hitchcock's ≠Gi pan research and their own excavation of the site, Brooks and Yellen (1987: 96) proposed that Sampson's 1960's excavation of Orangia 1 in the Karroo (Sampson 1968, 1978) provided strong support for ambush hunting from waterside blinds extending back to the MSA. For the last few kilometres before its confluence with the

Orange, the Berg River had cut a narrow gorge which opened out somewhat in its middle section. The archaeological site, about 15m from the present river and located just where the gorge narrows again, was a sealed horizon providing a cluster of eight semicircular and elliptical stone structures associated with a rich scatter of MSA lithics. The lithics include 11 'trimmed points', four of which were tightly clustered in one of the semi-circular structures, which were otherwise largely free of lithics (Sampson 1968, fig.16). The illustrated examples were partially bifacial with reduced butts (Sampson 1968, fig.24), suggestive of spear armatures. A line of torrent gravel and boulders suggested that the river was formerly 5m closer to the structures. Sampson (1978: 17) thought the gorge was used as a natural game funnel. The structures comprise several tiers of cobbles, all aligned to the stream; the six semi-circular examples range from 1.2m to 1.5m in diameter and closely resemble the ≠Gi pan blinds; and four were dug 30-60 cm into the soil (Sampson 1978: 21). Unfortunately, no organics were preserved and the site is now submerged by a dam.

At the time of publication, there was no archaeological or anthropological literature on Bushman ambush hunting, so Sampson (1968) proposed that the structures were sleeping hollows, despite having emphasised the advantageous location for hunting. He now accepts a hunting-blind interpretation (pers. comm. 21.12.92). However, in an unpublished conference paper, he questioned the association of the MSA lithics with the structures, suggesting that the latter were more likely to be terminal Pleistocene or early Holocene (Sampson 1988, cited by Thackeray 1992: 425, and pers. comm. 21.12.92). I do not know whether Sampson provided site-specific support for this revision, but there is nothing in the original accounts to suggest any Later Stone Age material, nor any basis for doubting the direct association between lithics and structures. Given that no MSA architectural features were known at the time, he was presumably being professionally cautious. Today, while MSA architectural features remain rare, they are not unprecedented (Barham *et al.* 2000; McDonald *et al.* 2016). Following Sampson's landscape interpretation of a game funnel, the blinds functioned as part of collective drives, suggesting probable diurnal use (but see Chapman 1971b: 50 for Bushmen using torches in nocturnal drives). Either way, Brooks and Yellen's proposed MSA antiquity to night ambush hunting remains compelling. More tenuous evidence concerns artificial pits in a palaeo-lake margin at Bir Sahara, excavation BS-12 (Campbell 1993). These ranged from 0.5m to 2m in diameter, the deepest of which was a stepped-in pit a metre deep (Wendorf *et al.* 1993a: 106). Reported as having been excavated to the water-level of the period, they were interpreted as shallow wells (Wendorf *et al.* 1993a: 106), dug in the dry season (Campbell 1993: 519). Early Late Pleistocene *Homo sapiens* was clearly capable of excavating pit blinds.

Faunal exploitation

From at least 400 ka, the ancestors of both Neanderthals and ourselves were collectively hunting medium to large sized animals, with mass-kills of bison at Atapuerca in Spain (Rodriguez-Hidalgo *et al.* 2017) and the selection of prime-age fallow deer in the Levant (Stiner *et al.* 2009). Several Levantine sites indicate similarly selective hunting across a range of species throughout the later Middle Pleistocene (Stiner 2005; Yeshurun *et al.* 2007). In what is now the Nefud Desert of Arabia, sometime between around 500 ka and 300 ka, hominins (and lions) are thought to have been ambush hunting wildebeest in a lake-margin setting (Stewart *et al.* 2019). In Africa, late Middle Pleistocene sites with fauna are rare. One such site is Bundu pan in the Northern Cape, thought to date between 200 ka and 300 ka (Kiberd 2006). The fairly small faunal sample – with signs of butchery and cooking – is dominated by wildebeest, equids and warthog (Hutson 2018). Warthog indicates that at least some of the procurement was diurnal.

In the European Late Pleistocene (beginning around 125 ka), evidence for jump-kill sites, other forms of collective drives and targeting of prime-age adults, all become more frequent (Marin *et al.* 2017; White *et al.* 2016). This is probably an artefact of improved archaeological visibility and faunal preservation rather than any major improvement in techniques. The zooarchaeological picture in Africa also dramatically improves. One of the most informative sites remains Klasies River Mouth on the southern Cape coast (Klein 1976). The dominant species is eland, totally disproportionate to their likely relative significance in the landscape (see also Marean *et al.* 2000). The eland sample is dominated by prime-age adults; while Klein inferred collective drives, the targeting of animals in peak condition seems more likely (Speth 2010: 64), equally if not more consistent with ambush hunting. Another prominent species is the historically extinct bluebuck, a smaller congeneric of roan and sable. Limited behavioural reconstruction suggests similarities with its congenerics (Faith and Thompson 2013). Possibly, like roan (see above), bluebuck was particularly susceptible to night ambush hunting. At Klasies and Blombos, small nocturnal and cathemeral antelope (grysbok and steenbok) are also significant (Dusseldorp and Langejans 2015). This was interpreted as suggestive evidence for snaring/trapping or diurnal net hunting, but an alternative hypothesis seems as valid. The predominant species taken by ambush hunting in the Dobe area was the similarly small dik-dik (Crowell and Hitchcock 1978), while in the Namibian Waterberg, the only species showing proportions of nocturnal drinking approaching that of eland were – along with gemsbok – the three, small antelope – duiker, steenbok, and dik-dik (Kasiringua *et al.* 2017: fig.5).

Intriguing as these shelter assemblages are, we need to focus on Late Pleistocene pan-margin sites where human hunting has been inferred. At the spring and pan margin site of Florisbad (Free State), the faunal analysis (Brink 1987) was based on combined samples from old and recent excavations, with the recent collections coming from an *in-situ* horizon with a hearth, dating to about 121 ka (Grün *et al.* 1996). With some evidence for butchery and hammerstone percussion on marrow-bones, the fauna is dominated by *Damaliscus* species (blesbok and extinct bastard hartebeest) and an extinct springbok; the high proportion of young adults among the *Damaliscus* was interpreted as consistent with selective hunting.

≠Gi pan (Botswana) is the ambush hunting site that provoked Crowell and Hitchcock's research (see above). Archaeologically, it provided Later Stone Age (LSA) and Middle Stone Age (MSA) horizons, the former including unique evidence for probable pit traps (≥1m deep, containing complete jaws and horn cores of large animals) and a small pit-hearth similar to the one Crowell and Hitchcock excavated in a recent hunting blind (Brooks 1984: 48). Rather than a pan-margin, the setting for MSA site use is thought to have been the margin of a recently dried river, perhaps focused on an ephemeral pool (Helgren and Brooks 1983: 188). This horizon provided a dating estimate of about 77 ka (Brooks *et al.* 1990: 62). Zebra and warthog dominate the associated faunal assemblage (Helgren and Brooks 1983); however, as it predominantly comprises teeth, it has not been subject to detailed zooarchaeological study. The high incidence of warthog again suggests a role for diurnal predation (lion or human). The inference of human hunting largely rests on very high frequencies of unifacial and bifacial points (Kuman 1989) and the claim for 'multiple examples of projectile impact damage' (Brooks *et al.* 2006: 239).

In Sudan, a very late MSA site (about 16 ka), at an isolated oasis in the Affad Basin, dry season hunting of waterbuck (*Kobus*) was inferred (Osypińska and Osypiński 2016). Seasonality was deduced on the basis of the overall faunal profile and the absence of very young waterbuck. The next Kobus age category, sub-adults, accounted for <5%. Although not stated, a prime-age adult dominated assemblage may be inferred.

At the palaeo-lake of Bir Tarfawi in Egypt, right at the end of the Middle Pleistocene around 135 ka (Nicoll 2018), the focus was on gazelle, particularly Dorcas gazelle (Gautier 1993). The principal ground for inferring hominin rather than lion predation was the spatial association with stone tools. Dorcas gazelles are reported as habitual nocturnal drinkers in the hot dry season (Ghobrial and Cloudsley-Thompson 1976). Dry season use was tentatively suggested (Gautier 1993: 143). The site's principal investigators argued for diurnal hunting, on the grounds that the risk from lions would have been too great for a nocturnal activity (Wendorf *et al.* 1993b: 570), but the foregoing ethnographic data suggests otherwise.

Circumstantial evidence for dry season use was inferred at two of the four sites and is implied at a third (≠Gi). Where age profiling was possible (Florisbad and Bir Tarfawi), the selection of prime age adults was inferred, which also seems likely at Affad. This is not only more consistent with some form of ambush hunting than tactical hunting (drives and/or jump-kills), but it suggests that animals were coming to drink in herds, allowing hunters to be selective.

Night ambush hunting as an evolutionary stable strategy

During dry seasons, plant foods tend to be scarce and game tends to be lean even by African standards. Humans need adequate supplies of carbohydrate and/or fat to avoid 'protein poisoning', the medium-term effect of converting lean-meat protein into energy, a metabolically costly process – the long-term effect of which is death by starvation (Speth 2010). Given the leanness of most game species during this season, one would predict preferential targeting of the fattest species (e.g. eland and zebra; Speth 2010) and – irrespective of species – intensive exploitation of marrow and brains.

For foraging Ju/'hoan in the 1960s and 1970s, the dry season was a time of rapid weight loss (Wilmsen 1989: fig.7.2) and lowest birth rates (Wilmsen 1978: fig.5). Dry season carbohydrate scarcity was even more acute in the central Kalahari, among the G/wi and G//ana (Tanaka 1980: 59, fig. 24; Silberbauer 1981: 199, fig.14). Intuitively, although the Hadzabe live in a better watered region, one would expect trends in the same direction (Marlowe 2010: 108). Paradoxically, however, women's body-fat percentages are highest at this time of year, attributed to peak returns from men's hunting (Marlowe and Berbesque 2009: 756), itself attributable to nocturnal ambush hunting (Marlowe 2010: 108). The Hadzabe have effectively turned a period of relative resource scarcity into one of absolute abundance.

The problems African savanna hunter-gatherers face in the dry season would generally have been more severe during glacial periods. During the two stages of our morphologically diagnosed speciation, there were two glacials; one between 310-255 ka (Marine Isotope Stage [MIS] 8), and the penultimate glacial – from 195-127 ka (MIS 6). For Africa, we only have environmental proxies from multiple regions across the continent for the last 150,000 years (Blome *et al.* 2012). These show that late MIS 6 was the only time when synchronous conditions from all four sampled regions prevailed for a substantial period (over 5,000 years), with arid proxies from before 150 ka to about 145 ka (Blome *et al.* 2012: fig.14). Where we have earlier records, from the Horn of Africa and South Africa, arid conditions extend more or less continuously to the beginning of the glacial at 195 ka, with just one, short, humid interval (Tierney *et al.* 2017; Partridge *et al.* 1998). MIS 6 populations in Savanna and Grassland Biomes would typically have faced problems of dry season caloric shortfall and the need to spare protein.

Allowing for the backdating of the two Jebel Irhoud crania (Hublin *et al.* 2017), and the two Omo crania (Vidal *et al.* 2022), it still seems that cranial capacities above 1400cc only became the norm during MIS 7 and MIS 6, coinciding with globularization of the cranial vault, the final morphologically diagnostic trait of our speciation (Bergstrom *et al.* 2021: 231, cf. Watts 2014: tbl.16.1). The slight increase contrasts with Neanderthals, where brain-size increase seems to have stalled during MIS 6 (Power, Sommer and Watts 2013). We can assume that any increase in brain size would have intensified maternal energy demands and obstetric risks. With dry season caloric shortfall being more pronounced during MIS 6, it follows that *Homo sapiens* mothers would have faced particular challenges during this glacial cycle.

The high returns from nocturnal, dry season ambush hunting by water-holes arise from the highly-localised distribution of a critical resource and resulting predictable behaviours of prey species, the concomitant high encounter rate, close range, and the cover of low illumination. These same factors make the strategy attractive to lions, with two critical differences: hominins require brighter hunting conditions and are themselves potential lion prey. While hominin ambush hunting is considered very ancient (Bunn and Gurtov 2014; Kubler 2015), nocturnal ambush clearly entails much greater risks and would be expected to be a late adaptation.

A wide range of measures could mitigate the threat: i) checking for recent lion spoor, ii) optimising available natural light (hunting around Full Moon), iii) stone-tipped rather than wooden-pointed spears, iv) a spear that could be accurately thrown over a short distance, v) having fire to hand, vi) at least a second pair of eyes (if only to alternate watches), ideally – two or three pairs watching over different game-trail approaches, and vii) ambush locations that, in addition to camouflage, provided some protection. Fire was not a prerequisite and, in some conditions, neither was a constructed blind; but for the strategy to become widespread and stable both options should probably have been available. The spear requirements seem to be the single most temporally significant variable. Thrust, stone-tipped spears in Africa probably go back 500,000 years, but the earliest compelling evidence for stone projectile points is at around 212 ka. A development from stone-tipped thrusting to short-distance thrown spears seems probable in the interim. The distance at which an animal could be seriously wounded or killed with such a weapon would typically have been less than ten metres. Recall that ≠Gi pan hunting blinds had a mean distance to game trails of 6.6 metres, just 3.3m to the nearest trail. Between around 100 ka and 80 ka, higher velocity (but lower kinetic energy) projectiles are inferred. These would have been of greatest benefit to diurnal pursuit hunting. This suggests a temporal window in which night ambush hunting was likely to have become significant between around 300 ka and 100 ka, with the strongest selection pressures between 195 ka and 145 ka.

Discussion

The sex-strike model proposed that through collective ritual performances, female cosmetic coalitions exploited menstruation as a signal of impending fertility to manipulate male behaviour (Power, this volume). In the proposed two stages to the evolution of group ritual, ritual power was created and encoded through 'blood' symbolism, based on a metaphor equating women's blood with the blood of the game animals (Knight and Lewis 2017). This generated a sub-set of predictions about the archaeological record of red ochre use (Watts 2009, 2014). In the second stage, with the final brain-size increase in our lineage creating renewed pressure on maternal energy budgets, what was required was significant improvement in hunting productivity, particularly in the context of glacially enhanced seasonal shortfalls in caloric intake. At this point, ritual performance would no longer be tied to real menstrual blood but occurring on a monthly basis; hence the prediction that, where locally or regionally available, red ochre should become a regular and ubiquitous feature of campsite occupations. In the nineties, we predicted that this shift in the ochre record should be evident by the glacial peak of MIS 6 (160-140 ka) (Knight, Power and Watts 1995: 81).

The presence of glittery specularite and red ochre at the back of Wonderwerk Cave (Northern Cape) provides compelling indirect evidence for fire-lit, brilliant, ritual display in the Fauresmith, spanning around 500 ka to around 300 ka (Watts *et al.* 2016). This is probably the earliest evidence for a ritual tradition, albeit at a local scale. From around 300 ka, a few more widely distributed sites begin to show regular use, but southern African cave and rockshelter campsites suggest that such regularity did not become ubiquitous until about 170 ka (Watts 2014; see also Val *et al.* 2021), consistent with the original prediction. It can now be proposed that such ritual performances drove a stabilisation and generalisation of lunar phase-locked night ambush hunting in savanna and grassland environments.

Dry season, night ambush hunting would have been the most important lunar scheduled hunting technique, but moonlight undoubtedly played a wider role in the scheduling of hunting and travelling. For example, Kalahari pursuit hunting of eland or giraffe typically took 5-10 days (Marshall 1959: 354 fn.1, 1961: 239); only some of this duration can be attributed to the time for arrow poison to take effect. Being away from a home-base for several days meant that such hunts were likely to occur during the Waxing Gibbous Moon, with the corollary that hunters returned around Full Moon.

Looking at hunting through the lens of lunar periodicity throws light on several otherwise unexplained features of Bushman and Hadza belief and ritual practice. Watts (2005) drew attention to Bushman myths where the origin of a sex-based division of labour was rendered in a lunar idiom connected to hunting and the |Xam Moon's creation being aetiologically explained (*inter alia*) as allowing them to hunt at night by waterholes. Among the Hadza, Woodburn (1964: 49) observed that at the height of the late dry season 'animals are being killed in large numbers at water holes. It is at this season that the formal opposition between the sexes is at its height'. The Hadza's most important ritual is the nocturnal *epeme* dance, normally held during the Dark Moon. It also requires a quorum of older and younger women, so tends to be further restricted to the dry season, the season of aggregation. One reason for holding the ritual is to help ensure the success of forthcoming hunting (Kohl-Larsen 1958: 121; Woodburn 1982: 190). This seasonal hunting productivity also occasioned the most frequent assemblies of men's secret society, also called *epeme*, involving the consumption of sacred (*epeme*) portions of meat from specified medium to large game animals (eland and zebra being exemplary). The culmination of the late dry season is the most propitious time to hold girls' collective initiation rituals, involving *inter alia*, the beating of men with sticks (Power 2015: 352). It was these three rituals that Woodburn was referring to in seeing the formal opposition between the sexes as most pronounced in the late dry season (Power 2015). In this context, the significance of Hawkes' 1991 demonstration of the productivity of dry season moonlit hunting transcends both economics and the 'show-off' hypothesis she went on to develop to explain why men focused on hunting large animals (Hawkes and Bleige Bird 2002); arguably, it underpins a unitary periodicity to economics, ritual, sexual politics and cosmology.

The strong implicit link between the Dark Moon *epeme* dance and Full Moon ambush hunting seems to inform a significant symbolic detail of *epeme* performances, concerning the *!ingiribe* bells on the male dancer's right leg, with the characteristic leg-stamp of the bells said to connote the knee-clicks of a mature eland bull (Skaanes 2017: 212). The clicks provide other eland with a reliable signal of social status (Bro-Jørgensen and Beeston 2015), but for human hunters, the sound would be most salient in the context of nocturnal ambush hunting, announcing the bull's approach in the darkness. Unusually, eland bulls have more fat than cows. Similar acoustic symbolism is reported as part of the ritual when a Ju|'hoan boy killed his first eland (Lewis-Williams and Biesele 1978: 129) and again during a Ju|'hoan girl's menarcheal ritual, as part of the Eland-Bull dance (Lewis-Williams 1977: 114). In both cases, the anthropologists inferred that the clicks were the sound of hoof-fall, but this was before any awareness of eland-bull knee-clicks; it seems likely that this was lost in translation, knee-clicks being far better indices of species and sex than hoof-fall. We have seen that of all the antelope that drink nocturnally, eland is the most habitual. The eland plays an important role in |Xam mythology about the Moon's creation (Lewis-Williams 1981), while other Bushman groups have a variety of beliefs relating eland to the Moon and the night (e.g. Geiss and Snyman 1986: 263; Sugawara 2001: 68, 76). Given the limitations of early Late Pleistocene hunting technology, it seems likely that seasonal nocturnal ambush hunting contributed to elands' disproportionate representation in southern Cape faunal assemblages, and it is quite plausible that the chain of eland-darkness-moon-fat symbolic linkages is of similar antiquity.

One of the most widespread Bushman beliefs was that the Moon must not be looked at when an animal had been hit (Bleek and Lloyd 1911: 67; Bleek 1920-22, notebooks 5 and 7; Watts 1998: Cat.7t.i, section 4; Bleek 1928: 16; Vedder 1937: 433-4). Breach of the taboo would result in the fat disappearing, or the animal recovering from the poison (through the curative power of Moon's water – dew), it being eaten by carnivores, and/or the hunter becoming sick – particularly in the eyes. This is generally explained in terms of the protracted uncertainty over whether the poison would have its desired effect, but explicit in Vedder's account and implicit in the others, is that the danger specifically arose when an animal was hit *in* moonlight. The temporal depth of moonlit night ambush hunting proposed here would suggest that the belief predates arrows and/or poison, as the hunter passed the rest of the night in his blind, before taking up any blood trail in the morning.

Conclusion

In savanna and grassland environments, before the invention of the bow and arrow, moonlit spear-hunting from ambushes by remaining water sources in the dry season would have been uniquely productive, primarily due to the behavioural regularities being exploited and the relatively short ranges involved. I have argued that the strategy probably post-dates 500 ka and that it was unlikely to have become significant before around 300 ka, perhaps closer to 200 ka. Two considerations suggest that this form of hunting may have become critical to *Homo sapiens* survival during the penultimate glacial period: fairly unremitting aridity between around 195 ka and 145 ka would have exacerbated dry season caloric shortfall, when maternal energy budgets were under renewed stress with the last period of brain-size increase.

That lunar-phase-locked hunting may have played an important role in the final phase of our African speciation is interesting in its own right and demands more thorough investigation. But it takes on greater significance for aligning so precisely with predictions derived from a pre-existing abstract model of a unitary origin to human symbolic culture. Recall that Knight's original model did not make any predictions of the ethnographic record concerning the role of lunar periodicity in extant hunting behaviours. Hawkes' Hadza data was an unexpected bonus that opened up this avenue of inquiry, which appears to provide a material basis to the symbolic and cosmological predictions that have already proved fertile ground for testing (Knight 1997; Power 2017; Power and Watts 1997; Sims 2005; Watts 2005, 2017).

The 'sex-strike' model holds that symbolic culture was not just revolutionary in its consequences but revolutionary at origin, by establishing that some things are sacred. Adding greater specificity to the form of the posited revolution, it now appears to have resulted from the combination of two strategic responses to the same material problem. The problem was that maximization of brain-case volumes overlapped with a glacial cycle that made meeting caloric needs in the late dry season exceptionally challenging. The two proposed responses were, on the one hand, the second stage of the hypothesised evolution of collective ritual driven by female coalitions, where 'blood' coded inviolability was raised to habitual performance; on the other hand, a seasonal strategy of collective, Full Moon ambush hunting – effectively turning a period of scarcity into one of relative if not absolute abundance (depending on local ecology).

Acknowledgements

I am totally indebted to Lionel Sims for introducing me to anthropology and to Knight's model; for improvements to the paper, I thank Bob Hitchcock, Elena Mouriki, Chris Knight, Camilla Power and the editors of this volume. I thank the University of Cape Town Manuscripts and Archives Library for access to Dorothea Bleek's notebooks.

References

Andersson, C. 1857. *Lake Ngami or Explorations and discovery during four years of wanderings in wilds of South-Western Africa*. London: Hurst and Blackett.

Ayeni, J., 1975. Utilization of waterholes in Tsavo National Park (East). *East African Wildlife Journal* 13: 305-323.

Backhouse, J. 1844. *A narrative of a visit to the Mauritius and South Africa.* London: Hamilton Adams.

Bagshawe, F. 1924-5. The peoples of Happy Valley (East Africa): Part II. *Journal of the Royal African Society* 24: 117-130.

Baines, T. 1864. *Explorations in South-West Africa.* London: Longman Green.

Barham, L., A. Pinto and P. Andrews 2000. The Mumbwa Caves behavioural record, in L. Barham (ed.) *The Middle Stone Age of Zambia, south central Africa*: 81-148. Bristol: Western Academic and Specialist Press.

Bergstrom, A., C. Stringer, M. Hajdinjak, E. Scerri and P. Skoglund 2021. *Origins of modern human ancestry*. Nature 490: 229-237.

Bleek, W. and L. Lloyd 1911. *Specimens of Bushman folklore.* London: Allen.

Bleek, D., 1920-1922. Unpublished notebooks, 'Interviews with !Kun, Naron, Auen, and Hei//kum prisoners in Windhoek Jail'. African Studies Library, University of Cape Town.

Bleek, D. 1928. *The Naron: A Bushman tribe of the central Kalahari.* Cambridge: Cambridge University Press.

Bleek, D. 1930. Unpublished Hadza notebooks. African Studies Library, University of Cape Town.

Blome, M., A. Cohen, C. Tryon, A. Brooks and J. Russell 2012. The environmental context for the origins of modern human diversity: A synthesis of regional variability in African climate 150,000-30,000 years ago. *Journal of Human Evolution* 62: 563-592.

Brink, J. 1987. The archaeozoology of Florisbad, Orange Free State. *Memoirs of the National Museum at Bloemfontein* 24.

Brooks, A. 1984. San land-use patterns, past and present: Implications for southern African prehistory, in M. Hall, G. Avery, A. Avery, M. Wilson and A. Humphreys (eds.) *Frontiers: Southern African archaeology today.* Cambridge Monographs in Archaeology 10, BAR International Series 207.

Brooks, A. and J. Yellen 1987. The preservation of activity areas in the archaeological record: Ethnoarchaeological and archaeological work in northwest Ngamiland, in S. Kent (ed.) *Method and theory for activity area research: An ethnoarchaeological approach*: 63-106. New York: Columbia University Press.

Brooks, A., P. Hare, J. Kokis, G. Miller, R. Ernst and F. Wendorf 1990. Dating Pleistocene archeological sites by protein diagenesis in ostrich eggshell. *Science* 248: 60-64.

Brooks, A., L. Nevell, J. Yellen and G. Hartman 2006. Projectile technologies of the African MSA: Implications for modern human origins, in E. Hovers and S. Kuhn (eds) *Transitions before the transition: Evolution and stability in the Middle Paleolithic and Middle Stone Age*: 233-255. Dordrecht: Springer Link.

Bro-Jørgensen, J., and J. Beeston 2015. Multimodal signalling in an antelope: fluctuating facemasks and knee-clicks reveal the status of eland bulls. *Animal Behaviour* 102: 231-239.

Bunn, H., L. Bartram and E. Kroll 1988. Variability in bone assemblage formation from Hadza hunting, scavenging, and carcass processing. *Journal of Anthropological Archaeology* 7: 412-57.

Bunn, H. and A. Gurtov 2014. Prey mortality profiles indicate that Early Pleistocene *Homo* at Olduvai was an ambush predator. *Quaternary International* 322-23: 44-53.

Campbell, A. 1981. A comment on Kalahari wildlife and the Khukhe fence. *Botswana Notes and Records* 13: 111-118.

Campbell, A., M. Main and R. Hitchcock 2006. Land, livestock, and labour in rural Botswana: The Western Sandveld region of Central District as a case study, in R. Hitchcock, K. Ikeya,

M. Biesele and R. Lee (eds) *Updating the San: Image and reality of an African people in the 21st century*: 183-228. Senri Ethnological Studies 70.

Campbell, Amy. 1993. BS-12: A site associated with West Lake 2 (1988 excavations), in F. Wendorf, R. Schild, A. Close and associates (eds) *Egypt during the Last Interglacial: The Middle Paleolithic of Bir Tarfawi and Bir Sahara*: 519-527. New York: Plenum Press.

Chapman, J. 1971a [1868). *Travels in the Interior of South Africa, 1849-1863 Volume I.* Cape Town: A.A. Balkema.

Chapman, J. 1971b [1868). *Travels in the Interior of South Africa, 1849-1863 Volume II.* Cape Town: A.A. Balkema.

Chazan, M., N. Porat, T. Sumner and L. Horwitz 2013. The use of OSL dating in unstructured sands: the archaeology and chronology of the Hutton Sands at Canteen Kopje (Northern Cape Province, South Africa). *Archaeological and Anthropological Sciences* 5: 351-363.

Churchill, S. 1993. Weapon technology, prey size selection, and hunting methods in modern hunter-gatherers: implications for hunting in the Palaeolithic and Mesolithic, in G. Peterkin, H. Bricker and P. Mellars (eds) *Hunting and animal exploitation in the Later Palaeolithic and Mesolithic of Europe*: 11-24. American Anthropological Assocation Archaeological Papers Number 4.

Churchill, S., R. Franciscus, H. McKean-Peraza, J. Daniel and B. Warren 2009. Shanidar 3 Neandertal rib puncture wound and paleolithic weaponry. *Journal of Human Evolution* 57: 163-178.

Clifford, B. 1930. A reconnaissance of the Great Makarikari Lake. *Geographical Journal* 85: 16-26.

Cooper, B. 1949. The Kindiga. *Tanganyika Notes and Records* 27: 8-15.

Cozzi, G., F. Broekhuis, J. McNutt, L. Turnbull, D. MacDonald and B. Schmid 2012. Fear of the dark or dinner by moonlight? Reduced temporal partitioning among Africa's large carnivores. *Ecology* 93: 2590-2599.

Crosmary, W.G., M. Valeix, H. Fritz, H. Madzikanda and S. Côté 2012. African ungulates and their drinking problems: Hunting and predation risks constrain access to water. *Animal Behaviour* 83: 145-153.

Crowell, A., and R. Hitchcock 1978. Basarwa ambush hunting in Botswana. *Botswana Notes and Records* 10: 37-51.

Cumming, R.G. 1850. *Five years of a hunter's life in the far interior of South Africa: with notices of the native tribes*. London: John Murray.

d'Errico, F., L. Backwell, P. Villa, I. Degano, J. Lucejko, M. Bamford, T. Higham, M. Colombini and P. Beaumont 2012. Early evidence of San material culture represented by organic artifacts from Border Cave, South Africa. *Proceedings of the National Academy of Sciences* 109: 13214-13219.

Douze, K. and D. Delagnes 2016. The pattern of emergence of a Middle Stone Age tradition at Gademotta and Kulkuletti (Ethiopia) through convergent tool and point techniques. *Journal of Human Evolution* 91: 93-121.

Dunn, E. 1931. *The Bushman*. London: C. Griffin and Co.

du Preez, J. and I. Grobler 1977. Drinking times and behaviour at waterholes of some game species in the Etosha National Park. *Madoqua* 10: 61-69.

Dusseldorp, G. and G. Langejans 2015. 'Trapping the past'? Hunting for remote capture techniques and planned coastal exploitation during MIS 5 at Blombos Cave and Klasies River, South Africa. *Analecta Praehistorica Leidensia* 45: 15-27.

Faith, J. and J. Thompson 2013. Fossil evidence for seasonal calving and migration of extinct blue antelope (*Hippotragus leucophaeus*) in southern Africa. *Journal of Biogeography* 40: 2108-2118.

Farini, G. 1886. *Through the Kalahari Desert*. London: Sampson Low, Marston, Searle, and Rivington.

Funston, P., M. Mills and H. Biggs 2001. Factors affecting the hunting success of male and female lions in the Kruger National Park. *Journal of Zoology* 253: 419–431.

Gaerdes, J. 1966-1967. Über Südwestafrikanische Pfeilgifte. *Journal of the South West Africa Scientific Society* 21: 33-89, with plates on pp.97-99.

Galton, F. 1853. *The narrative of an explorer in Tropical South Africa*. London: John Murray.

Gautier, A. 1993. The Middle Paleolithic archeofaunas from Bir Tarfawi (Western Desert, Egypt), in F. Wendorf, R. Schild, A. Close, and associates (eds) *Egypt during the Last Interglacial: The Middle Paleolithic of Bir Tarfawi and Bir Sahara*: 121-143. New York: Plenum Press.

Geiss, W. and J. Snyman 1986. The naming and utilization of plantlife by the Zu/'hõasi Bushmen of the Kau-Kauveld, in R. Vossen and K. Keuthmann (eds) *Contemporary Studies on Khoisan 1*: 237-346. Hamburg: Helmut Buske Verlag.

Ghobrial, L. and J. Cloudesley-Thompson 1976. Daily cycle of activity of the Dorcas gazelle in the Sudan. *Journal of Interdisciplinary Cycle Research* 7(1): 47-50.

Gordon, R. 1992. *The Bushman myth: The making of a Namibian underclass*. Boulder: Westview Press.

Gordon, R. 1997. *Picturing Bushmen: The Denver African Expedition of 1925*. Athens (OH): Ohio University Press.

Groman-Yaroslavski, I., Y. Zaidner and M. Weinstein-Evron 2021. Complexity and sophistication of Early Middle Paleolithic flint tools revealed through use-wear analysis of tools from Misliya Cave, Mount Carmel, Israel. *Journal of Human Evolution* 154: 102955.

Grün, R., J. Brink, N. Spooner, L. Taylor, C. Stringer, R. Franciscus and A. Murray 1996. Direct dating of Florisbad hominid. *Nature* 382: 500-501.

Harris, W.C. 1852. *The wild sports of southern Africa*. London: Henry Bohn.

Hawkes, K., J. O'Connell and N. Blurton-Jones 1991. Hunting income patterns among the Hadza. *Philosophical Transactions of the Royal Society of London Series B* 334: 243-51.

Hawkes, K., and R. Bleige Bird 2002. Showing off, handicap signalling, and the evolution of men's work. *Evolutionary Anthropology* 11: 58-67.

Hayward, M. and M. Hayward. 2012. Waterhole Use by African Fauna. *South African Journal of Wildlife Research* 42: 117–127.

Helgren, D. and A. Brooks 1983. Geoarchaeology at Gi, a Middle Stone Age and Later Stone Age site in the northwest Kalahari. *Journal of Archaeological Science* 10: 181-197.

Hitchcock, R. 1982. The ethnoarcheology of sedentism: Mobility strategies and site structure among foraging and food producing populations in the Eastern Kalahari Desert, Botswana. Unpublished Ph.D dissertation, Department of Anthropology, University of New Mexico, Albuquerque.

Hitchcock, R. 2017. Discontinuities in ethnographic time: A view from Africa. *Journal of Anthropological Archaeology* 46: 12-27.

Hitchcock, R., J. Yellen, D. Gelburd, A. Osborn and A. Crowell 1996. Subsistence hunting and resource management among the Ju/'hoansi of northwestern Botswana. *African Study Monographs* 17 (4): 153-220.

Hitchcock, R. and P. Bleed 1997. Each according to need and fashion: Spear and arrow use among San hunters of the Kalahari, in H. Knecht (ed) *Projectile technology*: 345-368. New York: Plenum.

Hitchcock, R., A. Crowell, A. Brooks, J. Yellen, J. Ebert and A. Osborn 2019. The ethnoarchaeology of ambush hunting: A case study of ≠Gi Pan, Western Ngamiland, Botswana. *African Archaeological Review* 36: 119-144.

Hodgson, T. 1977 (1821-1831). *The journals of the Rev. T.L. Hodgson, missionary to the Seleka-Rolong and the Griquas 1821-1831.* Johannesburg: Witwatersrand University Press.

Hodson, A. W. 1912. *Trekking the great thirst: Sport and travel in the Kalahari Desert.* London: T. Fisher Unwin.

Holub, E. 1881. *Seven years in South Africa.* London: Sampson Low, Marston, Searle, and Rivington.

Hublin, J.J., A. Ben-Ncer, S. Bailey, S. Freidline, S. Neubauer, M. Skinner, I. Bergmann, A. Le Cabec S. Benazzi, K. Harvati, and P. Gunz. 2017. New fossils from Jebel Irhoud, Morocco and the pan-African origin of Homo sapiens. *Nature* 546: 289-292.

Hutson, J. 2018. The faunal remains from Bundu Farm and Pniel 6: Examining the problematic Middle Stone Age archaeological record within the southern African interior. *Quaternary International* 466: 178-193.

Kasiringua, E., G. Kopij and S. Proches 2017. Daily activity patterns at water holes during the dry season in the Waterberg National Park, Namibia. *Russian Journal of Theriology* 16: 129-138.

Kiberd, P. 2006. Bundu Farm: A report on the archaeological and palaeoenvironmental assemblages from a pan site in Bushmanland, Northern Cape, South Africa. *South African Archaeological Bulletin* 61: 189-201.

Klein, R. 1976. The mammalian fauna of the Klasies River Mouth sites, southern Cape Province, South Africa. *South African Archaeological Bulletin* 31: 75-98.

Knight, C. 1991. *Blood Relations: Menstruation and the Origins of Culture.* New Haven and London: Yale University Press.

Knight, C. 1997. The wives of the Sun and the Moon. *Journal of the Royal Anthropological Society* N.S. 3: 133-153.

Knight, C., C. Power and I. Watts 1995. 'The Human Symbolic Revolution. A Darwinian Account', *Cambridge Archaeological Journal* 5: 75–114.

Knight, C. and J. Lewis 2017. Towards a theory of everything, in C. Power, M. Finnegan and H. Callan (eds) *Human Origins: Contributions from social anthropology*: 84-102. New York, Oxford: Berghahn.

Knight, M., A. Knight-Eloff and J. Bornman 1988. The importance of borehole water and lick sites to Kalahari ungulates. *Journal of Arid Environments* 15: 269-281.

Kohl-Larsen, L.,1958. *Wildbeuter in Ostafrika: Die Tindiga, ein Jager und Sammlervolk.* Berlin: Dietrich Reimer Verlag.

Kubler, S., P. Owenga, S. Reynolds, S. Rucina and G. King 2015. Animal movements in the Kenya Rift and evidence for the earliest ambush hunting by hominins. *Scientific Reports* 5:14011.

Kuman, K. 1989. Florisbad and ≠Gi: the contribution of open-air sites to study of the Middle Stone Age of southern Africa. Unpublished Ph.D. dissertation, University of Pennsylvania.

Lee, R. 1979. *The !Kung San: Men, women, and work in a foraging society.* Cambridge: Cambridge University Press.

Lewis-Williams, D. 1977. Believing and Seeing: An interpretation of symbolic meanings in southern San rock art. Ph.D. dissertation, University of Natal.

Lewis-Williams, D. 1981. *Believing and Seeing. Symbolic Meanings in Southern San Rock Paintings.* London: Academic Press.

Lewis-Williams, D. and M. Biesele 1978. Eland hunting rituals among the northern and southern San groups. *Africa* 48: 117-34.

Livingstone, D. 1857. *Missionary travels and researches in South Africa.* London: John Murray.

Lombard, M. and L. Phillipson 2010. Indications of bow and stone-tipped arrow use 64,000 years ago in KwaZulu-Natal, South Africa. *Antiquity* 84: 1-14.

Lombard, M. 2021. Variation in hunting weaponry for more than 300,000 years: A tip cross-sectional area study of Middle Stone Age points from southern Africa. *Quaternary Science Reviews* 264: 107021

Lombard, M. and S. Churchill, 2022. *Revisiting Middle Stone Age hunting at ≠Gi, Botswana: A tip cross-sectional area study.* Southern African Field Archaeology 1: 1-15.

Marean, C., Y. Abe, C. Frey and R. Randall 2000. Zooarchaeological and taphonomic analysis of the Die Kelders Cave 1 layers 10 and 11 Middle Stone Age larger mammal fauna. *Journal of Human Evolution* 38: 197-233.

Marin, J., P. Saladié, A. Rodríguez-Hidalgo and E. Carbonell 2017. Neanderthal hunting strategies inferred from mortality profiles within the Abric Romaní sequence. *PLoS ONE* 12: e0186970

Marlowe, F., and J. Berbesque 2009. Tubers as fallback foods and their impact on Hadza hunter-gatherers. *American Journal of Physical Anthropology* 140: 751-758.

Marlowe, F. 2010. *The Hadza: Hunter-gatherers of Tanzania.* Berkeley: University of California.

Marshall, J. 1958.Man as a hunter, part II, Huntsman of Nyae Nyae. *Natural History* 67(7): 376-395.

Marshall, L. 1959. Marriage among !Kung Bushmen. *Africa* 29: 335-65.

Marshall, L. 1960. !Kung Bushman bands. *Africa* 30: 325-55.

Marshall, L. 1961. Sharing, talking, and giving: Relief of social tensions among /Kung Bushmen. *Africa* 31: 231-249.

Marshall, L. 1999. *Nyae Nyae !Kung beliefs and rites.* Peabody Museum Monographs 8. Cambridge MA: Harvard University Press.

McDonald, M., M.Wiseman, M. Kleindeinst, J. Smith, N. Taylor, A. Wreschnig, A. Skinner and B. Blackwell 2016. Did Middle Stone Age Khargan peoples leave structural features? 'Site J', the forgotten settlement of the 'Empty Desert', Kharga Oasis, Egypt: 1933 and 2011. *Journal of African Archaeology* 14: 155-179.

Metzger, F. 1995 [1952]. *The Hyena's laughter.* Translated by P. Reiner. Windhoek: Kuiseb Verlag.

Milks, A., D. Parker and M. Pope 2019. External ballistics of Pleistocene hand-thrown spears: experimental performance data and implications for human evolution. *Scientific Reports* 9: 820.

Müller, H. 2005 (1912). A reconnaissance ride into the Kaukau Veld. Deutsche Kolonialblatt 23, in M. Guenther (ed.) *Kalahari and Namib Bushmen in German South West Africa*: 530-541. Koln: Rüdiger Köppe Verlag.

Neubauer, S., JJ.Hublin and P. Gunz 2018. The evolution of modern human brain shape. *Science Advances* 4: eaao5961

Nicoll, K. 2018. A revised chronology for Pleistocene paleolakes and Middle Stone Age – Middle Paleolithic cultural activity at Bîr Tirfawi – Bîr Sahara in the Egyptian Sahara. *Quaternary International* 463: 18-23.

Obst, E. 1912. Von Mkalama ins land der Wakindiga. *Mitteilungen der Geographischen Gesellschaft in Hamburg* 26: 2-27.

O'Connell, J., K. Hawkes and N. Blurton-Jones 1992. Patterns in the distribution, site structure and assemblage composition of Hadza kill-butchery sites. *Journal of Archaeological Science* 19: 319-345.

O'Driscoll, C. and J. Thompson 2018. The origins and early elaboration of projectile technology. *Evolutionary Anthropology* 27: 30-45.

Osypińska, M. and P. Osypiński 2016. Animal exploitation and behaviour of the latest Middle Stone Age in the Middle Nile Valley: Archaeozoological and taphonomic analysis of Late Pleistocene fauna from the Affad Basin, Sudan. *African Archaeological Review* 33: 107-127.

Packer, C., A. Swanson, D. Ikanda and H. Kushnir 2011. Fear of darkness, the full moon and the nocturnal ecology of African lions. *PLoS ONE* 6(7): e22285.

Partridge, T., P. deMenocal, S. Lorentz, M. Paiker and J. Vogel 1998. Orbital forcing of climate over South Africa: A 200,000-year rainfall record from the Pretoria Saltpan. *Quaternary Science Reviews* 16: 1125-1133.

Passarge, S. 1997 (1907). The Bushmen of the Kalahari, in E. Wilmsen (ed) *The Kalahari ethnographies (1896-1898) of Siegfried Passarge*: 127-218. Quellen zur Khoisan-Forschung. Köln: Rudiger Köppe Verlag.

Peters, J. and R. Vogelsand 2009. Losing the spoor: Hai||om animal exploitation in the Etosha region, in G. Grupe, G. McGlynn and J. Peters (eds) Documenta Archaeobiologiae. Tracking down the past: ethnohistory meets archaeozoology:103-185. *Jahrbuch der Staatssammlung für Anthopologie und Paläoanatomie München* 7.

Pontzer, H., D. Raichlen, T. Basdoe, J. Harris, A. Mabulla and B. Wood 2017. Mechanics of archery among Hadza hunter-gatherers. *Journal of Archaeological Science: Reports* 16: 57-64.

Porrat, N., M. Chazan, R. Grün, V. Eisenmann and L. Horvitz 2010. New radiometric ages for the Fauresmith Industry from Kathu Pan, southern Africa: Implications for the Earlier to Middle Stone Age transition. *Journal of Archaeological Science* 37: 269-283.

Power, C. 2015. Hadza gender rituals – *epeme* and *maitoko* – considered as counterparts. *Hunter Gatherer Research* 1: 333-358.

Power, C. and I. Watts 1997. The woman with the zebra's penis: gender, mutability and performance. *Journal of the Royal Anthropological Institute* N.S. 3: 537-560.

Power, C., V. Sommer and I. Watts 2013. The seasonality thermostat: female reproductive synchrony and male behaviour in monkeys, Neanderthals, and modern humans. *PaleoAnthropology* 33-60.

Power, C., I. Watts and C. Knight 2021. The symbolic revolution: A sexual conflict model, in N. Gontier, A. Lock and C. Sinha (eds) *The Oxford Handbook of Human Symbolic Evolution*. Oxford: Oxford University Press.

Raper, P and M. Boucher (eds) 1988. *Robert Jacob Gordon: Cape travels, 1777-1786*. Haughton: Brenthurst Press.

Raseroka, B. 1975. Past and present distribution of buffalo in Botswana. *Botswana Notes and Records* 7: 131-140.

Raven-Hart, R. 1971. *Cape of Good Hope 1652-1702. The first fifty years of Dutch colonisation as seen by Callers*. Cape Town: Balkema.

Reche, O. 1914. Zur Ethnographie des abflusslosen Gebeites Deutsch-Ostafrikas: auf Grund der Sammlung der Ostafrika-Expedition (Dr. E. Obst) der Geographischen Gesellschaft in Hamburg. *Abhandlungen des Hamburgischen Kolonialinstituts* Band XVII. Reihe B. Völkerkunde, Kulturgeschichte und Sprachen. Band 11. Hamburg: L. Friederichsen and Co.

Rots, V., C. Lentfer, V. Schmid, G. Porraz and N. Conard 2017. Pressure flaking to serrate bifacial points for the hunt during the MIS5 at Sibudu Cave (South Africa). *PLoS ONE* 12: e0175151.

Sahle, Y., W. Hutchings, D. Braun, J. Sealy, L. Morgan, A. Negash and B. Atnafu 2013. Earliest stone-tipped projectiles from the Ethiopian Rift date to >279,000 years ago. *PLoS ONE* 8: e78092.

Sahle, Y. and A. Brooks 2019. Assessment of complex projectiles in the early Late Pleistocene of Aduma, Ethiopia. *PLoS ONE* 14: e0216716.

Sampson, G. 1968. The Middle Stone Age industries of the Orange River Scheme area. *Memoirs of the National Museum at Bloemfontein* 4.

Sampson, G. 1978. The stone structures from Orangia, O.F.S. South Africa, in L. Freeman (ed) *Les structures d'habitat au Paléolithique Moyen*: 7-34. Union Internationale des Sciences Préhistoriques et Protohistoriques, IXe Congrès.

Sampson, G. 1988. *The flawed floor: Orangia I reconsidered in the light of recent MSA field research.* Paper presented to the 10th conference of the Southern African Association of Archaeologists, Johannesburg.

Selous, F. 1985 (1881). *A hunter's wanderings in Africa.* Alberton: Galago Publishing Ltd. Facsimile of 1st edition, Richard Bentley and Son.

Silberbauer, G. 1965. *Bushman survey report.* Gaberones: Bechuanaland Government.

Silberbauer, G. 1981. *Hunter and habitat in the Central Kalahari Desert.* Cambridge: Cambridge University Press.

Sims, L. 2005. The 'solarization' of the Moon: Manipulated knowledge at Stonehenge. *Cambridge Archaeological Journal* 16: 191-207.

Skaanes, T. 2017. Sounds in the night: Ritual bells, therianthropes and eland relations among the Hadza, in C. Power, M. Finnegan, H. Callan (eds) *Human origins: Contributions from social anthropology*: 204-223. New York, Oxford: Berghahn.

Sparrman, A. 1975 [1785-86]. *A voyage to the Cape of Good Hope.* Cape Town: Van Riebeeck Society.

Speth, J. 2010. *The paleoanthropology and archaeology of big-game hunting: Protein, fat, or politics?* Interdisciplinary Contributions to Archaeology. New York: Springer.

Stephenson, J. 2000. *The language of the land: Living among a Stone-Age people in Africa.* New York: St. Martin's Press.

Stewart, M., J. Louys, H. Groucutt, I. Candy, R. Clark-Wilson, P. Breeze, N. Drake, G. Price, Y. Al-Mufarreh, S. Soubhi, I. Zalmout, A. Alsharekh, A. Omari and M. Petraglia 2019. Taphonomic and zooarchaeological investigations at the Middle Pleistocene site of Ti's al Ghadah, western Nefud Desert, Saudi Arabia. *Quaternary Science Reviews* 218: 228-253.

Stiner, M. 2005. *The faunas of Hayonim Cave, Israel: A 200,000-year record of Paleolithic diet, demography, and society.* Cambridge (Ma): Peabody Museum of Archaeology and Ethnology.

Stiner, M., R. Barkai and A. Gopher 2009. Cooperative hunting and meat sharing 400-200 kya at Qesem Cave, Israel. *Proceedings of the National Academy of Sciences* 106: 13207-13212.

Sugawara, K. 2001. Cognitive space concerning habitual thought and practice toward animals among the Central San (|Gui and ||Gana): Deictic/indirect cognition and prospective/retrospective intention. *African Study Monographs, Supplement* 26: 61-98.

Tanaka, J. 1978. A study of the comparative ecology of African Gatherer-Hunters with special reference to San (Bushman-speaking people) and Pygmies. *Senri Ethnological Studies* 1: 189-212.

Tanaka, J. 1980. *The San hunter-gatherers of the Kalahari: A study of ecological anthropology.* Tokyo: University of Tokyo Press.

Tanaka, J. 1996. The world of animals viewed by the San hunter-gatherers in Kalahari. *African Study Monographs*, Suppl. 22: 11-28.

Tierney, J., P. deMenocal and P. Zander 2017. A climatic context for the out-of-Africa migration. *Geology* 45: 1023-1026.

Tindall, B. (ed) 1959. *The journal of Joseph Tindall, missionary in South West Africa 1839-55*. Cape Town: The Van Riebeeck Society.

Tindall, H. 1856. *Two lectures on Great Namaqualand and its inhabitants*. Cape Town: G.J. Pike.

Thackeray, A. 1992. The Middle Stone Age south of the Limpopo River. *Journal of World Prehistory* 6: 385-440.

Traill, L., J. Martin and N. Owen-Smith 2016. Lion proximity, not moon phase, affects the nocturnal movement behaviour of zebra and wildebeest. Journal of Zoology 299: 221-227.

Val, A., P. de la Peña, M. Duval, S. Bansal, F. Colino, J. Culey, T. Hodgskiss, P. Morrissey, A. Murray, M. Murungi, F. Neumann, K. Shadrach, K. Thompsen, M. van der Ryst, D. Witelson, J. X. Zhao and D. Stratford 2021. The place beyond the trees: renewed excavations of the Middle Stone Age deposits at Olieboompoort in the Waterberg Mountains of the South African Savanna Biome. *Archaeological and Anthropological Sciences* 13: 116. https://doi.org/10.1007/s12520-021-01302-7

Valeix, M., H. Fritz, A. Loveridge, Z. Davidson, J. Hunt, F. Murindagomo and D. Macdonald 2009. Does the risk of encountering lions influence African herbivore behavior at waterholes? *Behavioral Ecology and Sociobiology* 63: 1483-1494.

Valiente Noailles, C. 1993. *The Kua*. Rotterdam and Brookfield: A.A. Balkema.

Vedder, H. 1937. Die Bushmänner Südwestafrikas und ihre Weltanschauung. *South African Journal of Science* 334: 416-436.

Vidal, C., C. Lane, C. Asrat, D. Barfod, D. Mark, E. Tomlinson, A. Tadesse, G. Yirgu, A. Deino, W. Hutchison, A. Mounier and C. Oppenheimer 2022. *Age of oldest known Homo sapiens from eastern Africa*. Nature 601: 579-583.

Waguespack, N., T. Surovell, A. Denoyer, A. Dallow, A. Savage, J. Hyneman and D. Tapster 2009. Making a point: wood- *versus* stone-tipped projectiles. *Antiquity* 83: 786-800.

Watts, I. 1998. *The origin of symbolic culture: The Middle Stone Age of southern Africa and Khoisan ethnography*. Unpublished Ph.D. thesis, University of London.

Watts, I. 2005. 'Time, too, grows on the moon': Some evidence for Knight's theory of a human universal, in W. James and D. Mills (eds.) *The qualities of time*: 95-118. Oxford, New York: Berg.

Watts, I. 2014. The red thread: pigment use and the evolution of collective ritual, in D. Dor, C. Knight and J. Lewis (eds) *The social origins of language*: 208-227. Oxford: Oxford University Press.

Watts, I. 2017. Rain Serpents in northern Australia and southern Africa: A common ancestry? in C. Power, M. Finnegan and H. Callan (eds) *Human Origins: Contributions from social anthropology*: 248-271. New York, Oxford: Berghahn.

Watts, I., M. Chazan and J. Wilkins 2016. Early evidence for brilliant ritualized display: Specularite use in the Northern Cape (South Africa) between ~500 and ~300 ka. *Current Anthropology* 57: 287–310.

Weir, J. and E. Davidson 1965. Daily occurrence of African game animals at water holes during the dry weather. *Zoologica Africana* 1: 353-68.

Wendorf, F., R. Schild and A. Close 1993a. Middle Palaeolithic occupations at Bir Tarfawi and Bir Sahara East, Western Desert of Egypt, in L. Krzyzaniak, M. Kobusiewicz and J. Alexander (eds) *Environmental change and human culture in the Nile Basin and northern Africa until the second millennium B.C.*: 103-111. Poznan Archaeological Museum, Studies in African Archaeology 4.

Wendorf, F., R. Schild and A. Close 1993b. Summary and Conclusions, in F. Wendorf, R. Schild, A. Close and associates (eds) *Egypt during the Last Interglacial: The Middle Paleolithic of Bir Tarfawi and Bir Sahara*: 552-573. New York: Plenum Press.

Wikar, H.J. 1935 (1779). The journal of Hendrik Jacob Wikar, in E.E. Mossop (ed) *The Journals of Wikar, Coetsé and van Reenen*: 20-219. Cape Town: The Van Riebeeck Society.

Wilkins, J. and M. Chazan 2012. Blade production ~500 thousand years ago at Kathu Pan 1, South Africa: Support for a Multiple Origins hypothesis for Early Middle Pleistocene blade technologies. *Journal of Archaeological Science* 39: 1883-1900.

Wilkins, J., B. Schoville, K. Brown and M. Chazan 2012. Evidence for early hafted hunting technology. *Science* 338: 942-946.

Wilkins, J., B. Schoville and K. Brown 2014. An experimental investigation of the functional hypothesis and evolutionary advantage of stone-tipped spears. *PLoS ONE* 9: e104514.

Wilkins, J., B. Schoville, K. Brown and M. Chazan 2015. Kathu Pan 1 points and the assemblage-scale, probabilistic approach: a response to Rots and Plisson, "Projectiles and the abuse of the use-wear method in a search for impact". *Journal of Archaeological Science* 54: 294-299.

Wilkins, J. and B. Schoville 2016. Edge damage on 500-thousand-year-old spear tips from Kathu Pan 1, South Africa: The combined effects of spear use and taphonomic processes, in R. Iovita and K. Sano (eds) *Multidisciplinary approaches to the study of Stone Age weaponry*: 101-117. Vertebrate Paleobiology and Paleoanthropology Series.

Wilmsen, E. 1976. *Summary report on research on Basarwa in Western Ngamiland*. Gabarone: Ministry of Local Government and Lands.

Wilmsen, E. 1978. Seasonal effects of dietary intake on Kalahari San. *Federation Proceedings* 37(1): 65-72.

Wilmsen, E. 1989. *Land filled with flies*. Chicago: The University of Chicago Press.

Woodburn, J. 1964. *The social organization of the Hadza of northern Tanganyika*. Unpublished PhD dissertation, University of Cambridge.

Woodburn, J. 1968. An introduction to Hadza ecology, in R. Lee and I. DeVore (eds) *Man the hunter*: 49-55. Chicago: Aldine.

Woodburn, J. 1982. Social dimensions of death in four African hunting and gathering societies, in M. Bloch and J. Parry (eds) *Death and the regeneration of life*. Cambridge: Cambridge University Press.

Yeshurun, R., G. Bar-Oz and M. Weinstein-Evron 2007. Modern hunting behaviour in the early Middle Paleolithic: Faunal remains from Misliya Cave, Mount Carmel, Israel. *Journal of Human Evolution* 53: 656-677.

Enchantment in Stone

Chris Knight

When all humans everywhere were hunter-gatherers, the principle 'On Earth as it is in Heaven' was fundamental to all life. What needed to be organised on Earth had to follow the pre-ordained celestial patterns.

The principle was unavoidable for solid material reasons. In planning any large-scale undertaking, sequences and timings had to be agreed in advance. Looking skyward came naturally because nowhere else were time's intervals measured out. The Sun's predictable motions must have helped, but reliance on seasons and days would never have sufficed. Precision in fixing a date meant relying also on the Moon. A ceremony, for example, might be timed to coincide with the first New Moon following the flowering of the hawthorn or, much later, following the rutting of the deer. In that sense, we humans have always been astronomers.

There was a time when archaeologists viewed the builders of Stonehenge and other megalithic monuments in North West Europe as pioneers of the momentous transition to intensified farming, civilisation and a settled way of life (Sims 2006, citing Case 1969; Childe 1940; Runciman 2001). We now know that the builders were in fact cattle herders who still followed the Mesolithic hunting trails of their ancestors, migrating seasonally while continuing to hunt, forage and sometimes plant crops (Sims 2006, citing Edmonds 1999; Rowley-Conwy 1984; Thomas 1999; Whittle 1996; Zvelebil 1986). This new archaeological consensus led Lionel Sims (2006, 2009) to interpret Stonehenge, Silbury Hill and Avebury Stone Circle in a subtly different way. In his view, the megalithic monuments were built in order to construct hallucinatory worlds in direct contradiction of reality. The male elites who designed and constructed them needed ceremonial backing in order to preserve their rule while managing a risk-laden socio-political transition. Each step they took in betraying the old gods added to the pressure to present themselves through cosmic spectacle as guardians of the ancient ways.

The centrality of the Moon

There is now agreement that these monument builders, even while boldly innovative, were committed to preserving core cosmological traditions of their ancestors, reaching back many thousands of years (Barrett 1994; Bradley 1998; Thomas 1999; Tilley 1994, 1999; Whittle 1996). But there is less consensus as to what those traditions were. Did they involve systems for measuring time? And, if so, what methods were used? Perhaps the best-known attempt at a general understanding of Palaeolithic calendrical systems was Alexander Marshack's 1972 book, *The Roots of Civilization,* which emphasised the centrality of the Moon. Marshack followed his monumental book on lunar calendars with a steady stream of reports and articles reinforcing his claims.

Solarizing the Moon (Archaeopress 2022): 53–67

To a mostly sceptical academic audience, Marshack noted that carefully worked pieces of ivory or bone were sometimes marked by their Ice Age makers with regular notches made at different times, their clumping patterns suggestive of lunar periodicity. He went further by suggesting that zigzags, wavy lines and indications of 'flow' were used by artists to convey abstract notions of fertility and periodicity. In many cases, Marshack (1981, 1991) noted, such designs were marked in red ochre and set alongside vulvas and explicitly female imagery. But despite Marshack's meticulous work and much subsequent corroboration (see for example, Oldroyd 2003; Rappenglück 2015), his ideas about rituals organised to a lunar schedule were dismissed or forgotten until their recent qualified endorsement by archaeologists fluent in relevant hunter-gatherer research (for example, Hayden and Villeneuve 2011).

One problem with Marshack was that, as an archaeologist, he saw no reason to ground his claims in any part of evolutionary biology or human origins research. Without such a theoretical grounding, his critics could not understand why the Moon should be so central to Palaeolithic cultures. In response, Marshack (1990) could only point to humanity's advanced cognitive capacities. We were asked to believe that Ice Age humans connected lunar cycles with other significant periodicities simply because *Homo sapiens* now had the capacity to perceive and find meaning in such patterns. He was unable to suggest any deeper reason for the existence of the correlations he suspected. But as shown by Camilla Power (this volume) and also by Ian Watts (this volume), we now have compelling reasons for including lunar periodicity within the suite of environmental selection pressures and adaptive strategies responsible for shaping our emergence as a species. While Power explains how Moon-scheduled reproductive synchrony underpins the gender egalitarianism so characteristic of African hunter-gatherers, Watts explores the critical role played by lunar-scheduled night-stand hunting to the Hadza and other populations both recently and in the evolutionary past. Perhaps the most crucial fact is that the Moon directly affects the behaviour of key predator species known to have threatened our ancestors, prompting them to adopt defensive measures in response.

In *Human Origins: Contributions from Social Anthropology*, Power (2017) reconstructs the source cosmology at the root of African hunter-gatherer systems of ritual and belief. It quickly becomes clear just how pivotal the Moon's role has always been. Citing cross-cultural research by Watts (2005), Power notes by way of example the finding – predicted on theoretical grounds by Knight (1991) – that a girl's menstrual seclusion should be locked in step with the three nights of Dark Moon, while her emergence should coincide with the Moon's fattening and apparent resurrection. Power's model helps explain why fairy tales the world over echo this lunar pattern, in which initiation is likened to death followed by resurrection to new life.

Going beyond Marshack, Power brings together a range of findings from evolutionary biology, behavioural ecology and sexual selection theory to explain why, during the African Middle Stone Age, the Moon and menstruation so profoundly shaped ritual life. In her model, it is women themselves who orchestrate their own celebrations in response to a girl's first menstruation. This is grassroots resistance to male harassment or exploitation, with no need for ceremonial leaders or priests. Power points out that today's egalitarian hunter-gatherers in Africa still accord more significance to a girl's first menstruation ceremony than to the initiation of boys, presenting a compelling case for the antiquity of such rituals (Power 2017). Since the Moon is always involved, these understandings shed new light on Marshack's postulated lunar calendars for keeping track of ritually significant moments – findings which have been richly augmented in more recent years (see for example, Vavilova and Artemenko 2014). Previously, Marshack's idea of a lunar connection seemed excessively speculative. But if we accept Power's idea of a 'source cosmology', the burden of proof falls the other way. Marshack's findings, once considered unlikely, are precisely what current archaeological and evolutionary theory would lead us to expect.

Marshack's work was authoritatively re-evaluated in 2011. In their landmark paper, 'Astronomy in the Upper Palaeolithic', Brian Hayden and Suzanne Villeneuve concluded that, while much of Marshack's work was speculative and did not explore possible social reasons for keeping calendars, some of his more central ideas concerning the Palaeolithic existence of notations, seasonal scheduling and lunar recordings appear to have been well founded (Hayden and Villeneuve 2011: 351).

Crucially, the authors distinguish between simple astronomy and its more esoteric, complex forms, arguing that it was only hierarchically organised hunter-gatherers dominated by aggrandising elites who had political reasons to elaborate secret systems of astronomical knowledge. The implication is that when humans everywhere were egalitarian hunters and gatherers, astronomy would have been correspondingly simple. Central to the timing of all collective endeavours and ritual events, the Moon's changes would have been visible in the sky for all to see (*cf.* Knight 1991; Watts 2005).

In Western Europe during the Mesolithic and early Neolithic, the transition from a relatively egalitarian hunter-gatherer lifestyle to complexity and hierarchy was well under way. Hayden and Villeneuve (2011) provide an extraordinarily rich cross-cultural survey of historic accounts of hunter-gatherer groups of differing levels of complexity, defined in terms of settlement, population density and the onset of stratification. Their overview of Palaeolithic rock art, cave art and extant hunter-gatherer ethnography did much to enhance our understanding of the socio-political dynamics responsible for driving social elites to shift from simple observations of the Sun and Moon to much more complex astronomy. Their main point is that it is only hunter-gatherers who have begun developing elite structures of wealth accumulation and inherited rule who have an incentive to invest time and energy in detailed astronomical observation and secret knowledge.

When an aggrandising elite starts monopolising ritual power, a priest is often appointed to act as a calendar specialist to mark the solstices and to select the dates when ceremonies, rituals, feasting and dances would begin. Among the Chumash in North America, this specialist was known as the 'Sun priest'. Hayden and Villeneuve (2011: 336-340) explain why it is that priesthoods now begin celebrating the Sun at the expense of the Moon. While the Moon suffices to set a date in the near future, it is impossible to fix a date many years ahead without accurately marking the solstices. There was always a risk of conflicts and even bloodshed breaking out over the planning and timing of inter-regional ceremonies and feasts which required years of preparation. Getting the date right was a critically important means of creating alliances and displaying leadership and power. In fact, the accuracy of astronomical prediction could be a matter of life and death. Against this background, immense efforts had to be devoted to inventing complex rules for marking key seasonal events such as solstices while still accommodating the recalcitrant periodicities of the Moon. Such knowledge, kept secret within the priesthood, inevitably involved progressive reliance on solstices accompanied by deification of the Sun (Hayden and Villeneuve 2011).

According to Sims, this would have been the background to the building of Stonehenge and other megalithic monuments of Northwest Europe. Ritual leaders were faced with the challenge of switching from an ancient lunar calendrical system understood by everyone to a new and more secretive system based primarily on the Sun. An ingenious political strategy was to minimise the shock and disruption of this transition by conflating the Sun with the Moon. This meant designing a ritual theatre which would show how the Sun and Moon are merely aspects of each other. Initiates had to see with their own eyes that the Sun really was a hidden aspect of the Moon, its cycles stretching across time in accordance with laws known only to insiders. Intensified obedience to the Sun and its rhythms could then be presented as continued fidelity to the Moon (Sims 2006).

Sims built on the idea that as society became more male-dominated and stratified, shamans and ritual leaders became not only more divorced from the general population and secretive, but also more obsessively concerned with tracking risings and settings of constellations on particular horizons. Underlying all their concerns was an anxiety that events on earth might drift away from the pattern ordained by the heavens. Once people began to herd animals and sow crops, new imperatives tempted people to abandon their traditional rhythms. Seasonality was in danger of predominating over the ancient and revered pattern of ritual fidelity to the Moon. Somehow, as people switched over to calendars based on seasonality and hence ultimately on the Sun, they needed to convince themselves and each other that they were not breaking faith with the most ancient of heavenly commands.

The solution arrived at in Wiltshire was breathtakingly ambitious. Men set out to reconstruct the world as revealed to them during traumatic and elaborate ceremonies of initiation. They realised that they would have to reconfigure not only the entire landscape but the skyscape as well, so that the two could be brought back into alignment. The aim was to demonstrate that under a newly established social order with its secret rites and intensified patriarchal power, the harmonies previously sustained by a more gender egalitarian social order society could continue to be preserved. As long as an impression of cosmic order and continuity was upheld, society as a whole could be held together despite the profound economic changes that were by this stage well under way.

One myth only?

Only rarely will an archaeologist have the good fortune of Fabio Silva (2013, 2015) when he discovered how a surviving folktale concerning a star rising above a mountain range shed light on the location and orientation of prehistoric dolmens in Central Portugal. In the case of Stonehenge, we are unlikely to have such luck. But in a more general sense, informed analyses of folktales, place names and traditional religious assumptions in the approximate region of a prehistoric monument may provide a corrective to inappropriate reliance on assumptions specific to the archaeologist's own culture (see for example, Gazin-Schwartz and Holtorf 1999).

When the myths inspiring the construction of a ritual landscape are long forgotten, we have only the material evidence – the stones, bones, slopes, mounds and ditches to go on. These are richly informative but of course tell us nothing about the specific mythic narratives dominating the architects' minds. Perhaps we will never know. But just possibly we can. In a ground-breaking book, *An Amazonian Myth and its History*, the structural anthropologist Peter Gow (2001) showed how to use successive versions of myths to reconstruct historical events even when historical records are lacking. I hesitate to capture the subtleties of Gow's thinking while trying to be brief, but he sets out from Claude Lévi-Strauss' celebrated dictum that myths are 'instruments for the obliteration of time' (Lévi-Strauss 1970: 16).

Imagine a man standing on the deck of a boat in rough seas. In order to keep himself upright as the deck tips from side to side, he compensates by shifting his weight from one leg to the other. Gow's point is that although the figure is concerned only to keep upright, his shifting positions reflect in reverse the motions of the boat. The same applies, according to Gow, to communities whose traditional ways come under threat from external events. They strive to 'obliterate time' – that is, to preserve continuity with the past – by weaving narratives whose successive variants should help us reconstruct those events.

Gow's work in reconstructing history is based fundamentally on the insights of Lévi-Strauss (1970-1981), who developed what remains to this day the most fruitful methodology for the study of myth. It involves settling on a particular story, bringing to light its formal underlying structure and then showing how other myths – some superficially similar, some quite different – can be understood as variations on a theme. In the first volume of *Mythologiques*, Lévi-Strauss (1970) sets out from a particular myth – in this case, a Bororo story about a bird-nester – and treats it as M_1, his key. Believing that all humanity's magical narratives amount ultimately to 'one myth only' (Lévi-Strauss 1981), he might have chosen any other tale, but this is the one he starts with. Having made that personal choice, he brings out the myth's underlying structure and then, by examining one variant after another, seeks to reveal in extraordinary detail the nature of the template from which all are derived.

When it comes to the overall message of the myths, Lévi-Strauss (1978: 221-222) notes that they agree on one point. Menstruation once led to a situation of cosmic chaos which must never again be allowed. Academics have written a good deal about Lévi-Strauss' *Mythologiques*, but the passage in which he draws the threads together has been curiously ignored:

> ....the veil lifts to reveal a vast mythological system common to both South and North America, and in which the subjection of women is the basis of the social order. We can now understand the reason for this.... In her pristine innocence, [womankind] did not have monthly periods and gave birth suddenly and without warning. The transition from nature to culture demands that the feminine organism should become periodic, since the social as well as the cosmic order would be endangered by a state of anarchy in which regular alternation of day and night, the phases of the moon, feminine menstruation, the fixed period for pregnancy and the course of the seasons did not mutually support each other (Lévi-Strauss 1978: 221-222).

Lévi-Strauss takes it that the myths of all humanity concern 'the transition from nature to culture'. In order to secure the primacy of the cultural domain, women – who once menstruated haphazardly – must be made to bleed in an orderly way as trained and instructed by men. As he continues:

> So it is as periodic creatures that women are in danger of disrupting the orderly working of the universe. Their social insubordination, often referred to in the myths, is an anticipation in the form of the 'reign of women' of the infinitely more serious danger of their physiological insubordination. Therefore, women have to be subjected to *règles.* And the rules instilled into them by their upbringing, like those imposed on them, even at the cost of their subjection, by a social order willed and evolved by men, are the pledge and symbol of other 'rules', the physiological nature of which bears witness to the correspondence between social and cosmic rhythms (Lévi-Strauss 1978: 221-222).

Women must be kept down, say the myths, because their cycles are intimately connected with the Moon and the interconnected cycles of death and renewal on which all life depends. Women might menstruate too frequently or not frequently enough. 'But in either case, the sun and the moon, the heavenly bodies governing the alternation of day and night and of the seasons, would no longer be able to fulfil their function' (Lévi-Strauss 1978: 221-222).

If Lévi-Strauss is right, the unknown and unknowable myth which inspired the building of Wiltshire's stone circles must have been a variation on essentially the same theme. In that case, as Sims persuasively argues, the reason for building these megalithic monuments would have been to entrench the rule of men. One propaganda message sent out by the builders of Stonehenge seems to have been that men should be in charge because they alone could now control time. Unlike women with their menstrual potencies, according to this claim, men knew how to stop the Sun from setting – and even how to cause the Moon to pass through its phases not monthly but annually and in reverse (Sims 2006).

Avebury Stone Circle, Silbury Hill and Stonehenge were built to prevent women from ruling the world – or, rather, to accomplish the transition from rule by the Moon to a new and more narrowly solar calendar without risking social chaos. In my own work (for example, Knight 1991, 1997), I have stressed the fear – apparent in so many myths – that suppression of the Moon and its cycles will result in a calamitous loss of fertility. At whatever cost, life's cycles of renewal needed to be guaranteed despite the fact that the powers of menstruation and the Moon were being trimmed to fit new boxes designed to intensify male rule.

Building on Lévi-Strauss' argument, we might expect the myths and fairy tales of Europe to explore similar themes and be built around similar fears. It is worth bringing in here the thoughts of a classic writer on the topic of fairy tales, the psycho-analyst Bruno Bettelheim. In his book, *Symbolic Wounds*, Bettelheim (1955) argues that the female experience of bleeding without dying, in some cultures apparently envied by men, is central to rites of passage and to concepts of magic and divinity worldwide. In *The Uses of Enchantment*, Bettelheim (2010) shows how those episodes in fairy tales which seem most cruel and frightening – those involving death prior to rebirth – are in fact essential because they promise a way out from darkness and terror. In many traditional societies, a boy or girl discovers his or her own portal to another world while being initiated into adulthood. With their teenage heroes and heroines, brave enough to face death and conquer it, our most familiar fairy tales refer back to that terrifying yet magical experience.

The Sleeping Beauty

In what follows, I have selected a European fairy tale to serve as my key myth, hoping that just possibly it might illuminate the thinking behind such massive projects as Silbury Hill, Avebury Stone Circle and Stonehenge. While clearly sharing the same structure and revolving around similar themes, my chosen story cannot be interpreted as a call for the subjugation of women and their Moon. As if contradicting this message, it warns of the catastrophic consequences of repudiating women's lunar rule in favour of Sun-worship and male rule. As always, different versions exist. The French anthropologist Yvonne Verdier (1997) links Little Briar Rose to Little Red Riding Hood. Versions of the latter tale, she reports, remained until recently part of a living oral tradition in the Loire Valley, the Northern Alps and other parts of rural France. These tales of bloody events in a dark hut in the forest, Verdier argues, are in all cases inseparable from local and still remembered traditions of girls undergoing needlework apprenticeship while in menstrual seclusion.

The Grimms' version of 'Little Briar Rose', first published in 1812 and familiar to English speakers as *The Sleeping Beauty in the Woods*, tells of a king and queen who yearned for a child, immediately introducing us to concerns about fertility. As the story opens, the king has been unable to get his wife pregnant. The Queen fails to conceive until a frog jumps into her lap while she is bathing, promising her a daughter. The story continues:

> *Following the birth, the girl's parents celebrated with a feast, to which the Wise Women or Fairies were invited. There were thirteen of these in the kingdom, but the King invited only twelve because he had only twelve golden plates.*
>
> *The feast was held in splendour, whereupon the twelve fairies bestowed their blessings upon the child. The first promised virtue, the next beauty, the next wealth. Just before it was the turn of the twelfth fairy, the excluded thirteenth burst in. Seeing that no place had been laid for her, her blessing was instead uttered as a curse. 'The King's daughter', she declared, 'shall in her fifteenth year prick herself with a spindle and fall down dead.'*
>
> *The assembled guests cried out and begged the twelfth fairy, whose blessing had yet to be given, to undo the curse. Explaining that she was not sufficiently powerful, she instead softened it. Instead of dying forever when she pricked her finger, the girl would die only for a hundred years. Still not satisfied, the King ordered every spindle in the kingdom to be burnt.*
>
> *On her fifteenth birthday, while her parents were away, the princess climbed a stairway leading to a room in a tower where sat an old woman with a spindle, spinning her flax. Reaching out, the girl pricked her finger on the spindle and fell into a deep sleep. The King and Queen, who at this point arrived home, fell asleep with her. The horses slept in the stable, the dogs in the yard, the flies on the wall. The cook, who was about to box the ears of the scullery boy, left off and fell asleep. For a hundred years, the entire kingdom remained frozen in time while an impenetrable hedge of thorns grew around the palace. Hearing tales about a sleeping princess, young men would arrive, take out their sword and attempt to cut through. But all became impaled on the thorns.*

> *With the passing of the hundredth year, the deadly thorns turned to roses. The hedge parted of its own accord, allowing in a suitor who now entered the palace, stepped over the sleeping bodies and kissed the princess on her lips. She opened her eyes and the kingdom woke up with her. A royal wedding was held and the two lived happily ever after* (adapted from Little Briar Rose, Grimm and Grimm [1812] 1975: 237-41).

Any myth will be open to a range of interpretations. Verdier (1997) comments that on one level, the story tells of Prince Charming rescuing a helpless maiden from the clutches of a wicked witch. On that basis we might dismiss the entire narrative as woman-hating ideology (Dworkin 1974), one implication being that any powerful woman is likely to be a witch. If you are a girl, the way to get ahead is to lie on your back for as long as necessary, waiting for a prince to come and rescue you. If you are a boy, by contrast, decisive action is required. Wield your sword, conquer all obstacles and win your bride.

But as with any myth, it is important to pay close attention to the details. Lévi-Strauss (1970-1981) taught us that it is often the details in a story which seem most absurd that tell us most when properly understood. Take, for example, that frog in 'Little Briar Rose' who promises a baby to the Queen. This suggests a theory about where babies come from, and it is not from having sex with a man. To do justice to 'Little Briar Rose', we need to find an approach which brings out its internal coherence, showing how the whole story hangs together, its details connecting up to make consistent logical sense.

Interpreting the uninvited guest as a wicked witch leaves the remaining details of the story unexplained. This central figure, clearly the most powerful of all, is introduced to us as a 'wise woman' – one of thirteen who, traditionally, would be invited to give blessings to a baby girl. Why thirteen? Why does the king only have twelve plates? Twelve golden plates, thirteen wise women, a girl's pricked finger, a hedge of thorns, a hundred-year obliteration of time – not one of these details is explained by interpreting that wise woman as a wicked witch.

'Little Briar Rose' is a story filled with paradoxes and conflicts. It can be seen as an orally transmitted recollection of a time when society was on the cusp, threatened by patriarchy but still able to resist. According to my own interpretation (Knight 1987), the whole story reflects a struggle over who should mark out and control the passage of time. Should thirteen wise women retain their traditional control, or should they defer to a king? Should menstruation be considered a blessing – the thirteenth and most precious of all – or is it now to be rejected as a curse? And what about the Sun and Moon? Are the months of any year to remain what they always were, thirteen New or Full Moons? Or are they to be replaced by twelve man-made divisions, appearing in the story as twelve golden plates? Finally, where does power reside? Whose force ultimately prevails? Does power lie with the king who commands the destruction of all spindles – or with that thirteenth wise woman, senior figure in the princess' network of supportive kin, whose carefully preserved spindle succeeded in reaching the king's own daughter?

The narrative's most memorable images concern sharp spindles and thorns. When Little Briar Rose pricks her finger, the story-teller has no need to mention blood, which inevitably comes to mind. Yvonne Verdier (1997) links the spindle to the pins, needles and other prickly items found in little-known versions of 'Little Red Riding Hood'. Drawing on extensive fieldwork and research in regions of rural France, Verdier reports that these typically gruesome stories of a girl's bloody seclusion in the forest are widely known to be coded references to a girl's first menstruation. For Bettelheim (]1978] 2010: 232) too, it is clear that the bleeding is menstruation, in turn connected intimately with lunar time. In his words, 'The thirteen fairies in the Brothers Grimm story are reminiscent of the thirteen lunar months into which the year was once, in ancient times, divided... the number of twelve good fairies plus a thirteenth evil one indicates symbolically that the fatal "curse" refers to menstruation'.

If the thirteen wise women are Moons, their plates presumably of silver, then the king's golden plates must be twelve Suns, tokens of the new-fangled calendar apparently favoured by the king. The narrative makes quite clear that the thirteenth gift-giver is a wise woman like the others, from which we can infer that she has a blessing to give. It is only when this blessing is rejected that it turns into a curse. The myth seems to be accusing the king of being the enemy of fertility. First, he is unable to get his wife pregnant. And now he threatens to stop his daughter from becoming a woman. A moment's thought should clarify that menstruation, the blessing of fertility, is what the king with his solar calendar is repudiating.

A consistently menstrual interpretation along these lines would run as follows. The story reflects the contradictions faced by a society attempting to reconcile a newly introduced solar calendar with the concept of months or Moons. 'The earliest calendar year', writes Emily Lyle (1986: 243), 'was not the solar year of 365 days, but the lunar year consisting of twelve lunar cycles, to which an intercalary month was generally added every two or three years to keep the months in line with the natural seasons'. The number of days in a lunar cycle varies between twenty-nine and thirty – on average 29½ – so that a year was either 354 days (twelve lunar months) or 383½ days (thirteen lunar months). In other words, for as long as the year was divided up into observational lunar months – a sequence of directly-observed Moons – there was no way in which the number thirteen could be avoided. At the end of each twelve Moons, a part of the thirteenth always made its presence felt, and some place for it in the calendar had to be found.

The only way to establish the solar year as fixedly consisting of twelve month-like periods was to divide it into schematic months, arbitrarily adjusting the length of each to ensure that twelve of them totalled just 365 days. This, of course, is a feature of the modern Christian (Gregorian) calendar. The thirteenth month has been effectively suppressed. In folklore, however – at least in Europe – the suppressed month, and with it the number thirteen, remains associated with those older pagan traditions which took account not only of the Sun but of the Moon as well. This liminal, half-excluded thirteenth month finds reflection in 'the persistence of the number thirteen' as the standard number of witches ('Wise Women' or 'Fairies' as Grimm's tale puts it) in a coven in pre-Christian European traditions of ritualism (Murray 1921: 16.)

A dispute also exists as to whether menstruation should be considered a blessing or a curse. We may assume the existence of an early tradition according to which menstrual bleeding was associated with the Moon – and therefore with the number thirteen – and was considered a manifestation of women's ritual power. Menstruation was, in other words, included among the other blessings with which a woman could be endowed. The newer custom – and certainly the Christian one – has been to turn menstruation into a curse, just as the thirteenth month has been suppressed. In both respects, lunar time is being denied.

This, then, is the background to the story. The story itself tells of how a king just wanted his daughter to become the perfect bride. This would explain why the blessings offered by the good fairies are so consistently marital. Virtue, beauty and wealth – these are all qualities likely to attract a desirable suitor. No husband would be attracted by the menstrual condition of his bride, and so the thirteenth fairy with her special blessing is spurned. But menstruation is a force of nature and cannot be ignored. If suppressed, it simply makes its presence felt in malevolent form. The ultimate blessing now becomes the curse. In certain traditions, menstruation would involve a woman being set apart in some way, her seclusion conceived as a period of freedom from marital demands. So far removed is she from marital duties and domestic chores that from her husband's point of view, she might as well be in *another world*. Her blood carries her off into that world, as far removed from this one as heaven is unreachable from Earth. The injured and angered thirteenth fairy utters her curse. When the girl comes of age, no force on Earth can prevent her from bleeding. She will enter the world beyond and stay there.

Fortunately, as this curse is laid, the twelfth wise woman has yet to confer her blessing. Everyone implores her to undo the curse but, excusing herself, she explains that she is not as powerful as the thirteenth. The best she can do is commute the sentence to somewhere between normal monthly seclusion and permanent death. The royal couple will be subjected to the full rigours of the traditional menstrual spell but in exaggeratedly prolonged form. The traditional logic was for menstruation, particularly, we might suppose, a royal person's first-menstruation, to cast its spell widely and last for days on end but not for a hundred years. The century-long seclusion is a community's punishment for its attempt to escape seclusion altogether.

The menstrual spell is a cyclical occurrence, just as is seasonal change. Time, in the traditional view, is itself cyclical. The king, in attempting to destroy all spindles, is symbolically attempting to suppress the spinning by women of the threads of time – threads which wind like yarn around a spool. We may also infer that he is hostile to spinsterhood. Yvonne Verdier (1997) makes much of the fact that a traditional occupation for secluded women in rural France was needlework, sewing and spinning. English speakers are familiar with the term 'spinster' for a woman who opposes marriage, as if permanently in seclusion. The traditional concept, central to myths across the world, is that while in seclusion a woman is with her 'Moon Husband' at the expense of her earthly one (Knight 1997; cf. Lewis 2002: 103). When the princess explores the unfamiliar stairway and discovers the old witch spinning flax in her turret in the sky, she has defied her father and found her way back to that thirteenth blessing, conferred on her by the Moon.

The king was wicked to destroy all spinning-wheels and spindles, for lunar time cannot be suppressed. He should never have tried to set man-made legislation against the deeper laws of nature. It is in the nature of things that every girl will come of age and bleed, her cycle itself being among the most ancient of all clocks. And as the princess bleeds, the ancient power of the blood strikes out with a vengeance against all who had believed they could defy it. The whole palace, the whole kingdom is plunged into a deathly state. All normal domestic activities cease. It is as if time stood still. Those who believed that they could alter the ancient calendar, that they could abolish the thirteenth month, that they could suppress the hallowed logic of menstrual time are now put firmly in their place. They will be excluded from time's flow for a hundred years.

As the princess sleeps on, it is as if her blood had erected around her an impenetrable barrier to her ever getting married. Would-be suitors are kept at bay by a deadly hedge of thorns. She herself is now in menstrual seclusion of a particularly rigorous, long-lasting kind, with the whole palace in seclusion with her. But every period of seclusion – even a hundred-year one – must eventually expire. And when the time has come, lovers are free once more to approach. The spell breaks, the thorns give way to roses. The hedge parts, allowing the next young suitor to enter and deliver his kiss. The period of seclusion is over; the palace servants resume their domestic chores. Marital relations are resumed and are celebrated in the palace with a royal wedding and feast.

From the details of Little Briar Rose, Red Riding Hood and other traditional European fairy tales we can infer that many of them are not only pre-Christian but pre-Neolithic. It is a common feature that where magic is concerned, this comes not from farmland, from ploughing or from harvesting but from the wild – from the depths of the forest. It is different with Jack-and-the-Beanstalk, where we have a domesticated cow, a planted bean and a young man bleeding from the nose (Opie and Opie 1980: 212), all suggestive of ceremonies of initiation involving male menstruation (Knight 1987, 1991) in a later Neolithic context. Farming people often feel the need for magic in order to help the crops grow, but where this happens, they invariably fall back on more ancient traditions. The luck associated with the hunt may be transferred to serve agricultural ends, but in origin it belongs in a different world in which the unstable Moon is a more powerful clock than the predictable Sun.

Far from amounting only to patriarchal ideology, the story of Little Briar Rose tells of a power beyond that of any man, even a king. It is the power of the Moon and its rhythms of renewal, a central privilege of being female. So much has the king lost touch with this power that he has been unable to get his wife pregnant.

Frogs appear regularly in European fairy tales, and are seen as wet, periodic and rejuvenating – ugly creatures with a predictable tendency to metamorphose into a handsome prince. Frogs feature in Amazonian mythology, but in a different way. In a study of the Barasana Indians of northwest Amazonia, the links between metamorphosis, role-exchanging and menstruation are made explicit. One myth describes a certain Frog-Wife whose married life 'is divided into cycles of alternation between her husband's and her own natal community' (C. Hugh-Jones 1979: 166). In a valuable commentary, the ethnographer notes that the Frog Wife is 'metaphorically menstruating', her 'journeys home' being periods of menstrual seclusion. When she is with her own kin, she is 'dangerous' to her husband, and is, in fact, a Snake Woman (C. Hugh-Jones 1979: 166). In this state, we may compare her, then, with the 'false wife' of so many other myths and tales. Frogs and snakes are code terms for a wife who, in menstruating, has 'changed her skin' – in other words, changed her status, social identity or role. Hence among the Barasana, cycling women are potentially snakes, spiders and other 'skin-changing' creatures. A woman renews herself through menstruation, viewed as 'an internal changing of skin' (S. Hugh-Jones 1979: 183). Menstrual alternation, then, is metaphorically an exchanging of skin for skin, old life for new.

Where women have solidarity and power, as they do for example among the Kalasha of North West Pakistan, entering the women's house releases them from marital and domestic duties, giving them a freedom of movement which men also respect (Maggi 2004). But where men have succeeded in curbing such freedoms, we see this shift of power reflected in mythology. A heroic male succeeds in preventing his bride from leaving him periodically to return to her own kin. Cutting her off from that supportive kinship network, he isolates her in his own territory under his own close supervision and control. As a way of justifying his actions, the myths depict a woman's blood relatives in lurid terms, often as a venomous snake, many-headed dragon or other monster in constant need of blood (Knight 1991).

Elsewhere (Knight 1997) I have shown how one of Lévi-Strauss' key myths – a Plains Indian story concerning 'The Wives of the Sun and Moon' – makes sense in these terms, as a frog-wife is prevented by her husband from returning to her kin each Moon. Traditionally, I argued, women would make such visits as frogs or toads, metaphors for menstruation or pregnancy. A central mythological theme is that some heroic male sets out to end all such visits, now seen as a threat to the establishment of permanent patrilocal residence. This can only be understood if we make the underlying assumption that previously, hunter-gatherer women would remain with their supportive network of matrilineal kin, returning home particularly during menstruation or childbirth.

Concluding remarks

If we accept Lévi-Strauss' (1981) claim that humanity's myths amount in the end to 'one myth only', we might expect hunter-gatherers, horticulturalists and others to feel at home not only with Grimm's fairy-tales, but also with the myths of Aboriginal Australia or ancient Greece. I remember well an incident in 2004, when two hunter-gatherer Hadza men were staying with me in my flat in North London. They attended my evening class while I was giving a lecture on the story of Little Briar Rose. I had hardly begun reading it aloud when they shouted out, 'Oh, we've got that story!'. The details in their local variant were differently arranged, but they immediately recognised the structure and motifs.

Faced with Grimm's fairy tales, any hunter-gatherers could certainly draw significant comparisons with their own mythology – which itself is not a rigid doctrine of faith but a fluid social awareness, rich in contradictions, disputes and variations, and expressed through an indefinite number of myths and tales which have been overheard from neighbouring tribes, borrowed, exchanged, incorporated into more familiar tales, half-forgotten, distorted and amended in the manner common to story-tellers throughout the world.

There is no rigid, point-by-point, inevitable correspondence between any one particular myth and any one particular ritual sequence. Rather, a basically lunar logic is at a deep level governing the practice of magical ritual everywhere, spinning off practices and fairy tales in an endless variety of forms. If we can always discern what looks like a precise structural correspondence between myth and myth, myth and rite or one ritual and the next, it need not be because these elements are geographically or historically related. No one myth need stay anchored to one ritual, nor need any one localised ritual be explained by any one myth or set of myths. All are at the deepest level equally illuminating of one another because they all lead back to the same logical source. As products of a single lunar generator of collective practice and thought, all are, from an external patriarchal standpoint, absurdity or lunacy of much the same general kind.

Sims' success in making sense of the megalithic monuments of Wiltshire stemmed in large measure from his intuitions about the mind-set of the architects. None of us can claim to know what precise myths or rituals inspired their designs. But this hardly matters if the world's magical myths and fairy tales are variations on a theme. The builders of Stonehenge and Avebury were steeped in the mythology of their time and we can be sure that the Sun and Moon, life and death, Earth and sky followed heavenly constraints which have continued to shape mythological thought to this day. In an age of momentous transition, Wiltshire's priests and patriarchs feared the calamitous consequences of switching to a solar calendar and thereby losing touch with the Moon and its rhythms of fertility, death and renewal. Their project to 'solarize' the Moon – and, conversely, to preserve the Moon's properties even while attaching them to the Sun – was nothing if not ambitious. Cosmic mismatch culminating in loss of fertility was the overriding fear, driving the priesthood to temper, disguise and sanctify their new political rule by building mountains, transporting immense boulders and restructuring entire landscapes in an effort to set things right.

References

Barrett, J. 1994. *Fragments from Antiquity: an Archaeology of Social Life in Britain, 2900–1200 BC.* Oxford: Blackwell.

Bettelheim, B. [1978] 2010. *The Uses of Enchantment: The Meaning and Importance of Fairy Tales.* London: Vintage.

Bettelheim, B. 1955. *Symbolic Wounds.* London: Thames and Hudson.

Bradley, R.J. 1998. *The Significance of Monuments.* London: Routledge.

Case, H. 1969. Neolithic explanations. *Antiquity* 43: 176–86.

Childe, V.G. 1940. *Prehistoric Communities of the British Isles.* London: Chambers.

Dworkin, A. 1974. *Woman Hating. A Radical Look at Sexuality.* London: Dutton.

Edmonds, M. 1999. *Ancestral Geographies of the Neolithic: Landscapes, Monuments and Society.* London: Routledge.

Gazin-Schwartz, A. and C. Holtorf (eds) 1999. *Archaeology and Folklore.* London: Routledge.

Gow, P. 2001. *An Amazonian Myth and Its History.* Oxford: Oxford University Press.

Grimm, I. and W. Grimm [1812] 1975. *The Complete Grimm's Fairy Tales.* London: Routledge.

Hayden, B. and S. Villeneuve 2011. Astronomy in the Upper Palaeolithic? *Cambridge Archaeological Journal* 21 (3): 331–55.

Hugh-Jones, C. 1979. *From the Milk River. Spatial and temporal processes in northwest Amazonia.* Cambridge: Cambridge University Press.

Hugh-Jones, S. 1979. *The Palm and the Pleiades. Initiation and cosmology in northwest Amazonia.* Cambridge: Cambridge University Press.

Knight, C. 1987. Menstruation and the Origins of Culture. A reconsideration of Lévi-Strauss's work on symbolism and myth. Unpublished Ph.D. thesis. University of London, London.

Knight, C. 1991. *Blood Relations. Menstruation and the origins of culture.* New Haven and London: Yale University Press.

Knight, C. 1997. The wives of the sun and moon. *Journal of the Royal Anthropological Institute* 3 (N.S.): 133-153.
Lévi-Strauss, C. 1970. *The Raw and the Cooked. Introduction to a Science of Mythology* 1. London: Cape.
Lévi-Strauss, C. 1973. *From Honey to Ashes. Introduction to a Science of Mythology* 2. London: Cape.
Lévi-Strauss, C. 1978. *The Origin of Table Manners. Introduction to a Science of Mythology* 3. London: Cape.
Lévi-Strauss, C. 1981. *The Naked Man. Introduction to a Science of Mythology* 4. London: Cape.
Lewis, J. 2002. Forest hunter gatherers and their world: a study of the Mbendjele Yaka Pygmies of Congo-Brazzaville and their secular and religious activities and representations. Unpublished PhD thesis, University College London.
Lyle, E. 1986. Archaic calendar structure approached through the principle of isomorphism. *Semiotics* 61 (3/4): 243-257.
Maggi, W. 2004. *Our Women Are Free. Gender and ethnicity in the Hindukush.* Ann Arbor: University of Michigan Press._
Marshack, A. 1972. *The Roots of Civilization. The cognitive beginnings of man's first art, symbol and notation.* London: Weidenfeld and Nicolson.
Marshack, A. 1981. On paleolithic ochre and the early uses of colour and symbol. *Current Anthropology* 22 (2): 188-191.
Marshack, A. 1990. Early hominid symbol and evolution of the human capacity, in P. Mellars (ed.), *The Emergence of Modern Humans: An archaeological perspective*: 457-498. Edinburgh: Edinburgh University Press.
Marshack, A. 1991. The female image: a 'time-factored' symbol. A study in style and aspects of image use in the Upper Palaeolithic. *Proceedings of the Prehistoric Society* 57: 17-31.
Murray, M.A. 1921. *The witch-cult in western Europe.* Oxford: Oxford University Press.
Oldroyd, D. 2003. Feminine context of prehistoric notation systems, *The Accounting Historians Notebook:* 26 (2): 5.
Opie, I. and P. Opie, 1980. *The classic fairy tales.* St. Albans: Granada.
Power, C. 2017. Reconstructing a Source Cosmology for African Hunter-Gatherers, in C. Power, M. Finnegan and H. Callan (eds), *Human Origins: Contributions from Social Anthropology*: 180-202. New York & Oxford: Berghahn.
Rappenglück, M. 2015. Possible Calendrical Inscriptions on Palaeolithic Artifacts, In C. Ruggles (ed.), *Handbook of Archaeoastronomy and Ethnoastronomy:* 1205-1212. New York, Heidelberg, Dordrecht, London: Springer.
Renfrew, C. 1976. *Before Civilization: The radiocarbon revolution and prehistoric Europe.* Harmondsworth: Penguin.
Rowley-Conwy, P. 1984. The laziness of the short distance hunter: the origins of agriculture in western Denmark. *Journal of Anthropological Archaeology* 3: 300–324.
Runciman, W.G. 2001. From nature to culture, from culture to society, in W.G. Runciman (ed.) *The Origin of Human Social* Institutions: 235-254. Oxford: The British Academy.
Silva, F. 2013. Landscape and Astronomy in Megalithic Portugal: The Carregal do Sal Nucleus and Star Mountain Range. *Papers from the Institute of Archaeology* 22: 99-114.
Silva, F. 2015. 'Once upon a time...': When prehistoric archaeology and folklore converge. *Journal for the Academic Study of Religion,* 28, (2): 158-175.
Sims, L. D. 2006. The 'Solarization' of the Moon: Manipulated Knowledge at Stonehenge. *Cambridge Archaeological Journal,* 16 (2): 191-207.

Sims, L. D. 2009. Entering, and returning from, the underworld: reconstituting Silbury Hill by combining a quantified landscape phenomenology with archaeoastronomy. *Journal of the Royal Anthropological Institute.* 15 (2): 386-408.

Thomas, J. 1999. *Understanding the Neolithic.* London: Routledge.

Tilley, C. 1994. *A Phenomenology of Landscape.* Oxford: Berg.

Tilley, C. 1999. *Metaphor and Material Culture.* Oxford: Blackwell.

Vavilova, I.B. and T.G. Artemenko 2014. Ancient astronomical culture in Ukraine. 1: Finds relating to the Paleolithic era. *Journal of Astronomical History and Heritage,* 17(1): 29-38.

Verdier, Y. 1997. Little Red Riding Hood in oral tradition. *Marvels & Tales: Journal of Fairy-Tale Studies,* 11 (1-2): 101-23.

Watts, I. 2005. 'Time, too, grows on the Moon': Some evidence for Knight's theory of a human universal, in W. James and D. Mills (eds) *The Qualities of Time: Anthropological Approaches*: 95-118. New York: Berg.

Whittle, A. 1996. *Europe in the Neolithic: the Creation of New Worlds.* Cambridge: Cambridge University Press.

Zvelebil, M. 1986. *Hunters in Transition.* London: Cambridge University Press.

Part II:

Prehistory and Megalithic Monuments

Prehistoric Interest in Stations of the Sun and the Moon - Fact or Fiction?

Emília Pásztor

Introduction – contextual factors

The vast majority of archaeoastronomical research is dominated by the investigation of the alignment of structures towards the direction of the various special positions of the Sun and the Moon. Many scholars - including Lionel Sims - accept the common assumption that these stations were already known in prehistoric communities. Some go even further when they argue that these positions also served as orientation targets for Europe's prehistoric monuments. However, the meaning must be more complex. Therefore, Lionel Sims' scientific creativity for example, has rightly drawn attention to solarisation yet emphasised that remnants of the Moon's former veneration must also be found in monuments, including even those that were apparently dedicated to the Sun.

The social and ecological environment determines how we imagine the surrounding world, how we explain the celestial phenomena and how we use this acquired knowledge. Therefore, if we look for an analogy to the celestial knowledge of prehistoric Europe, firstly we must understand the way of life and the social conditions of the people who have lived in the studied area. Most social formations of late prehistoric Europe (Neolithic, Bronze Age, Early Iron Age) resembled more tribal assemblies rather than a highly hierarchical state organisation with a powerful ruler and persons specialised in spiritual life, as in the Near East (Harding 2000: 389; Iversen 2017; O'Shea 1996).

Many prehistoric societies in Europe have cultural elements, traditions or customs in common, such as the use of small clay figurines (idols) in the Neolithic, or the European-wide custom of deposition in the Bronze Age. However, archaeological research does not support the existence of a unified, organised religion, even within a single cultural group, but rather the presence of diverse religious behaviours despite these shared archaeological features. Although there are archaeological sites where rituals have been practised over a long period of time (for example near hot springs), archaeologists have not been able to prove clearly the existence of regularly repeated ceremonies and rituals governed by common principles, or the existence of a separate, specialised social stratum - like priests – in the majority of prehistoric Europe. Apart from the Mediterranean regions, religious activities are supposed to have taken place in a family circle or in a narrow community environment (Bradley 2005; Brück 2011; Pásztor 2011). As the saying goes, 'there's no accounting for taste'.

Ethnographic research provides the best examples of the role orientation can play in the life of a community. For example, traditional Japanese houses face south, more precisely they are trying to avoid the north with their facades (Hendry 1981: 217). The houses in the Indonesian village of Toraja face north where the rivers originate (Waterson 1994: 97). While, the Indian

Thakar and Warli tribes believe south is the direction of evil, thus, the doors of houses, the direction of beds cannot face south (Tribhuwan 2005). Examining the burial ceremonies of 31 traditional ethnic groups, anthropologist Christopher Carr argues that philosophical-religious beliefs play the most important role in designing burial rites, in addition to the social position of the deceased in the community. The preparation, treatment, orientation and the placement of the corpse and the spatial arrangement of the grave furniture provide the most useful information for the study of the religious world (Carr 1995: 157, 168, 188-89). Ethnographic records demonstrate that orientations, which can be considered dangerous *or* sacred, play an important role in countless ways:

- in the layout of dwellings and living space
- which direction the ceremony leader is turning during the ceremony
- as part of the funeral service (the orientation and arrangement of graves)
- the placement and orientation of sacred buildings/structures

The setting of directions and the importance of certain directions also depend on the way of life and social formation of the given societies. The use of the four cardinal directions (that is already an abstraction) is primarily characteristic of complex societies. Settled communities establish directions by the topographic features of their local environment. Rivers, streams, sunrise and sunset as independent natural phenomena play the most significant role in setting directions for such communities (Brown 1983: 136-137). Martin P. Nilsson also argues that the 'meaning of solstices can only arise among a people with a fixed dwelling-place, since a race which leads a nomadic life and changes dwellings and camps is without the necessary fixed points of observation' (Nilsson 1920: 312). Important directions are also established in connection with the given societies' mythology (death, a sacred place to found, ritual year ceremonies and so on), which can also vary according to rituals. For example, for the Khanty people, the Upper World is towards the south in a sacrificial ceremony, but it faces upstream in a death ceremony, even if the river happens to flow from the north (Leete 2017: 19).

All these data indicate that orientation - towards one or more directions - plays a major role in the culture of nearly every ethnic group. If ethnographic and anthropological research suggests the significance of certain directions, we can safely assume that the people of ancient cultures also considered certain directions important. Therefore, examining orientations is as important as any other study of past cultures. The most commonly used archaeoastronomical method is studying the orientation of monuments to reveal possible astronomical targets. The majority of archaeoastronomical orientation research argues that sunrises and sunsets at summer, and less often winter solstices, and even less frequently at equinoxes are likely to be the targets. Similarly, the directions of the Moon in similar positions are almost always targets, while the directions of the stars only sometimes. Nevertheless, if something has a communal importance, people celebrate it. Commemoration of the solstices was widespread in 19th century Europe. On this basis, archaeoastronomers feel justified in claiming that the 'highlighted' points of apparent solar and lunar motion had special significance in the past and that is why the monuments are aligned to them. However, many ethnologists argue that it is a cliché of European ethnographic research to associate the main festivities with the solstices and the equinoxes and the early European ethnologists were already sceptical about the theories of solstice celebrations in far ancient times.

This chapter aims to trace down the knowledge, the celebration and ritual use of the Sun and Moon's 'stations' in ethnographical and historical records as far back as possible, in order to find answers to questions like how far back in history does the celebration of solstices go, or were the lunar stations also recognised and celebrated alongside the time counting character of the Moon. It will also investigate ethnographic and historic cases in order to find alignments to these stations from later periods which can support the aforementioned assumption frequently used by archaeoastronomers.

Stations of the Sun

What do ethnographic cases reveal? At first glance, they may indicate that we are looking at an ancient tradition of celebrating the summer solstice because it was a widespread custom in 19th century Europe. Solstitial festivities are characterised by the ignition of bonfires in many folk traditions. Historical sources say that accounts of European fire festivals can be traced back to the Middle Ages, but their origins may be much older, dating back to a time well before we started to record time, as the anthropologist James G. Frazer said (Frazer 2015: 328-346). Bonfires are most often lit in spring and midsummer. The midsummer festival is characterised by lighting a bonfire, walking around fields and rolling a burning straw wheel. Many consider that flaming straw wheels are the symbol of the Sun's motion. Therefore, its mention in early literary sources is also thought to refer to the celebration of the solstice, although the text of the extant manuscripts is quite corrupt. It is reported in such a text dated to the 6th century, that Saint Christian Vincentius had witnessed a peculiar custom when suffering his martyrdom in Agen (Aquitaine, dép. Lot-et-Garonne), at the beginning of the 4th century. A flaming wheel was rolled out of a local temple down to a river, hit the water and was then reassembled in the temple (Hofeneder 2010: 103; Hutton 1996: 311; Zwicker 1934-6: 302-303).

Based on these resources, many researchers have argued that solstices played an important role in religion and traditional dramatic activities and that their origins might go back to as early as prehistoric Europe. This belief has surfaced throughout the 20th century with greater or lesser degrees of certainty and has become accepted by many archaeoastronomers as well. Furthermore, early ethnographical records proved the existence of rudimentary horizon calendars in Europe and North America (Nilsson 1920: 312-13) that marked important dates for communities by some of the Sun's positions at specific features on the horizon. Nilsson also writes in detail about how important days were defined:

> In Norway...On certain farms there was a definite stone, buried in the earth, to which the people repaired for these observations. They noticed when the sun rose and shone out above certain mountain peaks, or when its last rays touched this or that summit. They also observed the length of the shadow on the face of a cliff, or noted when it touched the brow of a mountain or a certain stone. Thence they were able to give the important days of the year, e. g. the festival of St. Paul or Candlemas. Our authority says that the observation was very inaccurate, so that the Christmas Day of the people might fall on January 2nd. But it was not so bad as that, since they still followed the old style (Nilsson 1920: 317).

This humble and easy to learn method used for calendric purpose was still in practice across Europe even in the 20th century (Koleva 2003: 43; Moszyński 1967: 162; Vaiškūnas 2003: 33-34). Beside landmarks, the Sun might also have been observed with the help of poles as the memory of such practices has survived in Lithuanian folklore (Vaiškūnas 2003, 33).

Based on evidence such as this, many archaeoastronomers feel justified in claiming that the certain horizontal points of the apparent solar and lunar motions made such an impression on ancient communities that they oriented their monuments towards them. However, we must be aware that bonfires, fire jumping and the use of flaming wheels were commonplace in European customs and they were not tied exclusively to summer solstice rituals (Frazer 2015: 328-346; Nilsson 1920: 287; Gailey 1977; Van Gennep 1949). Fire jumping activities with bonfires were also performed in the Balkans for example, on the feast of the Prophet Elijah (20th July) or on the feast of St. Constantine and Helena in May (Dömötör 1983: 140-143). Among the Serbs, the custom of lighting fires at the feast of St. Ivan is not limited to the day of the saint, it lasted until the day of Elijah and the primary purpose was to avert danger (Liungman 1938: 551-552).

Jacob Grimm, in his *Deutsche Mythologie* also describes two distinct times in the summer for the lighting of fires but in the north of Germany, they took place at Easter. Midsummer fires with their relevant games took place only in the south of Germany (Billington 2008: 42). Even the practice of rolling down burning wheels does not mean an exclusive solstice ritual. In the German town of Lügde (North Rhine-Westphalia), a spectacular tradition is carried out, known as the Osterräderlauf, or 'Easter-wheel-run' on Easter Sunday. Similarly, burning oak wheels are rolled down the slopes of the Osterberg or 'Easter-mountain' (Sermona 2008: 338).

Are these fire festivals really an ancient custom? As suggested earlier, many ethnologists argue that it is a cliché of European ethnographic research to nearly always associate the main festivities with solstices and equinoxes. However, this 'straightforward' association, even in the 19th to 20th centuries, fits predominantly with the summer solstice. As for the winter solstice, there are many other factors that play a role in determining the date of winter festivals. Also, spring festivities cannot be matched to the spring equinox and there are no traditional dramatic customs during the autumn equinox. That is why European ethnologists from the early 20th century (Chambers 1903; Marót 1940: 146; Nilsson 1920) were highly sceptical about solstice theories.

Studying the ancient Lithuanian calendar festivals from the 14th to 20th centuries, Arūnas Vaicekauskas also argues that the role of midsummer or St. John's Day (Lith. Joninės) in the festive peasant calendar is overrated in scientific and, especially, popular literature. There are parts in Lithuania where this festival was not even celebrated (Vaicekauskas 2014: 115). Sandra Billington (2008), folklorist-historian, has made a thorough examination of the usual argument that medieval midsummer traditions in northern Europe descended from ancient pagan customs in Germany and Scandinavia which included a ritual at the summer solstice. She has, however, not found any clues in Nordic and Saxon literature that support the conclusion that original Germanic traditions had been concerned with the Sun's summer station. The Anglo-Saxon literature also lacks records about the significance of summer solstice (Billington 2008: 42). She also added that:

> In fact, we have no record of customs at the summer solstice in Germany until the seventh century AD, and none from Scandinavia until the end of the first millennium when St John's Eve became one of the Christian feast days on which Olav Trygvason, after his conversion, allowed drinking festivals. The absence of recorded pagan activity at this solstice is in marked contrast to substantial material for Yule (Billington 2008: 44).

Those people living near the Arctic Circle have probably been more observant of the motion of the Sun, as the difference between winter and summer solar movements is more striking there. Therefore, it is widely presumed that they have known and considered solstices important. However, there are some notable exceptions. Even the use of the phrase 'midsummer' in written sources does not mean self-evident identity with the summer solstice. The Icelandic Calendar was divided into two six-month seasons and summer began after the spring equinox. The halfway point in the Nordic summer 'quite clearly was not June, but July, and since the midpoint was after the sun's turning, no solstitial meanings were, nor could be, built into the Icelandic' calendrical system (Billington 2008: 44). The calendar used by the Vikings was quite practical in denomination. The months of June and July were both called Lida, meaning 'pleasant or navigable'. These well-lit months and safer seas were essential to sail south for their survival instead of having festivals during this time (Billington 2008: 45). Billington also draws attention to the fact that 'had midsummer been a festive day, one would have expected its inclusion by writers such as Snorre. This lack, plus Snorre Sturlason's silence on activity at the summer solstice and similar silence from the earlier Procopius, leads to the strong probability that *originally there were no ancient pagan festivals at all in Scandinavia at high summer*' (Billington 2008: 44, author's emphasis).

The connection with solstices and equinoxes is not certain even in cultures where time is connected to the four turning points of the year. Kustaa Vilkuna, who researched the four turning days in the old calendar of the Finns and Estonians, argued that although the days were not far from the solar 'stations', the short and long days were of no particular significance to the peasants. If we look at the multi-year average, the coldest days are in approximately mid-January and the hottest ones in mid-July. Here the turning days correspond more to the weather and farm work rather than to the course of the sun (Vilkuna 1961).

However, there are many sun symbols in rock carvings and artefacts in Scandinavia and it is also well known from their sagas that they worshipped the Sun. Sandra Billington mentions that:

> Olaus Magnus wrote that savage peoples in the polar regions had not only given thanks to the sun for "light to oppose the darkness" (which would seem to refer to Yule), they had also given thanks for "warmth to dispel the immeasurable cold". Warmth, of course, does not return with the light in January, therefore any religious celebration must have come later in the year. The beginning of summer was not fixed to any one day but was "determined by signs, the opening of flowers, the arrival of birds". Events were not in time, they were times, and the festival for the beginning of summer was not held until the event actually happened. The event itself created the moment in time... Grimm's material on combats between winter and summer makes the beginning of the

> warm season one of the most significant in the Germanic year, with the defeat of the people's greatest enemy, winter, played out in these mock battles (Billington 2008: 46).

Following the footsteps of Chambers (Chambers 1903: vol. I, 112–13), Billington argues that these pagan games in Germany eventually shifted to June 24th, when a festival of probably Pre-Christian-Roman origin, dedicated to Fors Fortuna, was celebrated. It could have been adopted through German groups who had lived in the south of the country while serving in the Roman legions and who later brought this newly acquired knowledge back to their homeland when they finished their service. This cultural mixture of customs involving pagan heritage became so disturbing for the Christian church among the peoples of north-west Europe that by the 7th century they were banned (Billington 2008: 49). As a conclusion she argues:

> The evidence on the type of customs that did take place at midsummer is consistent. So much so that it leads to the conclusion that, whereas ancient winter and spring festivals were based on events, and on the experience and needs of pagan societies, games at the summer solstice could only develop once time was seen as a separate entity. Games at the midsummer solstice used the sun's example of rise and fall to reflect satirically on human aspiration and on human claims to power, law and order; therefore, the tradition could only come into being once the abstract concept of time had become a feature of social thinking (Billington 2008: 51).

There are also solstitial traditions on the Eastern and South-eastern part of Europe to which pre-Christian roots are attributed. The East Slavic summer festival of Ivan Kupala takes place on the eve of the feast day of St. John the Baptist (23-24 June). The Christian holiday of St. John the Baptist was, however, actually added to the festival with the adoption of Christianity. V. Ivanov and V. Toporov demonstrated, in their investigation on symbolism related to the Ivan Kupala festival, that the personality of Ivan Kupala, like other mythological characters across Central-Eastern Europe and Western Asia named after John the Baptist or the prophet Elijah, is the artificially Christianised avatar of the storm and lightning god known in the mythology of many Indo-European speaking peoples (Ivanov and Toporov 1974: 217-242). The semi-pagan Balts also celebrated the cult of their storm god 'Swats Parkauns' (Saint Perkunas) on the day of John the Baptist as late as 1734 (Tuite 2004: 481-482). On these holidays, however, the exact day of the solstice was uninteresting. The period was important when light (and warmth?) was at its peak when the summer was flourishing. These holidays therefore consisted not of a single day, but of a scattered series of holidays, until, as Billington writes above, the use of the calendar fixed the holiday to an exact time. This is also why the day of St. Elijah, who was also identified with the storm god, was celebrated later, not on the exact day of the summer solstice.

The winter solstice is characterised by the shortest day and the longest night. It is also usually close to the coldest winter period. The ritual behaviour of this period is more related to the re-appearance or intensification of light rather than to the exact position of the turning point of the solar disk on the horizon. The time around winter solstice is equal to the period of darkness in the year which was associated in Eastern European popular religion with the visit of the dead. According to archaic beliefs that have survived in certain parts of Central Europe, the dead bring fertility to the living (Pócs 2015: 508). Here, the relation to the Sun is not so emphasised, unlike in areas further north, where the intensification of the sunlight after the winter solstice signified the triumph of light over darkness. Procopius in the 6th century gives details of Scandinavian men gathering on a mountain top in the darkness, awaiting the first signs of returning light in January. The momentous event was celebrated with a festival once light had again illuminated human settlements (Gunnell 1995: 122).

Winter folk customs involving rituals celebrating the revival of the light and world, also apotropaic and fertility magic, can be found in almost all peoples of the Central and South-Eastern European region. They include the special greeting rite known koleda / koliada / Colindă (in Romanian) / regölés (in Hungarian) to which pre-Christian roots are attributed; the remnants of Roman festivals and the carnival-like Saturnalia and Calendæ Ianuariæ. The origin of the word has been uniformly derived from the prefix Calendæ Ianuariae since Petru Caraman's 1928 dissertation (Caraman 1983). The performances of the koleda rite, however, do not focus on the position of the Sun disk, it is not even mentioned in the songs, in which they wish good for the future in the darkest period of the year. Noel Robertson (1984) emphasises the importance of winter solstice when holding a winter Poseidon festival in Greece, the origin of which she dates back to the Mycenaean era. Though bonfires are also lit at this feast, the rites of the festival are not devoted to the Sun, but rather to rouse Poseidon and bring the rushing waters.

The question then arises as to whether solstices were actually known and/or celebrated in ancient times. The official Sun god of the late Roman Empire and the patron saint of the soldiers was Sol Invictus (Invincible Sun), whom the Roman emperor Aurelian (reign 270-275 AD) adopted as the official religion alongside traditional Roman cults on December 25th in 274 AD. It seems that the feast of *Natalis Invicti* in Rome must be seen as the anniversary of the birth of the Sun and the dedication of the temple to the Sun. This date was chosen because this is the day when one can witness one of the most dramatic moments of the Sun's course. For the Romans, the winter solstice was much more important than the summer solstice (Noiville 1936). However, the scientific discussion about the influence of the cult of Deus Sol Invictus on Christianity is highly controversial. This influence is assumed to be responsible for shifting the celebration of the birth of Christ to the 25th of December, which had until then been held on the day of Epiphany, the 6th of January. The celebration of the birth of the Sun god which was accompanied by a profusion of light and torches and the decoration of branches and small trees, had captivated the followers of the cult to such a degree that even after they had been converted to Christianity, they continued to celebrate the birth of the Sun god (Halsberghe 1972: 174).

The Celts are usually said to have worshiped the Sun and therefore, it is generally assumed that they must have observed and celebrated the solstices. However, this was not the case at all. The Celts did not celebrate solstices and equinoxes, instead the most important dates for them were the turning points of winter and summer: 1 May (Beltane) and 1 November (Samhain) together with the midpoints of these two seasons: 1 February (Imbolc) and 1 August (Lughnasa). In Ireland, an equinoctial feast called Michaelmas was popularised in many regions only after the arrival of the Normans and the introduction of Christianity (Monaghan 2004: 15, 28).

Andreas Hofeneder also claims that:

> The available source material for a Celtic sun cult is very scanty. The most expressive sources, namely the ancient literary testimonies, ignore this phenomenon almost completely. It is also beyond doubt that the Celts revered a sky god whose most prominent attribute was the cosmic symbol of the wheel. This divine figure, which is not clearly perceptible before Roman times and which was equated with the Roman sky god Iupiter, can be determined in the absence of written sources only quite vaguely. Gallo-Roman religion is a hybrid and very complicated mixture of Celtic and Roman-Mediterranean elements. Hence, archaeological findings from the imperial time can be used only with considerable reservations as a means of determining the religious concepts of the Pre-Roman Iron Age... About a Gaulish sun cult Caesar did not say a word... A solar cult with an elaborated mythology and complicated rites, as it is attested in ancient Egypt and old Iran, in India and among the Aztecs, the ancient Celts never had (Hofeneder 2010: 104).

The ancient Greeks of the eastern side of the Mediterranean Basin demonstrated more interest in the knowledge of solstices. According to Ptolemy, Hipparchos compared Aristarchos' observation with his own very accurate observation at the end of the 43rd year of the third Callippic period (135 BC), 145 years later and concluded that Aristarchos of Samos had observed the summer solstice in 280 BC (van der Waerden 1986). Meton the Greek astronomer is even said to have observed the summer solstice in Athens in 432 BC (Bowen and Goldstein 1988: 40). Also, the summer solstice is mentioned in Hesiod's Works and Days (Evelyn-White 1914: 663–665) and he reckons the time with days from it:

> Fifty days after the [summer] solstice,
> when the season of wearisome heat is come to an end,
> is the right time for me to go sailing . . .

Hesiod the ancient Greek poet is generally thought to have been active between 750 and 650 BC, around the same time as Homer. Thus, peoples of ancient Europe were aware of the days of the solstices - which are easy to follow on the horizon by noticing their turning point - but the question is whether they considered them important and celebrated them?

Myths, legends, and tales tell about many events, phenomena and customs that had a significant impact on a community. If these sources contain remnants of customs and beliefs about the Sun and the Moon dating back to the ancient past, they may indicate the importance of the Sun and Moon stations. Martin West argues that Indo-European poetry and myth kept the memory of a winter solstice festival (Mahāvrata) when there was a symbolical struggle for the round white sheepskin that symbolised the Sun. In certain Indian rituals the Sun was also represented by a wheel or a gold plate (West 2007: 213). The winter solstice is also considered to be the beginning of the new year in the Hindu Ṛgveda collection of Vedic texts, whose oldest parts may date back to 1200 BC (Schmidt 1968: 135). However, there are some researchers who are sceptical about this by saying 'if only the winter solstice could be proven beyond doubt' (Falk 1997: 82). It is hard to find more exact examples than these. Other Indo-European mythological studies do not even mention solstices or equinoxes (Arvidsson 2006; Gamkrelidze and Ivanov 1995; Lincoln 1986; Mallory 1991; Woodard 2006). The motif-index of folk-literature by Thompson mentions only two cases. A Hawaiian myth tells about the causes of seasons when deities push the Sun back and forth at solstices. The other is an Irish myth that mentions a feast at midsummer (Thompson 1955-1958: V70). Sandra Billington's words sum up the problem:

> One thing that can be done today to reduce a twenty-first-century bewilderment is to disentangle sun-worship from the summer solstice. When there was sun-worship, this was not practised at midsummer, and, when midsummer became a festival, it was either when sun-worship had been superseded by Christianity or a few centuries earlier among some pagan tribes that accepted the Roman calendar (Billington 2008: 52).

Stations of the Moon

Like the solstices, there are turning points for the Moon as well. However, they are not repeated every year, but every 18.6 years. In addition, the turning points of the Moon are shifted during the 18.6 year-cycle, meaning that they are always at different times, in different seasons and in different months. As a result, the horizon and the seasons did not reflect these events in an easy to remember way for prehistoric people. Therefore, the period when the Moon is seen again at the major and minor points would have required continuous year counting, which did not exist in Neolithic and Bronze Age Europe.

Martin P. Nilsson, a Swedish scholar, studied time reckoning worldwide in tribal communities, among peoples with traditional lifestyles. He recorded that the naming of the months and lunar days revealed what these peoples had observed about the Moon. Within a month, the names of the lunar days refer either to the appearance of the Moon on that particular day or the specific activity people do when the Moon rises. These names rarely or almost never indicate where exactly the Moon rises on the horizon (except when it is very close to the horizon, for example, 'it falls on the forest'). The names also never mention the Moon's major and minor points, meaning that they never specify how far the Moon moves in one direction or another during the year. Unlike when observing the movement of the Sun, people did not note the exact location of the moonrise during each month and/or year. They only focused on the behaviour of the Moon within a month and the names were often changed depending on its activity and appearance (Nilsson 1920).

In addition to short-term time reckoning, the Moon played a more significant role in religion and magic. Among the different phases of the Moon, two stand out with special prominence - the first appearance of the crescent of the New Moon in the evening twilight and the duration of the Full Moon. Both events are joyfully greeted and celebrated among many peoples. Celebrations during the time of the Full Moon are due not only to the full light of the Moon but also to the universal idea that everything that is to prosper belongs to the time of the waxing Moon (Nilsson 1920: 151-154). There is no trace of any structure's orientation towards the Moon stations in ethnographic records.

In rites, the Sun is mainly referred to through the sunrise or sunset but without giving special significance to the solstices. In the case of the Moon, the New moon and the Full Moon are the most important and celebrated by many peoples (Nilsson 1920: 151-154). There is a reference to them even in the Bible:

> The Book of Psalms 81: 4. Blow the horn on the new moon, on the day of our feast...
>
> Chronicles II. 2: 4. ... offer a fire offering every morning and evening on the days of the new moon...

This could indicate that the Moon might have played a more important role in orientations than the Sun. Nevertheless, instead of the Moon stations - minor and major standstills - the Full moon and the New Moon phenomena should be taken into consideration. Curt Roslund and his co-authors argue that the observations of the rising of the first Full Moon or the sightings of the first lunar crescent, which followed the vernal equinox, were instrumental in orienting the passages of passage tombs in the administrative district of Evora in central Portugal (Roslund *et al.* 2000). Further studies have supported the possible significance of New Moon and Full Moon at specific times in the year. C. M. da Silva found that the spring Full Moon would account for the distribution of orientations of megalithic dolmens in Alentejo, Portugal (da Silva 2004). F. Pimenta also noticed that the main axes of the megalithic enclosures of the same region were aligned to the autumn Full Moon (Pimenta and Tirapicos 2008). F. Silva and F. Pimenta have developed and expanded the notion of crossover (when the rise and set positions of the Sun and Full Moon cross over each other) which happens annually rather than at the long intervals between the lunar standstills, in order to suggest such targets be considered by archaeoastronomers and ethnographers (Silva and Pimenta 2012).

Conclusion

The thorough examination of historical and ethnographic sources does not clearly support the general significance of the Sun and Moon stations in ancient times. Societies must have recognised the regularity of the Sun and Moon's motion and the role of their landmarks to predict the times of these events in the early periods of human history. However, it can no longer be proven that these extreme solar and lunar stations were also generally celebrated or even aligned to. When studying the orientation of ancient structures, the importance of the Sun's turning points should not be seen as implicit: this has led to false assumptions that communities would always align their monuments towards the sunrise and/or sunset of these periods. Many graphs representing the orientations of such structures, especially for a large number of monuments, clearly do not support this assumption.

According to ethnographic records, the purpose of orientations is very diverse. Many directions can be important during magical/ritual actions, in which random selections can prevail as well. The conclusion is that, following the guidance of ethnography, the orientation of structures depends on the purpose for which they were used; so it is first necessary to clarify the function and role of a particular monument before finalising the interpretation of the data. This, however, doesn't mean that investigating the relation between the stations of the Sun and the Moon and the orientation of prehistoric monuments is of little or no avail. Although ethnographic and historical data do not confirm the legitimacy of such a connection, their existence cannot simply be excluded either. The monuments investigated may be up to thousands of years older compared to the earliest literary sources. In the case of prehistoric monuments, we must also take into consideration the use of any tools that could help obtain further information about the communities who were responsible for erecting them.

However, the rites are never simple in real life and it is very difficult to present their peculiarities through prehistoric archaeological artefacts. Therefore, the results of Lionel Sims work offer an excellent example of how to proceed, because his research masterfully combines the methods of three disciplines - anthropology, archaeology and archaeoastronomy - and offers new interpretations and meanings for some of the well-known British prehistoric monuments. He argues that the monuments have a complex meaning and their relationship to certain key horizon points of the Sun and the Moon indicates an important transition in the belief system - the solarisation of the Moon. The complex orientations of monuments followed the intention of investing the Sun with the Moon's former religious significance (Sims 2006, 2015). He could be right.

References

Arvidsson, S. 2006. *Aryan Idols. Indo-European Mythology as Ideology and Science.* Chicago and London: The University of Chicago Press.

Billington, S. 2008. The Midsummer Solstice As It Was, Or Was Not, Observed in Pagan Germany, Scandinavia and Anglo-Saxon England. *Folklore* 119 (1): 41-57.

Bowen, A.C. and B.R. Goldstein. 1988. Meton of Athens and astronomy in the late fifth century BC, in E. Leichty, M. de J. Ellis, and P. Gerardi (eds) *A scientific humanist: studies in memory of Abraham Sachs*: 40–81. Philadelphia: University Museum, University of Pennsylvania.

Bradley, R. 2005. *Ritual and Domestic Life in Prehistoric Europe.* Abingdon: Routledge

Brown, C.H. 1983. Where Do Cardinal Direction Terms Come From? *Anthropological Linguistics* 25 (2): 121-161.

Brück, J. 2011. Fire, Earth, Water: An Elemental Cosmography of the European Bronze Age, in T. Insoll (ed.) *The Oxford Handbook of the Archaeology of Ritual and Religion.* Oxford: Oxford University Press.

Caraman, P. 1983. *Colindatul la români, slavi şi la alte popoare. Studiu de folclor comparat.* Bucharest: Editura Minerva.

Carr, C. 1995. Mortuary practices: Their social, philosophical-religious, circumstantial, and physical determinants. *Journal of Archaeological Method and Theory* 2: 105–200.

Chambers, E.K. 1903. *The Medieval Stage* I-II. Oxford: Classic Books.

Dömötör, T. 1983. *Naptári ünnepek - népi színjátszás* [Calendar holidays - folk acting]. Budapest: Akadémia Kiadó.

Evelyn-White, H.G. (trans) 1914. *Hesiod. The Homeric Hymns and Homerica with an English Translation, Works and Days.* Cambridge: Harvard University Press; London: William Heinemann Ltd.

Falk, H. 1997. The Purpose of Ṛgvedic Ritual, in M. Witzel (ed.) *Inside the Texts, Beyond the Texts*: 69 – 88. Harvard Oriental Series, Opera Minora Vol 2. Cambridge: Department of Sanskrit and Indian Studies Harvard University, Distributed by South Asia Books, Columbia.

Frazer, J.G. 2015 [1922]. *The Golden Bough: A Study in Magic and Religion.* Enhanced Media Publishing.

Gailey, A. 1977. The Bonfire in North Irish Tradition. *Folklore,* 88 (1): 3-38.

Gamkrelidze, T.V. and V.V. Ivanov 1995. *Indo-European and the Indo-Europeans. A Reconstruction and Historical Analysis of a Proto-Language and a Proto-Culture.* Berlin and New York: Mouton de Gruyter.

Gunnell, T. 1995. *The Origins of Drama in Scandinavia.* Woodbridge: D.S. Brewer.

Halsberghe, G.H. 1972. *The Cult of Sol Invictus.* Leiden: E. J. Brill

Harding, A.F. 2000. *European societies in the Bronze Age*. Cambridge: Cambridge University Press.
Hendry, J. 1981. *Marriage in Changing Japan*. London: Croom Helm.
Hofeneder, A. 2010. Vestiges of sun worship among the Celts, in A J. Gail (ed.) Sun Worship in the Civilisations of the World. *Pandanus 10': Nature in Literature, Art, Myth and Ritual* (4) 2: 85–107.
Hutton, R. 1996. *The Stations of the Sun: A History of the Ritual Year in Britain*. Oxford and New York: Oxford University Press.
Ivanov, V.V. and V.N.Toporov 1974. *Issledovanija v oblasti slavianskix drevnostej: leksich. i frazeol. voprosy rekonstruktsii tekstov*. Moscow: Nauka
Iversen, R. 2017. Big-Men and Small Chiefs: The Creation of Bronze Age Societies. *Open Archaeology* 3: 361–375.
Koleva, V. 2003. Measuring time in the Central Rhodopes, in M. Blomberg, P.E. Blomberg and G. Henriksson (eds) *Calendars, Symbols, and Orientations: Legacies of Astronomy in Culture. Proceedings of SEAC 9. Uppsala Astronomical Observatory, Report no. 59*: 41-44. Uppsala: Uppsala University.
Leete, A. 2017. Landscape and Gods Among the Khanty. *Journal of Ethnology and Folkloristics* 11 (1): 19–38.
Lincoln, B. 1986. *Myth, Cosmos, and Society. Indo-European Themes of Creation and Destruction*. Cambridge, MA and London: Harvard University Press.
Liungman, W. 1938. *Traditionswanderungen Euphrat-Rhein I-II. F.F. Communications No. 119*. Helsinki: Suomalainen Tiedeakatemia.
Mallory, J.P. 1991. *In Search of the Indo-Europeans - Language, Archaeology and Myth*. New York: Thames and Hudson.
Marót, K. 1940. Rítus és ünnep. [Rite and Festivity] *Ethnographia* 51: 143–184.
Monaghan, P. 2004. *The Encyclopedia of Celtic Mythology and Folklore*. New York: Facts on File, Inc.
Moszyński, K. 1967. *Kultura ludowa Słowian*. Tom II kultura duchowa. Warsaw: Książka i Wiedza.
Nilsson, M. P. 1920. *Primitive Time-Reckoning*. Lund: C. W. K. Gleerup
Noiville, J. 1936. Les origines du Natalis Invicti. *Revue des Études Anciennes* 38 (2): 145-176.
O'Shea, J. M. 1996. *Villagers of the Maros. A Portrait of an Early Bronze Age Society*. Boston: Springer US
Pásztor, E. 2011. Prehistoric sky lore and spirituality, in D. Gheorghiu (ed.) *Archaeology Experimenting Spirituality?*: 89.117. Cambridge Scholars Publishing.
Pimenta, F. and L. Tirapicos 2008. The orientations of central Alentejo megalithic enclosures. *Archaeologia Baltica* 10: 234–40.
Pócs, É. 2015. The Living and the Dead at the Time of the Winter Solstice in Central Eastern European Beliefs, in T. Minniyakhmetova and K. Velkoborská (eds) *The Ritual Year 10. Magic in Rituals and Rituals in Magic*: 507 – 518. Innsbruck – Tartu: LM Scholarly Press.
Robertson, N. 1984. Poseidon's Festival at the Winter Solstice. *The Classical Quarterly*. 34 (1): 1-16.
Roslund, C., Y. Kristiansen and B. Hårdh 2000. Portuguese passage graves in the light of the Easter moon. *Fornvännen* 95: [1]-12.
Schmidt, H.P. 1968. *Bṛhaspati und Indra: Untersuchungen zur vedischen Mythologie und Kulturgeschichte*. Wiesbaden: Harrassowitz.
Sermona, R. 2008. From Easter to Ostara: the Reinvention of a Pagan Goddess? *Time and Mind* 1 (3): 331–344.
da Silva, C.M. 2004. The spring full moon. *Journal for the history of astronomy* 35 (4): 475-478.

Silva, F. and F. Pimenta 2012. The Crossover of the Sun and the Moon. *Journal for the History of Astronomy* 43 (2): 191-208.

Sims, L.D. 2006. The 'Solarization' of the Moon: Manipulated Knowledge at Stonehenge. *Cambridge Archaeological Journal* 16 (2): 191-207.

Sims, L.D. 2015. Out of Africa: The Solarization of the Moon, in *SEAC 2011 Stars and Stones: Voyages in Archaeoastronomy and Cultural Astronomy*: 200-206. Oxford: Archaeopress/British Archaeological Reports.

Thompson, S. 1955-1958. *Motif-index of folk-literature: a classification of narrative elements in folktales, ballads, myths, fables, mediaeval romances, exempla, fabliaux, jest-books, and local legends.* Bloomington: Indiana University Press.

Tribhuwan, R.D. 2005. *Tribal Housing Issues*. Delhi: Discovery Publishing House.

Tuite, K. 2004. Lightning, Sacrifice, and Possession in the Traditional Religions of the Caucasus (Continued from Anthropos 99,2004: 143-159). *Anthropos* 99 (2): 481-497.

Vaicekauskas, A. 2014. Ancient Lithuanian calendar festivals. Kaunas: Vytautas Magnus University.

Vaiškūnas, J. 2003. Some aspects of Lithuanian folk observations of the sun during the summer solstice period, in M. Blomberg, P. E. Blomberg and G. Henriksson (eds) *Calendars, Symbols, and Orientations: Legacies of Astronomy in Culture. Proceedings of SEAC 9. Uppsala Astronomical Observatory, Report no. 59*: 33-39. Uppsala: Uppsala University.

Van Gennep, A. 1949. *Manuel de folklore français contemporain. Tome premier IV 2, Les cérémonies périodiques, cycliques et saisonnières Cycle de mai, la Saint-Jean.* Paris: Editions A. and J. Picard.

Vilkuna, K. 1961. Wochenrechnung und Teilung des Jahres in zwei oder vier Teile. *Finnisch-Ugrisches Forschungen* 34.

Vries, J. de. 1956. *Altgermanische Religionsgeschichte*. Berlin: W. De Gruyter.

van der Waerden, B.L. 1986. Aristarchos's observation of the summer solstice. *Isis* 77 (1): 103-104.

Waterson, L. 1994. *The Living House, an Anthropology of Architecture of South-East Asia*. Singapore: Thames and Hudson.

West, M.L. 2007. *Indo-European Poetry and Myth*. Oxford: Oxford University Press.

Woodard, R.D. 2006. *Indo-European Sacred Space. Vedic and Roman cult.* Urbana and Chicago: University of Illinois Press.

Zwicker, J. 1934-6. Fontes Historiae Religionis Celticae. Rotterdam: De Gruyter.

The Sun and the Moon: Double Alignments in the Iberian Peninsula

A. César González-García

Introduction

I first met Lionel at the SEAC conference held in 2005 in Isili, Sardinia. In the beautiful setting of the small island village, I presented a paper discussing a dichotomy between solar and lunar alignments in several megalithic compounds in the western and central Mediterranean (González-García *et al.* 2007). The two facts are a remarkable coincidence given the strength the lunar argument has gained in the last decade thanks particularly to Lionel's powerful élan.

Possibly, due to the natural prominence of the Sun, or perhaps due to a western cultural bias, and in spite of some remarkable efforts (like Alexander Thom's), the orientation of megalithic monuments has been primarily connected with the solstices and equinoxes. Lockyer, for instance, indicated that the main axis of Stonehenge had long been known to be oriented to the summer solstice sunrise (Lockyer [1894] 1964: 89-91). In spite of this, already during these early times, some voices claimed for other possible relations. In the case of Stonehenge, Admiral Somerville (see for example Somerville 1927) indicated that such directions could also be linked with the lunar extremes and some stars.

As seen from a particular location on Earth (away from the Polar regions), the Sun is observed on a particular band of the sky during the year. If we concentrate on sunrise for the ease of explanation, the Sun appears to move between two extreme positions, the solstices. For the northern hemisphere, summer solstice is where it gets the further northern rise (and set), and it is at this time of the year when the Sun travels the longest path on the sky. Conversely, at winter solstice and for the northern hemisphere it rises further to the south and travels the shortest journey during those days in the heavens.

Indeed, the path of the Sun coincides with several stars, but also with the Moon. The Moon's movements are rather more complicated than those of the Sun as seen from Earth. The Moon travels around the earth on slightly more than 27 days. Depending on the reference we take, either the background stars or the orbit of the Moon, the period is slightly different. However, because of the movement of the Moon around the Earth, and of the Earth-Moon system around the Sun, the Moon is illuminated in various ways presenting phases of illumination, at different times. The overall movement, the synodic month, is nearly 29.53 days on average (see for example González-García and Belmonte 2019 and references therein for a recent review).

Moreover, the orbit of the Moon is nearly co-planar to that of the Earth around the Sun, although there is a very small tilt (i) of a bit more than 5°. This small tilt has various peculiar and important consequences. The first is that it precludes having a solar and lunar eclipse every month. If the orbit of the Moon would be coplanar with (or the tilt would be less than

1° with respect to) the ecliptic, we could expect to have some sort of eclipse every month. However, the tilt means that the synchronicity needed for having a solar or lunar eclipse appears only when the line of nodes, the intersection of the plane of the lunar orbit and that of the Earth, aligns with the Sun-Moon-Earth system. This happens variably, but at least four times a year.

It also means that the extreme positions of the Moon are going to be different from those of the Sun. Depending on the configuration of the lunar orbit, there would be a maximum angle of $|\varepsilon + i|$, where ε is the inclination of the rotation axis of the Earth with respect to the ecliptic. In our time, this would be nearly 29°. However, due to the gravitational and tidal forces of the Earth and the Sun, the line of nodes of the lunar orbit describes a receding movement in 18.6 years. That means that the Moon can reach the maximum declination ($|\varepsilon + i|$) for slightly more than two years, every 18.6 years. Also, conversely it will, for a couple of years, be near the minimum declination ($|\varepsilon - i|$) 9.3 years after that maximum.

This complicated scheme of movements, cycles and phases have rendered the Moon a complicated object to deal with in cultural astronomy studies (see for instance Schaefer 2017; González-García and Belmonte 2019). The ease of following its movements and the conspicuousness of the Sun make it the preferred 'target' of most interpretations. As indicated above, this predilection might crystalise from a western preference for utility and practicality: the orientation towards the Sun can be directly linked to a calendrical purpose; however, the lunar one is rather more difficult. However, Lionel has attempted to advocate fiercely for lunar explanations in some of the most recognisable British monuments, most notably Stonehenge and Avebury (see for example Sims 2006 and references thereafter). The background for this is that although lunar orientations could be rendered as less 'useful', they could provide more powerful explanations with ethnographic parallels.

A key argument in Lionel's interpretation is that there can be double solar-lunar alignments in those (and other) megalithic monuments and that they can be considered at the same time (see, for example, Sims 2006: 204, Sims 2007: 312-316, Sims 2010: 13). Such double alignments appear due to the nature of the solar and lunar movements indicated above and they have commonly been interpreted as a dichotomy between either the Sun or the Moon (as rightly indicated by Lionel himself, this was rarely -if ever- interpreted both at the same time; see for instance Sims 2006: 201). A notable case for instance is that of Stonehenge, where some parts are connected with the Sun, like the main axis, while others are connected with the Moon, like the station stones (see, for example, Ruggles 1999: 35-41). Lionel, on the contrary, following on from North (1999), advocated that they were both possible and recognised at the same time (Sims 2006). In particular, one paradigmatic example of this idea would be the double orientation of Stonehenge's axis as viewed from the Heel Stone. The main axis, as seen through the lower passage of the Trilithons, faces winter solstice sunset, while the orientation towards the window of the large Trilithon would be towards the minor standstill, and in particular the so-called, Dark Moon, producing the darkest night at that time.

From such reading of the data, and imposing an anthropological interpretative scheme based on a particular understanding of several present and past facts in different societies (Knight *et al.* 1995), Lionel concluded that this might indicate a 'solarization' of previous lunar rituals or cults (Sims 2006: 203-204). The lunar orientation appears to be almost hidden compared to the solar one, but it is still there because it had to be. According to this scheme, in a progressive movement at the time of the introduction of the new productive processes, a previously female-based lunar ritual, was gradually being challenged and changed to a male-centred solar one. However, Lionel somehow postulated (Sims 2006: 204-205) that during the transition stage and, to make the change acceptable to all parts of the society, the Sun had to be invested with the attributes of the Moon. Therefore, the double alignments were a reflection of such and perhaps a tool to adopt the new solar based cult and the new economy. Indeed, Lionel's hypothesis was based basically on the Dark Moon plus winter solstice coincidence, for instance at Stonehenge. However, a broadening of the basis towards any double lunar plus solar alignment could still render support for the 'solarization of the Moon' hypothesis in a general sense.

I asked Lionel at several venues and in private discussions that if such an interpretation was true, one should see other examples at other areas apart from the British Isles of such 'double alignments'. I know Lionel carried out some research in the last years in Iberia, especially in Palaeolithic sites, but I would like to take a step forward and review a few examples in search of the double alignments in the area of the Iberian Peninsula. In short, what follows is a data driven approach to Lionel's proposal: 'the solarisation of the Moon' and the possibility of double Sun-Moon alignments.

I am not going to argue in favour or against the anthropological interpretation, as I believe that first one should consider if its basis, in this case the existence of such double alignments, is firm or not. The issues raised are admittedly controversial, but I feel they deserve to be exposed and discussed, especially in honour of Lionel's ideas. If lunar alignments alone are difficult to argue, a double alignment is even more challenging. The following lines include a number of speculations that I would like to take in order to explore the possibility of Lionel's hypothesis. I hope the reader may bear with me for the sake of the argument.

Iberian Peninsula and the Balearics

Michael Hoskin (2001) and his collaborators measured a large fraction of the megalithic chambers In the Iberian Peninsula and the Balearics during the last decades of the twentieth century. One of the main conclusions of their effort was that most of them opened towards the eastern half of the horizon, with a clear predisposition for the solar range. In fact, Hoskin proposed that this was due to a preference for pointing these structures towards the rising Sun on the day of the start of construction. For the cases where the custom was not followed, Hoskin proposed a relaxation of the norm by pointing the megalith towards the Sun climbing in the sky.

This scheme, however, left a number of open questions that needed to be answered. For example, one of the most prominent monuments in the south of the Iberian Peninsula is Menga. This is a chambered megalithic tomb with massive orthostats under a prominent tumulus and its entrance and main axis (see below) faces farther north than any positions reached by the rising Sun or Moon. In addition, although very small in number compared with the sheer quantity of megalithic monuments facing eastwardly in Iberia, there is a number of them facing west, especially in the Balearic Islands. Also, a number of megaliths appear to be facing nearly south or, at least far enough towards south as to be consistent

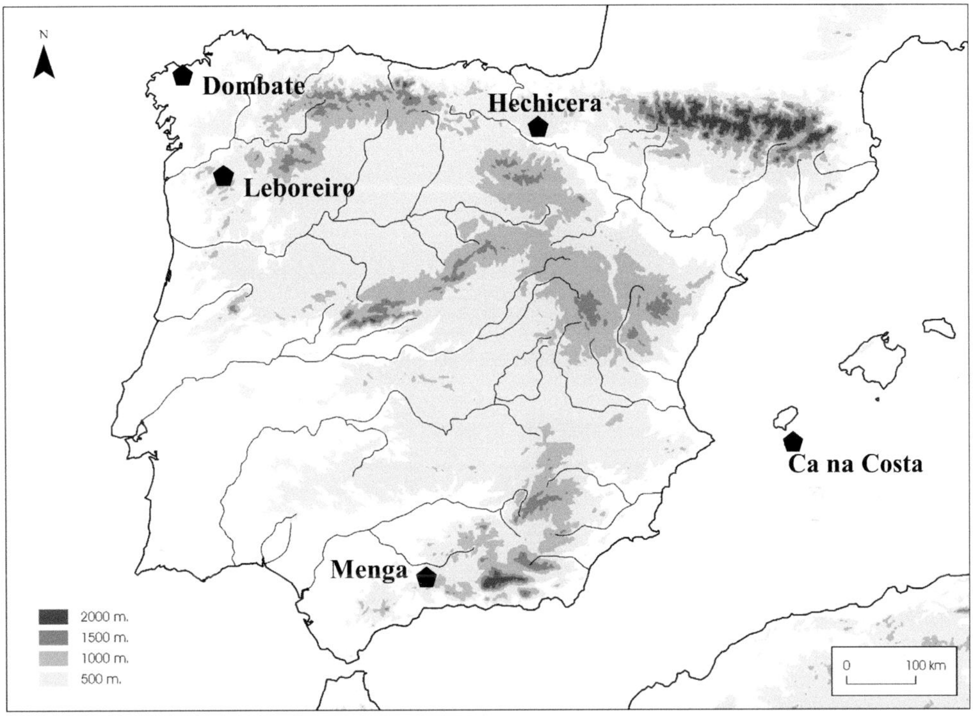

Figure 1. Location of the five sites considered in the text.

with the Sun climbing hypothesis. Three of them will be reviewed here to indicate that they could be hints towards a lunar explanation that in the end could be interpreted following Lionel's framework. Finally, two other sites are included where, although the orientation of the megalithic chambers is towards the eastern half, the western part of the sky could also be relevant (see Figure 1).

Menga

One of the largest and best-known megalithic monuments in the Iberian Peninsula is the Cueva de Menga dolmen. Located in Antequera, in the province of Málaga, it is the oldest megalithic monument of a complex of at least three different chronologies in this neighbourhood (see González-García 2018, Lozano *et al.* 2014 and references therein for a recent review). The megalithic chamber of Menga is formed by 12 pairs of orthostats of between 3.5 to 5 metres in height, plus a capstone at the end. They define an elongated chamber some 10 metres in length, slightly less wide at the entrance than at the back, without a real corridor. The three roof slabs are massive and have to be supported by four pillars in the centre of the chamber. Excavations during the last decade have uncovered a number of very interesting facts, the most fascinating among them is the presence of a well some 18 metres deep near the back of the chamber (Lozano *et al.* 2014).

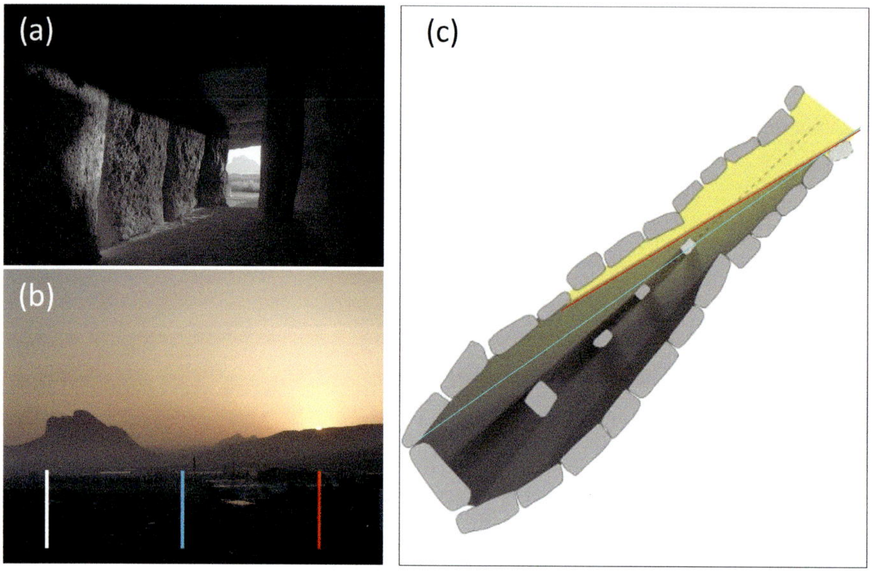

Figure 2. (a) Menga megalithic chamber, formed by massive slabs, faces the peculiar hill on the local landscape called 'Peña de los Enamorados'. (b) The northeast horizon as seen from Menga at the summer solstice sunrise. The vertical white line indicates the orientation of the main axis of Menga, the red line the summer solstice sunrise and the blue line the lunar northernmost rise. (c) Indicates the area illuminated by the Sun at the summer solstice sunrise (red line, and yellow area) and that of the Moon (cyan line). Images by courtesy of J. A. Lozano (a&b) and modified from Lozano et al. 2014.

The orientation of Menga is several degrees away from the northern-most positions of the Sun and Moon (see Figure 2). In fact, the orientation is towards one of the most conspicuous and peculiar elements of the local landscape, the Peña de los Enamorados hill. Certainly, this hill resembles the profile of a head or face, but it also is a very prominent area for archaeological remains. The slabs to the northern side of the chamber seem to present more polished sides than those to the south, and this north side appears straighter than the southern one. As a consequence of this and of the general orientation of the tomb, only the northern side would be directly illuminated by the Sun during a period of several days before and after summer solstice (Lozano *et al.* 2014).

At the lower slopes of the Peña de los Enamorados, there are a number of rock shelters with numerous rock art paintings and engravings, possibly older or at least contemporaneous of the construction and use of Menga (Rogerio-Candelera *et al.* 2018). Finally, quite recently, archaeologists have unearthed a megalithic chamber in this area possibly contemporary with Menga (García Sanjuan 2020, private communication). In summary, Menga is not only facing the most prominent feature of the local landscape but also a possibly significant one for the local population at the time. One that was linked to a sacred area from previous generations, and the orientation is perhaps indicating a link with the ancestors of the Menga population.

In this regard, the fact of the north side as being the only part illuminated by the Sun during midsummer could perhaps suggest some relevance. However, the Sun would only illuminate slightly more than half of the northern wall: it would not be completely illuminated at that time. Conversely, due to the slight change in orientation indicated above, the northern wall would be completely illuminated by the Full Moon during midwinter, in the years where the Moon is near major lunar standstill. It could also be argued that the northern side would be illuminated by the last crescent before and after the summer solstice, again with the same periodicity as indicated above. In this sense, we could suggest that the builders of Menga could at the same time be linking the prominent hill of their ancestors (Peña de los Enamorados), the dying Moon -understood as the Moon before New Moon, or even the Dark Moon as proposed by Lionel for Stonehenge, for instance, and the rising Sun, in a very peculiar way.

Ca Na Costa

The dolmens in the Balearic Islands present the only group with orientations consistently towards the west in Spain (Hoskin 2001; Hoskin and Morales-Núñez 1991; González-García and Belmonte 2010). Their orientation seems to be closer to the customs found in southern France than to the ones in the neighbouring areas of the Iberian Peninsula (González-García and Belmonte 2010). In fact, in some cases this orientation has been linked with the first visibility of the crescent Moon (González-García *et al.* 2007).

Ca Na Costa is the only dolmen found on the island of Formentera. Formentera is rather small, only 17 km from east to west and some 14 km from north to south. In the centre, there is a lagoon of salty waters and next to it appears the Ca Na Costa dolmen (see Figure 3). This is formed by a rather small chamber defined by seven orthostats on a circular socket and a narrow corridor. The megalithic structure is supported by a circular platform of rubble and this in turn by 24 orthostats, defining a system similar to the radii of a cartwheel. All this is placed on top of a stony platform. The entrance to the chamber was through a perforated stone, now broken. The material remains recovered from the site (a few human bones, pottery and beads) indicate that it was possibly erected at the time of the local Bronze Age. This was the time of the first settlement in the island (Fernandez *et al.* 1976) and it has been termed as the local epi-bell beaker period, at the turn of the second millennium BC (see for example, Sureda 2018).

The orientation of Ca Na Costa, according to Hoskin and Morales-Núñez (1991), is 268°. However, they indicated that they could not measure the orientation on site so they relied on the original excavation plans, corrected by magnetic declination. In spite of this, the actual orientation, measured by the author in two independent seasons (2005 and 2011; with a Suunto 360 tandem of compass plus clinometer), corrected by magnetic declination and reanalysed through aerial ortho-photography is 252.4°±0.6° (three readings, 253°, 252.75° and 252° with magnetic compass, plus a reading of 251.75° from the ortho-photography), with a horizon altitude of 0.25°. The corresponding declination (-13.7°) is again consistent with the setting Sun or the setting Moon.

González-García *et al.* (2007) indicated that the western orientation for the megalithic monuments in southern France could be better explained (and fitted) by the orientation towards the first sighting of the crescent Moon in the west rather than to any solar orientation.

This is especially so for those monuments in that area that had orientations to the south of the solar setting limits. González-García and Belmonte (2010) found that the megalithic monuments in the Balearic Islands shared orientations with those of southern France. The orientations and also the archaeological remains therefore support a possible common origin of this cluster of megaliths. If we apply the same scheme for Ca Na Costa, where the western orientation could be linked with the first crescent, this would mean a date near mid-February or the end of October. To this, it should be added the possibility that the monument was oriented to the setting Dark Moon.

If we include the possibility that the setting Sun illuminates the interior of the chamber, the combination of the narrow entrance and the corridor define a window of visibility (Silva 2014; or window of illumination) between declinations -2° and -24.6°, then this means that for the whole period between autumn equinox and spring equinox, the setting Sun would directly illuminate the interior of the chamber.

Finally, the inspection of the location of the megalithic passage grave might provide further relevant data. In this regard, it is interesting to take a look at the surrounding landscape. Ca Na Costa is located only 5 metres above sea level and 40 metres from the shores of the salty lagoon. Thus, the gentle slopes of Formentera dominate the surrounding landscape. In spite of this, on the southeast, the highest summit of the island, Sa Mola, can be spotted. The direction of this peak is 130.9° (alt=1°; dec=-30°). This means that the southernmost rising of the Moon could be seen on top of it. The profile of nearby Ibiza dominates the north and north-western horizon. Particularly prominent, as seen from Formentera, is the sight of Es Vedrá, a massive islet off the southwest coast of Ibiza. Its profile would be quite conspicuous from the area of Ca Na Costa on the northwest. The direction of the highest part of Es Vedrá is 306° (alt=1/4°; dec= 26.8°). The orientation is not directly that of the northernmost setting of the Moon, but it could be related to the setting of the Moon (or even, perhaps Venus).

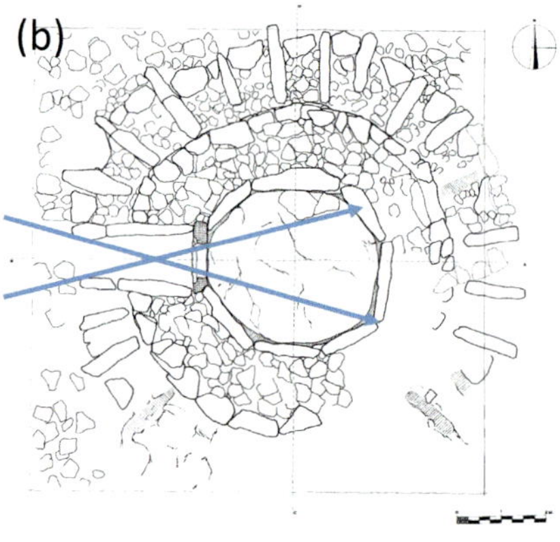

Figure 3. The Ca na Costa megalithic burial chamber in Formentera. Left, excavation plan. Notice the radiated structure of the outer orthostats. According to the excavators, this peculiarity helped the preservation of the megalith, as it was believed to be an ancient 'solar clock' by the locals. The blue lines indicate the illumination window, for details see text. Images A.C. González-García.

If we now apply an interpretative scheme similar to that proposed by Lionel, we could argue that the possibility exists that the layout of Ca Na Costa and its locations were deliberately chosen so that the setting Sun could illuminate the area for the dead and for the ancestors, during the time of the year when the nights are longer. The combination of the setting Sun, plus the setting of the Full Moon in coincidence with Es Vedrá might point to a relevance for nighttime for the rituals that might have taken place at the site, with a prominent role for the Moon. Such a role could still be advocated for, and even highlighted, in the case of the importance of the first crescent visibility (or the setting Dark Moon), in the direction indicated by the corridor entrance.

Chabola de la Hechicera

Chabola de la Hechicera (Sorceress' Shack) also presents a peculiar orientation compared to the rest of passage graves in Iberia. It forms part of a small cluster of passage graves in the vicinity of the river Ebro, in the Rioja Alavesa wine region. Chabola is a passage grave formed by a polygonal chamber with seven orthostats. A broken covering stone appears today on top of the rear part of the chamber. Three pairs of orthostats form the corridor, nearly 5 metres long and slightly less than 1 metre wide. It is segmented in two parts by a closing stone.

Figure 4. Chabola de la Hechicera dolmen, in northern Spain. The dolmen has a peculiar orientation, facing the Valley of Ebro River to the southeast. It is located on a plain with the Sierra de Cantabria to the north (a). The singular peak of Lapoblación mountain appears very prominently to the northeast end of this sierra as seen from Hechicera (b). (c) Summer solstice sunrise happens on the slopes of this mountain, which is also the last one to be illuminated at sunset (d). Images A.C. González-García.

Archaeological excavations in the 1930s and 1970s recovered a number of severely damaged human remains together with stone tools, ceramics and beads from both the chamber and the corridor. In the upper layers there were also some metallic elements and decorated ceramics perhaps indicating the long use of the chamber (from 3800 BC to 1100 BC in several phases and stages; Narvarte Sanz 2005: 88-99). A tumulus of nearly 26 metres in diameter covered the structure but did not completely hide the chamber and the corridor. The tumulus is truncated next to the entrance of the passage grave by a paved atrium with flat slabs. It is also delimited on the east side by a stone wall which is not symmetric to the western side (Martínez–Torres *et al.* 2014).

According to Michael Hoskin (2001: 236), the orientation of the passage grave is 143°, and the altitude of the horizon in that direction is 0.75°, rendering a declination of -35.8°. This orientation was confirmed by the author on a recent visit to the monument (see González-García 2021). Such a declination is a long way from the solar range contrary to the general custom in this area of north-central Spain, where the corridors opened towards the south or south-southeast. The width of the corridor allows for a window of visibility ranging from azimuths of 131° to 166°. The northern extreme of this opening, with a declination of -29°, would allow the marginal visibility of the lunar southern extreme.

Also, when inspecting the local landscape an interesting topographic feature catches our attention. At the north-eastern extreme of the Sierra de Cantabria, the chain of mountains that constrains the Ebro valley to the north of this area, the Castillo de Lapoblación (1.243 m.a.s.l.), appears particularly prominent from the location of Hechicera. Interestingly, the corridor of Chabola is almost perpendicular to the direction where we can see the Lapoblacion Mountain. The corridor seems to be facing the most distant horizon as seen from this spot, facing the Sierra de Iregua to the southeast and the slopes towards the river Ebro valley.

The ethnography of the name of this megalith might provide further relevant information. The name of the site, Chabola de la Hechicera (Sorginaren Txabola in Basque) or Sorceress' Shack, connects this site to a commonplace in Basque folklore, the Sorceress (Vegas Aramburu 1991; Gordón Peral 2008). In particular the legend of Hechicera, which could be traced back at least to the beginning of the 19th century (Vegas Aramburu 1991), says that this was the shack of a Sorceress who at night on Saint John's day (June 24th) turned anybody who came along her way into stone.

As indicated above, the orientation of the main axis of Hechicera is far from any solar orientation looking out from the interior of the structure. However, the northern horizon is extremely interesting. Towards northeast appears the prominent shape of the Lapoblación Mountain. The peak of this mountain has an azimuth of 58° and declination near +25° and thus is nearly perpendicular to the corridor entrance, as mentioned above. The summer solstice sunrise would be visible on the slopes of this prominent peak as seen from Hechicera. Interestingly, at summer solstice, the Sun sets on the westernmost slopes of the Sierra and the last rays illuminate Lapoblación (Figure 4d), while the rest of the landscape is already in shadows. The next morning the Sun rises from the slopes of this peak in a stunning way (Figure 4c).

Could it be that the summer solstice sunrise and sunset features might be connected with the marginal orientation of the corridor towards a lunar rise at the southernmost position for this period? It certainly could be, and such a possibility might render some support for the double lunar-solar hypothesis. We could argue that in this way the shortest night, would be further illuminated by the summer Full Moon at an almost no-darkness period. Perhaps this was the propitious moment to connect with the ancestors at the Hechicera dolmen. Indeed, such a slight possibility might indicate a transitional step towards substituting a lunar-based cult, with only a marginal importance to such a lunar event, with perhaps a more prominent role for the solar one. However, the direct orientation of the corridor is far from that lunar event. Indeed, this positioning could have been for the above reason of diminishing the role of the lunar event. But one could also argue that this was connected to other facts (see González-García 2021). In a number of cases, we do see dual/opposition orientations to the Sun and the Moon as a possibility.

Dombate

Possibly as one of the most well studied exemplars of the seven-stone passage graves in Northwestern Iberia, Dombate presents a number of very interesting features. The first to be noted here is that the large monument hides an older and smaller simple dolmen which was composed of seven orthostats defining a simple chamber elongated towards the entrance. That first megalith was covered by a tumulus that was incorporated by the larger one of 'new' Dombate just a few decades later (perhaps a century). The new seven-stone chamber with a

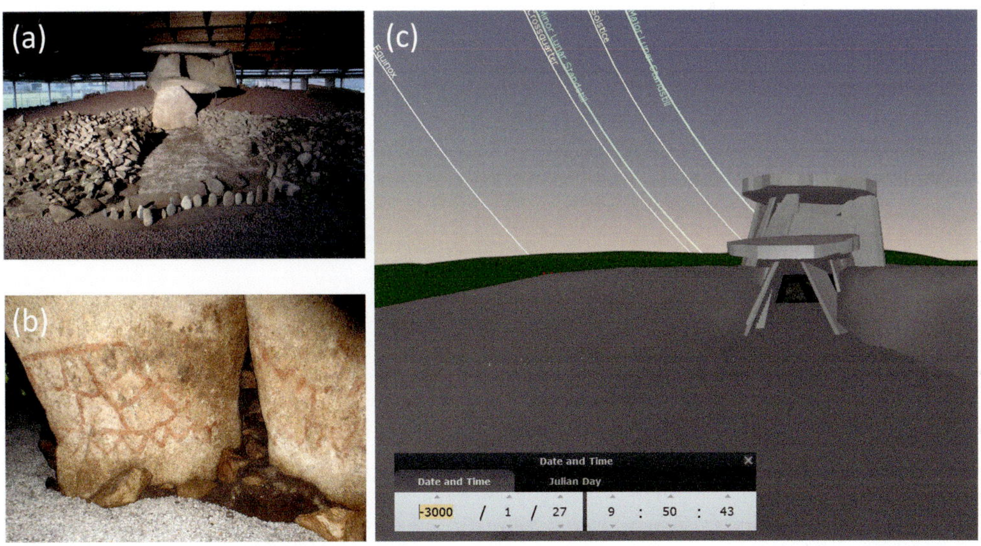

Figure 5. (a) Dombate, in northwest Spain, is a large passage grave with an elaborate decoration (b) and evidence of a ritual for the ancestors. (c) It has an orientation towards winter solstice sunrise. At that time, the rising Sun illuminates the paintings on the back stone, and at that time, the people who gathered at the entrance to perform rituals could have witnessed the setting of the Full Moon just behind the massive megalithic chamber.

passage was erected during the first half of the fourth millennium cal BC (Alonso and Bello 1997). A big mound (c. 24 metres in diametre) was built and partially covered with a crust of medium size stones. All orthostats in the chamber and corridor of the passage grave are decorated with paintings — black and red linear motifs and dots over a white background — and engravings. These decorations seem to be contemporary to the date of construction of the monument. The lower level is better preserved throughout the monument and the motifs depicted there seem much more complex. Big red bands delimit irregular spaces, which are smaller and more varied in the chamber. Further, a total of 20 idols were identified, 17 of them standing in situ and forming a line in front of a series of flat slabs that were placed in the manner of a threshold right at the entrance of the corridor.

The orientation of Dombate to face the winter solstice sunrise is the most frequent we could find in the area. In fact, it has been argued that this orientation produces an illumination event in the innermost area of the chamber, in such a way that only for a short period around the solstice, the first rays of the rising Sun would directly illuminate the red crisscrossed paintings, and only in this area (González-García *et al.* 2019). The authors argue that this phenomenon could indicate a deliberate attempt to highlight a particular moment devoted for the dead, something that might also explain the presence of the stone idols, as possibly the area where they are placed might be the one where the rituals were carried out.

Interestingly, the perspective from this particular point of view might also present a singular connection with the Moon. Figure 5c shows a reconstruction of Dombate inserted in a digital terrain model in the planetarium software Stellarium (2021). There we can see what the participants might have witnessed at the time of winter solstice. It is interesting that at the time of sunrise they could have also spotted the setting of the winter Full Moon — defined as the Full Moon closest to the solstice — just behind the chamber of Dombate. Despite the arguable uniqueness of the major lunar standstill, in the case of Dombate, and given the size of the chamber, such an event would happen for most winter Full Moon settings in the lunar setting cycle. It might have been possible then for them to notice and realise this interesting fact. An interpretation along the lunar plus solar proposal might suggest that the Moon (Full in this case, not Dark) was thought to set inside the area for the ancestors, while the Sun is being reinforced at the moment when it will start spending a longer time in the sky. In this sense, it could be understood as a moment of change from the lunar dominated nights to the solar strength that announces the fertility of spring.

Leboreiro

All cases investigated so far have been individual cases. Finally, I would like to include here a review of a necropolis where both solar and lunar events could be linked to the orientations and location of megalithic mounds. Leboreiro is located at the frontier between Spain and Portugal in a Sierra with a mean altitude of nearly 1200 metres above sea level. According to the paleo-environmental research, the Sierra was first inhabited by the end of the 5th or beginning of the 6th millennium BC (Jorge *et al.* 1997, 119). It houses well over a hundred mounds in less than 20 km^2, being one of the densest concentrations of mounds in Iberia. A number of them (at least 15) include megalithic chambers, with simple dolmens as well as passage graves and some also house depictions of megalithic art. The sizes of the tumuli are varied with some of them being rather small while others present are quite sizeable.

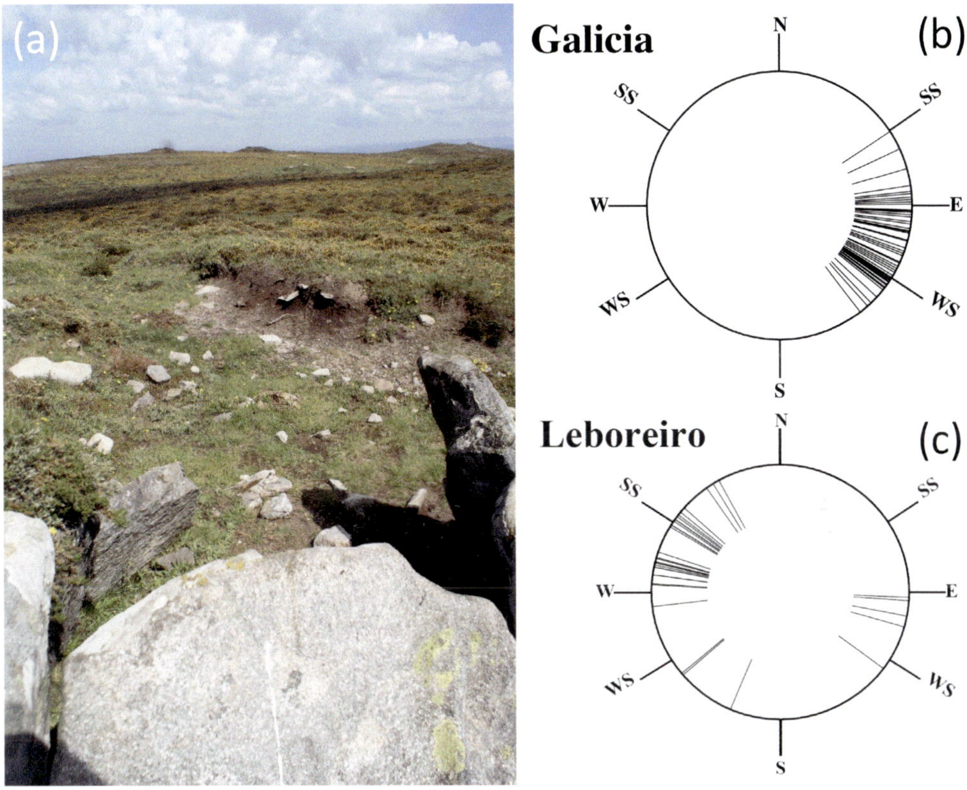

Figure 6. (a) Mota Grande, as seen from one of the dolmens in the area. (b) Most megalithic chambers in Galicia open to face a short arc in the horizon from east to winter solstice sunrise. (c) Mota Grande in Leboreiro is seen normally on the western skyline, between west and summer solstice sunset.

The largest and most prominent one is the one called Mota Grande, well over 50 metres in diameter and above 5 metres in height. It is located at the summit of one of the local hills near the Spanish-Portuguese border.

Mota Grande is intervisible with 42 out of the 120 mounds identified within its vicinity (see Figure 6a). Thirty-eight of those monuments have Mota Grande on their skyline. This is 90% of the intervisible sample. González-García *et al.* (2017) measured the orientation and altitude of the horizon of Mota Grande as seen from each of those thirty-eight mounds. The orientation is in most cases towards the western part of the horizon (Figure 6c).

Mota Grande appears aligned to either summer solstice sunset (or marginally towards the major northern standstill) or at a declination between 10° and 12°. In other words, it is almost a mirror image of the most frequent orientations for the megalithic chambers in Galicia (Figure 6b). In summary, in Leboreiro, Mota Grande could be indicating either summer solstice sunset or the sunset sometime between mid-April and end of August. Conversely, it could also indicate the setting of the winter Full Moons (if we consider this phase as more relevant than any other).

Until recent times the villages next to Leboreiro housed one of the later examples of seasonal house movements in the Iberian Peninsula. At a time near mid-spring (end of April to beginning of May), the peoples of the local parishes moved their households towards the upper areas of the Sierra together with their flocks in order to secure the pastures for them in the heat of summer. The movement was reversed at the end of summer, near the end of August. We believe this could be related to the orientations described above, in spite of the large time span. Interestingly, it might provide a link with the elusive secondary concentration towards -12° in the orientation of chambers and c. 12° in the alignments towards Mota Grande. As indicated above, the concentration of alignments towards Mota Grante connected with a declination of c. 12° could be related to the sunsets in mid-April and the end of August in coincidence with the movement of population and cattle towards the Sierra. The largest concentrations of the orientation of chambers for Galicia occur at -23°, usually assumed to be the winter solstice and around -12° which could have been connected with sunrise around mid-February or the end of October. However, it should be noted that this area, above 1200 m.a.s.l., would be covered by snow from the end of autumn until the start of spring.

Here, at 1200 metres of altitude, the harsh weather conditions in winter, when this area is full of snow, would hamper performing a relevant ritual at that time, besides which the evidence of the transhumant movement indicates that the dates around the end of April and mid-August would have been preferred. It is clear that the situation has changed a lot in 6000 years, but this gives us a hint that possibly such orientations and alignments could be connected with the economy, social time and rituals of the ancient inhabitants of the area. This poses a big question mark on the assumption that the orientation of the chambers should be always linked with the rising Sun. The orientations in this case could be more easily explained by a lunar hypothesis. In this case, for the Sierra, we could argue the possibility of a double alignment, with the setting Sun on particular summer dates, occurring on top of a prominent mount with the chambers facing the Full Moon at those times.

Discussion

We have seen a number of sites in Iberia where we could argue in favour of the existence of double alignments towards the Sun and the Moon. As we argued in the introduction this was one of the requisites to start a discussion in favour of Lionel's hypothesis. However, is this enough? It is true that Lionel's own proposal for Stonehenge, for instance, only took into account the Dark Moon plus winter solstice sunset double alignment. Arguably, in the present paper I've expanded this requirement to include, not only the Dark Moon, but also the possibility of considering other lunar phases. Some of the sites presented so far do include the fact that at the same time or very nearly, both the Sun and the Moon could be interpreted as being part of the ritual that could have taken place at the site. Others include innovative readings of the local landscape that might allow a solar and a lunar event to be part of those rituals. Finally, at others, the location indicates that such double alignments might exist.

Table 1 includes a summary of the solar and lunar events that might be linked to each site and a broad chronology for each of them. The oldest monuments do already include the possibility that the orientation worked in both directions. In the case of Dombate the location of the idols might indicate that the area next to entrance but outside the megalithic structure had some relevance for the ritual that might have taken place at the site. If so, a careful inspection of the idols might point to them facing towards winter solstice sunrise. However, it could be of interest that at the same time the people could witness the illumination of the paintings at sunrise and the setting of the Moon at sometimes almost at the same time. This could arguably be the strongest case for the 'solarization of the moon' in Iberia so far: the Sun might get the strength to overcome the longest nights from the Moon when it visits the ancestors inside the megalithic chamber. Indeed, this is rather speculative, but also quite suggestive as well. In fact, this scheme of double alignments could apply not just to Dombate but also to most of the seven stone antas. Is this the relic of an ancient lunar-based cult changed to a solar one?

Leboreiro could perhaps include some clues as well. Here the interpretation of the orientations presented is admittedly rather elaborate. On the one hand, we have the general orientation of megalithic chambers in Galicia. The entrances seem to always face the sector from east to winter solstice sunrise, with a preference for the latter, with a concentration towards declinations c. -12°. The chambers in the sierra do belong to this scheme. Mota Grande is located in the sierra at a prominent spot so that it can be seen defining the skyline in most cases between west and summer solstice sunset. However, there is a logical problem: the sierra at nearly 1200 m.a.s.l. would be impracticable during most of autumn, winter and the start of spring. Then, if we assume that somebody had to be present to witness the possible astronomical event linked with the orientation, then that cannot be facing the rising Sun, but most probably the rising Moon, and in particular the Full moon. If so, and if the location of Mota Grande is connected with the setting Sun, a beautiful picture arises, where the sites of the mounds are chosen so that they have a large mound at their back at sunset, but they might be facing the Full Moon rise at the same time. The times they appear to mark would be coincidental with the later movements of local peasants up the sierra to bring the cattle there during the 'summer' months. The fact that both elements, the orientation and the location indicate an intertwined understanding of time, space, the Sun and the Moon renders support to this interpretation. Does it support a substitution of an older lunar cult by a solar one? One cannot be certain.

Menga is one of the most prominent sites in southern Iberia and houses one of the most peculiar orientations. It is clearly topographical, but as we have seen it could be linked, if anything, more easily with the Moon, but we cannot discard the Sun either. In this case, one possibility we argue for is a last visibility of the Moon together with the sunrise. It could be argued that the waning Moon was seen moving northwards by the people who built Menga and it could be understood that the Dark Moon happened on the Peña de los Enamorados, where their possible ancestors might have come from. In this sense, the fact that later local

Site	Date	Event
Dombate	IV millennium BC	Sun-Moon opposition
Leboreiro	Late IV millennium BC	Sun-Moon opposition
Menga	III millennium BC	No Sun, no Moon; marginally lunar-solar
Hechicera	III millennium BC	No Sun, no Moon; Solar, marginally lunar
Ca na Costa	II millennium BC	Solar, marginally lunar

Table 1: Summary of the sites, dates and lunar-solar possibilities discussed in the text.

monuments such as Viera and El Romeral were connected to solar orientations could render some support to the substitution hypothesis.

The case for Hechicera, on the other hand, could arguably be rather similar to the ones in Galicia, but now with no synchronicity of the Sun and the Moon. There is, though, the possibility that the shortest night was a 'no darkness time' if we account for the summer solstice Full Moon. I am not certain if this renders support to Lionel's hypothesis or not, but it could be a mirror image of his 'darkest night' proposal, for the Dark Moon on winter solstice case in Stonehenge. Finally, the case of Ca Na Costa is a cumbersome one. The orientation could be connected with the Sun and some particular dates. However, as argued elsewhere, such orientations could also be motivated by the first sight of the Crescent Moon. If this is true, we could argue that these orientations could also be adding some further support to the lunar-solar hypothesis.

Indeed, double Sun-Moon alignments were the basis for one of the imaginative explanations for the orientation of the dolmens in the Alentejo (Portugal) and Extremadura (Spain) regions. There, more than 170 seven stone antas, very similar to Dombate, were measured. The data shows that all face systematically towards a part of the horizon where there is always a Sun rising event (Hoskin 2001; Belmonte *et al.* 2016). It can be shown that the same area would also be connected to the Moon and Marciano da Silva (2004) showed that the pattern of orientation could be explained by the crossover of the Sun and the Moon. This means that a combined solar-lunar movement could be the basis for the interpretation of these orientations. Further support for the role of the Moon in combination with the Sun, could come from the study by Belmonte and Hoskin (2002: 86-89) of the plaque idols found in some of the antas. These idols are schist plaques with a geometrical decoration that includes eyes and slightly anthropomorphic representations. They are normally found at chalcolithic sites and tholoi, but often at the corridors of the seven stone antas and in secondary uses of the chambers. Belmonte and Hoskin counted the geometric forms and found that the most frequent numbers are those of the cycles of the Moon as related to the solar year.

This is preliminary research to apply Lionel's hypothesis. However, is this enough to argue for a backup of his other statement on the change of roles? Leaving apart the fitness of the anthropological ideas that Lionel's proposal rest upon, the solar plus lunar combination opens an interesting and rich interpretative frame. First, we must clarify that the cases explored here are by no means exhaustive nor fully representative. They are but five out of several hundred megalithic monuments in the region. However, they present a possibility of the existence of double alignments. It is clear that 'Occam's razor' might still make most of us prefer the pure solar interpretation in most cases. However, the fact that these cases might open new possibilities for interpretation, including the holistic understanding of orientation and location, should be considered when acquiring new data. In any case, it must be clear that the possibility of the double orientations having at the same time a lunar and solar phenomenology, given the large time span presented here, at least precludes a rapid substitution of a lunar cult by a solar one. It seems that, if all the assumptions made hold, such substitution was done over a very prolonged period, possibly at different rhythms and scales and with varying degrees of depth. Nevertheless, the same could be said of different aspects of the change from a hunter-gatherers' economy to a fully Neolithic one.

My personal feeling is that in order to go as far as proposing that the orientations and alignments render support to the change of roles, one would need much further information. Although most of this information must come from a new and fresh consideration of the archaeological data, some may come from orientation data as well, for instance, from Mesolithic sites. We are now starting to have early Neolithic and late Mesolithic data from cemeteries in Catalonia, one of the first sites where the Neolithic economy appeared in Iberia. It would be interesting to see if the orientation, location and other finds in these sites are more closely connected to a lunar-based cult than to the solar one. New data will appear for sure in the near future that might help us clarify the issue and new approaches will be opened by new considerations from an anthropological perspective. One thing that I am sure about is that, thanks to Lionel, we will look into it with different minds.

References

Alonso Mathías, F. and J.M. Bello Diéguez 1997. Cronología y periodización del fenómeno megalítico en Galicia a la luz de las dataciones por carbono 14, in A. Rodríguez Casal (ed.) *O Neolítico atlántico e as orixes do megalitismo*: 507–20. Santiago de Compostela: Universidade de Santiago de Compostela,

Belmonte, J.A. and M. Hoskin 2002. *Reflejo del Cosmos. Atlas de Arqueoastronomía del Mediterráneo Antiguo*. Madrid: Equipo Sirius.

Belmonte, J.A., A.C. González-García and M. Hoskin 2016. Serial nominations for the AWH initiative: The paradigm of seven-stone antas and beyond, in Piero Benvenuti (ed.) *Astronomy in Focus*, Volume 1, Focus Meeting 2 XXIXth IAU General Assembly, August 2015, Proceedings of the International Astronomical Union, 11(A29A): 102-104. doi:10.1017/S1743921316002490

da Silva, C.M. 2004. The Spring Full Moon. *Journal for the History of Astronomy* 35: 475-478.

Fernández, J.H., L. Plantalamor Massanet and C. Topp 1976. Excavaciones en el Sepulcro Megalítico de Ca na Costa (Formentera). *Mayurqa,* 15: 108–136.

González-García, A.C. 2018. Light and Shadow Effects in Megalithic Monuments in the Iberian Peninsula, in C. Papadopoulos and H. Moyes (eds) *The Oxford Handbook of Light in Archaeology*. Oxford University Press online. DOI: 10.1093/oxfordhb/9780198788218.013.6

González-García, A.C. 2021. Diachrony and the big picture: Chabola de la Hechicera, a peculiar orientation and a sacred landscape, in E. Boutsikas, S.C. McCluskey and J. Steele (eds), *Advancing Cultural Astronomy: Studies in Honour of Clive Ruggles*: 167-188. New York: Springer.

González-García, A.C. and J.A. Belmonte 2010. Statistical Analysis of Megalithic Tomb Orientations in the Iberian Peninsula and Neighbouring Regions. *Journal for the History of Astronomy* 41: 225–38. https://doi.org/10.1177/002182861004100205

González-García, A.C. and J.A. Belmonte 2019. Lunar Standstills or Lunistices, Reality or Myth?. *Journal of Skyscape Archaeology* 5(2): 177-190.

González-García, A.C., L. Costa-Ferrer and J.A. Belmonte, 2007. Solarists vs. Lunatics: Modelling Patterns in Megalithic Astronomy. In M. Zedda and J.A. Belmonte (eds), *Light and Shadows in Cultural Astronomy*: 23–30. Cagliari: Stampa.

González-García, A.C., F. Criado-Boado and B. Vilas 2017. Megalithic Skyscapes in Galicia, in *The Marriage of Astronomy and Culture, a special issue of Culture and Cosmos* 21(1) and (2): 87–103.

González-García, A.C., B. Vilas-Estévez, E. López-Romero and P. Mañana Borrazás 2019. Domesticating Light and Shadows in the Neolithic: The Dombate Passage Grave (A Coruña, Spain). *Cambridge Archaeological Journal* 29 (2): 327–343.

Gordón Peral, M. Dolores. 2008. Los Megalitos en la Cultura Popular: la Toponimia Megalítica. *Boletín del Instituto Andaluz del Patrimonio Histórico* 67: 108-115.

Hoskin, M. 2001. *Tombs, Temples and their Orientations: a New Perspective on Mediterranean Prehistory*. Bognor Regis: Ocarina Books

Hoskin, M. and J.J. Morales-Núñez 1991. The Orientations of the Burial Monuments of Menorca. *Journal for the History of Astronomy* 22, *Archaeoastronomy* (16): S15-S42.

Jorge, V.O., A.M. Baptista, E.J. Lopes Da Silva and S.O. Jorge 1997. *As mámoas do Alto da Portela do Pau*. Porto: Sociedade Portuguesa de Antrapologia e Etnologia.

Knight, C., C. Power and I. Watts 1995. The human symbolic revolution: a Darwinian account. *Cambridge Archaeological Journal* 5: 75–114.

Lockyer, J.N. [1894] 1964. *The Dawn of Astronomy*. Cambridge (MA, USA): The MIT Press.

Lozano, J.A., G. Ruiz-Puertas, M. Hódar-Correa, F. Pérez-Varela and A. Morgado 2014. Prehistoric engineering and Astronomy of the great Menga Dolmen (Málaga, Spain). A geometric and geoarchaeological analysis. *Journal of Archaeological Science*, 41: 759-771.

Martínez-Torres, L. M., J. Fernández-Eraso, J. A. Mujika-Alustiza, Á. Rodríguez-Miranda, and J.M. Valle-Melón 2014. Geoarchaeology and Construction of the La Chabola de la Hechicera Megalithic Tomb, Elvillar, Northern Spain. *Geoarchaeology: An International Journal* 29: 300-311.

Narvarte Sanz, N. 2005. *Gestión Funeraria Dolménica en la Cuenca Alta y Media del Ebro: Fases de Ocupación y Clausuras*. Instituto de Estudios Riojanos: Logroño (Spain).

North, J. (1996). *Stonehenge: Neolithic Man and the Cosmos*. New York: Harper Collins.

Rogerio-Candelera M.A., P. Bueno Ramírez, R. de Balbín-Behrmann, M.I. Dias, L. García Sanjuán, M. Larsson Coutinho, J.A. Lozano Rodríguez, A.Z. Miller, A.W. Pike, C.D. Standish, M.I. Prudêncio, A.L. Rodrigues, J.M. De la Rosa Arranz and D. Gaspar, 2018. Landmark of the past in the Antequera megalithic landscape: A multi-disciplinary approach to the Matacabras rock art shelter, *Journal of Archaeological Science* 95: 76-93.

Ruggles, C. 1999. *Astronomy in Prehistoric Britain and Ireland*. New Haven (CT): Yale University Press.

Schaefer, B.E. 2017. The Utter Failure of the Lunar Standstill Myth in Archaeoastronomy. Paper presented at the joint 10th Meeting of the Inspiration of Astronomical Phenomena (INSAP X), 11th Oxford Symposium of Archaeoastronomy and Ethnoastronomy (Oxford XI) and 25th Annual Meeting of the European Society for Astronomy in Culture (SEAC XXV), Santiago de Compostela, Spain, 18th–22nd September.

Silva, F. 2014. A tomb with a view: new methods for bridging the gap between land and sky in megalithic archaeology. *Advances in Archaeological Practice* 2 (1): 24–37.

Sims, L. 2006. The 'Solarization' of the Moon: Manipulated Knowledge at Stonehenge. *Cambridge Archaeological Journal* 16(2): 91-207. DOI: 10.1017/S0959774306000114

Sims, L. 2007. Lighting up dark moon: ethnographic templates for testing paired alignments on the sun and the moon, in M. Zedda and J.A. Belmonte (eds) *Light and Shadows in Cultural Astronomy*: 309-318. Cagliari: Stampa.

Sims, L. 2010. Coves, Cosmology and Cultural Astronomy. In N Campion (ed.) *Cosmologies*: 4-28. Bath: Sophia Centre Press.

Sims, L. 2016. Forum: What is the Minor Standstill of the Moon? *Journal of Skyscape Archaeology* 2 (1): 67–76. https://doi.org/10.1558/jsa.v2i1.30212

Somerville, B. 1927. Orientation. *Antiquity* 1: 31-41.

Stellarium 0.21.0, viewed April 2021, <https://stellarium.org/>

Sureda, P. 2018. Una punta de tipo Palmela en Formentera (Islas Baleares). Nuevos datos para el estudio del primer poblamiento humano y su metalurgia. *NAILOS Estudios Interdisciplinares de Arqueología* 5: 202-217.

Vegas Aramburu, José I. 1991. Atribución Mágica de los Dólmenes Vascos y su Posible Explicación. *Cuadernos de Sección. Antropología-Etnografía* 8: 77-86.

Zotti, G. and A. Wolf. 2018. Stellarium version 0.18.0. *Journal of Skyscape Archaeology*, 4(1), 154–158. https://doi.org/10.1558/jsa.36102

The Long Dark Night: Neolithic Ritual as Palimpsest

John Grigsby

Introduction: Cheetham's Law

In order to begin addressing Lionel Sims' contributions to archaeology, I need to start by introducing a concept I am going to call 'Cheetham's Law'. Cheetham's Law is named after Paul Cheetham of Bournemouth University who made this candid observation to me some years ago whilst on a field trip to Avebury. He said that breakthrough ideas in a field tend to come not from those already established in that field (i.e., professors or professionals) but from 'newcomers' - either those just starting out or those who have arrived late and come in from another discipline. On asking why this was, he answered that the latecomers brought with them ways of thinking from their own discipline that enabled them to see through old entrenched (and wrong) ideas in the new, whereas the young had not yet learned to abide by those same old, entrenched ideas. In short both parties, both types of newcomer, were not yet aware of what they were *not* supposed to think. Established ideas have a habit of becoming dogma and remain mostly unchallenged; this is not just a case of the 'Emperor's new clothes', where the frailty of an entrenched idea (the nakedness of the emperor) is evident to all, but where no one (except a child – Cheetham's 'newcomer') speaks out, for fear of judgement (though this is often the case); it is more often, I would argue, that those lacunas in thought are simply not seen, as it is a basic psychological dictum that 'a man sees what he wants to see and disregards the rest', as Simon and Garfunkel (1969) put it – often wholly unconsciously.

Back to front

A case in point occurred to me recently when investigating an old house for an archaeology report I was writing. I am no expert in medieval architecture, but I was handed this project being told it was an anomaly, the cross-wing of this particular medieval hall was in the wrong place, at the high-end (where there was a nice carved dais-beam preserved); the house included many other odd features, odd because they seemed to be set in the wrong place. I, however, looked at the plan and saw immediately that the description in the Heritage Listing was wrong: the dais-beam was in fact the low-end beam. This example had been overlooked and recorded erroneously as a dais-beam at the high-end of the hall, and all subsequent work done in the house had carried on this assumption. I did not, at that point, know that carved low-end beams were a rarity and therefore usually to be discounted... in other words I did not know what *not* to think, and hence had solved the enigma through my ignorance. Previous surveyors had not been unable to *un-see* the description of this beam as the dais-beam, and as a result had concocted a whole raft of reasons for the odd design of the house. The truth was they were looking at it back to front. Once this was realised, every previously odd feature of the house was resolved.

Stonehenge is, in terms of design, a timber building made permanent in stone, complete with redundant woodworking joints (Atkinson 1979: 177). And like the medieval hall house above, it is usually, wrongly, viewed back to front (North 1996: 468–70). Generations of scholars, from Stukeley onwards, have argued for the alignment of Stonehenge and other ritual sites of the Neolithic and Early Bronze Age on the midsummer sunrise (Atkinson 1979: 93–7). Stukeley noted that Stonehenge aligned on 'the point where the Sun rises, or nearly, at the summer solstice' (Stukeley 1740: 56) and from this time forward such alignments became the focus of many studies. What Lionel has referred to as a 'Motley crew' of archaeoastronomers (Sims 2020) has continued to promulgate a solar theory. And this became the 'dais-beam' of prehistoric archaeoastronomy and continues to exist in the popular imagination, given the public preoccupation with midsummer. But it is not just the fact that, as John North, one of Lionel Sims' intellectual heroes, pointed out, the monument was meant to be viewed from the north-east, looking through the monument towards the setting midwinter Sun (North 1996: 459) that was so much the issue (more of that anon), it was that a whole precipice of reconstructed prehistoric belief had been built upon this wrong assumption. Like the anomalous hall built strangely around the 'dais-beam', so the edifice of ideas concerning the beliefs and rituals of the Stonehenge builders have been built on the shaky foundations of the rising midsummer Sun; and John North and Lionel Sims, like the child in the tale of the emperor's new clothes, saw fit to speak up. Just as North was not an archaeologist but a historian of science (a 'latecomer', in 'Cheetham's Law') so too Lionel, who looked at Stonehenge anew, was not an archaeologist but an anthropologist and saw what others had not seen; indeed, saw what *could not be seen*. Let me explain.

Archaeology is the science of the hidden - an occult science, if you will. It is a study of the past through remains that, for the most part, lie hidden under the dust of centuries. Yet there is an irony here in that the objects of this study, when found, are the material remains of a culture and usually its most permanent and lasting objects; the hard-wearing, most visible; what the archaeologist lacks is the ephemeral, the fleeting, the immaterial and the invisible – the remnants of a culture least suited to remain preserved in sand and earth. It is difficult, then, for an archaeologist to examine the invisible; but Lionel Sims is such a scholar and his study of this occult science is truly a study of the hidden. His work looks as much at what cannot be seen and never could remain; the immaterial; the implied rather than the explicit, so where other scholars had looked to the visible orb of the Sun in alignments, Lionel, following North, looked to the dark winter nights and brought with him thinking from another discipline, that of anthropology, that would allow him to see what had remained invisible... both metaphorically to generations of scholars and literally – the Dark Moon.

So, what lies behind his ability to see in the dark?

Matriarchal origins

Lionel's interest was sparked by a theory of the origins of culture, a palaeoanthropological model that suggested early hunter-gatherer societies were based on a matriarchal system - a theory championed by anthropologist Chris Knight in his *Blood Relations* (1991). His theory suggested a culture ruled by the phases of the Moon, something Marshack (1972a, 1972b) had suggested through early archaeological evidence; the model theorises a seclusion of the females at Dark Moon and during this period of dark to full was the time when the men went hunting. The argument runs that this seclusion was a ruse by the females to garner increased support from males in provisioning their offspring. By synchronising their ovulatory cycles and concealing ovulation they maximised parental interest and lessened the chances of husbands cheating. Menfolk would hunt under a waxing Moon while the women were secluded. Full Moon saw the surrendering of game, feasting and marriage (with the husband going to his wife's camp). These periods of aggregation and separation follow a lunar logic. In a way it put men at the mercy of the Moon.

The point here is not to analyse that theory or comment on its veracity, only to note its importance in the development of Lionel's thinking. The idea of a past/lost matriarchal system is not new, nor limited to the palaeolithic hunter-gatherers. Others, such as Marija Gimbutas (1974: 34) have attributed the same matriarchal rule to later cultures, i.e., the Old European culture of the first farmers in the Balkans and Danube valley (c. 7000 BC to the start of the second millennium BC). But, *contra*-Gimbutas, Sims, after Knight, suggested that the advent of farming and cattle-rearing was when the change to patriarchal rule began in earnest:

> In particular, the shift from a hunter's bride-service to a cattle owner's bride-price led to a reversal in socio-political marital relations, with a significant deterioration in women's status. Women became the chattels of men's cattle exchanges (Sims 2013: 184).

Anthropological evidence of cattle-rearing tribes in Africa such as the Dinka of Southern Sudan showed a male-dominated society in which women were seen in terms of exchange with social status counted in heads of cattle. For Lionel, farming marked the advent of the male-dominated system. At some point the old system collapsed. So, he decided to look for evidence of it, predicting:

> that Neolithic and Early Bronze Age beliefs would display a complex logic which simultaneously respects and transcends an ancient cosmology which in its astronomical aspects had focused on the Moon. By extension, this also implies that the Neolithic and Early Bronze Age introduction of solar symbolism was to modify and transcend earlier engagement with the Moon *(Sims 2006: 193).*

Stonehenge seemed to be a good place to start his search. Might traces of the old lunar system be hidden away beneath the farming rites preserved at such a site? For old powers were not just cast away unthinkingly; the thrall of superstition meant that once powerful (and hence dangerous) ideas were not simply ousted but integrated, controlled, nullified, tamed... exactly what Knight reasoned had happened to flesh and blood women with the demise of hunter-gathering, hence the uncanny power of the Moon. Was there evidence of the sublimation of such rites, or even an attempt to take control of them at Stonehenge?

Exits and entrances

Lionel's close reading of North's work revealed lunar imagery present in this supposedly 'solar' site, such as its 29.5 stones in the outer trilithon circle, representative, it could be argued, of the synodic month (Sims 2016: 472). There were also hints in its structure that contrary to popular belief it was not meant to be entered to see an external sunrise, but was meant to be viewed from without, from a position revealed by a double arc of trilithons and leaning lintels that seemed to converge on a spot beside the so-called heel stone (North 1996: 447). And it was from this viewpoint that the forest of stones that was Stonehenge morphed into a solid, impenetrable barrier save for two apertures, an upper and lower window, discovered by John North (1996: 474 and Figs. 170–176). In this wise, a seeming disparate ring of doorways became a solid structure like the passage grave of Newgrange in Ireland, with its lightbox above the blocked doorway that allowed a single beam of light on midwinter morning to penetrate its inner chamber (O'Kelly 1982: 125). As at Newgrange, Stonehenge boasted a narrow entrance revealed by a heavenly body at midwinter.

This appearance makes total sense in relation to surviving myths and folktales; Lionel is a lover of fairy tales (especially the interpretations of Structuralist Vladimir Propp (1928)) and the belief that myth can be decoded, offering clues to a lost past. For me, too, myth is a way pointer to a lost culture. With this in mind, here I will refer to a myth entitled *Aided Chon Roi* – 'The Death of Cu Roi' (Best 1905; Stokes 1905), an Irish myth, to show how clues about ancient sites and possible astronomical use, might lay within surviving mythical imagery. It recounts how one Cu Roi mac Dairi had aided the men of Ulster in a raid, but because he was not paid for his services, he seized the plunder, namely a woman named Blathnat (Flowers), the three cows of luchna (that could each produce the milk of 30 cows) and a cauldron.

The Ulster hero Cúchulainn, lover of Blathnat, pursues him. He meets with Blathnat and arranges a ruse by which Cu Roi can be killed and Blathnat, her cows and her cauldron rescued. Blathnat advises Cu Roi that he should build an enclosure for his stronghold of *standing stones*, accordingly he sends his men away to fetch building materials leaving his stronghold undefended. Blathnat has agreed that when Cu Roi is most vulnerable, she will send a signal to Cúchulainn by pouring the milk of her magical cows down the river (henceforward named 'Finnglas (White Flecked)') that runs through the stronghold. Blathnat bathes Cu Roi and binds his hair to his bedpost, then pours the milk and opens the stronghold doors. Cúchulainn, seeing the signal of the milky river, enters the stronghold of pillar stones, cuts off Cu Roi's head, and so regains the spoils lost to Cu Roi, though in the earliest extant version (Cross and Slover 1936) Blathnat subsequently dies at the hands of her husband's seneschal. It is the old tale of journeying to the underworld and winning the bride (for however tragically short a time – other brides, like the Welsh Olwen, have a happier ending, (see 'The tale of Culhwch and Olwen' in Jones and Jones 1957) with the cow, the magical vessel, stealing the treasure from the dragon.

Cu Roi's stronghold, built with pillar stones, is suggestive of a stone circle: it is described in the tale 'Bricriu's Feast' thus:

> In what part of the globe whatsoever Cu Roi should happen to be, every night o'er the fort, he chanted a spell, till the fort revolved as swiftly as a mill-stone. The entrance was never to be found after sunset (Cross and Slover 1936).

The turning fort moves in a manner suggestive of the sky revolving around the pole. The inability to find its entrance after sunset in the tale is the result of a magical trick to make it impregnable, yet it suggests a more complex origin: does it only revolve at night or is this just when the motion of the stars in the dark sky make it appear so? Is, then, the entrance visible by day as it is marked by the rising or setting point of the Sun (something not visible after nightfall?); if so, the fort might only be 'entered' when the Sun had marked the point of entry/

exit, i.e. when the right conjunction had taken place between it and the heavens. This reminds us of North's Stonehenge, set under a turning sky, drum-shaped like a millwheel and with an entrance not visible after sunset, as the setting sun shows the doorway. It suggests ingress into the sacred enclosure is only permitted at a certain time of year – the winter solstice. And this is the time the drama is set to take place: the rescue of the cows and women and cauldron of milk (a treasure trove of lunar analogues, one could argue).

To return to Stonehenge, the Sun, yearly, at midwinter 'enters' the monument – it penetrates the lower 'window' (North 1996, 446). Here it is visible for the few days either side of the solstice, as if held in position in the sky; but there was more – for Stonehenge was built on a slight rise and in climbing that rise along the avenue, an observer approaching the stones at sunset could ascend at a pace that would counterbalance the setting Sun (North 1996: 451–2; Sims 2006: 194), keeping the solar disk still in the heavens, thus seeming to stop time itself. This fits another Irish myth that recounts the birth of the god Aenghus: Aenghus ('one-strength') is the son of a deity named the Dagdae and is conceived during an adulterous liaison with the cow-goddess Bóand ('White Cow'; see Swift 2003: 56) (also known Eithne) aided by the magic that sees the Sun appear to stand still in the sky. According to the Tochmarc Étaíne:

> Elcmar of the Brug [Brú na Bóinne, that is, Newgrange] had a wife whose name was Eithne [Bóand], the Dagdae worked great spells upon Elcmar as he set out, that he might not return betimes (that is, early) and he dispelled the darkness of night for him, and he kept hunger and thirst from him. He sent him on long errands, so that nine months went by as one day, for he had said that he would return home again between day and night. Meanwhile the Dagdae went in unto Elcmar's wife, and she bore him a son, even Aengus, and the woman was whole of her sickness when Elcmar returned, and he perceived not her offence, that is, that she had lain with the Dagdae (Bergin and Best 1938: 143).

The spell performed by the Dagdae is astronomical:

> He brought her to the birth in a single day.
> It was then they made the Sun stand still
> to the end of nine months — strange the tale —
> warming the noble fine grass
> in the roof of the perfect firmament.
> (poem 3 Bóand II, trans Stokes 1894).

The magical stilling of the Sun when a creative act occurs suggests the solstice, which literally means 'sun-standing-still', when the Sun no longer moves along the horizon (that is, it is seen to visibly rise and set at the same location on the horizon for a few days around the solstice). At Stonehenge this magical feat was made visible even more dramatically by the act of walking along the avenue that seemed to stop the Sun from setting. Time was stilled by an active ritual act. At Newgrange, a place for the dead, the effect was more passive, requiring no external movement or engagement with the monument but Newgrange was a place of sunrise rather than sunset, when the great cycle of nature had started again, arguably at a point further along the ritual process.

This 'stilling' phenomenon at Stonehenge, however, was not limited to the Sun. There were two trilithon 'windows' at Stonehenge, according to North (1996: 446–447), one above the other, and while the Sun was visible through one each year, the Moon became visible through the other one once during the 19-year Metonic (lunar) cycle. Every 19 years the setting full Moon would be viewable as a line, a sliver of silver, through the upper window during what astronomers refer to as the Southern minor standstill, located 30 degrees south of west (North 1996: 473). This was perhaps echoed by the 19 stones in the inner bluestone circle within the trilithon horseshoe of Stonehenge.

But what Lionel did was to ask whether there were also occasions when the *Dark* Moon and the Sun passed through their respective windows at the solstice? One might ask why no one had asked this before, but the answer is probably because in such a scenario the Moon, logically, would be invisible, appearing in the window when obscured by the light of the Sun. Anthropologists, however, such as Sims and Knight, are happier contemplating the Dark Moon - it might not be visible, but its symbolism makes it important. The coincidence of Dark Moon and winter solstice had a combined symbolic potency that went beyond its relative invisibility to the naked eye.

Darkness visible

If the alignment of Stonehenge marked the longest night of the year, then its pairing with a Dark Moon, as Lionel suggested, would be on the longest and darkest night of the whole 19-year Metonic cycle: a night with no Moon.

Was, then, this alignment about darkness rather than light? If so, it suggests a myth recorded in the metrical Dindshenchas concerning the origin of the name of Dowth, the neighbouring passage grave to Newgrange:

> A king held sway over Erin, Bressal bó-dibad ['extinction of cows'] by name. In his time a murrain came upon the kine of Erin, until there was left in it but seven cows and a bull. All the men of Erin were gathered from every quarter to Bressal, to build them a tower after the likeness of the Tower of Nimrod, that they might go by it to Heaven. His sister came to him and told him that she would stay the sun's course in the vault of heaven, so that they might have an endless day to accomplish their task. The maiden went apart to work her magic. Bressal followed her and had union with her: so that place is called Ferta Cuile from the incest that was committed there. Night came upon them then, for the maiden's magic was spoilt. 'Let us go hence,' say the men of Erin, 'for we only pledged ourselves to spend one day a-making this hill, and since darkness has fallen upon our work, and night has come on and the day is gone, let each depart to his place'.' Dubad (darkness) shall be the name of this place for ever', said the maiden. So hence are Dubad [Dowth] and Cnoc Dubada named (The Metrical Dindshenchas, 78; trans Stokes 1894).

Here the stopping of the Sun (not specifically referred to as the solstice in the text, but this can be inferred) at a ritual monument accompanies an incestuous union, in the manner of Nut and her brother Geb in the Heliopolitan Egyptian tradition, which is the creative act *par excellence* (Hooke 1991: 72). While the incest motif in the Egyptian tradition is wholly positive, in Irish it is not, causing the end of the magical state; however, this is likely to be a later (Christian) gloss, rather than part of the original myth – for recent DNA analysis of human remains in the Boyne valley necropolis has shown incest was practised amongst the elites, perhaps to keep the bloodline pure as was the case amongst Egyptian royalty. The authors note: 'Socially sanctioned matings of this nature are very rare, and are documented almost exclusively among politico-religious elites – specifically within polygynous and patrilineal royal families that are headed by god-kings' (Cassidy *et al.* 2020: 1). This myth, located at a Neolithic ceremonial site, suggests both a 'time' for its actions – the solstice – and a preoccupation with darkness that fits the site mentioned, as the chamber of one of the satellite tombs at Dowth (Dowth south) is aligned, like Stonehenge, on the winter solstice sunset (Ruggles 1999: 129).

If Dowth 'darkness' was the place of solstitial sunset, Newgrange might correspond to the place where the light was born at sunrise. Newgrange's Gaelic name *Brú na Bóinne* can be translated as 'Womb of Bóand/White Cow' (eDiL 2019) which suggests the passage grave symbolised the belly of the cow-goddess Bóand from whom Aengus was born (expressed in the Sun's rays appearing in the chamber on the morning of the winter solstice?).

The Dark Moon hypothesis of Lionel Sims might elicit some disagreement from those who might ask why a monument might be built to align on something that could not be seen. However, this is to ignore another intriguing aspect of the alignment that occurred before the 'darkness visible' of the midwinter Dark Moon: due to the relative rotation of Earth, Sun, and Moon, when the Moon is once more visible in the same part of the sky as a month before, it is not in the same phase, but an earlier one - 2.2 days earlier, to be exact (Sims 2016: 468). This means that if viewed through an aperture, a Full Moon, for example, when next seen through the same aperture, will be 2.2 days from full, a waxing gibbous Moon. If one could *only* see the Moon through such a gap, one would believe the phases of the Moon occurred in reverse order to that which one would observe if watching its daily changes naturally. It is like a strobe effect where the wheels of a speeding car seem to be going slowly backwards despite their forwards motion. The Moon seen moving forward in the heavens when viewed through the 'magic' window at Stonehenge in the months leading up to the minor lunar standstill, can be seen going back in time, slowly. The lintel doorways of Stonehenge act, then, as a time machine, slowing and reversing the phases of the Moon, reversing history. Mythologist Mircea Eliade would suggest such a 'time-machine' was built to take one back to the time of the gods, the time of creation. In his view the myth behind such temples was a cyclical festival/ ritual of rebirth, such as the Ancient Near Eastern *Heb Sed* (jubilee) in Egypt and the *Akitu* (barley sowing) in Mesopotamia (Eliade 1971: 55–58; Frankfort 1948: 313–318; Gaster 1950: 34–49); ceremonies of a cosmogonic or seasonal nature, reflecting an ongoing concern with (re-)establishing order and performed within temples that mirrored the wider cosmos. They involved rites of sacrifice and dismemberment symbolising the destruction and re-creation of the cosmos and linked with the death and rebirth of the land. Such ritual sites of the Near East had a clear astronomical basis - the Ptolemaic texts in the temple of Edfu describes the pharaoh's actions in the *Heb Sed* court thus:

> He runs crossing the ocean
> And the four sides of heaven,
> Going as far as the rays of the Sun disk,
> Passing over the earth,

> Giving the field to its mistress (Frankfort 1948: 86).

Eliade argued that all sacred buildings mirrored the cosmos: 'Every construction or fabrication has the cosmogony as paradigmatic model' (Eliade 1957: 45), and that such sites sought to express the idea of a 'timeless', ideal state – built to reflect the conditions of the *illo tempore* (Eliade 1971: 4), a kind of Edenic, pre-fall state, literally pre-history. Such a return to a primordial state of union back to a beginning, a time before creation, is perhaps suggested in the long dark night before the creation of Sun and Moon...hence the need to turn back time and return to the longest darkest night when neither Sun nor Moon existed. This is a rewriting of the mythic past, an escape from history back to an idealised beginning. But Lionel has another interpretation. This turning back of the clock was perhaps more subversive. If the Moon was the clock of the heavens and dictated women's power, then what did it mean if such sites aimed to somehow turn back the clock of the Moon; dismantle its progress; control it? It is, in Lionel's view, an attempt to stop progress and hem in women. It is an attempt to reverse the progress of the Moon that gave women their power; it enables one to look through the 'magic' window and slow, stop and reverse the Moon; the power of the Moon is thus imprisoned, like Sleeping Beauty in the fairy tales (see Chris Knight's essay in this volume); and it is the cattle barons of Salisbury Plain who take this female cult and turn it on its head with the objective of investing the Sun with the Moon's former cultic significance.

> This bracketing of winter solstice sunset with Dark Moon suggests, by extension of the principle of identity, a coding in which winter solstice sunset is invested with the property of Dark Moon...and by abstracting one Dark Moon from the twelve others in any one year, winter solstice provides the annual anchor for estranging ritual from a monthly to an annual cycle (Sims 2006: 203-204).

The window at Stonehenge harnesses the power of the Moon and lends it to the solar year. But one window is not enough to build a theory on, so Lionel continued to look elsewhere for evidence – this time at Avebury.

By the light of the Silbury Moon

North had argued (1996, 274) that the nearby site of Avebury, Britain's largest stone circle set in a larger monumental landscape, was aligned on the midwinter sunset and southern major lunar standstill, the latter event occurring some nine years after the minor standstill at Stonehenge. But, as at Stonehenge, Lionel's investigations (Sims 2009) went one step further; his approach was a literal approach on foot, up the Beckhampton Avenue through the main Avebury circle and along the West Kennet Avenue towards the Sanctuary; after all, an avenue was meant to be walked. Lionel's approach to landscape as experiential is based on a phenomenological perspective, looking at the experience of being within a landscape, on its effect on the individual – an approach championed by others such as Paul Devereux (2001, 2003).

Silbury Hill, the largest man-made Prehistoric mound in Europe and built to the south of the great Avebury henge, Lionel noted, was so-placed as to be obscured for the most part, in a landscape of hills, valleys and different vistas (Sims 2009: 393–395). However, from certain, limited, viewpoints the terraced flat top of the hill was revealed to be in seemingly deliberate relationships with the hills behind it. Lionel (2020) suggests it may have been periodically cleared of grass, perhaps every nine or nineteen years to reveal the underlying chalk, making a bright, white line on the horizon (Sims 2009: 400). This, he suggests, is a model of the crescent Moon (Sims 2009: 403), and his argument hinges on the placement of the Moon in this crescent phase as seen from the vistas in the landscape.

When seen to the east at Fox Covert at the start of the Beckhampton Avenue, the Silbury Moon is in the place of the rising Moon (waning) as seen just before sunrise. Days later, such a rising crescent is obscured by the Sun, so this chalk-analogue represents a Moon just before Dark Moon. The second viewing position is of the Silbury Moon as from the north after having crossed the winterbourne stream. From here the Silbury Moon is in line with the horizon, suggesting you are looking at a Moon that has set, yet is still, paradoxically visible...

> There is only one place from which the Moon under the horizon can still be seen. That place is the underworld. Descending along the two avenues at these places, which includes the requirement to cross a winterbourne river (Lincoln 1991: 62-75), was an embodiment designed by the builders as a metaphor for entering the underworld (Sims 2009: 21).

Having entered the underworld by crossing the Winterbourne, like some native river Styx, the next view of the hill is a view 80 degrees west from the southern circle within the main henge, beside the so-called obelisk; this view is also of a Moon in a position where it could never be seen in actuality, only if one were in the underworld (i.e., below the horizon). The next visible sighting of the hill is as a crescent on the western horizon seen from the east of the hill; this would relate to the Moon as a waxing crescent, seen in the west just after the Sun has set, but still in the underworld as the hill-terrace remains in line with the horizon. The final view Sims uncovered was from the wooden palisades just east of the hill in the valley floor; the view here is 30 degrees north of west and aligns on the extreme northern minor limit of the Moon.

The Silbury Moon is seen from here peeping over the oak palisade in Ritual enclosure 1 in West Kennet palisades, which has the river Kennet running through it, which makes us think of the river Finnglas running through Cu Roi's fort in the tale mentioned earlier in this essay. This tale which involved the rescue of the woman and the three magical cows from the underworld, is suggestive of a seasonal return of fertility after winter, the rescuing of the Sun (a female entity in Indo-European myth) from the abyss of the underworld and tied to the appearance and position of the Milky Way on this long dark night (Grigsby 2018: 244, 282). Lionel would argue the taking of the woman is seizing the power from the Moon and that the very structure of the monument is about such annexation (Sims 2013: 12, 180).

The Sun sets on the western horizon and rises in the east, so travels west to east through the underworld, at least as we 'experience' it. In Lionel's model, the Moon-analogue at Avebury, however, is last seen waning on the east, then when next seen 'rising', it is on the western horizon, so it journeys *backwards* through the underworld. This journey through the Avebury underworld accompanied by the heavenly bodies is not unlike the Edfu texts mentioned above that see the Pharaoh in the *Heb Sed* ritually traversing the sky, specifically the region known as the *Duat*, equated with the underworld (Naydler 2005: 17). It is a Hero's journey through an underworld realm, an initiatory journey through a symbolic, cosmic ritual landscape. Is

Avebury a vast initiation site? Lionel says yes – one that embodies the defeat of the Moon's power and its annexation into a solar pattern, one that concurrently disempowers the status of womenkind (Sims 2013: 16). He envisions senior men taking young men round the landscape as an initiation rite, revealing the secret that the Avebury 'Moon' is different from that seen in the sky, as when spied through the vistas of the monument, just as through the trilithon window at Stonehenge, it is reversed; here the power of the Dark Moon, once a monthly occurrence has been displaced by a Dark Moon seen once every 19 years.

One could find issues with certain technical aspects of this theory – there is the fact that Silbury wasn't built as a single structure, but in stages, over time, so it couldn't have acted, initially, as a horizon marker. Also, the line in the sky formed by the platform which Lionel suggests is an analogue of the crescent Moon is flat – though this doesn't necessarily negate it being lunar – for might it then closer ape the flat line of the Moon as viewed through the narrow trilithon window at Stonehenge? That is a possibility. There is also the question of whether Silbury Hill may have only been flattened in the Medieval (possibly Early Medieval) period (Malone 1989: 102); if so, might the hill-top originally have been more rounded, perhaps better representing a full or crescent Moon? But if so, then it would have always been visible above the horizon, and therefore never in the 'underworld' at all. But these issues are mostly 'possibles', not solid rebuttals; indeed, Lionel argues that his theory:

> has explained nearly thirty features of Silbury Hill in its Avebury monument complex with a single model of lunar-solar conflation. Critics will have to come up with either errors in the data or an alternative and more compelling interpretation of so many features (Sims 2009: 21).

Lionel sees Silbury Hill as a myth experienced in the landscape, in which the observer has agency and is an active, creative participant. It is like an Anthony Gormley installation, experienced as a felt landscape, that makes the invisible visible, enabling the experiencer to see what can normally not be seen - the Moon in the underworld.

The counter-revolution

This idea of the defeat of an older (lunar? female?) power finds support in the fact that many myths can indeed be read as showing such an overthrow of the feminine. Many Indo-European myths (stemming from at least the fourth millennium BC), for example, seem to tell of a creation of the cosmos through the destruction of a male figure named 'Twin' by another named 'Man' (Lincoln 1975: 139); but as I have argued, this is a relatively late and corrupted version of an originally very different creation myth (Grigsby 2018: 47–75). The 'newer' myths attempt to obscure and displace earlier ones that had a much greater female emphasis, as Wendy Doniger says:

> In studies of Indian mythology, the Ṛgveda is usually taken as the beginning; but it would be misleading here to begin with the Vedas, for by the time they were being composed (c.1200 BC) a major power shift had already taken place. In the earlier, Indo-European period, there appeared in myth and ritual an important goddess... She survives in the Ṛgveda in the figures of Urvaśi, Saraṇyū, and Yamī, each appearing in a single obscure hymn (Doniger 1980: 79).

Some scholars, such as Puhvel, are dismissive of an original female presence in the myths, stating that 'It seems this...male-female myth is of a trite and transitory anthropogonic kind, with the female a mere folkloristic foil to her brother' (Puhvel 1987: 64). However, Near Eastern myths display similar male-female pairings without the female element being regarded as a mere foil (Hooke 1991). The extant Indo-European androcentric myths are a later cultural adaption (Grigsby 2018: 63, 75; Wiseman 1995: 92), bearing little resemblance to the original, oldest strata of these myths, yet remnants remain hinting at more ancient forms; the myths are a palimpsest beneath which the older versions can just be discerned.

Lionel (Sims 2006) sees in the very fabric of Stonehenge this same palimpsest, of patrilinear replacing matrilinear cults, writ large in stone and reflecting an ongoing concern that he believes started much earlier than the Bronze Age, with the demise of hunter-gatherer cultures many thousands of years before. That distant victory over the power of the Moon/woman remained in myth and ritual, still undermining the lunar logic of the hunter-gatherers – what he has called a Neolithic *counter*-revolution against egalitarian hunter cultures (Sims 2020). For the Moon could not be got rid of. Man is a superstitious animal; one suspects there was a fear that time itself would somehow stop if the natural lunar pattern were interrupted... and so there had to be sublimation and inclusion rather than elimination, but under solar domination. Accordingly:

> Neolithic rituals would have been drawn from a time-resistant syntax of sacred power ultimately derived from Palaeolithic hunter-gatherer cultures...In embracing and adapting this ancient rule to the logic of northwest European pastoralists... strictly lunar scheduling to ritual could be reduced and estranged into solar cycles at lunar standstills whilst preserving the phase properties associated with the synodic month (Sims 2006: 204).

Such a theory makes Sims heir to a long line of free-thinking individuals, often ignored by the academy, who have approached archaeological questions uniquely, via myth and anthropology (examples, then, of 'Cheetham's Law'), and who have found evidence, as Doniger and myself have in Indo-European myth, for the removal or demotion of the feminine (Doniger 1980: 79). Robert Graves in his 'The White Goddess', suggests such a conflict was preserved in an ancient Welsh poem named the 'Battle of the trees', and occurred in Bronze Age Wessex, at the 'necropolis' of Stonehenge, and that it was a war of words that saw the change in an alphabet that ousted one set of gods from the national omphalos, effecting the rise of male gods over the Goddess (Graves 1948: Chapter 2). In this he echoes Gimbutas, who likewise promulgated the idea of a peace-loving matriarchy in Old Europe ousted by Kurgan warriors from the Black Sea (Gimbutas 1989: 318). My own work suggests that Neolithic myth displays less evidence for a 'matriarchy' ruled over by a goddess than Gimbutas posits, rather a more equal male and female pairing on a Near Eastern model, but it nevertheless identifies a similar obfuscation of feminine roles by the time of the advent of the Bronze Age (Grigsby 2018: 71–72) - some level of androcentric replacement occurred whether it was at the extreme level Gimbutas paints or not. What is debatable is *when*.

Interestingly, an earlier, palaeolithic date for this paradigm-shift is suggested by another academic *pariah*, Stan Gooch. For Gooch, the matriarchy and its lunar wisdom, celebrations based on the number 13 and the linked symbolism of blood, red ochre and Moon, were linked to Neanderthal Man, and the conflict was between them and Homo Sapiens. His '*Cities of Dreams*' (Gooch 1989) identifies the same patterns in the myths as Propp, Knight and Sims, but theorises their origins lay earlier in prehistory. Lionel would argue that as hunter-gatherers, early Homo Sapiens lived in a similar lunar culture as Gooch suggests for Neanderthal Man, and that therefore the conflict was not between mankind and Neanderthals but between hunter-gatherers and cattle-herders after the advent of farming, when the psychology of the tribe had changed, indeed, *had* to change. Farming needed different timescales than hunting; and the solar year was more useful for planting than a solely lunar one. What is more, the males were ever-present, not away hunting for half the month; the dynamic of society would have changed, irrevocably.

Analysis of western myth, then, shows evidence of a growing misogyny in which the female comes to be seen as a commodity; yet they also reveal their roots in older myths that show her as more than a bargaining-piece for cattle, more than a prize. Myth is a palimpsest that records, despite attempts to scratch it from the pages, the original role of woman; it tells us she is there, and that she was obscured. Lionel sees the stone circles of Britain as colossal and lasting attempts in stone to write this new narrative. Whether such sites held the Dark Moon for worship or control is ultimately debateable, but either way it is still darkly present; though it remains in academic circles, as it does in myth - obfuscated, hidden, occult and ignored. With Gooch and Graves, Sims joins the company of thinkers who stand apart from the field and instead peer into the darkness, into this palimpsest of the past, in search of the traces of an earlier way of being, a clue to a lost cultural ethos that history tried to eradicate.

Lionel Sims' interpretations peer behind the face of things to focus on what cannot be seen, or barely seen - on the occluded and the obscure. Unlike many others in the field, he revels in what is implied, hidden and dark, and his work acts as a foil to mainstream speculations – a 'shadow' in the Jungian sense - a rich and mercurial counterpoise – that opens-up vistas into worlds of ritual and belief - vistas usually left undisturbed. It is a method that leaves some of his contemporaries uncomfortable, for like the dais-beam mentioned at the start, it suggests they have all been looking at things the wrong way around.

References

Atkinson, R.J.C. [1956] 1979. *Stonehenge*. London: Hamish Hamilton.

Bergin, O. and R.I. Best, 1938. Tochmarc Etain. *Ériu* 12 (2): 137–196.

Best, R.I. (ed.) 1905. The tragic death of Cúrói mac Dári. *Ériu* 2: 18–35.

Cassidy, L.M. *et al.* 2020. A dynastic elite in monumental Neolithic society. *Nature* 582: 384–388.

Cross, T. and C. Slover 1936. *Ancient Irish Tales*. Figgis: Dublin.

Devereux, P. 2001. *Stone Age Soundtracks*. London: Vega.

Devereux, P. 2003. *Spirit Roads: An Exploration of Otherworldly Routes*. London: Vega.

Doniger, W. 1980. *Women, Androgynes and Other Mythical Beasts*. Chicago: University of Chicago Press.

eDIL 2019. An Electronic Dictionary of the Irish Language, based on the Contributions to a Dictionary of the Irish Language (Dublin: Royal Irish Academy, 1913-1976), viewed March 2019, <www.dil.ie>.

Eliade, M. 1957. *The Sacred and the Profane: The Nature of Religion*. New York: Harcourt.

Eliade, M. 1971. *The Myth of the Eternal Return: Cosmos and History*. Princeton: Princeton University Press.

Frankfort, H. 1948. *Kingship and the Gods: A Study of Ancient Near Eastern Religion of Society and Nature*. Chicago: University of Chicago Press.

Gaster, T. 1950. *Thespis: Ritual, Myth, and Drama in the Ancient Near East*. New York: Henry Schuman.

Gimbutas, M. 1974. *The Goddesses and Gods of Old Europe*. Los Angeles: University of California Press.

Gimbutas, M. 1989. *The Language of the Goddess*. New York: Harper and Row.

Graves, R. 1948. *The White Goddess: a Historical Grammar of Poetic Myth*. London: Faber & Faber.

Grigsby, J. 2018. Skyscapes, Landscapes, and the drama of Proto-Indo-European myth. PhD Thesis, Bournemouth University, <http://eprints.bournemouth.ac.uk/32226/>

Gooch, S. 1989. *Cities of Dreams*. London: Aulis.

Hooke, S.H. 1991. *Middle Eastern Mythology*. London: Penguin

Jones, G. and T. Jones (Trans) 1957. *The Mabinogion; with an introduction by Gwyn Jones and Thomas Jones*. London: Dent.

Knight, C. 1991. *Blood Relations: Menstruation and the origins of culture*. London & New Haven: Yale University Press.

Lincoln, B. 1975. The Indo-European Myth of Creation. *History of Religions*, 15 (2): 121–145.

Malone, C. 1989. *Avebury*. London: English Heritage.

Marshack, A. 1972a. Cognitive aspects of Upper Paleolithic engraving. *Current Anthropology* 13: 445–477.

Marshack, A. 1972b. *The Roots of Civilization. The cognitive beginnings of man's first art, symbol and notation*. London: Weidenfeld and Nicolson.

Naydler, J. 2005. *Shamanic Wisdom in the Pyramid Texts*. Vermont, USA. Inner Traditions.

North, J. 1996. *Neolithic man and the Cosmos*. London: Harper Collins.

O'Kelly, M.J. 1982. *Newgrange: Archaeology, Art and Legend*. London: Thames & Hudson.

Propp, V. 1928. *Morphology of the tale*. Leningrad

Puhvel, J. 1987. *Comparative Mythology*. London and Baltimore: John Hopkins University Press.

Ruggles, C. 1999. *Astronomy in Prehistoric Britain and Ireland*. New Haven and London: Yale University Press.

Simon, P and A. Garfunkel 1969. The Boxer. USA: Columbia.

Sims, L. 2006. The 'Solarization' of the Moon: Manipulated Knowledge at Stonehenge. *Cambridge Archaeological Journal* 16 (2): 191-207.

Sims, L. 2009. Entering, and returning from, the underworld: reconstituting Silbury Hill by combining a quantified landscape phenomenology with archaeoastronomy. *Journal of the Royal Anthropological Institute*, 15: 386–408.

Sims, L. 2013. Interpretation through emergence: reconstituting the lost complexity of the late Neolithic/Early Bronze Age cosmovision by multi-disciplinary method. PhD thesis (by publication and production) University of East London

Sims, L. 2016. What is a lunar standstill? *Documenta Praehistorica* XLIII:467–478

Sims, L. 2020 The Solarisation of the Moon Interpreting the Stonehenge and Avebury Monuments. Online lecture, 29 June 2020, <https://www.youtube.com/watch?v=t6TdNb5TP7w>

Stokes, W. 1894. The prose tales in the Rennes dindshenchas. *Revue Celtique* 15: 272–336, 418–484.

Stokes, W. 1905. The Eulogy of Cúrói (Amra Chonroí). *Ériu* 2: 1-4.

Stukeley, W. 1740. *Stonehenge: a Temple restor'd to the British Druids*. London: Innys & Manby.

Swift, C. 2003. The gods of Newgrange in Irish literature & Romano-Celtic tradition, in G. Burenhult and S. Westergaard (eds) *Proceedings of the Stones and Bones Conference in Sligo, Ireland, May 1-5, 2002*: 53-63. Oxford: BAR International Series 1201.
Wiseman, T.P. 1995. *Remus: A Roman Myth*. Cambridge: Cambridge University Press.

Entangling the Cosmos: Astronomy of the Ancestral Pueblos - Sacred Skyscapes and Medicine Bundles

J. McKim Malville

The rising or setting of the Sun and Moon over sacred features on the horizons of the American Southwest may have been experienced primarily as performances, i.e. as hierophanies rather than horizon calendars. Building upon the ideas of Timothy Pauketat, I suggest that the archaeoastronomy of the Ancestral Pueblos can often be understood as a bundling of the Sun, Moon, landscape, ritual, pilgrimages, great houses and most of the other features that we archaeoastronomers have studied. Such bundles, not individual alignments, are the key to accessing the sacred realms of Native American people. Cosmic power resided in convergences of human bodies, souls and objects, which were symbolically wrapped in a bundle. When opened the bundle became a portal with entry to the seen and unseen superhuman powers in the cosmos. Experiencing a sunrise/sunset or moonrise/moonset from a special location may have been equivalent to the opening of such a bundle. Theories of bundling are applied to Chaco Canyon, New Mexico with special attention to Piedra del Sol and the Headquarters site 29SJ514 and 29SJ515.

> In its structured spaciousness, the canyon proper and the region beyond seem to have gathered moving bodies and beings and ordered them into a series of great nested bundles (Pauketat 2013b :45).

Bundling

Power and meaning among ancient cultures were created by the crossing of the world-lines of people at places that eventually became sacred. The greater number of intersecting lines, the greater their entanglement and the more powerful and significant those intersections became. We are born into an entangled universe. Snowflakes, fractals, scale independence and so on, all reveal a universe that is intertwined and interdependent. We are entangled by vibrating strings of space-time with ancient colliding black holes, billions of years in the past. This is what we have been given, but what about that which we make, how we entangle ourselves? Much has already been interwoven for us, but how much do we create ourselves? Weaving and entanglement are going on continuously. In his book *Lines, A Brief History*, the British anthropologist Tim Ingold (2007) speaks of knotted or intersecting lines in a space-time network that is created by movement. The world line of the Earth, to which we humans are attached, is a helix, a curve that does not return to the same point in four-dimensional space time. Projected onto flat space that helix can look like a closed circle. Likewise, cyclical gatherings of people at solstices or pilgrimage destinations may look like they occur on closed circles, but they are not really closed. They are spirals moving outward in ever increasing arcs. People are changed by such movement: changed by the hierophanies they experienced; changed by sunrises, moonrises and powerful skyscapes. These are cosmic events that are bursting with time and change.

The archaeologist Tim Pauketat shares Lionel Sims' interest in the partnership of archaeology and cultural astronomy. He suggests in his book, *An Archaeology of the Cosmos: Rethinking Agency and Religion in Ancient America* (2013a), that bundles can be useful metaphors for how we experience and explore issues in cultural astronomy. Pauketat encourages those of us in cultural astronomy to seek bundles of beings, events, and things as opposed to the standard fare of searches for (often single) alignments. To explore the details of a bundle, during which one gathers together all of the related astronomy, archaeology, and anthropology, is another version of Geertz's (1973) thick description. Bundling is a focused form of thick description. It increases our opportunities for the kind of anthropological theorising for which Lionel Sims (2006) was well known.

The bundles of indigenous people of the Americas are collections of objects that represent a particular culture's history, its experiences and its place in the cosmos. From the Shawnee in the North American midcontinent, north and west to the Blackfeet in the High Plains, and south past the Navajo and Pueblo peoples, to the Aztecs in central Mexico, the Maya in Mesoamerica and the Inca in South America, people kept their most meaningful and powerful possession called 'medicine' or fetishes in bundles, packs, sacks or bags (Pauketat 2013a: 44). Among the Arikara in North Dakota, the [the] sacred bundle was a shrine that symbolized the history of a particular band within the total history of the tribe. Bundles were powerful and sacred, connecting the people to mysterious and powerful forces of the cosmos. Opening them could have been an encounter with the supernatural, understood as an actual re-enactment of the original transfer of knowledge from the supreme being (Zedeno 2008: 368).

Bundles are entanglements and intersections of world-lines, and they acquire agentive power of their own and become more than metaphors. Some of these bundles of time, people and skyscapes may have been woven into our space-time web without conscious intention; part of the inevitable entanglement of the world. Many bundles may have been carefully chosen and contain signifiers that reveal layers of embedded meaning in a culture. Geertz, in particular, encourages us to follow a chain of signifiers to reveal fundamental traditions, beliefs and intentionalities (Geertz, 1973). These bundles grow in agentive power and sacrality with the number of repeated entanglements (Pauketat 2013a: 41).

In the mortuary crypts of Pueblo Bonito, the largest of the Great Houses of Chaco Canyon, Pueblo Bonito excavators found more than 300 prayer sticks (Plog and Heitman 2010). Hopi and Zuni prayer sticks are multi-valent bundles associated with very practical aspects of life as well as moral and ethical beliefs. In addition to prayers involving clouds, rain and corn, prayer sticks relate to remarkable efforts by the Zuni and the Hopi to benefit all animate and inanimate beings (Wallace 1966).

Today, the celebration of either the winter or summer solstice officially opens when the Zuni North Priest announces that all adults are to make prayersticks. They may consist of six feathers including downy eagle, duck and tail feathers of four summer birds tied to carved, peeled and then painted red willow or narrow-leaf cottonwood sticks. Red willow is chosen because its roots are connected to a common root stock. The making of willow prayersticks thereby connects all Zunis together into the common root stock of Zuni society. Men plant turquoise prayersticks for the Sun Father and women plant yellow prayersticks for the Sun Father's younger sister, the Moonlight-Giving Mother (Tedlock 1983: 93-94).

The breast feather of the eagle is said to symbolise falling rain; thus, the bundling together of corn, clouds, and moisture relates to human survival and a successful harvest. The moral responsibility of the Zuni Rain priesthood transcends the human community and is an example of how all-encompassing the bundling of prayer sticks can be. Beyond survival, prayer stick rituals reveal a respect for all forms of life and concern for the long and happy lives of all beings (Fulbright 1992: 229).

Bundling in Chaco Canyon

The ruins of the 21 known Great Houses in Chaco Canyon are intersections of many world-lines. In the northern and oldest areas of Pueblo Bonito, the suite of rooms 28, 32 and 33 contain bundles (Kennett *et al.* 2017). The large quantities of ritual items, as well as their placement in the rooms, suggest intentionality that extends beyond burial offerings. These appeared to be collections of offerings to deities as well as ritual objects that could access those deities and 'bring them forth' (Plog and Heitman 2010: 19625). Room 33, in particular with its turquoise, flutes, wooden ceremonial staffs, cylinder jars, and conch shell trumpets seems to have been a bundle of objects that had great meaning and ritual efficacy.

Eleven burials identify an apparent matriarchal line of descent, which lasted for nearly three centuries. A 40-year-old man was buried with a conch shell trumpet and large shells from the Pacific coast. He was adorned with more than 11,000 beads and pendants made of turquoise and more than 3,000 made of shell. On top of him was a two-foot layer of sand, another body, wooden planks and then 12 more bodies; the bones mixed together. Flutes, ceremonial staffs, more turquoise, stores of ceramic vessels, remains of South American parrots and jewellery were found nearby. The elite group of 11 had been buried in the same tiny room over the course of 330 years, starting around the year AD 800 and continuing to around AD 1070.

Sometime after the death of the last member of the matriarchal line of descent, around AD 1075, large changes began to happen in Chaco Canyon. A total eclipse passed over the Canyon on July 11, AD 1097, which could also have played a role in some of these changes. Pueblo Bonito had originally been oriented to the south-southeast following a tradition that was manifest in the McPhee Pueblo (AD 840-880) after which Pueblo Bonito may have been copied (Lekson 2008: 100-102). This large structure was reoriented to the cosmos by means of the construction of a north-south wall that divided the plaza sometime after AD 1100 (Windes 2003: 26-28). The construction of that wall may have been what Eliade has described as 'cosmicization....to repeat the paradigmatic work of the gods, a re-establishing of a close connection with the cosmos and its powers' (Eliade 1987: 32). That north-south wall may have represented Eliade's *axis mundi*, thereby providing a symbolic opening to the realms of the sky. Who could doubt the intimate connection between the Great House and the heavens, because when standing at the southern end of that wall at night one could follow its line to that area of the heavens around which the stars revolve? The new, cardinal orientation replaced that of the earlier single matriarchal power, enabling the structural recognition of two moieties, associated with the east and west halves of the plaza. The precision (180.7°; Munro 2011) with which the new dividing wall is oriented indicates the significance of the change. To reach that kind of precision, required serious commitment, probably using a technique similar to the Indian circle method (Malville 2008). There are two other apparent cases of cosmicization that occur among the late Bonito Great Houses built after AD 1100: (1) Tsin Kletsen was placed due south of Pueblo Alto, as first pointed out by Fritz (1978, 1987) and (2) New Alto was built north of Casa Rinconada.

On 17 October 1259 AD another total eclipse of the same saros occurred at the Pot Creek Pueblo south of Taos. Fowles (2013: 137-190) suggests that it may have triggered a similar socio-political transformation as summer and winter moieties appeared. Prior to AD 1250 the area contained fragmented family compounds. By 1270, the new spatial structure of the village revealed a change wherein people who once were opposed to each other transformed their differences into a new social organisation that brought them into parallelism with the cosmos (Fowles 2013: 141).

In Chaco Canyon after the eclipse of AD 1097, a new respect for the Sun appears to be manifest in the Great Houses that were constructed after approximately AD 1100. It is possible that the total eclipse was not viewed as dangerous. Rather, it may have revealed the hidden glory of the Sun's corona. The vast majority of people in antiquity, and indeed today, only experienced a partial eclipse, and it is understandable that in the past it was understood to be dangerous and fearful. As the Moon began to bite into the Sun, often it seemed they were viewing a damaged Sun, a solar deity who could be the loser in its battle with darkness. But, for those got a brief glimpse of the Sun totally covered by the Moon, the effect could have been an extraordinary revelation of another face of the Sun god. It could have changed their understanding of the Sun forever. After AD 1100 new Great Houses were built at locations where the rising and setting Sun interacted with special features of the landscape, suggesting attention to a theophany, a juxtaposition and bundling of celestial and terrestrial deities (Munro 2011; Munro *et al.* 2017). Could this event also occurring during the drought of the 1090s AD, have triggered an ideological shift in Chaco?

Figure 1. Piedra del Sol (29SJ514) a. From west; b. North-east face (photos by author).

Construction of Great Houses in Chaco ceased around AD 1130. Lekson (2015) argues that the centre of power of the Great House culture moved to the Aztec Empire. In addition, there may have been a migration from Chaco to Zuni between AD 1125 and 1225 (Kintigh *et al.* 2004). After the abandonment of the Great Houses by their primary residents, certain of the Great Houses were reoccupied, such as Pueblo Bonito, which shows evidence for ritual use of its kivas, some of which had been converted to Mesa Verdean style. The visitors appear to have had more interest in the ritual uses of the Great Houses than as residences (Windes 2003). If Great Houses were built to inspire awe, they would have succeeded for these visitors. They may have been so impressive and sacred, that they chose not to live in them.

It is not apparent whether the people occupying Chaco Canyon at this time were remnants of the original residual population or whether they had migrated into the Canyon during the mid-12th century megadrought or at the beginning wet period around 1180 AD. There may have been visits by pilgrims, for whom the canyon and its Great Houses continued to be sacred. Visitors and pilgrims appear to have brought with them some of their own ritual traditions in the Mesa Verde period in the late 1100s, that appear as pecked basins and grinding slicks in sites such as Piedra del Sol, 29SJ514, the Gallo Cliff Dwelling, 29SJ540, and Loaf Rock 29SJ555.

Figure 2. Theodolite in front of the spiral July 1992. Note the vertical outermost portion of the spiral as it climbs the rock (photo by author).

Astronomy at Piedra de Sol, 29SJ514

Two miles east of Pueblo Bonito, close to the Visitors' Center, Piedra del Sol appears to be a bundle of memories of rituals and solar events. The north-east face of Piedra del Sol contains a spiral petroglyph that is one of the most complex interactive astronomical petroglyphs in Chaco Canyon (Figure 2). The western end of the rock appears to have been an observing station for June and December solstice sunset. Its pecked basin and grinding slick may be part of a network of solar rituals that developed at Mesa Verde and elsewhere during the Pueblo III period. The south face may depict the only total solar eclipse that was visible in the Canyon during the years of the Great House Culture.

The spiral

My own exploration of Piedra del Sol started in the summer of 1992 when archaeologist Jim Judge at Ft. Lewis College and I organised a three-week summer school in archaeoastronomy held jointly with the University of Colorado and Ft. Lewis College. We had about 12 participants in our field school, one of whom was Rick Watson, a professor of archaeology at Rio Grande College in Farmington. During our three-day stay in Chaco Canyon, Rick located the spiral petroglyph on the north-east face of a free-standing rock just 200 metres east of the Visitors' Center, and for a few months we identified the rock as 'Rick's Rock'. The site had already been recorded as 29SJ415, and we have subsequently identified it as Piedra del Sol (Cornucopia *et al.* 1996; Malville 2005, 2008). During that month of July, we noticed a pyramidal rock on the northeastern horizon at a distance of 68.5 metres and speculated that around June solstice the rising Sun might reach the tip of the rock and that its shadow might fall on the spiral. Measurements with a theodolite indicated that the rock and spiral might mark solstice, but to be certain we needed to observe the shadow on June solstice. However, solstice had already occurred that summer, and we needed to wait a year to test our supposition. We enlisted the help of park ranger G. B. Cornucopia to document it the following June.

The spiral petroglyph has a diameter of 43 cm and contains 13-14 turns. An observer can stand in front of the spiral and look directly outward. While the shadow on the spiral has a diffuse penumbra, limiting the precision of its position, direct observations of the Sun above features of the horizon are limited only by the visual acuity of the observer. As viewed from the spiral, the Sun reaches the top of the horizon rock approximately two weeks before solstice. When the upper limb of the Sun just clears the top of the horizon rock, the tip of the shadow of the rock reaches the centre of the spiral. On the day of solstice, the Sun rises in a distinctive notch on the horizon (Figure 3). The message here is that two weeks before solstice seem to have been more important than solstice itself. The spiral has *not* been placed to align with the horizon rock on the day of solstice. Zeilik (1985a: S3) has argued that, 'the anticipatory aspect of sun watching is the most important feature of the sun watcher's job, far more important than its confirmatory aspect'.

The 'anticipatory' event is more complex than simply allowing residents sufficient time to prepare for a solstice festival. The period initiated 14-15 days before the solstice is the synodic period of the Moon, those 29.5 days when the Moon cycles though all its phases. Ethnography of the Hopi and Zuni offers some clues about the meaning and function of this kind of anticipation. For the Hopi the exact date of solstice was needed, which the site eminently

Figure 3. Views outward from the centre of the spiral. a. June 5 - as it rises the Sun follows the left-hand side of the rock; b. June 20 (photo by G.B. Cornucopia, with permission).

provides, when the Sun is directly seen rising in a distinctive notch on the horizon to the north of the horizon rock. Solstice is the time of the maximum and minimum of the solar cycle, when the Sun changes its course. It was an especially important time in winter for the ancestral Pueblos, anticipating the end of winter and warming of the earth.

The Zuni sought a balance of the Sun and Moon. A strong Sun balances a weak Moon, a 'New Moon' at summer. A strong Moon, a 'solarized Moon' balances a weak Sun at winter solstice (Tedlock 1984; Zeilik 1985a, 1985b, 1986). Zuni ritual traditions come from their emergence myth involving a bipartite cosmos; upper and lower worlds, balancing summer and winter, day and night. The lunar phases of birth, death and resurrection are symbolically linked to cosmic darkness, women, plants, fecundity, death and rebirth. The Moon is always changing, whereas the Sun always maintains a single shape. In Zuni tradition the Sun Father sent a part of himself, in the form of twin sons, deep into the Earth's interior to bring their ancestors to the Earth's surface. The two divine twins emerged unchanged, leading the Zuni ancestors out from the dark underworld into the blinding daylight of the Sun Father (Tedlock 1972: 225-57). In the process the people were transformed from raw into cooked people also called daylight people.

Piedra del Sol would have provided the Sun watcher everything he needed, especially the transformative blinding sunlight when Sun appeared above the horizon rock. The two-week period before solstice gave the right amount of time to identify the New Moon closest to solstice. The *astronomical* New Moon is Dark and has never been seen except during a total eclipse, when it is precisely between the Sun and Earth. The *calendrical* New Moon refers to the appearance of the first slender Crescent Moon on the western horizon, just before it sets, first visible 15 hours after the astronomical New Moon (Schaefer,1996), and this is what the Sun watcher was waiting for after the Sun appeared above the horizon rock.

Not only did the horizon rock establish the onset of the synodic period surrounding solstice, but its shape is wonderfully appropriate for a ritual sunrise. The angle of its northern side above the horizon is 55°, which is within a degree of the co-latitude of Chaco. The result is that the path the Sun follows at sunrise is parallel to the edge of the rock. Thus, some two weeks before and after summer solstice, the Sun climbs along the northern edge of the horizon rock

Figure 4. Two views of the steps leading to the small platform on the southwestern end of Piedra del Sol (photo by author).

and reaches its tip. This remarkable phenomenon could not have been missed by the creators of the spiral petroglyph and must have added to its ritual power. These two sunrises at the horizon rock, separated by some 30 days approximately, bookend the synodic cycle of the Moon, 29.5 days, the full range of time during which the Moon cycles through all its phases.

Thus, the calendrical New Moon, whenever it occurs during that period is guaranteed to be the New Moon closest to June solstice. An interesting caveat is that the first slender crescent cannot be observed from the northeast side of Piedra del Sol. The Sun watcher needed a view of the western horizon and would have established a second observing station on the western side of Piedra del Sol where steps have been cut leading to a small platform (Figure 4).

The two entangled spirals

Fajada Butte lies 1300 metres to the south of Piedra del Sol. The three-stone slabs and their spiral are in a direct line-of-sight with Piedra del Sol. The spiral behind the three slabs on Fajada Butte is smaller, 24 cm x 36 cm, placed on the rock face behind the slabs and more carefully made. There is no prominent natural feature on the horizon of the area around the three-slab spiral that could be used to establish the date of June Solstice. It thus could not have been used as an autonomous calendrical device. The most likely possibility is that the date of summer solstice was acquired from Piedra del Sol by direct line-of-sight signalling. The Fajada Butte three-slab spiral also marks December solstice with two shafts of light that bracket the spiral. The information for that may have come from the Headquarters site, 29SJ515 which is 300 metres away from Piedra del Sol. It is a Late Bonito house, which was constructed sometime after AD 1090. This was a time that appeared to have an enhanced interest in and devotion to the Sun. Nine of the 12 Late Bonito Great Houses that were in the canyon during this time were placed at locations such that the solstice Sun could be seen joined with notable features of the horizon (Munro 2011; Munro *et al.* 2017).

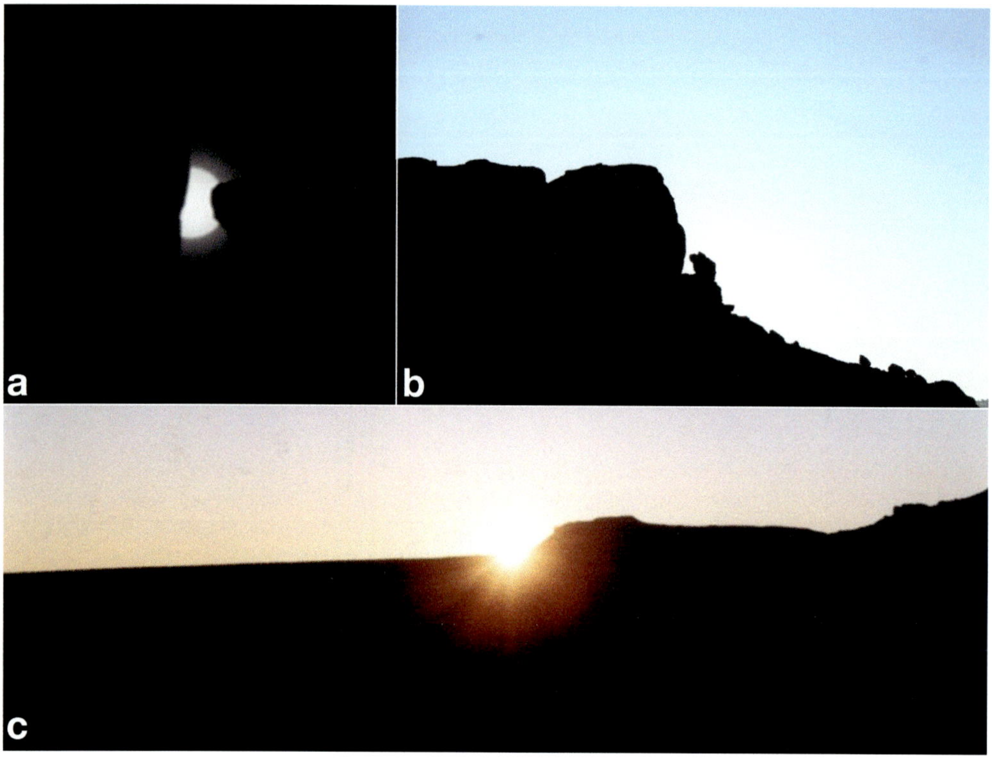

Figure 5. a. December solstice sunrise at Headquarters site (photo by author).; b. Southwestern horizon of Headquarters site (photos by A. Munro, with permission). c. View from the western face- sunset on December 7 1993 (photo by G.B. Cornucopia, with permission).

With an area of 886 square metres the Headquarters site is smaller than Wijiji (2535 sq metres) and larger than New Alto (645 square metres). One burial and Mesa Verde Black-on-white sherds were found in refuse above the floor (Vivian and Mathews 1965: 81). Nearby is Headquarters #2 at the base of the talus slope, which was apparently occupied during the Mesa Verde phase. Approximately 77% of the sherds were Mesa Verde Black-on-white (Vivian and Mathews, 1965: 81). Munro (2011) has shown that the eastern and western horizons of Headquarters #1 could have provided a nearly complete set of dates throughout the year except for June solstice and an anticipatory marker for December solstice. The latter two dates could have been provided by the Piedra del Sol. As Munro suggests (2011: 161) 'An integrated solar calendar kept using these two stations would provide coverage of the entire year. Both of these sites have a line-of-sight to the three-slab "sun dagger" shrine on Fajada Butte'.

A remarkable feature of December solstice sunrise at the Headquarters site is the projection on the ground of a shaft of light produced by a horizon feature, which is about 10 arc minutes wide, at its smallest, at an elevation of 8.3° above the horizon. As the Sun rises the shaft of light moves across the footprint of the house from west to east. If the house was one storey high, the shaft of light would have moved across the roof. It is likely that the location for the Headquarter site was chosen because of this remarkable phenomenon (Munro 2011: 158-160). Residents of the Headquarters house must have been aware of the Piedra del Sol spiral and, indeed, they may have been responsible for its construction. Both sites have reflexive solar phenomena, containing both cause and effect, with direct views of the Sun and shadows cast by the foresights, and they may have functioned as a single ritual centre combining both winter and summer solstices.

A connection between Piedra del Sol, the Headquarters site and the three-slab spiral on Fajada Butte has fascinating implications. That site may have been associated with and established by those who inhabited the 30-35 rooms and one kiva on the upper ledges of Fajada Butte, 29SJ296/297. The presence of manos grinding stones, utility ware, burned maize cobs, and hearths indicate these remote rooms were occasionally used as residences. The large amount of Mesa Verde Black-on-white ceramics suggests substantial use of these rooms in the late AD 1100s and AD 1200s, i.e. Pueblo III. Their inaccessibility suggests they were used as temporary safe havens for residents of the canyon during the dangerous times of the late AD 1100s and 1200s, similar to those sites discussed by Haas and Creamer (1996). It seems quite possible that residents of the Headquarters site and the Gallo Cliff Dwelling (29SJ540), from which maize cobs have been dated to AD 1180 (Benson 2010), climbed Fajada Butte for protection. The three-slab spiral may have been produced during that period. The fleeting appearance of the shaft of light (the so-called sun dagger) suggests the phenomenon was discovered serendipitously by people living near the top of the butte in the period around summer solstice. By itself, the Fajada spiral cannot be dated, but it is possible that the creation of the three-slab spiral was

Figure 6. South face. Note the petroglyph that may be an image of the Sun with a coronal mass ejection present during the eclipse of AD 1097 (photo by author).

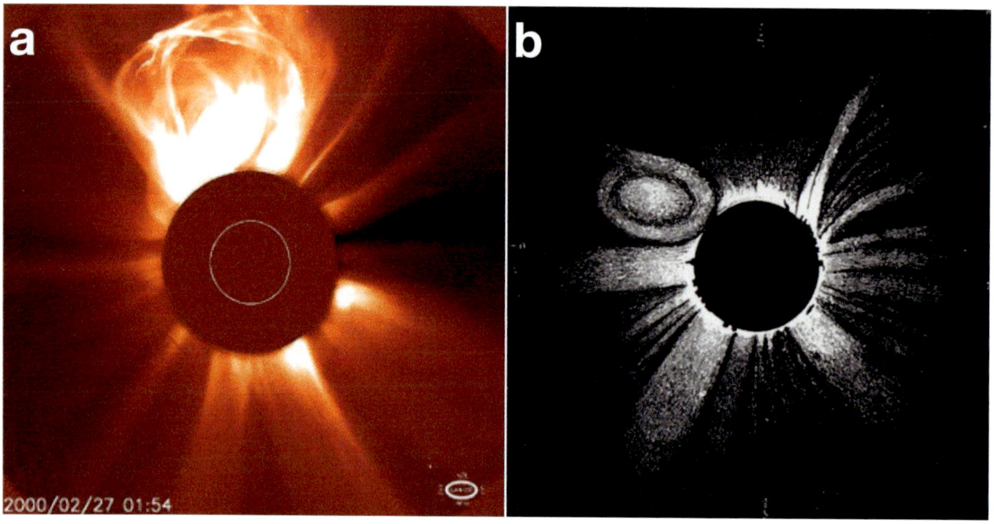

Figure 7. a. Coronal mass ejection (SOHO spacecraft, NASA); b. Temple's drawing of the eclipse, and a coronal mass ejection, of July 1860.

a collaborative venture involving residents of the Headquarters site, Gallo Cliff Dwelling and other dwellings in the canyon sometime in the Pueblo III period.

South face

Around the corner from the spiral is a rock panel containing a variety of figures, such as flute players, stick figures, human figures, and a very striking and unusual circular object with curved lines at its edge (Figure 6). As a solar astronomer I was struck by its similarity to the solar corona at the time of coronal mass ejections, when great eruptions of gas pass through the corona, and sometimes impact the earth causing aurora, magnetic storms, and disturbances of the ionosphere (see Figure 7).

Perhaps, I thought, only a solar astronomer could find beauty in such a petroglyph. Was it possible that a solar eclipse had been depicted by this petroglyph? Soon I learned about the already mentioned total eclipse of July 11, AD 1097, the only total solar eclipse to cross the Canyon during its Great House phase (AD 875 to 1140). Occurring in mid-afternoon with duration slightly greater than 4 minutes when the Sun was high in the sky with an altitude of 58°, the eclipse was well placed for admiring the beauties of the solar corona. Could a coronal mass ejection have occurred during those 4 minutes? It was a hypothesis that could be tested. If a high degree of solar activity did not occur close to AD 1097, my idea was probably wrong. Recent studies now indicate that a maximum of solar activity occurred in AD 1098 based upon the presence of cosmogonic isotopes. These isotopes of Berillium-10 and Carbon-14 are produced in the atmosphere when it is bombarded by cosmic rays produced by the Sun. Also the number of naked eye sunspots and the number of nights with auroral activity peaked around AD 1098.

This eclipse was close to the beginning of a period of very unusual sunspot activity associated with the so-called Medieval Maximum (AD 1100-1250) (Vaquiro and Malville 2014). This eclipse occurred during the drought of AD 1090-1100 when Chaco culture was undergoing major changes, transitioning from the so-called Bonito Period to the Late Bonito period, when Great Houses of a different style were built. The appearance of the solar corona may not have been a dangerous omen but an extraordinarily beautiful revelation of another side of the sacred Sun, a view of Father Sun that no one had witnessed before. That experience may have had a profound effect upon the residents of Chaco Canyon. It is particularly interesting that in India this was a time of construction of temples, which included references to the Sun god, Surya, having been afflicted by leprosy, which probably refers to the large number of naked-eye sunspots during this period of high solar activity (Malville and Swaminathan 2005).

There are flute players on the petroglyph panel that may have been related to the Sun also. The Sun plays a major role in the Blue and Drab Flute Societies of the Hopi. These two societies have one day each in winter and summer for special prayer offerings to the Sun called Tawa Baholowu (Voth 1912). The summer ceremony of the Drab Flute Society in June involved quartz crystals for throwing rays of sunlight into a medicine bowl. Flutes may have played a role in bringing up the Sun. Additionally, near to the putative solar petroglyph is a detached circular petroglyph to the upper left that may represent the planet Venus, which was the brightest object in the sky during the eclipse, lying 34° east of the Sun with a magnitude of -4.0. The sudden appearance of brilliant Venus during a total eclipse is often a spectacular and dramatic phenomenon.

The South-West face

The third face of Piedra del Sol contains features that imply explicit connections with solar ritual that occurred in Mesa Verde in the late 1100s and 1200s AD. A pecked basin with a diameter of 8 cm and a depth of 5 cm is contained on the detached shelf in front of the west face of the rock at Piedra del Sol (Figure 8) (smaller pecked basins are also known as cupules). The basin is similar to more than 200 related objects in Mesa Verde (Malville and Munson 1998) as well as at other Pueblo III sites.

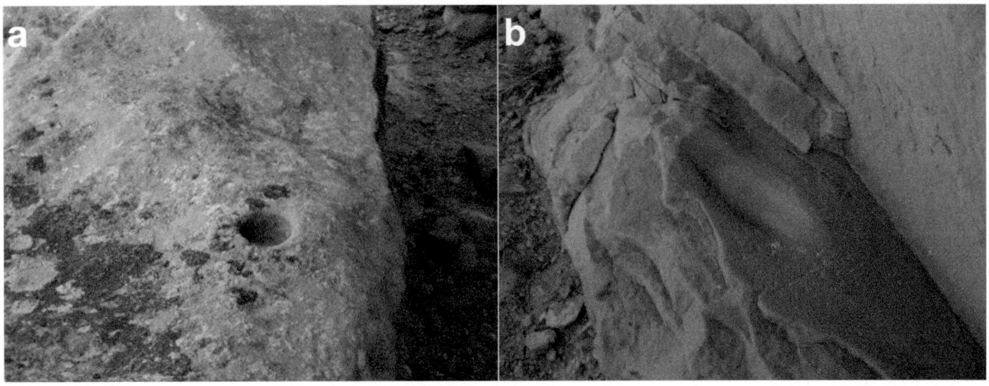

Figure 8. The southwest face: a. Pecked basin-cupule; b. Grinding slick (photos by author).

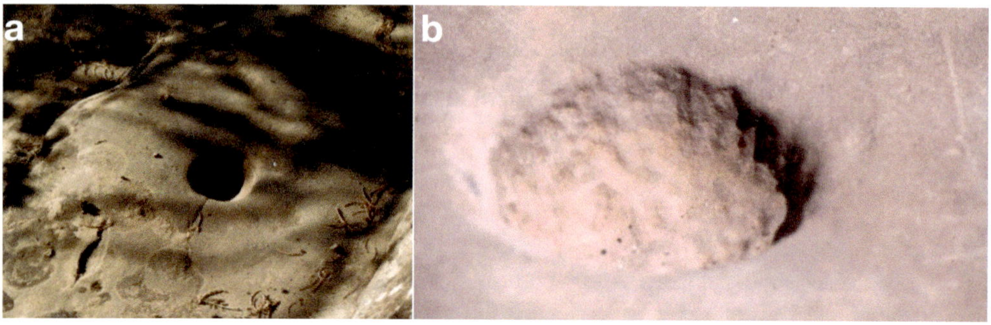

Figure 9. Platform with the Pecked Basin at Cliff Palace (photo by author).

As viewed from the platform next to the pecked basin, the Sun sets on the southwest horizon just south of a cliff as observed on December 8, 1996, establishing an approximate lunar synodic period surrounding December solstice. That platform may also have been the station for observing the first appearance of the New Moon closest to June Solstice. Behind the pecked basin, a narrow corridor provides access to a bedrock grinding feature with a length of 30 cm and width of 12 cm and is set on a slightly downward sloping ledge.

The pecked basin and grinding slick on the southwest side of the rock must be related to the multiple grinding slicks and pecked basins at the Gallo Rock Shelter (29SJ540) some 4000 feet to the east. This small structure has four rooms and a kia with a total area of 66 square metres. Two sets of maize cobs were analysed giving dates of 1177±12 AD (9) and 1196±15 AD (10), which coupled with the rock features, firmly places this small site in the late 1100s AD (Benson 2010). The grinding sicks (Figure 10a) are comparable in length and width to those of Mesa Verde and Grand Gulch. The similarity with these Pueblo III sites, further enhances the late date for the those features in Piedra del Sol.

The similar grinding features in Mesa Verde have average lengths of 20-30 cm and widths of 10-13 cm (Malville and Munson 1998). They may have been used for grinding corn or semi-precious stones for offerings to the Sun. This combination of a pecked basin and a grinding feature is found at several sites on Mesa Verde, which may have been used for solar rituals appearing in the late AD 1100s (Malville and Munson 1998). In Mesa Verde, at the southern end of the Cliff Palace enclosure, just where the modern trail heads upwards to the canyon rim, there is a smooth trapezoidal platform, at the centre of which is a pecked basin with a diameter of 8 cm and depth of 3 cm. A person standing on the platform over the basin can view the winter solstice Sun setting over the centre of the Sun Temple (Figure 9).

At the upper end of Cliff Canyon, the cave MV-502, containing 5 pecked basins and 10 grinding features, is so located that it provides a view of sunrise over Cliff Palace on the morning of winter solstice (Malville and Munson 1998: 9). Balcony House, occupied between approximately AD 1195 and AD 1275, contains 16 basins and 11 grinding slicks. A cave near Balcony House, MV-611 contains a rock with the same kind of multiple grinding slicks we find at Grand Gulch and Gallo Cliff Dwelling (Figure 10c). Another example of the combination of a basin and grinding slick is the Far View Cross, located at the edge of the canyon to the east

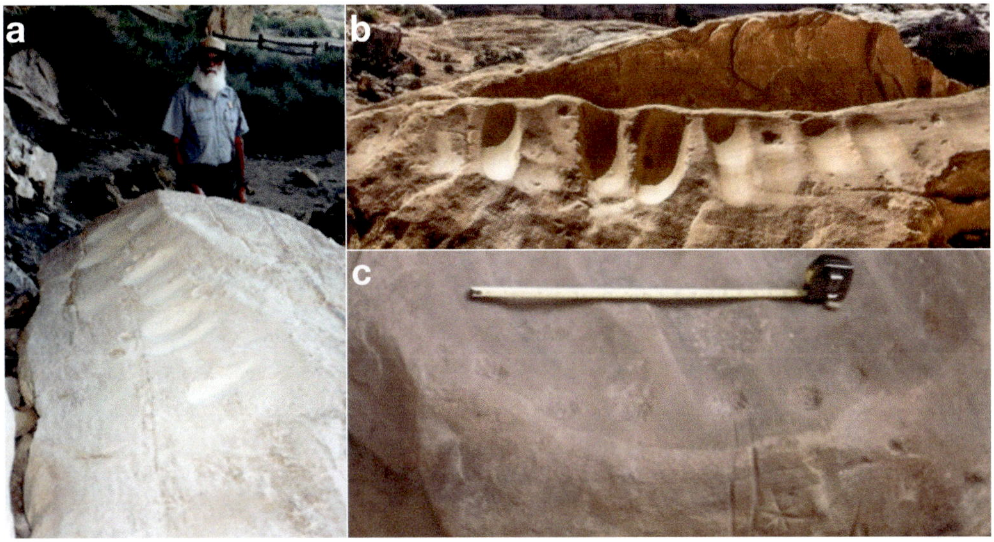

Figure 10. Multiple grinding slicks and pecked basins. a. Gallo Cliff Dwelling 29SJ504 (photo by G.B. Cornucopia and Cherilyn Morrow, with permission); b. The Perfect Kiva, Grand Gulch, Utah (photo by Todd Martin, with permission) c. MV-611 adjacent to Balcony House, Mesa Verde (photo by author).

of Far View House and Mummy Lake. This feature consists of a central basin with a diameter of 12 cm and four troughs or grinding slicks which enter the basin. Material may have been placed in these troughs for ceremonial grinding and then pushed into the central basin. From the basin, the June solstice Sun can be seen rising above the La Plata peaks (Malville and Munson 1998: 22-23). Ten basins form a network of sightlines between major sites in Mesa Verde including Sun Temple, Sunset House, Cedar Tree Tower Cliff Palace, Oak Tree House and Step House. Altogether we have documented 196 pecked basins in 11 sites in Mesa Verde (Malville and Munson 1998).

Another place with an abundance of basins and grinding slicks is some 150 km to the west of Mesa Verde in Grand Gulch in Utah, where we have documented 106 pecked basins and 187 grinding slicks. The most dramatic example of astronomy is found in the large echoing cliff enclosure that contains the Perfect Kiva (Figure 10b). The rock that contains multiple grinding slicks and pecked basins faces December solstice sunrise. There are 12 grinding slicks with an average azimuth of 124.5°. With a 9-degree horizon, the December solstice Sun rose at an azimuth of 129.4°. The acoustics of this cave is such that many people grinding together would have produced dramatic music at sunrise. Similar combinations of basins and grinding slicks are found at the Pot Creek Pueblo, a.k.a. T'aiöna (Fowles 2013). These basins and grinding slicks (also described as cupules and ground slicks) are part of the Pueblo IV ceremonial landscape, involving multiple shrines with isolated boulders containing small cupules or ground slicks dating to the late thirteenth to fourteenth centuries (Fowles 2013: 178-179). Among the Tewas, women pecked cupules at sunrise 'to attract the attention of the "Sun God"' (Jeançon 1923: 70).

Time, space, and hierophanies

A total solar eclipse can provide a brief glimpse of the extraordinary beauty of the normally hidden face of the solar deity. The petroglyph itself on the south face of Piedra del Sol may be a memory of those few minutes of the eclipse and the recollection of a hierophany, which is perhaps akin to opening a sacred bundle. Another solar hierophany may have been the view of the Sun climbing to the top of the horizon rock. Combining that with the Moon's 29.5-day synodic period produces a profoundly powerful metaphor. In its death the Moon appears to be subject to the same universal law of birth and death as plant and human life. As Eliade observed (1958: 154), 'This perpetual return to its beginnings, and this ever-recurring cycle make the Moon the heavenly body above all others concerned with the rhythms of life'. In Piedra del Sol the cycle of birth and death of the Moon is contained within the two hierophanies of the Sun.

> The sacred manifests itself as a power or force that is quite different from the forces of nature. A sacred tree, for instance, is not worshipped for being a tree. Neither is a sacred stone adored, in and of itself, for its natural properties as a stone. These objects become the focus of religious veneration because they are hierophanies, revealing something that is no longer botanical or geologies but "wholly other" (Eliade and Sullivan 1987).

According to the anthropologist Alfonso Ortiz (1977), the Tewa people attach no importance to historical and linear time. Pueblo people attempt to be part of cyclic, rhythmic time, a pattern of endless repeating cycles. Tewa tradition contains the concept of 'spatialisation' of time, which is the turning of time into space. Events of sacred time such as solstices and eclipses can be anchored in rock, thereby providing a glimpse of ever-present and simultaneously existent time.

Cyclic hierophanies have been bundled into the ever-present landscape of Piedra del Sol, which, unlike time itself, could be traversed back and forth on special occasions. These endlessly repeating cycles of circular time, the death of the Moon followed by its rebirth as a slender crescent, the death and rebirth of the Sun at winter solstice with the assistance of the solarised Moon and, indeed, even the death and reemergence of the Sun at an eclipse, are contained in that rock.

> Or say that the end precedes the beginning,
> and the end and the beginning were always there
> Before the beginning and after the end,
> And all is ever now (Eliot 1941).

The spatialisation of time is only part of the human encounter with stone and Sun. The stone remains unchanged, outside of time, but 'bundled fields never remain static' (Pauketat 2013b: 53). People are part of the bundle. In the cyclical experience of the skyscape of Piedra del Sol, mediated by its horizon calendar, indelible time enters people's lives as they may be transformed by the reciprocity of the connection with the Sun and Moon. Piedra del Sol provides an entirely new kind of bundling in which the fullness of the Moon, its synodic cycle, is bundled between the two apparitions of the Sun at the top of the horizon rock. The combination of intentionality and serendipity is remarkable: the horizon rock is in the right place to mark both June solstice and the synodic period of the Moon; the slope of the horizon rock is equal to the co-latitude of the site and there is a horizon feature that just happens to mark the lunar synodic period surrounding winter solstice. Nearby, the Headquarters site contains unusual reflexive light and shadow markers of winter solstice (Munro 2011: 258-261). To our modern eyes, these seem to be coincidences, but to traditional societies nothing can be truly coincidental: all are part of the entangled bundle of Piedra del Sol/Headquarters.

Conclusions

Piedra del Sol and the Headquarter site may have functioned as a single ritual centre. The light and shadow effects on the spiral and the winter solstice image that moves across the Headquarters site may have been manifestations of the sacredness of the Sun but also of light itself, as is evidenced in the Zuni emergence myth. Both places provided reflexive hierophanies at their respective solstices. The climb of the Sun along the northern edge of the horizon rock and the crowning of the rock by the Sun is a unique interaction between the solar deity and the sacred landscape. The most parsimonious interpretation is that the spiral was produced by the occupants of the nearest habitation structure, Headquarters site, built sometime after AD 1100, perhaps as late as AD 1180. The three-slab spiral of Fajada Butte may have been produced by residents of the canyon who sought refuge on its high ledges. That spiral may date to the late 1100s AD or 1200s. An ideological shift around AD 1100 may have been associated with the re-orientation of Pueblo Bonito, the death of the last member of the matriarchal line of leaders, the eclipse and the construction of late-Bonito Great Houses. A further ideological shift is evident in the Mesa Verde phase in Chaco which is evidenced by re-occupation of portions of the Great Houses, Mesa Verde Black-on-white sherds, and the appearance of pecked basins and grinding slicks.

It is not surprising that a powerful hierophany can produce the kind of spiritual magnetism that persists as further ritual, astronomical sightlines and bundling. Before closing this chapter, I suggest three further examples of hierophanic bundling involving astronomy of the Ancestral Pueblo. (1) The combination of Cliff Palace, the window and pictographs of the Four-Story Square Tower, pecked basins and the Sun Temple in Mesa Verde, involve both Sun and Moon. They may be part of a larger ritual landscape that includes a processional way connecting Mummy Lake with Cliff Palace and Sun Temple (Benson *et al.* 2014; Malville 1993). (2) At Chimney Rock, the Great House and the rock towers associated with the Divine Twins of Pueblo tradition, are bundled with multiple sightlines to the Sun and to the standstill Moon and may have been a pilgrimage destination within the Chaco system (Malville 2004). (3) The largest known site of the ancestral Pueblo, Yellow Jacket Pueblo, 5MT5, was occupied from AD 1050 to the end of the 1200s. The pueblo covers 100 acres and bundles together a variety of archaeoastronomical features in its multiple room blocks, kivas, towers, reservoir, north-south processional avenue, sacred ash cave, sightlines to the winter and summer solstice sunrises and a dramatic pre-solstice sunrise over Lizard Head Peak (Malville 2006). Around AD 1180, when the population of 5MT5 increased by a factor of ten, kiva rows were rotated toward the ash cave away from cardinality. These three sites, plus Piedra del Sol-Headquarters, demonstrate the benefits of searching for bundles in cultural astronomy.

Acknowledgements

G. B. Cornucopia has played a major role in documenting the complex features of Piedra del Sol, and I thank him for the many insights that he has shared about Chaco Canyon and its astronomy. I am very grateful to John Ninnemann for his commitment to photographic documentation of astronomy throughout the Ancestral Pueblo world. Andy Munro has played a large role in elucidating the meaning of the Late Bonito Great Houses and has made some very worthwhile suggestions on this paper. Cherilynn Morrow has organised a comprehensive investigation of Piedra del Sol, which has led to a more detailed understanding of this remarkable rock of the Sun and its surroundings.

References

Benson, L. V. 2010. Who provided maize to Chaco Canyon after the mid-12th-century drought. *Journal of Archaeological Science* 37: 621-629.

Benson, L.V., E.R. Griffin, J.R. Stein, R.A. Friedman and S.W. Andrae 2014. Mummy Lake: an unroofed ceremonial structure within a large-scale ritual landscape. Journal of Archaeological Science, 44: 164-179.

Cornucopia, G.B., J. Malville and R. Watson 1996. The Three Faces of Piedra del Sol (29SJ514), Chaco Canyon. Paper presented at the Oxford V Conference, August 3-9, Santa Fe, New Mexico.

Eddy, J.A. 1974. A nineteenth-century coronal transient. *Astron.* Astrophys, 34: 235.

Eliade, M. 1958. *Patterns in Comparative Religion. New York: New American Library.*

Eliade, M. 1987. *The Sacred and the Profane.* New York: Harper & Row.

Eliade, M. and L.E. Sullivan 1987. Hierophany. In *The Encyclopedia of Religion.* New York: New American Library.

Eliot, T. S., 1958. Burnt Norton. *The Complete Poem and Plays 1909-1950.* 121. New York: Harcout, Brace and Company.

Fowles, S. F. 2013. *An Archaeology of Doings, Secularism and the Study of Pueblo Religion.* Santa Fe: School for Advanced Research Press.

Fritz, J. M. 1978. Paleopsychology Today: Ideational Systems and Human Adaptation in Prehistory, in C.L. Redman (ed.) *Social Archaeology: Beyond Subsistence and Dating*: 37-59. New York: Academic Press.

Fritz, J. M. 1987. Chaco Canyon and Vijayanagara: Proposing Spatial Meaning in Two Societies, in D.W. Ingersoll, and G. Bronitsky (eds). *Mirror and Metaphor*: 314-349. Lanham: University Press of America.

Fulbright, J. 1992. Hopi and Zuni Prayer-Sticks: Magic, Symbolic Texts, Barter, or Self-Sacrifice? *Religion*, 22: 221-234.

Geertz, Clifford. 1973. Thick Description: Toward an Interpretive Theory of Culture, In *The Interpretation of Cultures*:3-30. New York: Basic Books.

Haas, J. and W. Creamer 1996. The Role of Warfare in the Pueblo III World, in M. Adler (ed.), *The Prehistoric Pueblo World, CE 1150*-1350: 205-213. Tuscon: University of Arizona Press.

Ingold, T. 2007. *Lines: A Brief History.* London: Routledge.

Jeançon, J.A. 1923. *Excavations in the Chama Valley, New Mexico.* Washington, DC: Smithsonian Institution Press.

Kennett, D. J., S. Plog, R.J. George, B.J. Culleton, A.S. Watson, P. Skoglund, N. Rohland, S. Mallick, K. Stewardson, L. Kistler, S.A. LeBlanc, P.M. Whiteley, D. Reich and G.H. Perry 2017. Archaeogenomic evidence reveals prehistoric matrilineal dynasty. *Nature Communications* volume 8, Article number: 14115.

Kintigh, K.W., D.M. Glowacki and D.L. Huntley 2004. Long-term settlement history and the emergence of towns in the Zuni area. *American Antiquity* 69: 432–456.

Lekson, S.H. 2008. *A History of the Ancient Southwest.* Santa Fe: School for Advanced Research.

Malville, J.M. 1993. Astronomy and Social Integration Among the Anasazi, in J.E. Smith and A. Hutchinson (eds), *Proceedings of the Anasazi Symposium*, 1991: 155-166. Mesa Verde Museum Association.

Malville, J.M. 2004. The Many Meanings of Chimney Rock, in J. McKim Malville (ed.), *Chimney Rock: The Ultimate* Outlier: 1-22. Lexington Press.

Malville, J.M. 2005. Ancient Space and Time in the Canyons, in *Canyon Spirts: Beauty and Power in the Ancestral Puebloan World,* essays by S.H. Lekson and J.M. Malville with photographs by J.L. Ninnemann: 65-86. Albuquerque: University of New Mexico Press.

Malville, J.M. 2006. The Cosmic and the Sacred at Mesa Verde and Yellow Jacket, in D. Noble (ed.), *The Mesa Verde World: Explorations in Ancestral Pueblo Archaeology*: 85-91. Santa Fe: School of American Research.

Malville, J.M. 2008. *Guide to Prehistoric Astronomy in the Southwest.* Denver: Johnson Books.

Malville, J.M. and G.F. Munson 1998. Pecked Basins of the Mesa Verde. *Southwestern Lore*, 64: 1-35.

Malville, J.M. and R.N. Swaminathan 2005. Surya Puja in South India, in V.D. Chamberlain, J. Carlson, and M.J. Young (eds), *Songs from the Sky: Indigenous Astronomical and Cosmological Traditions of the* World: 310-319. West Sussex: Ocarina Books.

Munro, A M. 2011. *The Astronomical Context of the Archaeology and Architecture of the Chacoan Culture.* PhD Thesis, Centre for Astronomy, School of Engineering and Physical Sciences, James Cook University, Townsville.

Munro, A.M., T. Hull, J.M. Malville, F.J. Mathien and C. Morrow 2017. Investigation of Solstice Horizon Interactions at Chacoan Monumental Architecture. *Culture and Cosmos*, 21: 151-171.

Ortiz, A, 1977. Some Concerns Central to the Writing of 'Indian' History. *The Indian Historian* 10: 17-22.

Pauketat, T. 2013a. *An Archaeology of the Cosmos: Rethinking Agency and Religion in Ancient America.* New York: Routledge.

Pauketat, T. 2013b. Bundles of/in/as Time, in J. Robb and T. Pauketat (eds), *Big Histories, Human Lives: Tackling Problems of Scale in Archaeology*: 35-56. Santa Fe: School for Advanced Research Press.

Plog, S. and C. Heitman 2010. Hierarchy and social inequality in the American Southwest, A.D. 800-1200. *Publications of the National Academy of Sciences*, 107:19619-19626.

Schaefer, B. 1996. Lunar Crescent Visibility. *Quarterly Journal of the Royal Astronomical Society*, 37: 759.

Sims, L. 2006. The Solarization of the Moon: Manipulated Knowledge at Stonehenge. *Cambridge Archaeological Journal,* 16 (2): 191-207.

Tedlock, B. 1983. Zuni Sacred Theater. *American Indian Quarterly* 7: 93-109.

Tedlock, D. 1972 *Finding the Center: Narrative Poetry of the Zuni Indians.* New York: Dial Press.

Vaquero, J. and J.M. Malville, 2014, Piedra del Sol: The Solar Eclipse Petroglyph in Chaco Canyon. *Mediterranean Archaeology and Archaeometry,* 14 (3): 189-196.

Vivian, G.R. and T. Mathews 1965. Kin Kletso: A Pueblo III Community in Chaco Canyon, New Mexico. Technical Series 6 (1): 1-115. Southwest Parks and Monuments Association: Globe, Az.

Voth, H.R. 1912. Tawa Baholawu of the Oraibi Flute Societies. Publications of the Field Museum of Natural History. Anthropological Series 11 (2), Brief Miscellaneous Hopi Papers.

Wallace, A C. 1966. *Religion: An Anthropological View.* New York: Random House.

Windes, T.C. 2003. This old house: construction and abandonment at Pueblo Bonito, in J.E. Neitzel (ed.), *Pueblo Bonito: Center of the Chacoan World*: 14-32. Washington D.C.: Smithsonian Books.

Windes, T.C., R.M. Anderson, B.K. Johnson and C.A. Ford 2000. Sunrise, sunset: sedentism and mobility in the Chaco East Community, in J. Kantner and N. Mahoney (eds), *Great House Communities across the Chacoan Landscape*: 39-59. Tuscon: The University of Arizona Press.

Zedeno, M. N. 2008. Bundled Worlds: The Roles and Interactions of Complex Objects from the North American Plains. *Journal of Archaeological Method and Theory.* 15:362-378.

Zeilik, M. 1985a. The ethnoastronomy of the Historic Pueblos, I Calendrical Sun Watching. *Archaeoastronomy Supplement to the Journal of the History of Astronomy*, 8: S1-S24.

Zeilik, M.1985b. Sun shrines and Sun Symbols in the U.S. Southwest. *Archaeoastronomy Supplement to the Journal of the History of Astronomy* 9: S86-S96.

Zeilik, M. 1986. The ethnoastronomy of the Historic Pueblo, II Moon Watching. *Archaeoastronomy Supplement to the Journal of the History of Astronomy*, 10: S1-S22.

Hats Off To Lionel: The Moon's Vertical Descent into Robin Hood's Ball and Other 'Dualities'

David Fisher

Throughout our lives we all wear different hats that make up our identity, some we don out of duty, while others arise from our interests and passions. Some reflect our inner selves which we prefer to keep private, yet others are our public and professional personas. Such a multidimensional talented person was Lionel Sims. I was initially introduced to Lionel Sims, Professor Emeritus, University of East London, at the 2012 annual SEAC conference, held in Ljubljana, Slovenia. I quickly became aware of his immense scholarly knowledge and passion for his research. A man of sharp wit and intellectual curiosity he was quick to jump into a spirited debate with both feet – 'getting down and dirty with the facts'. I was a participant at the centre of such heated discussions with Lionel on several occasions, (on some occasions he 'actually' allowed me to win, just once in a while).

Our professional and personal relationship grew as I had the privilege of collaborating with Lionel on several presentations and papers (Fisher and Sims 2017; Sims and Fisher 2020). However, our initial introduction began in the most unusual manner when we were both independently presenting papers at the Ljubljana conference. As I walked down the aisle to the podium, I passed Lionel, seated in one of the end-of-row seats, leaning forward in intense concentration ready to do battle with the facts presented. I began my presentation by setting out the background of my research into solar and lunar orientations of Scottish stone rows through the generation of 3D dimensional computer simulations (Fisher 2013: Figure 1).

Beginning to warm up, I reached a point in the presentation when I was expounding upon particular 3D animations illustrating aspects of the Sun and Moon respectively, riding down and up the tops of the megalithic monuments; in this specific instance that of the summer solstice sunrise along the top of one of the stones located at Dunamuck Farm (Figure 1). To my utter surprise Lionel, quite literally, jumped out of his seat into the aisle, with an elated grin from ear to ear, while furiously pumping the air, and loudly hissing "Yes, yes, yes". As I stated previously, a passionate man about his research our Lionel. Appreciative of his animated response, I was nevertheless, perplexed at his overt reaction. All became crystal clear when Lionel eventually took the podium to present his paper where he outlined part of his hypotheses regarding the lunar minor and major limits and solstices that may feasibly be oriented across the tops of the stones within the Avenue leading to Avebury Stone Circle (see Figure 2, Sims 2013). Surprisingly, these orientations were similar to those I had previously demonstrated for the Scottish sites. I realised at once, that although we had never previously corresponded with one another regarding our research, our individual findings regarding aspects of celestial orientations as they related to the tops of megaliths were in concurrence and thus our professional collaboration began.

Solarizing the Moon (Archaeopress 2022): 135–143

Figure 1. Summer Solstice sunrise at Dunamuck Farm, Argyll and Bute, Scotland. Image by author.

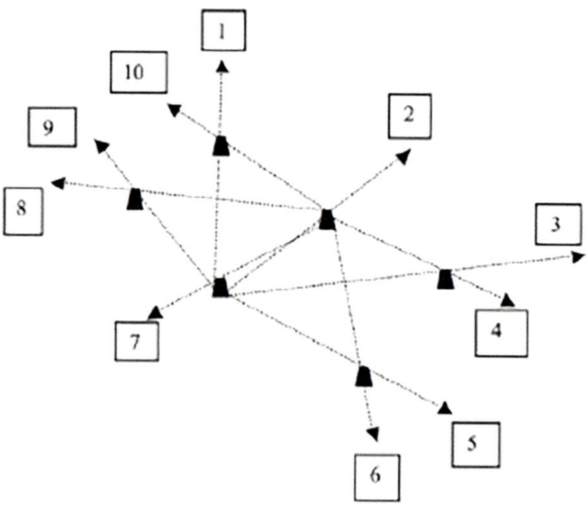

Figure 2. Ten possible alignments across adjacent stones from a central pair of stones (Sims 2013, 241) © Permission granted 03/2021

Lionel first approached me, with a degree of scepticism and apprehension, regarding the possibility of 3D modelling Stonehenge and its Palisade. He was aware of modelling from a general representation of the subject matter but was concerned with the accuracy of orienting monuments with solar and lunar events dating back 3000-4000 years. My response was to send him a copy of my research where such topics are dealt with in quite some detail (Fisher 2019). I guess his reticence was assuaged, because after a couple of weeks he contacted me to ask when we could start our collaboration. In the course of developing this paper Lionel copied me on his work on the 'Solarization of the Moon' (Sims 2006), out of which evolved a paper for presentation entitled 'Modelling Lunar Extremes' (Fisher and Sims 2017). Both this paper and 'Through the dark vale: interpreting the Stonehenge Palisade through inter-disciplinary convergence' (Sims and Fisher 2020) were eventually presented, at the SEAC Bath Conference in 2016.

Modelling Stonehenge

Lionel and I then agreed to apply the same techniques to analyse the wooden palisade associated with Stonehenge (Gaffney *et al.* 2012: 147-155). The techniques employed for the Argyll sites and consequently for this investigation comprised of photogrammetric 3D computerised re-construction of the individual megaliths and associated landscape artefacts. The re-constructed structures were then placed within a 3-dimensional topography, created from OSGB digital terrain models (DTMs), to their geographic (GPS) positions and orientations. The 3D models were tested against the celestial events as they would have been for time periods ranging from 3500 BC to 1500 BC, thereby generating visually assessable computer images for any potential solar, lunar and planetary associations. In the case of the palisade at Stonehenge the dates for testing celestial orientations was constrained by the considered date of construction that corresponds to Stonehenge 3rd phase (2600 BC to 2400 BC).

For Stonehenge, the palisade no longer exists, only the post holes which were first uncovered by Vatchers in 1967 (Cleal *et al.* 1995: 155-161) during the underpass excavation. Plus, a lengthy photographic undertaking of the megaliths at Stonehenge was not possible. However, my initial foray into determining whether the techniques described above could even be considered for such work was conducted by constructing a 3D model of Stonehenge in the early 1980's by scanning a copy of the Official Ground Plan of Stonehenge available as a foldout survey site plan contained within Fred Hoyle's (1977) book *On Stonehenge*. An accurately scaled 3-dimensional model of the Stonehenge megaliths utilising the extensive dimensional data available at the time was then created. In addition, through personal correspondence, English Heritage were kind enough to provide me with a copy of the data from the 2012 laser scan of Stonehenge with the intention to make any necessary adjustments to the original Hoyle plan-based model to that of the laser scan where required. No alterations were necessary to the model I had created from the original.

The palisade and Robin Hood's ball

Lionel hypothesised that a correlation between Stonehenge, its avenue, the palisade and a distant Neolithic construction which is situated atop of a hill to the north west of Stonehenge and known as Robin Hood's Ball, may exist (see Sims and Fisher 2017). A 3-D model of the palisade was constructed by combining the layout plan provided by Gaffney and sized to their

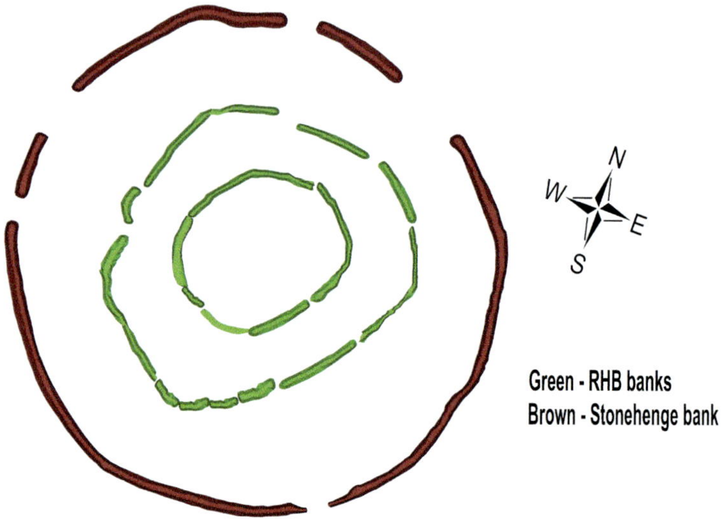

Figure 3. Scale adjusted comparison of the banks of Robin Hood's Ball and Stonehenge (RHB banks rotated by 20 degrees). Image by author.

height based upon an analysis conducted by Sims. Robin Hood's Ball (RHB) comprises of a double bank, double ditch arrangement with the ditches situated exterior to each bank; see Figure 3. On initial inspection of the RHB site plan (Richards 1990) a similarity to the bank and ditch of Stonehenge became evident. Due to this similarity the bank and ditch, from the Stonehenge model, mentioned above, was adapted for use in developing the banks of RHB. Here the first unexpected discovery became evident; by rotating the bank and ditch features from Stonehenge by 20 degrees clockwise it was an almost perfect fit. Only minor modifications to the model to match the RHB site plan were necessary – a mirror reversal, bank-to-ditch ditch-to-bank of that of the Stonehenge site - raising the aspects of duality, discussed in Sims and Fisher (2017).

One hypothesis put forward by Sims was the association between the Moon, features of the palisade and RHB as one walks along the Avenue, especially the stretch around Stonehenge Bottom - now marshy and possibly a watery pool in Neolithic times - where the Avenue turns left to ascend toward Stonehenge. To aid in visualising this walk, a sequence of images was created via computer simulation, each image set at a stride distance of 2 feet, a steady processional pace and with a viewing height set to the average Neolithic human person's height of 5' 6" (1.67 m) above ground. The sequence of walking down the Avenue commenced as the Moon, during its setting at the time of its most northern limit; (erroneously termed a lunar standstill (see Fisher and Sims 2017: 207-216)), appeared directly above Robin Hood's Ball. For the descent down the Avenue, one can imagine the beating of a drum, to instigate a steady processional pace. From the slight angle of the Avenue towards the north from true west by 27 degrees, in combination with the degree of the descent of the Avenue towards the point at which it bends and heads up toward Stonehenge, the second discovery is exposed. The Moon at its northern maximum declination is seen to descend vertically into Robin

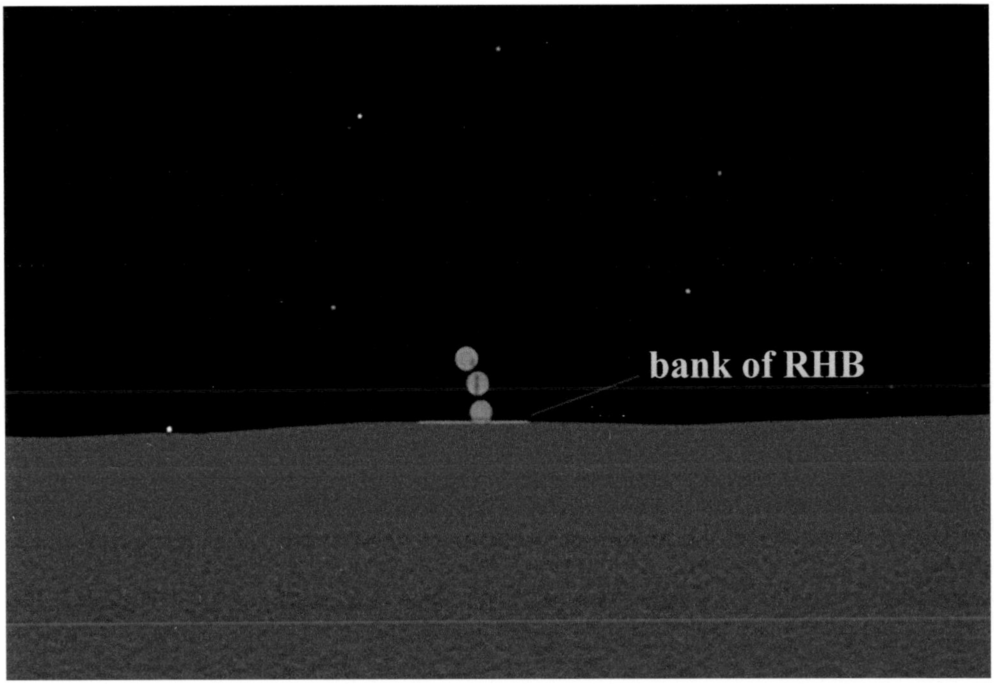

Figure 4. Vertical descent of the Moon into Robin Hood's Ball. Image by author.

Hood's Ball, see Figure 4. If we accept the lunar phenomenon presented here, as a cause of the Avenues descending path, then the Stonehenge complex expands northwest to Robin Hood's Ball.

The first thought is: pure coincidence, the avenue was used to transport stones to the monument site. But was it only that? As mentioned earlier the Avenue begins at Kings Barrows and descends to what could have been a pool of water, before turning almost 90 degrees, rising again toward Stonehenge. If stones were being transported from the river Avon to their final destination it would not be necessary to drag them downhill only to drag them up again, when by reviewing the contours of the landscape it would be far easier to follow the contour of the ground with only a minor incline to attain their final destination. Therefore, the avenue has to have another or associated purpose other than just stone transportation.

A geophysical survey conducted by Darvill and colleagues (2013) uncovered what is thought to be ice-age generated runnels that run down the Avenue in the direction of the solstices' rise and setting and hence why the location for Stonehenge was chosen. There are two issues with such conjecture. The first stones erected at Stonehenge were the four station stones that were more oriented to the Moon than the Sun (Hoyle 1977: 44-45), therefore not a solstice orientation. Secondly, with several thousand years between the ice age and the commencement of construction at Stonehenge these runnels would not be evidentiary unless the topsoil was removed, as Darvill and colleagues exposed whilst digging a trench across the avenue, begging the question how would the builders of Stonehenge know they even existed?

The avenue as it rises toward Stonehenge is demarked by raised earth on either side. If one applies water to the surface of downland chalk its coefficient of friction becomes that of ice (see Babcock 1996). We can assume the builders of Stonehenge experienced the effect of water on chalk, so if we conjecture they cleared the soil away from the underlying chalk, creating the raised earth on either side, then what would have been a pool at the base of the ascent may have had significance. Maybe this was a point at which ceremonial activity could have occurred prior to the ascent to the monument which incorporated the wetting down of the bluestones in readiness to slide the stones with greater ease uphill toward the monument. Having the chalk now exposed I hypothesised that natural weathering over time would wash the geologically weaker chalk away, resulting in the ridges and runnels until the eventual re-covering of top soil.

The Preseli Hills

Lionel's influence on me is not just limited to these specific papers, because as I was developing my paper on megalithic sites surrounding the Preseli Hills (Fisher 2018), Lionel's concept of 'duality' came to mind. This concept resonated with me when I came to realise that the celestial orientations of the megalithic sites in Wales also contained aspects of duality. The sites to the

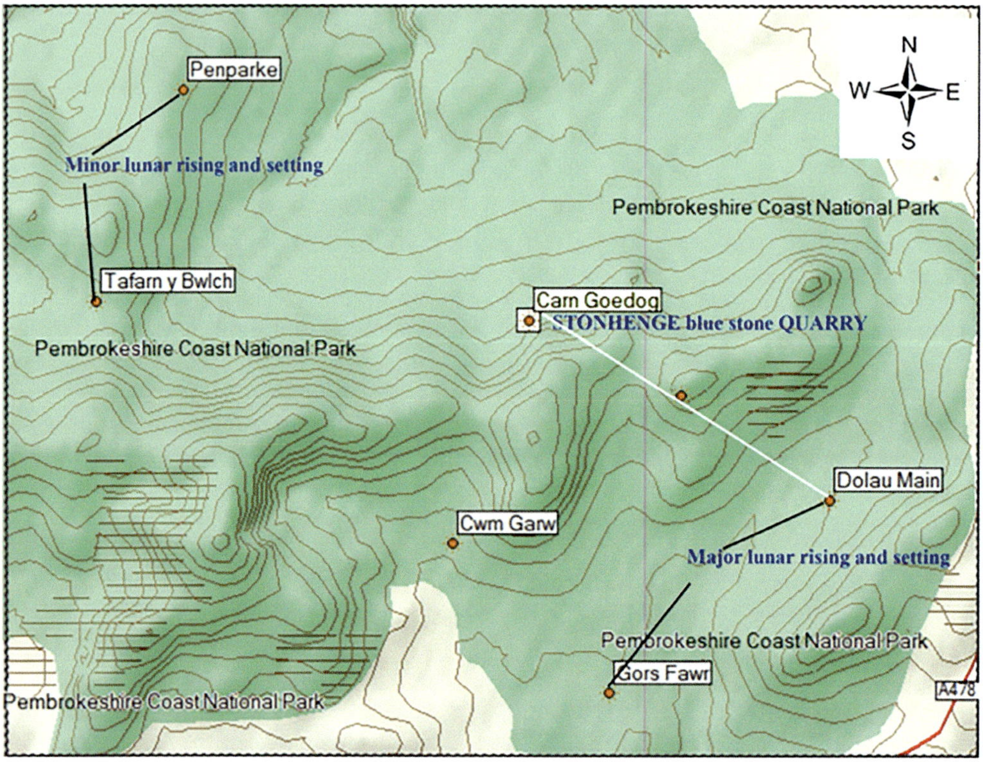

Figure 5. Asymmetrical Duality Map with Major lunar setting from Dolau Main pointing to Carn Goedog Quarry (derived from Mapsource).

south of the Preseli Hills show a preference for the major lunar rising and setting, whereas those to the west and northwest, have a prevalence toward the minor rising and setting of the Moon. Triangular shaped stones at Penparke and Gors Fawr (see Figure 5) provide these opposites in orientations and also that these triangular stones reside on opposing sides of the Preseli Hills. This led to two conjectures, the first being that the communities across the region were connected and the second being compliant with duality as described by Sims (Sims and Fisher 2020) where each monument horizon is paired with another monument's matching but reversed horizon. The horizon alignments are also combined asymmetrically with their reverse equivalent in paired monuments whose design configurations overlap each other (Sims and Fisher 2020). One key example is the stone row at Dolau Main, Wales (Fisher 2018: 157-164) whereby the setting point on the horizon of the northern lunar limit indicated by these stones, is in direct orientation of one of the quarries from which the bluestones originate (Pearson *et al.* 2019), Figure 6. What, if an even more impressive and awe-inspiring sight when transporting the first bluestones to be moved to the Stonehenge site is the lunar sphere's vertical descent into Robins Hood's Ball, to consecrate the site. I leave the reader to cogitate the possibility.

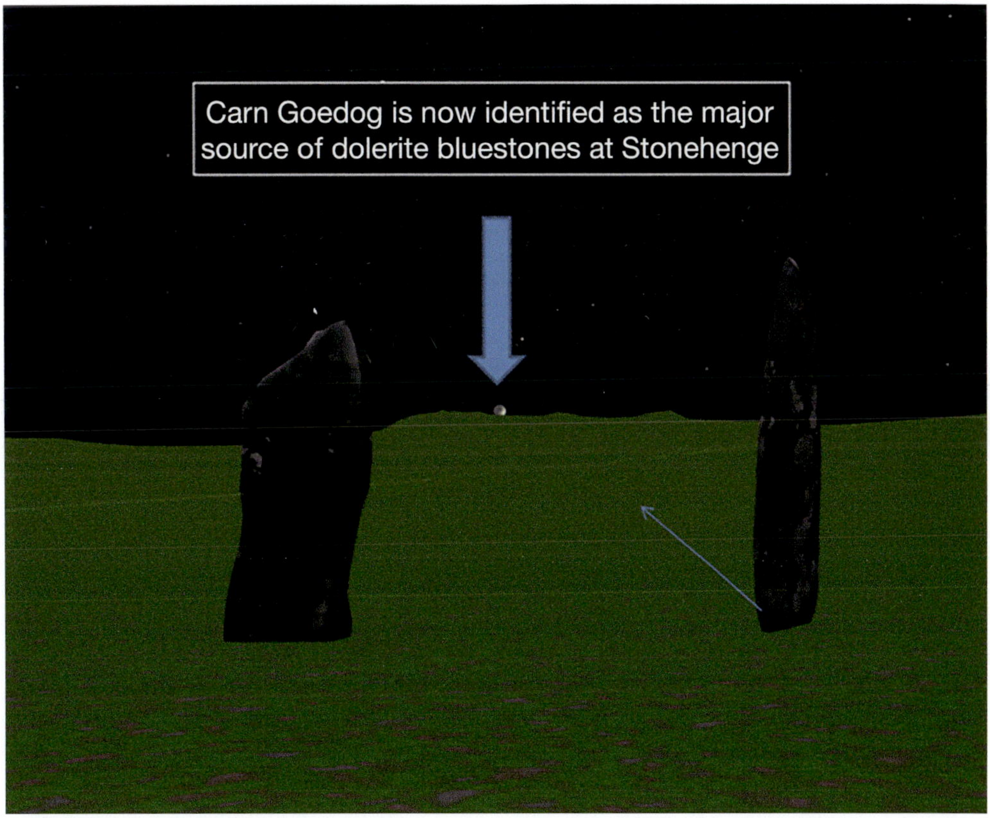

Figure 6. Face of Dolau Main stone oriented toward the setting Moon at its Northern Maximum Limit. Image by author. For Carn Goedog reference see Pearson, *et al*, 2019.

Concluding remarks

Lionel's influence will continue with me into the future and with it my collegiate respect and the deepening of our friendship. It has been an honour to 'walk the walk, talk the talk' and get 'down and dirty with the facts'. I doff my cap to you Lionel, bravo!

> Myself when young did eagerly frequent
> Doctor and Saint, and heard great Argument
> About it and about: but evermore
> Came out by the same Door as in I went.
>
> With them the Seed of Wisdom did I sow,
> And with my own hand labour'd it to grow:
> And this was all the Harvest that I reap'd –
> I came like Water, and like Wind I go.
>
> (From The Rubáiyát of Omar Khayyam)

References

Babcock, D.D. 1996. The Coefficient of Kinetic Friction for Curling Ice, in The Physics Factbook, viewed January 2019, < https://hypertextbook.com/facts/2004/GennaAbleman.shtml>.

Cleal, R.M.J., K.E. Walker and R. Montague 1995. *Stonehenge in its landscape: twentieth-century excavations English Heritage Archaeological Report 10.* London: English Heritage.

Darvill, T., F. Lüth, K. Rassmann, A. Fischer and K. Winkelmann 2013. Stonehenge, Wiltshire, UK: High Resolution Geophysical Surveys in the Surrounding Landscape, 2011. *European Journal of Archaeology* 16 (1): 63-93.

Fisher, D.A., 2013. Employing 3-Dimensional Computer Simulation to Examine to Celestial Dating of Scottish Megalithic Sites in *Ancient Cosmologies and Modern Prophets: Proceedings of the 20th Conference of the European Society for Astronomy in Culture*: 143- 155. Ljubljana: Slovene Anthropological Society, EBSCO publishing.

Fisher, D.A. 2018. Stone Rows of Preseli Hills. *Mediterranean Archaeology and Archaeometry* 18 (4): 157-164. doi: 10.5281/zenodo.1478024

Fisher, D.A. 2019. *The Phenomena of Argyll Stone Rows Revealed Through 3D computer Simulation.* Oxford: BAR publishing.

Fisher, D.A. and L. Sims 2017. Modelling Lunar Extremes. *Journal of Skyscape Archaeology* 3 (2): 207-216. doi: 10.1558/jsa.34686

Gaffney, C., V.Gaffney *et al.* 2012. The Stonehenge Hidden Landscapes Project. *Archaeological Prospection* 19(2): 147-155. doi: 10.1002/arp.1422

Hoyle, F. 1977. *On Stonehenge*. San Francisco: Freeman and Co.

Omar Khayyam, 1859. *The Rubáiyát of Omar Khayyam* trans. Edward Fitzgerald. London: Collins.

Pearson, M., J. Pollard, C. Richards, K. Welham, C. Casswell, C. French, D. Schlee, D. Shaw, E. Simmons, A. Stanford, R. Bevins and R. Ixer 2019. Megalith quarries for Stonehenge's bluestones. *Antiquity* 93 (367): 45-62. doi: 10.15184/aqy.2018.111

Richards, J. 1990. *The Stonehenge Environs Project*. Historic Buildings and Monuments Commission for England. London: English Heritage.

Sims, L. 2006. The 'Solarization' of the Moon: Manipulated Knowledge at Stonehenge. *Cambridge Archaeological Journal* 16 (2): 191-207. doi:10.1017/S0959774306000114

Sims, L. 2013. Monuments as Myths or Myths as Monuments, in I. Šprajc and P. Pehani (eds) *Anthropological Notebooks. Ancient Cosmologies and Modern Prophets: Proceedings of the 20th Conference of the European Society for Astronomy in Culture.* Ljubljana: Slovene Anthropological Society, EBSCO publishing.

Sims, L. and D.A. Fisher 2020. Through the dark vale: interpreting the Stonehenge Palisade through inter-disciplinary convergence. *Journal of Skyscape Archaeology* 6 (1): 5-29. doi: 10.1558/jsa.38690

Fire-drills in the Neolithic Near East

Estelle Orrelle

Introduction

Elliptical stone and clay rods in the Pottery Neolithic (PN) period in the Near East have been regarded as drill bits. This comes in contrast to researchers who suggest they have a symbolic function as models of phalli (Gopher and Orrelle 1996: 261; Stekelis 1972: 45) I suggest that drawing on the prehistoric propensity for double meanings and the cultural context of ritual fire lighting, it is possible to assign both functions to these artefacts. This is supported by aspects of Indo-European mythology and cultic sources. As a background to the pyrotechnology in Neolithic times in the Near East, I consider a specific ritual context, namely, the birth of Agni.

Cylindrical objects of fired clay and stone are found in Pottery Neolithic sites in the Jordan Valley and over an extended geographical area of the Near East. These objects are all cylindrical in shape and many have one conical end, while some rare examples have two biconical (pointed) extremities. Most are found fragmented. Large numbers of these have been found in the Yarmukian Pottery Neolithic sites (first half of sixth millennium BC) of Sha'ar HaGolan (Garfinkel 1993; Freikman 2006) and Munhata (Gopher and Orrelle 1995) and at Nahal Zehora ll, (Gopher and Eyal 2012: 1186).They also appear in sites with no Yarmukian material such as Pottery Neolithic A (Lodian) of Jericho (Holland 1983: fig 367: 16) and Teluliyot Batashi (Kaplan 1958: 19 fig 9: 30. The length of the complete items averages *c.*47mm with the diameter being *c.*13mm. A full description of these artefacts, their characterisation and their distribution can be found in Goren-Inbar *et al.* 2012.

Function

Stekelis, suggested that these items were cultic in function, following their resemblance to phalli (Stekelis 1951, 1972). Garfinkel 1993 assigned them a 'clay pestle' function; Garfinkel and Miller (2002: 262) a 'clay rod' and Freikman (2006) called them 'cylindrical clay objects'. Stekelis (1972) and Gopher and Orrelle (1995) interpreted them as models of phalli and Gopher and Eyal (2012: 1186) as masculine symbols and phallic representations.

Offering a different interpretation, Goren-Inbar *et al.* (2012) see the function of these items as the elliptical bit components of a fire drill related to a distinct evolutionary phase in pyrotechnology, including the introduction and the extensive use of 'mechanical' drills. They present a reconstruction of their technology and mode of use: the rotation and friction of the drill transmits energy, i.e. heat, into the socket of a fireboard surface to produce sparks. Their article is problematic for a number of reasons. Firstly, the authors do not provide any evidence that such drill bits would be able to ignite any material. Secondly, the article was weighted towards the technological. The drill bit and fire drill were regarded as the earliest evidence of a complex technology of fire ignition which they assign to an advanced pyrotechnology in Neolithic times (Goren-Inbar *et al.* 2012: 4). They do not examine the significance of the replacement of the two-stick method of fire-making by a ceramic item, which is an important ritual material that was used for vessels and figurines. Thirdly, the genital imagery present in ethnographic and religious symbolism was given scant mention.

I suggest that drawing on the prehistoric propensity for double meanings and the cultural context of ritual fire lighting, it is possible to assign both functions to these items. As a background to the pyrotechnology in Neolithic times in the Near East, I consider a specific ritual context, namely, fire sacrifices.

Fire making

The authors claim that the role of fire became more visible during the Pre-Pottery Neolithic Age A (*c.* 11,750–10,500 cal BP) and particularly in the Pre-Pottery Neolithic B (PPNB; *c.* 10,500–8400 cal BP) and that the widespread distribution of rods illustrates the regular use of this particular method of fire making. Worship or deification of fire (also pyrodulia, pyrolatry or pyrolatria) is known from various religions and survives in the religions of peoples of Central Asia in their rituals from shamanic origins to Vedic tradition and Buddhist Tantra. Fire has been used to offer and to make sacrifice to please the gods.

The best known and most fully documented early ritual system in the world is the Vedic religion. Kaliff (2005: 79) claims that Indo-European religion can provide a good analogy because of its long well documented record. The Vedic ritual was handed down orally and is known from writings from *c.*1000 BC onwards. Ancient texts lay down specific instructions for the ritual in handbooks for their performance (Staal 2001[1983]: 29-40).

In the text below I shall consider a specific ritual context, namely, the ritual of fire kindling, creating the god of fire as an analogy for an interpretation of fire rituals in the Southern Levant. The significance of such rituals is well documented in the Vedic tradition, and Vedic culture is a rewarding context for comparisons and a source of inspiration for interpretations. I shall also attempt to show that the archaeological material provides strong evidence that fire rituals were practised in the prehistoric Southern Levant. I describe the fire sacrifice of the Vedic god Agni as an analogy for an interpretation of the archaeological contexts (see Barrelet 1968). For this I use the name of the god Agni as it appears in the record, but naturally we cannot know the name of the recipient of the sacrificial ritual in the Levantine context.

Although the early presence of the Indo-Europeans in the Near East has not been unequivocally proven, the legitimacy of using an analogy from Vedic religion is supported by Adams and Otte (1999) subscribing to the Paleolithic continuity paradigm; a hypothesis suggesting that the Proto-Indo-European language (PIE) can be traced back to the Upper Paleolithic (*c.*50,000–12,000 BC) several millennia earlier than the Chalcolithic or Neolithic periods (*c.*5500–4500 BC). Relating to the theory which explains the spread of Indo-European language as being associated with the spread of farming out of the Near East (Renfrew 1990), Adams and Otte have posited an early Indo-European presence in the Near East. During the Younger Dryas, the authors claim, populations clustered in moist sites, population refuges such as the Jordan Valley (Adams and Otte 1999: 74, 77; Wright 1993), the find location of many of the artefacts discussed here. However, the debate on the possible Anatolian origins of the Indo-Europeans is still being waged. The recent DNA evidence linked to the presence of the Caucasian Hunter-Gatherer component in all IE groups might further support such a proposition (Heggarty 2015).

Agni fire ritual

The ritual surrounding the god Agni is relevant in providing supporting evidence for the cultural context of this technology. Agni, an important Vedic god, is the god of fire and is worshiped in domestic and ceremonial contexts. The sacred texts describe how Agni is created daily in a fire making ritual - the fire sacrifice of a divinity who represents fire, who is even fire itself.

> Agni is brilliant, golden, has flaming hair and beard, three or seven tongues, his face is light, his eyes shine, he has sharp teeth, he makes a cracking noise, and leaves a black trail behind. He is fond of clarified butter, but he also eats wood and devours the forest. In fact, he eats everything (Staal [1983] 2001: 73).

The proper offering to Agni, and hence all the gods, is ghee, which is clarified butter. The Rig Veda makes frequent mention of a ladle or offering spoon used for distributing the libation as sacrificial instrument/ utensil (*sruca or agnihotrahavani*).

Archeological evidence for butter-making includes models of churns appearing in small numbers in the Wadi Raba assemblages of the Nahal Zehora sites (Gopher and Eyal 2012: 721). A unique item, a spoon, was found at Yarmukian layers at Munhata (Garfinkel 1993: 55 A3, Figure 29, 1-3).

Fire drill

The lighting of the New Fire was called *Agnyadheya* ('lighting of fires') and this was an important preliminary at all Vedic sacrifices. Instructions for the sacred method for kindling the ritual fire by friction are recorded in sacred texts of the Vedic tradition of which the oldest, the Rig Veda, dates back to *c.*1500 BC and have remained remarkably consistent up until modern times. The ancient Brahmans used a spindle called *matha* or *pramatha,* 'to bring out friction to light the holy fire (Joly 1876)'. The sacred *fire-drill* (*agnimathana*) for procuring the fire has a penetrating action created by male and female parts - symbolic of *Agni's* daily miraculous birth. He is ever-young and immortal, because the fire is re-lit every day.

Vedic fire drill

The fire drill has a cruciform shape closely related to that of the Cross and the entire apparatus was called *sioastika*. As a character 卐 or 卍 is a geometrical figure and an ancient religious icon in the cultures of Eurasia, used as a symbol of divinity and spirituality in Indian religions (Clarke 1894). The arms of the cross are of equal length and perpendicular to the adjacent arms, each bent midway at a right angle (Pant *et al.* 2007: 231; Goblet d'Alviella 2000 [1894]) forming a swastika motif.

The spindle or *pramantha* had a cord with which the priest gave it an alternating rotary motion from right to left and from left to right. In rotating the spindle, one end of it rested in a depression made at the intersection-point of two crossed pieces of wood (Joly 1876). The father of the sacred fire was named Twastri, the divine carpenter who made the *sioastika* and the *pramantka* (Snodgrass 1992: 82-3), the mutual rubbing of which produced the divine babe Agni.

Boards

Drills use a board with sockets, usually lined up in a row, for the bit to drill into the surface of the board (see refs in Goren-Inbar *et al.* 2012). Grooving or notching of the board assists in gripping the drill bit and also creates guttering in order to allow the accumulation of sawdust (or clay) (Goren-Inbar *et al.* 2012: 5). Drilling enlarged the sockets; surface grooves were made to accommodate the tinder and an area around it, the fire pan, was hollowed out for tinder to catch the spark from the heated dust and complete the process of ignition (Goren-Inbar *et al.* 2012: 6).

Several fragments of stone blocks with notches made of limestone were found at Kfar Hahoresh and assigned to the Middle PPNB (*c.* 8800–6500 BC) (Goring-Morris 2005). These are regarded as 'fireboards' associated with the production of fire (Goren *et al.* 2012: 6). The authors speculate that the PPNB and PN rods from Shaar Hagolan were drilled on the cavities of limestone artifacts from PPNB Kfar HaHoresh (Goren-Inbar *et al.* 2012: figs 5 and 6). However most of the rods come from PN contexts suggesting that the systematic use of fire drills predates the PN finds at Sha'ar HaGolan. It is also possible that what have been described in the literature as game boards may have in fact been fire boards (see for example, Eirikh-Rose 2017; Simmons 2007: 158).

Using the analogy of the components of the drill used to create Agni, we may regard the father as the main phallic element and the mother the receptacle. The incisions marking a firepit on the limestone fragments, at Kfar Hahoresh (Goring-Morris 2005), though incomplete, seem to indicate an oval vulva shape, supporting a female role for the fire boards. Goren-Inbar *et al.* (2012: 7) claim that they lack the boards that were the counterpart of the fired-clay cylindrical artefacts in the PN, and rely on markings such as striations, to support the contention that extensive friction took place. As the 'receptacle' for the rods from PN Shaar Hagolan came from PPNB Kfar Hahoresh where no rods were found, what then was the female receptacle used in PN Shaar Hagolan?

I suggest that evidence for 'fire boards' *does* exist in the Pottery Neolithic Shaar Hagolan site. Drilled cavities of *c.*20 mm near or beneath the eyes appear on the so called 'pebble figurines' from this site and other Yarmukian sites (Garfinkel *et al.* 2010: 123–216, 132) suggest a drilling action on an article regarded as female. In Shaar Hagolan some 62% of these items bear signs of exposure to fire (N=35) (Garfinkel *et al.* 2010: 127), reinforcing the idea that male drilling action on the female artefacts caused a fire simulating the birth of the fire god Agni.

Assimilation of vulva and mouth cavities

Garfinkel *et al.* (2010: 130) regarded these drilled cavities as 'mouths'. They appear on some 40% of the total pebble figurines; these 'mouths' might be deep cylindrical holes or circular cuplike depressions The incised markings, straight and curved incisions on the stone blocks from Kfar Hahoresh, depict vulva imagery (Goren-Inbar *et al.* 2012 Fig.6: 2–3). Striations and hollowed areas on the PPNB fireboards may also have been made to accommodate pubic hair as tinder (see below).

The pebble figurines, regarded as female bearing drilled cavities supposedly formed by the friction of the male drill, match the expectation of the sexual symbolism inherent in the kindling of ritual fire. They also appear in the same PN sites as the clay rods.

Special clay and use of clay

A distinctive characteristic of the Pre-Pottery Neolithic B (PPNB, *c.*8500–6750 BC) is the increased use of clay (Biton 2010; Biton *et al.* 2014). An analysis of fragments of vessels

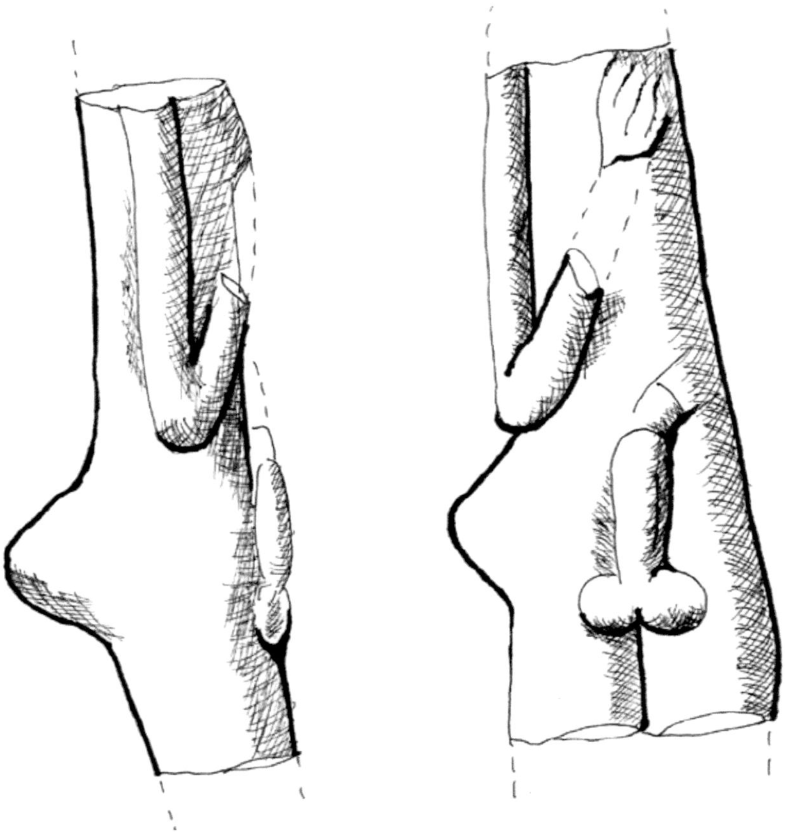

Figure 1. Male Cylindrical figure from Munhata (after Yizraeli-Noy 1999 No. 53).

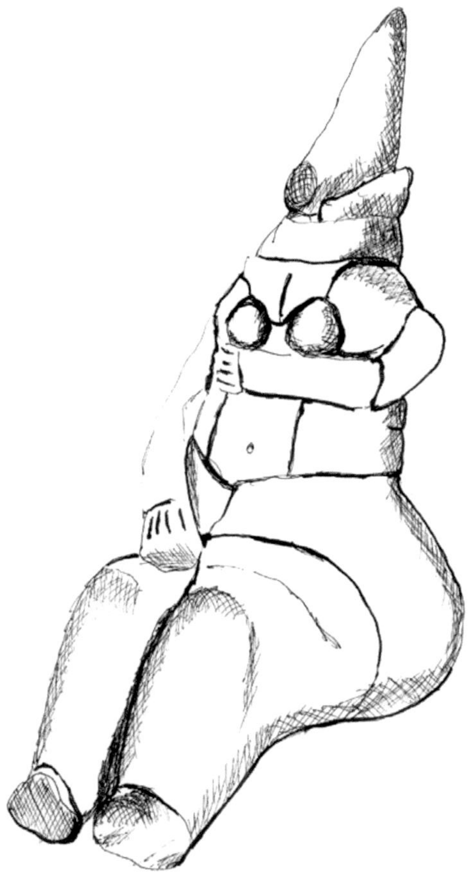

Figure 2. Reconstruction of large statue from Shaar Hagolan (after Garfinkel *et al.* 2010: 18).

from Kfar Hahoresh revealed that they were made of material unavailable on site, manufactured on a sporadic basis for limited purposes. Since ceramic rods were not part of the PPNB clay repertoire it seems that the technological innovation of clay used for rods belongs to the early Pottery Neolithic period, Yarmukian culture.

The PN rods from Munhata and Shaar Hagolan were made of select raw material; a dense, special light grey to white paste containing a high percentage of chalky matrix and well levigated. A similar clay was used for modeling male cylindrical figurines (Garfinkel 1995: 44). There were soot marks (1995: 20) on the buttocks of cylindrical male figs (Figure 1). A large human statue was made of such pure whitish clay (Figure 2, Garfinkel *et al.* 2010:18).

At Shaar Hagolan and at Munhata the clay differs greatly in both fabric and colour from the clay used for pottery. Thus, the cylindrical objects are characterised by their high-quality fine-grained clay (Freikman 2006). Assuming that the interpretation of rods as part of a fire drill is accepted, then we must ask why this, which is in fact an elaboration of the ritual, was adopted in place of the two wooden sticks method previously recorded as used to ignite Agni and why were clay implements used to kindle fire?

The use of clay in lighting the ritual fire does not appear in the Rig Veda, but a reference to clay associates it with death (Leeming 2005: 235). Goren-Inbar *et al.* (2012: 5) find support for a technological function for these items based on the frequency of the rods and their lack of artistic decoration. Nevertheless, I reject the automatic assumption that the lack of 'artistic decoration' is equated with a technological function. In fact, as we shall see below it was rather the use of the material, clay, and of a specific type of clay that lent these artefacts both a technological *and* symbolic function.

The selection of unusual clay at Shaar Hagolan (rods, statue and male cylindrical figurines) and Munhata (rods and male cylindrical figurines) and the use of a fire drill may provide the answer to why clay parts were integrated in the fire kindling implements and explain the linkage between the selection for fine clay for rods and figurines. The answer to this linkage lies in a myth.

Mythology

At the root of all the legends about the fire drill, the *pramantha*, is a primitive myth, the myth of the miraculous birth of the one universal fire stolen from the Sun or produced by the fire drill. The presence of the myth is further supported by the linkage between the selection of special clay for the fire drill bit and figurines in Munhata and Shaar Hagolan.

The Pottery Neolithic figurines made of the fine clay were well executed as opposed to the three very schematic anthropomorphic figurines 'pillar figurines' recovered from PPNB Kfar Ha Haresh (Biton 2010: Table 2.2), the site where the limestone 'boards' were found. Schmandt-Besserat (2013: 135) notes that the cuneiform accounts of magic rituals from the ancient Near East reveal that creation could be effected through the act of modelling clay. In some creation myths, several attempts were made to create a man. The first attempts were said to be without gender and incapable of reproducing. The figurines from KHH may represent such defective attempts, while perhaps the Yarmukian figurines represent the successful creations.

Fire drills and the creation of the first human are linked in the Greek myth of 'Prometheus' whose has been associated with pramantha. Prometheus is 'the fire-bringer', just as is the *pramantha* (Müller [1895-1910] 2001). In some traditions, Prometheus made the first man from clay. The 'creation of man from clay' is a miraculous birth theme that recurs throughout world religions and mythologies. Schmandt Besserat (2013: 135) confirms that, 'The ancient Near East cuneiform texts reveal that the act of modeling clay was associated with the ultimate power: the creation of life'. Although it is not stated, the dust containing the spark to light the tinder, may have been part of the clay used to form humans.

The linkage between the selection of special clay for the fire drill bit and figurines in Munhata and Shaar Hagolan seems to support the presence of this myth associated with the action of the ceramic rods. However, the creation myth of the first human being made of clay does not appear in Vedic texts.

Sexual symbolism

Goren-Inbar *et al.* (2012) note the symbolic connotations that the fire drill may have held, in particular, their representation of the male and female sex organs. The ritual surrounding the god Agni is most relevant to providing supporting evidence for the sexual symbolism surrounding the kindling of ritual fire (Staal 2001[1983]). In some Hindu symbolism, Agni's parents are said to be the two components of the fire drill used to start the fire, - the father the main phallic element and the mother the receptacle. His parents are the two *aranis*, or fire sticks, with his father represented by the upper stick and his mother by the lower. When rubbed together swiftly, these sticks create fire. It is sometimes said that Agni destroyed his parents when he was born because they could not care for him. Müller 2001 [1895-1910]: 305) notes that *pramantha* seems to be used in the concrete sense as the male organ.

In descriptions of the ritual, women's pubic hair is described as the tinder that lights the fire. For example, the sexual act of intercourse in the Vedic sacrifice of *yajna* is described as an offering by a man where the lower part of a woman is the (sacrificial) altar and her hairs the (sacrificial) grass (Radhakrishnan 1997: 321). Brahamanas also interpret the ritual in sexual terms (Faure 1998: 52) - her pubic hair the smoke. In Vedic sacrifice, the *Ashvamedha* (or Horse Sacrifice) often associated with Tantric practices, the woman is also equated with the earth.

Genital imagery in tools

Genital imagery is present in the assemblage of tools from the Neolithic period (Orrelle 2014: 83). For example, the oval transected shape is regarded both as a vulva (see for example, Stekelis 1972: Pl 56-58; Gimbutas 1991: 223; Marshack 1991: 297; Avner 2002: 69, Avner *et al.* 2019: 29, Orrelle *et al.* 2020) and shaft-straighteners or sharpener/whetstones (Wright 1992: 73; Dorrell 1983: 512; Yizraeli-Noy 1999; Gopher and Orrelle 1996). In this respect, shaft-straighteners are imbued with sexual metaphor as Mithen *et al.* 2005 suggested for pestles. Their shape is that of a vulva and acts as a tool when paired with a male hunting tool – an arrow. They are present from the Natufian period. The shapes and actions of this paired tool kit signal coitus.

Concluding remarks

While we cannot name the god created in this fire ritual, the linkage between clay, rods, male figurines, statues; sexual symbolism, creation myths, evidence of butter making and pebble figurines with drilled cavities seems to match the legends and textual descriptions of an early version of the Agni myth. Since 'phallic rods', 'female mother boards', spoon and domesticated cattle appear at the same site, an Agni fire kindling and sacrifice can be proposed.

Sexual symbolism is a constant strand in the ritual fire making; the fire is kindled by the friction of the male and female parts of the drill and the female boards, the bodily imagery of the female pubic hair as tinder. The use of clay in the male element of the drill links the phallic rods of the drill to the male figurines and the unique statue from Shaar Hagolan and the female stone recipient to the female pebble figurines. This ritual use of fire drill with a ceramic element seems to be an elaboration of the two-stick method of kindling and a change in ritual which related to the myth of the creation of humanity from clay that appeared in the Yarmukian period. It marks a possible Near Eastern deviation from the Indo-European cosmological and mythological principles which were to underpin ritual systems in Europe (Kaliff 2005: 79).

This complex of meanings surrounding the fire drill, supported by textual and archaeological evidence, includes a core creation myth attached to the symbolism of clay and gives new meaning to the Yarmukian period when the new pyrotechnology marks a departure from Vedic fire kindling with wooden sticks. In particular, it demonstrates the necessity of looking beyond the two options of match or phallus that Goren-Inbar *et al.* (2012) debate, and the need to investigate the cultural and archaeological background to present a fuller meaning for these items. If according to the myth, humans were created by gods and could be formed out of clay by man, it assumes that men had access to divine skills; a formidable advantage in the growth of hierarchical power in the Pre-Pottery Neolithic B and Yarmukian culture.

Finally, I would like to say that what a pleasure it has been to learn from Lionel. His skill and insight in looking beyond the bare archaeological facts and having the scholarship and knowledge to interpret them gives us the hope to be able to present a fuller, more rounded account of the past. In my work, I feel privileged to have been influenced by him.

References

Adams J. and M. Otte 1999. Did Indo-European languages spread before farming?. *Current Anthropology* 49: 73-77

Avner, U. 2002. Studies in the Material and Spiritual Culture of the Negev and Sinai Population during the 6th–3rd millennia BC. PhD. dissertation, The Hebrew University, Jerusalem.

Avner U., M. Shem-Tov, L. Enmar, G. Ragolski, R. Shem-Tov and O. Barzilai 2019. Neolithic Cult Sites in the Southern Negev, Israel, in: H. Goldfus, M. I. Gruber, S. Yona and P. Fabian (eds) *Isaac went out. . . to the field" (Genesis 24:63): Studies in the Archaeology and Ancient Cultures in Honor of Isaac Gilead.* BAR International Series. Oxford: Archaeopress

Barrelet, M.-Th. 1968. *Figurines et reliefs en terre cuite de la Mésopotamie antique, I: Potiers, termes de metier et proceeds de fabrication et production.* Paris: Institute Français d'Archéologie de Beyrouth.

Biton, R. 2010. The Clay Repertoire from Pre-Pottery Neolithic B Kfar HaHoresh: Not Just the Usual Bull. MA Thesis, The Hebrew University of Jerusalem Institute of Archaeology.

Biton R., Y. Goren and N. Goring-Morris 2014. Ceramics in the Levantine Pre-Pottery Neolithic B: Evidence from Kfar HaHoresh, Israel. *Journal of Archaeological Science* 41: 40-748

Clarke, D.R. 1894. *The Cross and its Symbolism.* Societas Rosicruciana in America.

Dorrell, P.G. 1983. Appendix A: Stone vessels, tools and objects, *Jericho V*, in K. Kenyon and T.A. Holland (eds) *Jericho V*: 485-576. London: British School of Archaeology in Jerusalem.

Eirikh-Rose, A. 2017. 9000-Year-Old Fire Starting 'Panel' Attests To advanced Technology In Prehistoric Israel, viewed March 2021, <https://www.biblicalarchaeology.org/daily/news/ancient-fire-making-israel/>.

Faure, B. 1998. *The Red Thread. Buddhist approaches to sexuality.* USA: Princeton University Press.

Freikman, M. 2006. The Assemblage of baked clay items of Sha'ar Hagolan: a Pottery Neolithic site in the Jordan Valley. MA dissertation, Jerusalem, The Hebrew University.

Garfinkel, Y. 1993 The Yarmukian Culture in Israel. *Paleorient* 19(1): 115–133

Garfinkel,Y. 1995 *Human and animal figurines of Munhata (Israel).* Paris: Association *Paleorient.*

Garfinkel Y., D. Ben-Shlomo and N. Korn 2010. *Sha'ar Hagolan Volume 3. Symbolic dimensions of the Yarmukian culture: Canonization in Neolithic Art.* Israel Exploration Society and the Sha'ar Hagolan Expedition.

Garfinkel, Y. and M.A. Miller 2002 *Sha'ar Hagolan Vol. 1. Neolithic art in context.* Oxford: Oxbow Books.

Gimbutas, M. 1991 *The Civilization of the Goddess: The World of Old Europe.* San Francisco: Harper Collins

Goblet d'Alviella, Count E. 2000 [1894] *Symbols Their Migration and Universality.* Mineola, NY: Dover Publications.

Gopher A. and E. Orrelle 1996. An alternative interpretation for the material imagery of the Yarmukian, a Neolithic culture of the sixth millennium BC in the Southern Levant. *Cambridge Archaeological Journal* 6 (2): 255-279

Gopher A. and E. Orrelle 1995 *The Groundstone Assemblages of Munhata a Neolithic Site in the Jordan Valley - Israel - A Report.* Les Cahiers des Missions Archéologiques Françaises en Israel 7. Paris: Association Paléorient: Paris

Gopher A. and R. Eyal 2012. The Pottery Assemblages at the Nahal Zehora Sites: A Summary, in A. Gopher (ed.), *Village Communities of the Pottery Neolithic Period in the Menashe Hills, Israel. Archaeological Investigations at the Sites of Nahal Zehora,* Vol.2: 697-744. Sonia and Marco Nadler Institute of Archaeology Tel Aviv University.

Goren-Inbar N., M. Freikman, Y. Garfinkel, N. Goring-Morris and L. Grosman 2012. The Earliest Matches, *PLoS ONE* 7 (8).

Goring-Morris, A.N. 2005. Kefar HaHoresh, in E. Stern (ed.), *The new encyclopedia of archaeological excavations in the Holy Land Jerusalem*, Israel: Exploration Society and Simon & Schuster.

Heggarty P. 2015. Ancient DNA and the Indo European Question *Diversity Linguistics Comment.* Language structures throughout the world. (blog post).

Holland, T.A. 1983. Miscellaneous small finds from Jericho, in K.M. Kenyon and T.A. Holland, *Excavations at Jericho V: The Pottery of the Tel and other finds*: 814-818. Oxford: The British School of Archaeology in Jerusalem.

Joly, N. 1876. The Early History of Fire *Popular Science Monthly* 10. Translated from the French by J. Fitzgerald.

Kaplan, J. 1958. Excavations at Teluliot Batashi, Nahal Soreq. *Eretz Israel* 5: 9–24.

Kaliff, A. 2005.The Vedic Agni and Scandinavian Fire Rituals A Possible Connection. *Current Swedish Archaeology,* 13: 77-97.

Leeming, D. 2005. *Oxford Companion to World Mythology*. Oxford: Oxford University Press.

Marshack, A. 1991 The female image: a time-factored symbol. A study in style and aspect of image use in the Upper Palaeolithic. *Proceedings of the Prehistoric Society* 57: 17-31.

Mithen S. J., B. Finlayson and R. Shaffrey 2005. Sexual symbolism in the Early Neolithic of the southern Levant: pestles and mortars from WF16. *Documenta Praehistorica* , 32: 103-110.

Müller, M. 2001 [1895-1910]. Vedic *Hymns Part 2 Hymns to Agni Mandalas 1-V The sacred books of the east,* Vol. 46. Richmond, Surrey: Curzon Press Ltd.

Orrelle, E. 2014. Material *Images of Humans from the Natufian to Pottery Neolithic Periods in the Levant.* BAR International Series 1832. Oxford: Archaeopress.

Orrelle E., U. Avner, L. Kolska Horwitz and M. Birkenfeld. 2020. Snakes of Stone: A Unique Stone Artefact from the LPPNB of Nahal Roded: 110. *Neo-Lithics* 20.

Pant, M. and F. Shūji 2007. Stupa and Swastika: Historical Urban Planning Principles in Nepal's Kathmandu Valley. Singapore: National University of Singapore Press .

Radhakrishnan, S. 1997. The *Principal Upanishads.* New Delhi: Harper Collins Publishers India.

Renfrew, C. 1990. Archaeology *and Language. The puzzle of lndo-European Origins.* Cambridge: Cambridge University Press

Schmandt-Besserat, D. 2013. The Human Clay Figurines and Ancient Near Eastern Magic, in D. Schmandt-Besserat (ed.), *Symbols at 'Ain Ghazal*: 113-166. Jordan: *'Ain Ghazal Excavation Reports.*

Simmons, A.H. 2007. *The Neolithic Revolution in the Near East: Transforming the Human Landscape.* Tucson: The University of Arizona Press.

Snodgrass, A. 1992. *The Symbolism of the Stupa.* Delhi: Motilal Banarsidass Publishers.

Staal, F. 2001 [1983]. *Agni, The Vedic Ritual of the Fire Altar 2.* Asian Humanities Press.

Stekelis, M. 1951 A new Neolithic industry: The Yarmukian of Palestine. *Israel Exploration Journal* 1: 1–19.

Stekelis, M. 1972. *The Yarmoukian Culture of the Neolithic period.* Jerusalem: Magnes Press.

Wright, K. 1992. *Ground Stone Assemblage Variations and Subsistence: Strategies in the Levant 22,000-5,500 B.P.* PhD thesis submitted to the Department of Anthropology, Yale University.

Wright, H.E Jr. 1993 Environmental Determinism in Near Eastern Prehistory. *Current Anthropology* 34: 458-69.

Yizraeli-Noy, T. 1999. *The Human Figure in Prehistoric Art in the Land of Israel.* Jerusalem: Israel Museum Publications.

Part III:

Theory

Human Beings in Cosmic Lifeworlds: Anthropology, Ecospheres and Cultural Cosmologies

Michael A. Rappenglück

The anthropology of archaic astronomy: Lionel Sims' approach

Lionel Sims (Figure 1), in his many contributions, has repeatedly emphasised the importance of anthropological questions and answers for cultural astronomy, particularly concerning prehistoric sites (see for example Stonehenge or the West Kennet Palisades in the Avebury Monument Complex, England). The prehistory of astronomy has been and is being researched from the perspective of contemporary sciences with their sophisticated, highly instrument-intensive methodology. Sims is concerned with the core of cultural astronomy which is informed by anthropology in various facets of its sub-disciplines.

Sims' great commitment to the consideration of the peculiarly human component as an essential feature of cultural astronomy is obvious. For him, the statistical methodology

Figure 1. Lionel Sims on the trip to Delphi (SEAC 2013 conference, Athens) and at Stonehenge (SEAC 2016 conference, Bath). Photos by Michael A. Rappenglück.

Solarizing the Moon (Archaeopress 2022): 157–181

of archaeoastronomy is of great value and indispensable. But he also makes clear that this scientific approach is not sufficient to explore the ideas of humankind's place in the world and the web of interactions between the world and humans, as conceived and lived by societies in prehistory and early history (Sims 2016). For him, the interdisciplinary and multidisciplinary methodology, in the sense of a pan-human project, offers the appropriate approach to the everlasting question of 'what is it to be human?' (Sims 2020a: 23–24). Thus, supported by a variety of modern methods he is also concerned with revisiting the old questions of the 19th/20th century philosophical anthropology about human nature and human's position in the cosmos, using the formulation of testable hypotheses to work out approaches to gain solutions. Always open to even unusual interpretations, he insists on comprehensible arguments that can be substantiated by scientifically collected and discussed facts (Sims 2002). Sims repeatedly expresses his concern, orally and in writing, about the future development of the subject of cultural astronomy (Sims 2010, 2016, 2020b). He emphasises the essential but often missing linkage of an acceleratingly growing corpus of empirically collected data with anthropological questions and interpretations (Sims 2016). In the historical roots and developmental trajectories of the discipline of cultural astronomy, with its use of vague terminology and narrowly defined theoretical foundations at times, he recognises major limitations to the possibilities for development and the acquisition of knowledge in this field (Sims 2016). Important to Sims is the approach of phenomenology, structuralism and mythology in interplay with archaeoastronomy and anthropology (see for example his analysis of the West Kennet Palisades in the Avebury Monument Complex in Sims

Figure 2. Lionel Sims on the trip to Nemea (SEAC 2013 conference, Athens) and lecturing at Stonehenge (SEAC 2016 conference, Bath). Photos by Michael A. Rappenglück.

2013 or his 'Decoding Cryptic "Astronomies"' in Sims 2021). In his view, immersing oneself in the magical thinking and actions of archaic cultures can also be a further approach for interpreting archaeoastronomical relics (Sims and Holbrook 2014).

A special pedagogical concern for Sims is that the practice of cultural astronomy including anthropology should feature in educational programmes, not only for students and experts but also for everyone. In this sense, he was, among other things, responsible as a longstanding Vice-President of the European Society of Astronomy in Culture (SEAC) and head of its Educational Committee (Sims 2017). In this pedagogical work for anthropology and cultural astronomy, Sims notes that the combination of scientific theory and practical fieldwork achieves the greatest success in understanding the issues (Sims 2020a: 28–29).

I remember many discussions with Lionel, fierce and profound in substance, often controversial yet always finding similarities, but in any case with joy, enthusiasm and humour. When he lectures, his enthusiasm and commitment to the cause are felt (Figure 2). Impulsively, he reaches forward into the ramifications of various trains of thought. He wants to approach the essence of humankind's relationship to the cosmos and in doing so also touches on the ultimate questions, about life and death (see for example, Sims 2006: 204, 2009, 2020c; Sims and Fisher 2020), which accompany us all and shape us as human beings. Taking up Sims' fundamental question about the relationship between anthropology and cultural astronomy, in terms of content, structure and methodology, one can formulate the concept of cultural cosmology by incorporating existing approaches and an interdisciplinary and transdisciplinary methodology, going beyond this (Rappenglück 2021). It is about how cultures position themselves with their image of humankind in cosmic lifeworlds.

Cultural astronomy / cultural cosmology: Range of topics and methodology

In its history, there have been repeated attempts to define the range of topics and methods in archaeoastronomy (see for example, Aveni 1986; Magli 2020: 101-124; McCluskey 2004; Pedersen 1982; Ruggles 1993a; Sinclair 2005). Other reviews provide information on the content and scientific standards of the subject (see for example, Gummerman and Warburton 2005; Magli 2020; Ruggles 1993b, 2005, 2011a, 2015). This dispute has been urgent for several decades and remains open today. Of particular importance has been the discussion and critique of the methods used (see for example, Aveni 2006; Bialas 1988, 1989; González García 2013; Rappenglück, B. 2013; Rappenglück 2013a, 2020a; Ruggles 2011a; Sims 2007, 2010, 2016; Sims and Holbrook 2014). A distinction has also been made between green and brown archaeoastronomy (Aveni 1989: 1). While the former is mainly concerned with alignments and uses statistical methods, the latter is more anthropological. How can one proceed in a methodologically sound and sufficiently precise way to conduct scientific research in this field and not always 'move in the same circles' (Ruggles 2011a)? Important work on cultural astronomy and on positioning archaeoastronomy as a research discipline has been published over the years by Stanislaw Iwaniszewski (see for example, Iwaniszewski 1995, 2003, 2010). The range of topics in archaeoastronomy/cultural astronomy around the globe with relation to all periods since the Palaeolithic has become very extensive (Rappenglück 2020a, 2021). Today, it is also increasingly evident that the subject matter is not exhausted by examining ancient understandings of astronomy alone but needs to be grasped more comprehensively with cosmological and cosmopractical models of human embeddedness in, and in relation to, the world (Rappenglück 2014a, 2014b, 2018a, 2018b, 2019a, 2020b; Ruggles 2015).

The way forward could be the field of *cultural cosmology* (Figure 3) as the study of cosmologies in cultures, exploring and reconstructing human perceptions of the cosmos and their interpretation related to humanity's position in the universe (Rappenglück 2020a; 2021). As such it essentially includes cosmologies, cosmogonies, and cosmopraxis (in architecture, chronology, orientation and navigation, ecology, economy, politics, sociology, religions and so on) of prehistoric, historic, and/or recent cultures. The term cosmopraxis is used in the context of studies on the cosmology of Andean peoples (Arnold 2018; De Munter 2016; De Munter and Note 2009; Tickner and Querejazu 2021) and has been used for the practice of divination in ancient Greek culture, too (Bartoletti 2019). While the term *cosmology* aims at the creation of a kind of 'map' of the world and the term *cosmogony* encompasses the world's

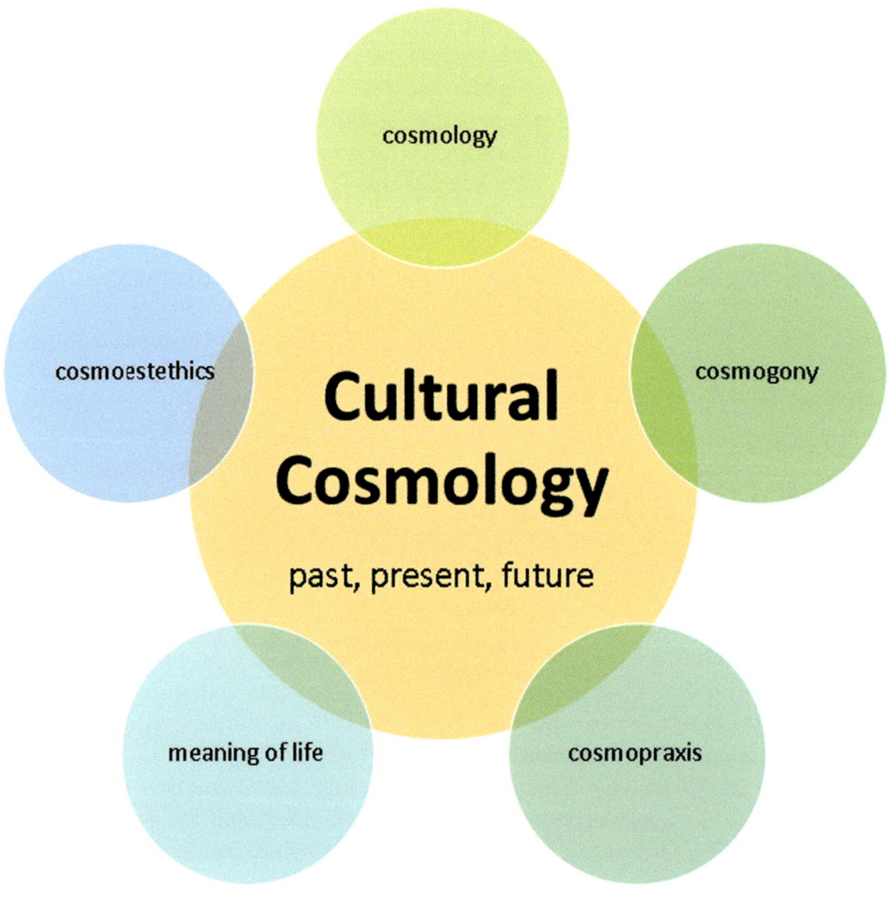

Figure 3. The *integral method*. Graphic: Michael A. Rappenglück

transformations, the term *cosmopraxis* describes how human beings interact with the world, experiencing it in doing, feeling and becoming. With the term *cosmopraxis*, for example, the arts, rituals, or spiritual experiences that relate to the cosmos can also be included in cultural cosmology. In a way, the terms reflect the dual human communicative structure: the content aspect and the relational aspect (Watzlawick *et al.* 2014).

A cultural cosmology aims to reconstruct archaic prehistoric and historical cosmologies as well as the analysis of various contemporary cosmological models in their relevance to anthropological questions. Depending on the object of research, the diversity of topics, questions and methods listed require the inclusion and combination of results of different fields like archaeology, astronomy, geosciences, biology, chronobiology, chronology, semiotics, cultural and social anthropology, ethnoscience, symbolism, mythology and religious studies. It is also necessary to deal with the world view of other and especially prehistoric cultures. This includes looking at ancient concepts, such as astrology, mantic and so on. Cultural cosmology is thus described in terms of its range of topics as well as its interdisciplinary and transdisciplinary methodology (Rappenglück 2020a, 2021). Concerning methodology, cultural cosmology is transdisciplinary at best, but in any case, must be interdisciplinary.

Some words about an 'Integral Methodology' as a scientific approach

The integral methodology to be applied is interdisciplinary and transdisciplinary (Figure 4). It is based on a systems theory model (Rousseau *et al.* 2018) and follows the principle of coherence (BonJour 1985; Rescher 1973; Thagard 2000) to increase the probability of a hypothesis or theory. In particular, the methodology follows the so-called hermeneutic spiral as a process of securing integrative understanding (Stegmüller 1986). The term hermeneutic

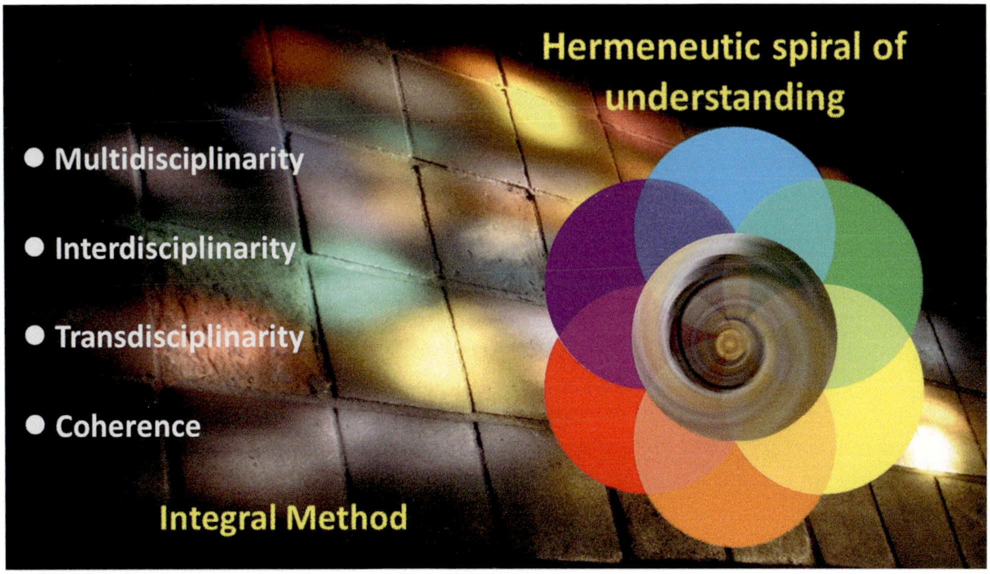

Figure 4. Simplified concept of *cultural cosmology*. Graphic: Michael A. Rappenglück.

spiral describes a double movement towards a progressive elucidation of the facts: previous knowledge, assumptions and what is already understood individually, are constantly brought into relation with the object of investigation and corrected. Based on the improvement, the process of understanding is continued.

The first ideas for an integral methodology have already been developed (Rappenglück 1999, 2013a) and implemented. It is not simply a matter of collecting results and methods from different sciences (multidisciplinarity), critically examining them and bringing them together or combining them (cross/interdisciplinarity), but of integrating them in a transdisciplinary way (Rousseau *et al.* 2018: 47–62). Important basic subjects are four-subfield anthropology (cultural anthropology, archaeology, biological anthropology and linguistic anthropology), religious studies, history (including the history of science and technology) and astronomy. There are also a large number of other natural sciences and humanities, which are added as needed. Since the worldviews of cultures that existed before the modern era or still survive today were characterised by a holistic and ecomorphic perception and interpretation of the world related to human life and the lifeworld, such a methodological and substantive approach may be more appropriate for reconstructing ancient cosmologies as well as an understanding of cosmopraxis that still exists today (Rappenglück 2009, 2013b, 2014b).

The first step of the integral methodology consists of a phenomenological approach (Van Manen 2016). One's own observation as a primary source of knowledge takes precedence over second-hand information (secondary sources) whenever possible. Already at this first step, it is necessary to be clear about the fact that there are different types of sensory perception and neuronal processing, which differ from person to person and even more so if one goes far back in time. The perception of space, time, body, living beings, environment and so on, shows differences and similarities in temporal development (see for example, Bogdanovic 2018; Ingold, 2011a; Rappenglück 1999, 2019a, 2020a). Possible variants would have to be discussed at this stage.

When using secondary sources, it should be ensured that they are reliable, following scientific standards. Research should be conducted using as many different senses and tools as possible: everything, whether overt or still hidden, can be of importance for later evaluation and interpretation, even if it is not understood now. In addition to a purely rational perspective, the value of one's own emotional experience can also be significant. The specific temporal distance to the cultural epoch being studied, concerning linguistic, historical, biological/psychological and other aspects, must be considered. That can be called the 'hermeneutic difference' (Gadamer 1972: 270-305). Attention should be paid to the recognition that the environment and the way of life can change significantly over time. In any case, even (quantitatively measured) 'facts' (González-García 2013: 50) do not meet the truth *per se*. They are based not only on the necessary disclosed assumptions (equipment, measurement procedures, circumstances during measurement, selection of starting positions and boundary positions, environmental conditions in the respective epoch and so on) but also on assumptions that are unknown or unconsciously hidden at the time of observation and measurement. Therefore, it is necessary to avoid preconceived ideas by careful phenomenological description, by defining classes of characteristics and by observing modes of perception. This requires refraining from pre-judging the data and instead adopting an open-minded approach, as well as a willingness to be receptive to the characteristics of the object.

One should also be aware of the psychology of perception (human sensory perception, information processing in the brain, fantasies, imaginations and so on). The various pitfalls of brain delusions as known from perceptual psychology need to be considered. Knowledge of the laws of Gestalt, perceptual psychology and cognitive psychology are helpful (Bollnow 2010; Galotti 2018; McBride and Cutting 2019; Wearden 2016). In research, the first difficulty to overcome is the diversity of human perception and cognition. It is always important to remember the properties of cognitive illusions, one's hidden preferences, biases and epistemological interest (Chabris and Simons 2011). It is the task of scholarship to bring these to the fore, to reflect on them and to discuss the presuppositions of the respective approaches, assumptions and types of personal preferences and prejudices. Thus, training is needed to recognise ambiguous illusions, separation of figure and ground as well as figure-ground inversions, fictions and problems of context. If a decoration could be read as figurative writing, the focus should be on iconographic syntactic, semantic and pragmatic consistency. Astronomers are familiar with different types of such cognitive illusions, for example, the perception of patterns in the arrangement of stars (asterisms/constellations), shapes or faces in the lunar disc or Martian canals. Depending on the context (semantic, pragmatic) of the respective cultures, a certain star pattern (syntax) is interpreted differently. Moreover, the people of the Upper Palaeolithic already intentionally used these cognitive illusions to illustrate several levels of meaning in single representations (Alpert 2008: 119–92). This increases the number of traps one can fall into. Finally, one needs to know about emotional bias - we have hidden likes and dislikes - as well as the ecological basis of our thinking (Gibson 2015; Hergovich 2018). Moreover, there is evidence that, at least during the Upper Palaeolithic, those who created the artwork had a certain spatiotemporal perception that was different from the average person today (Azéma *et al.* 2015; Rappenglück 1999: 115, 215-218). Hunter-gatherers of the Upper Palaeolithic were able to observe and depict the behaviours of animals (Rappenglück 1999, 2015a, 2015b), sometimes much better than in modern times. As hunters and gatherers, they had a sense for dynamic processes, which they illustrated in their artworks, such as by dissolving continuous movements into a superimposition of successive images (which can be reversed into a 'film'). Furthermore, three-dimensionality was experienced through movement, giving rise to the concept of hodological space (Bollnow 2010: 156–57; Lewin 1934; Rappenglück 1999: 218). These cognitive abilities of the peoples of the Upper Palaeolithic strongly influenced their perception of astronomical phenomena (Rappenglück 1999). Similarly, humans as a species, whether groups or individuals, may have possessed different weights of sensory perception and neural processing at other times.

In a second methodological step, a comprehensive detailed analysis and description of the method(s) used must be carried out for each research subject with the required accuracy. The following question words are helpful for this: what? where? when? who?. The phenomenological approach is accompanied by using a neutral description. Scepticism towards others and one's own conscious and unconscious subliminal interpretations, which in phenomenology are called 'epoché' in the sense of becoming aware and refraining from assumptions and prejudices, is necessary. Not only must the pitfalls of cognitive illusions (see above) be considered, but also prejudices and sweeping statements such as, scientific mainstreams that can be right or wrong, one's own and others' particular interests ('preferences', 'expectations', 'assessments'). Questions, hypotheses, definitions, terms, categorisations, experiments, instruments and methods should be sound and well defined.

The use of today's technical measuring instruments and computers tempts us to accuse ancient cultures of great deficiencies in their observations and results or, conversely, to attribute extreme abilities to them. To avoid both misconceptions, it is necessary to correlate the postulated abilities of these cultures with the archaeological and anthropological knowledge available according to the current state of knowledge. A kind of 'experimental archaeoastronomy' is also helpful here: how could one make which observations with which instruments?; what mistakes are made in the process?; what conclusions were possible for the 'experts' of the time?. The first steps to answer these questions, for example in relation to the Palaeolithic, already exist (Rappenglück 1999, 2019b). It is necessary to carry out appropriate experiments with replicas of objects which can be interpreted as measuring aids. Reference can also be made to instruments known in ethnoastronomy. In this way, replicas and the practical use of such simple measuring instruments give us the possibility of determining the handling and the errors of these aids.

In a third methodological step, references are made visible (relation): the relationship of the parts is important here. At this stage, a multidisciplinary and interdisciplinary methodology is very important. The current state of knowledge about the respective cultural environment (living environment and living practice) must be considered: four-field anthropology is helpful here. If the focus is on a unique research object or only a few cases and the statements made about them, then a rich and differentiated context is particularly important. It is necessary to address and describe the research object as precisely as possible, to localise and date it and to place it in the context of its former living environment. Individual and collective skills of different levels of detail and complexity can coexist in different places of the same epoch. Cultures, which are not based on our scientific, technical and industrial way of life, have perspectives and approaches to their world that are different from ours. However, amongst these different ways, they can achieve a considerable level of knowledge and skills that should not be considered subordinate to our cultural level. These cultures integrate different domains of meaning into their artefacts and their worldviews, making extensive use of symbolic, mythic and ritual forms of representation. It is necessary to consider the characteristics of the people of the respective epoch, their lifeworld and life practice, to develop the cultural framework in which astronomical knowledge may have been relevant. In which landscapes did people live and move? What was the prevailing climate? What were the flora and fauna like? What were the characteristics of the respective human species? What form of society and economic system existed? What skyscape was to be seen? These questions and others are important for astronomical reconstructions, for example, the visibility of celestial objects, orientation and time-reckoning abilities of cultures.

Qualitative and quantitative methods can and must be used together. An example of this is the combination of the semantic meaning of cosmological myths with a quantitative analysis by clustering (Thuillard *et al.* 2018). Another example would be the merging of personal and community experiences of observing celestial phenomena with their pictorial representation. However, care must be taken to ensure that quantitative or qualitative methods are used appropriately and not excessively one or the other. Consideration should be given to how the components and methods are intertwined (overlap, entanglement), whether complementary (complementarity, polarity), or contradictory (inconsistency, dichotomy). If sufficiently large and standardised data sets are available, statistical methods (univariate, bivariate, multivariate), can be used to gain knowledge. Statistical hypothesis testing and

Bayesian statistics are particularly important when a smaller amount of information and the degree of belief in an event form the basis. It is important to discuss the accuracy, errors and reliability of observations, categorisations, measurements, calculations, data processing, transmission and translation, sources and references. Error calculation helps determine the tolerance range of measured quantities and in scientific data verification. However, the over-extension of statistics as the mother of all methods is flawed. An example of this is provided by Sweatman and Tsikritsis (2017). Statistical methodology and cluster analysis are important and necessary (González-García 2013), but require a well-structured, well-defined, and comprehensive database and collection method. Moreover, the problems and paradoxes of statistics must be considered (Stegmüller 1973). If this is not done rigorously and seriously, errors and fallacies occur (Campell 1987; Gardenier and Resnik 2002), ending up with the danger of drawing wrong conclusions and passing them off as scientifically confirmed. In any case, the hypothesis developed from the data should be verifiable and testable. It should not be 'immunised' against testing. The same applies to theories. Despite the multidisciplinary and interdisciplinary methodology, care should be taken to ensure that the assumptions are reasonably frugal. However, the following also applies heuristically: do not perform unfounded mental acrobatics and do not follow the desire to 'smooth' when contradictions arise. Contradictions that are taken seriously are a source of deeper questions and lead to reconsidering naturally accepted answers again and again.

Finally, a fourth step leads to synopsis and integration using a transdisciplinary methodology based on general systems theory (Rousseau *et al.* 2018). This approach is based on an activity-knowledge-guidance model that shows the main elements of a system of different disciplines and their interactions with each other. The model is built up from a knowledge base (data, theories, methodologies) that enables the activity scope (exploration, development, application), which in turn affects the knowledge base. A guidance framework (domain view, worldviews, terminology) sets the conditions for the activity scope, which in turn can be modified by the latter. Finally, the knowledge base provides the raw material for the guidance framework, with the latter challenging the former (Rousseau *et al.* 2018, especially Fig. 2.1).

The interpretation of the data follows two further questions: why and how did people do this? This approach requires that the diversity of data and methods from the humanities and natural sciences be used in a complementary way, strictly considering the particularities and circumstances of each. It is necessary to relate research results to the meaning and function of astronomical objects, phenomena, and processes: astronomical objects, images, and concepts can be used as linguistic codes (such as cosmograms, symbols, myths, emblems, allegories, and so on) to convey other contents. Astronomy then serves as a tool for the actual purpose, which is on an ecological, economic, social, political, or spiritual level. This is exactly the approach that Lionel Sims follows in his life's work (see literature). For him, ancient astronomy is primarily located in the life world of ancient cultures. Therefore, answers to the question of why and for what purpose the observation of the sky and the sense of oriented buildings and other objects, must be approached not only astronomically but also with a reference to anthropology. The results can be classified as quasi-astronomical. Here, low quantitative accuracy is sufficient, with high demands on the qualitative model. If astronomical phenomena, processes and structures are in the foreground, a different picture emerges: for this purpose, observatories are built and measuring instruments and methods, exact time calculation and navigation techniques and exact cartography of the starry sky are developed. The results can be classified as exact-astronomical but are associated with various side issues. For the interpretation(s) it is essential to perceive, elaborate and relate several levels of meaning (synopsis). It is also necessary to know the phenomenon of equifinality: different processes can lead to similar phenomena or results. Contradictions, inconsistencies and circular conclusions of the respective interpretation(s) are to be disclosed, discussed, and, if possible, classified under a new approach.

Ecosystems, life conditions, Lifeworlds and anthropology

The human life of the individual and within communities takes place under spatial, temporal, material, energetic, biological, and communicative *living conditions* that are set and limited by the respective stages of evolution of the very late Earth system during the Pleistocene, Holocene and Anthropocene. Living conditions are differentiated in *ecosystems*. The term *ecosystem* refers to a natural structure that develops as an interacting system consisting of different living organisms (biocenoses, biotic factors) and the different parts of the environment (biotopes, abiotic factors and physiotopes) in which this system exists (Rappenglück 2014b: 237–41). Ecosystems that are influenced by humans include the complex relationships that humans have with nature as part of the kingdom of living things. The natural conditions of life are also extended by the specific anthropological characteristics and cultural frameworks during the unfolding of human evolution. The reconstruction of the respective living conditions is a prerequisite for research in cultural cosmology. A distinction must be made between the term 'living condition' and the term 'lifeworld' (Kraus 2015). Living conditions refer to material and immaterial, natural and cultural framework conditions for sustaining life (Kraus 2015: 4). Lifeworld includes the subjective view and construction of the 'world' based on living conditions (Kraus 2015: 4). After its first uses in the 19th century in the philosophy of life, especially with Wilhelm Diltheys' idea of *life nexus* (Dilthey 1991; Makkreel 1982), the concept of lifeworld has its roots in the phenomenological philosophy of Edmund Husserl (Husserl 2008; Husserl and Held 2007), supplemented by sociological, constructivist, epistemological and existential anthropological extensions in the works of Maurice Merleau-Ponty (Merleau-Ponty and Landes 2012), Alfred Schütz (Schütz and Luckmann 1974), Jan Patočka (2016), Jürgen Habermas (1989), Hans Blumenberg (Arnold 2020), Bernhard Waldenfels (2005), Klaus Held (2012), Michael Jackson (Jackson and Piette 2017), Björn Kraus (2015) and also in the writings of Otto Friedrich Bollnow (2010). The concept of the lifeworld is closely related to that of *weltanschauung* (worldview, cosmovision). Exploring different worldviews and systematising the terminology of worldviews can be helpful for cultural cosmology (Jones 1972; Kearney 1988; Schäfer 2004; Underhill 2009). The phenomenological approach together with hermeneutics, structuralism, semiotics, comparative mythology, anthropology (at least as the holistic four-field approach, including archaeology, biological and physical anthropology, cultural anthropology and linguistic anthropology), religious studies and ecology are essential to the subject of cultural cosmology. Quantifying and qualitative methods must be used on an equal footing. First approaches to integrative holistic research in this sense already exist (Henty *et al.* 2017; Henty and Brown 2020; Ingold 2011a, 2011b; Rappenglück 1999; Tymieniecka 2013). Different lifeworlds to a certain extent correspond to a plurality of ontologies, each representing perspectives of human communities/societies on their respective ecosystem; today also extended to the planet Earth and extended further to the cosmos (see, for example, Abramson and Holbraad 2014; Mackenzie *et al.* 2017; Viveiros de Castro 1998). However, there must be a core that forms the hermeneutic horizon of understanding. Without this common basis existing at one time, understanding is not possible. But what is incomprehensible at one time concerning the perceptual and thinking capacities of an individual or a culture may be comprehensible at another time.

Cultural cosmology encompasses the position of humans in the cosmos and to the cosmos. Humans and the world embody a fundamental polarity and complementarity (Webb 2012). Therefore, in addition to the respective ecosystems in which people live, the anthropological specifics of human existence (during evolution until today) must be considered. With the emergence and unfolding of human self-consciousness, based on the abilities of reasoning, language and counting, the dichotomy of the world into complementary subjective and objectifiable realities emerged and grew. As a result, the original instinctive integration into the ecosphere was reduced - world-openness (Gehlen and McMillan 1988) - and the genus Homo was released into a freer way of dealing with the world, which at the same time led to a progressive distancing from the natural world. Until today, cultures served to compensate for the dwindling embeddedness in the natural world by providing systems of order and orientation. Humans developed certain models for understanding the functionality of the ecosystems as well as the human position in them and the interaction with them (Douny 2014; Gonzales and Gonzalez 2010; Kohn 2013; Rappenglück 2009, 2013b, 2014a, 2014b, 2018a; Wilcock *et al.* 2013). These concepts manifest themselves as *cultural cosmologies*. Occasionally, the term *eco-cosmology* is also used for this subject (Doda Doffana 2019; Kumar Sarma 2011), but cultural cosmology seems more appropriate, since not only is the respective ecosystem connected to the respective cosmology, but also anthropology and the respective culture. Concerning ideas of this kind that are still alive today, the term *living astronomy* or *living geography* is also used (Haverkort and Hiemstra 1999). However, these designations (and similar ones) are not appropriate, since the ancient cosmologies claim a comprehensive interpretation of the world - according to the experience and knowledge of the respective society.

A characteristic of ancient lifeworlds is that people understand the ecosystem in which the culture exists as a connection of different entities that interact with each other. The spatiotemporal structure of the lifeworld is usually not experienced and culturally expressed as a continuous process, but as a set of events (Da Silva Sinha 2019; Ong 1969), forming a netlike force field, which establishes the living context (Magowan 1997). Entities, for example, rocks, objects, plants, animals and humans and also spiritual beings, can merge into each other (Athayde *et al.* 2016: 16). There is also often the view that this dynamic-living web of interaction is a cosmic living being (Rappenglück, 2018a). The soul-spiritual and the material cannot be separated from each other but are transformations of a single cosmic being of nature. Human existence is in ongoing and dynamic 'dialogue' with the essential structures and processes of the ecosystems in which humans live (Strang 2005).

Living beings (plants, animals) and the manifestations of inanimate matter could have the rank of persons (Comba 2014; Guenther 2015, 2020; Hill 2013). Between these beings and humans not only communication would be possible, but also a change of the first-person perspective. Perceptions and experiences of different entities could be accessible simultaneously, though they do not lose their individuality (Athayde *et al.* 2016; Willerslev 2004a, 2004b). This also justifies the respect for the autonomy of living beings and inanimate nature, which was also considered to be alive, and the respect of humans towards them (Athayde *et al.* 2016: 16). Related to this is also the idea of the interconnectedness of all beings and the lineage of ancestor beings in which the world unfolds (See for example, Awienagua 2017; Duli 2018; Janowski 2020;Rappenglück 2009, 2013b; Tamisari 1998; Treadwell 2017). Close-to-nature communities and societies recognise a living being in the world, permeated by spiritual forces and entities; a sacred landscape that also encompasses other spheres in the underworld and heaven (Jodry and Santoro 2017; Rappenglück 2007, 2020b; Singh 2009; Strang 2004).

Humankind and the World: cultural cosmologies

Today, certain ancient cosmologies are still present and play an important role in the everyday life of rural people. Increasingly, these ideas are being given attention and importance in development programmes. Archaic cultures and even today's human communities that still live close to nature have tried to synchronise human life with this fundamental ecosystem. In these views, the world is a spatiotemporal domain of interacting, 'bundled' forces, usually as individual and collective beings (Pauketat 2012).

Against the background of the special functionality of human self-consciousness and parallel to the progressive reduction of instincts, humans became gradually aware of being separated especially from the ordinary natural world. The anthropological concept of 'eccentric positionality' (Plessner 1975) describes very well the human feeling of no longer being in the middle, of being centred. Instead, the human being experiences his/herself in a special way taken out of the natural order. Humans try to transform wilderness (chaos) into culture (cosmos) and to replace the realm of the unknown with the well-known for grounding and stabilising their self-confidence and that of their culture. To do this, it is necessary to constantly integrate one's own habitat into existing ecosystems and to orientate oneself within them. It is therefore very understandable why ancient cultures around the world conceive of caves, sacred architecture, dwellings, such as a tent, a hut, a house, temples, funerary monuments, a village or a city, and finally even the entire landscape as spatiotemporal replicas of the cosmos, reflecting conceptions of cosmovisions in the human habitat (Rappenglück 2014b).

Since humans essentially need a renewed 'centring', cognitive and pragmatic models that are closely linked to the respective cosmologies have been developed over time. They have also served to answer people's fundamental questions about the structure of the world and the mysteries of life and death. The structure and the web of interactions of the respective ecosystems become well-ordered and habitable lifeworlds under the model of the associated cosmology. Wild nature is 'domesticated' by and for humans and provided with evaluations and meanings, with the semantics of complexes of 'meaning' by cultural cosmology. By literally domesticating their world through cosmology in the true sense of the word (Latin *domus*: house), humans establish systems that guide and orientate them, thereby transforming the anthropologically given eccentric positionality (Fischer 2000; Plessner 1975: 288–348) into centred life. The human body however actually embodies the centre and at the same time the starting point of all experience and knowledge. Bodily existence related to the embodiments (things), appearances and forces of the world is an essential component of any cultural cosmology whose claim is not to remain purely abstract. In the dimension of corporeality and moving bodies, individuals and cultures also experience dwellings and landscapes (Bollnow 2010; Lawrence 1990: 473; Merleau-Ponty and Landes 2012; Tamisari 1998). With the growing depth of time and space, however, this kind of understanding will only be medially communicable to a very limited extent today as related to the Earth system, interplanetary, galactic, or cosmic systems. Up to now, only a few astronauts in Earth's orbit and on the Moon have been able to experience near space in the flesh. Since the bodily centre with the first-person perspective usually defines a topocentric system of cosmology (Holenstein 1972), it is clear that for any cultural cosmology, places and events are more essential than abstractions such as spaces and times (Tamisari 1998: 250). This remains valid for future planetary abodes. Ancient cosmologies, however, often contain the idea (experience?) that a change of the first-person perspective is possible through entanglement with other entities, for example, animals (Hamel 2020; Leder 2012; Mazard 2016; Praet 2009; Saniotis 2019).

One of the fundamental conditions of human existence is to set up living spaces - to dwell - or to have special (spiritual) experiences of being in extraordinary places (Rappenglück 2014b). The structure, arrangement and weighting of living spaces, their classification and embedding in the fundamental orders of space and time are activities that have occupied people since the Palaeolithic. The human activities for this are expressed symbolically, mythically and ritually in objects, buildings and landscapes in a sensual-symbolic way. In them, the perception of orders in space and time as well as dealing with them (feeling, reflection) is addressed. The expansion and transformation of the 'normal' world of life at the 'interfaces' - birth, death, otherworldly existence, ecstasy - to other sensed areas of experience, connected with the existential human questions about the why and wherefore of the world and the position of human beings in it, are also addressed. Ancient cosmologies (including cosmogonies) can be understood as holistic, multi-layered models of evolving human ecosystems, which in symbolic-mythical-ritual expression help to make the world worth living in, but also help to transcend it spiritually. They are also used to derive systems of social, political and religious differentiation as well as order, especially hierarchy. They serve to authorise and legitimise power structures. The gaining and maintaining of power are achieved through control of space and time (cosmic forces), which are secured through astronomical knowledge and measurement procedures. Cosmologies and forms of rule correlate: monocentric worldviews, for example, geocentric or heliocentric, go together with monarchical forms of government (Malecka 1999, Pankenier 1995; Rappenglück 2016; a good example is Louis XIV [1638-1715], the Sun King), while polycentric worldviews can present concepts or real democratic forms of domination. The latter connection is documented from Graeco-Roman times to the present (Coates 2018; Patomäki 2010; Tatlow 2018).

For archaic and ancient cultures, the lifeworld was spatiotemporally organised. It formed a chronotopos, a term that was first applied to biology and then to literary studies in connection with the topic of general relativity, but which excellently reflects the view of archaic and ancient cultures (Bakhtin *et al.* 1982; Frank 2015; Günzel 2010: 294-304). The cosmological model located the human being in the (life) world. It also provided a 'housing' in which humans could move and develop according to their given abilities: localisation, orientation and navigation (Rappenglück 2014a, 2014b, 2018b, 2019a, 2020a). With the temporal component, the model also offered incorporation into processes of transformation, development, and synchronisation. Time calculations and later constructed calendar systems helped to align celestial processes with earthly processes (maritime, biological, meteorological, and social-economic rhythms), which had already been observed very closely since the Palaeolithic (Rappenglück 2015a, 2015b). The aim was to grasp the interaction, conflict and competition of forces and powers in the world and to derive rules from this as to when and how action should be taken: the 'right moment' was aimed at optimising effects. Heaven with its phenomena and processes also determined times of the sacred (sacred times) and every day (profane times), of rest and action (vita contemplativa / vita activa). In addition to the intention of understanding and influencing the present spatial-temporal network of effects, people also wanted to interpret future events from the processes in the heavens and the processes in the cosmos (mantic/divination; astrology) to determine directions for action (Becker 1981; Campion 2012; Hogrebe 2005; Maul 2013).

Archaic and ancient cultural cosmologies worldwide and through all epochs were based on the view and awareness of the principle of correspondences: the cosmic spheres - the upper world (heaven), the middle world (earth) and the lower world (underworld) - mirrored each other in their structures and processes. Cosmic phenomena, processes and objects became 'earthbound' and tangible: in the landscape, in architectural monuments, on objects, clothing, in the fine arts, in games, in religious, social, political symbols, myths and rituals, partly up to the present day (Rappenglück 2013b, 2016, 2018b). The cosmological models used astronomical language and concepts (*'the astronomical code'*) to make human life (individual and society) understandable in the given ecosphere. They also served to make the embeddings, the references and the transitions in and to a spiritual-transcendental background comprehensible. This cosmological framework and the references to it served to keep human life in as good a harmony as possible with the processes of nature and the principles revealed in them, so that people could maintain and develop through the spatiotemporal change (Geertz 2003; Girardot *et al.* 2001; Melo and Saito 2013). Since at least the Upper/Middle Palaeolithic time, this action results in cosmological holistic models that enable integration, orientation and estimation, shared by members of certain social groups, within changing ecospheres.

Conclusion

The archaic and ancient views of the lifeworld were essentially based on the unity of the network of forces in the world with which these societies felt connected. Heaven was important, but it was only one aspect of their respective world, which contained at least Earth and the underworld or was divided into many different cosmic spheres in between. The view of the cosmos was interrelated with the way people existed in the associated lifeworlds and ecosystems. Their cosmologies were *ecomorphic*, modelled on their lifeworlds. It is, therefore, more appropriate to refer to the discipline which studies them not as archaeoastronomy or cultural astronomy, but as cultural cosmology, as a generic term for various sub-disciplines. From the discussions on content and methodology, the scope and methodology of such a research field can be determined as taking up previous approaches from archaeoastronomy to cultural astronomy and integrating them with a transdisciplinary methodology. In his studies, Lionel Sims has charted this path. Cultural cosmology deals with the self-understanding of a culture in its world (cosmos). This definition also makes it possible to include the ongoing cosmic change of perspective that began in the modern era (15th/16th century) - geocentrism, heliocentrism, galactocentrism ... multiverse, or from the singularity of the position of the Earth and humankind in the cosmos to the plurality of worlds (Figure 5). The tremendous global technical, scientific and economic development of modern times and modernity led to a growing alienation of humanity from the life processes of planet Earth. This also created numerous problems that threaten the diversity of life and thus humanity in the long term. The rapid development of the earth system sciences (Butz 2004; Jacobson 2011) however, together with the growing need for solutions to global problems, interestingly lead back to

Figure 5. An illustration of the location of Earth in the Universe. It consists of a series of nine frames that show annotations with the names of astronomical objects (in white) and their distance from Earth (in purple). The blue text indicates the object found in the previous frame. Some items have no distance attached while others are rough approximations or averages due to variances in research findings. Many of the objects and visible distances are inaccurate as they have been increased substantially for illustration purposes. The purple text indicates the real astronomical distances in several units: kilometres, light years, kilo light-year, and mega light-years. Credit: Andrew Z. Colvin, CC BY-SA 4.0.

Figure 6. The future of *Cultural Cosmology*. Buzz Aldrin on the moon, July 21, 1969. Credit NASA, Project Apollo Archive - AS11-40-5903; A Martians view: Bright 'Evening Star' seen from Mars is Earth, sol 529 (Jan. 31, 2014). Credit: PIA17935 (zoomed in) and PIA17936, NASA/JPL-Caltech/MSSS/TAMU); PIA21260: Earth and its Moon, as seen from Mars, November 20, 2016, Credit: PIA21260, NASA/JPL-Caltech/Univ. of Arizona; The day the Earth smiled: sneak preview - Earth and its Moon seen from Saturn by space probe Cassini, July 19, 2013. Credit: PIA17171, NASA/JPL-Caltech/Space Science Institute; Distant Galaxy GN-z11 in GOODS North Survey, Redshift 11.1, as seen 13.4 billion years in the past, 11 February 2015 and 3 April 2015, by HST, ACS/WFC WFC3/IR. Credit: STScI-PRC16-07a, NASA, ESA, P. Oesch (Yale University), G. Brammer (STScI), P. van Dokkum (Yale University), and G. Illingworth (University of California, Santa Cruz).

the connection of the different earth spheres, the interacting network of life forms, and a communicative world sphere. But contrary to most of the ancient worldviews, the cosmos is now gigantically expanded in space and time. This makes a future cultural cosmology difficult, but not hopeless. At the same time, however, modern techniques make it possible to translate distant spaces and times, other worlds and realities into perception and, within limits, a kind of experience.

With the moon flight of Apollo 8, the first colour image of the Earth rising above the Moon (Earthrise) was taken on 24.12.1968 by William Anders (Photo ID: NASA: AS8-14-2383). This image, the later (since Apollo 17, 1972) 'Blue Marble' photographs of the Earth, as well as the images taken from great distances by space probes (Voyager 1, 6 billion km away, 14.2.1990; Cassini-Huygens, 1.45 billion km away, 19.7.2013), referred to as 'Pale Blue Dot', are meant to promote a 'planetary' consciousness (Figure 6). With a focus on the 'blue planet' as the only ecosphere and home of humankind to date, the advance of space travel into interplanetary space and the simultaneous extreme widening of the view into the diversity of the structures of the cosmos, the theme of a cultural cosmology is formed anew (Biemann 2015). The core question is how humans, earth, and cosmos relate to each other

References

Abramson, A. and M. Holbraad (eds) 2014. *Framing Cosmologies: The Anthropology of Worlds.* Manchester: Manchester University Press.

Alpert, B.O. 2008. *The Creative Ice Age Brain: Cave Art in the Light of Neuroscience.* New York: Foundation 20, 21.

Arnold, F. 2020. *Die Architektur der Lebenswelt: Entwürfe nach der philosophischen Anthropologie Hans Blumenbergs.* Originalausgabe. Klostermann Rote Reihe 128. Frankfurt am Main: Vittorio Klostermann GmbH.

Arnold, D.Y. 2018. The Andean material world, in L.J. Seligman and K.S. Fine-Dare(eds)*The Andean World*: 143-160. Milton: Routledge.

Athayde, S., J. Richard Stepp and W.C. Ballester 2016. Engaging Indigenous and Academic Knowledge on Bees in the Amazon: Implications for Environmental Management and Transdisciplinary Research. *Journal of ethnobiology and ethnomedicine* 12 (26): 1–19. https://doi.org/10.1186/s13002-016-0093-z

Aveni, A.F. 1986. Archaeoastronomy: Past, Present, and Future. *Sky and Telescope* 72: 456–460.

Aveni, A.F. 1989. Whither archaeoastronomy?, in A.F. Aveni (ed) *World Archaeoastronomy*: 3-12. Cambridge University Press, Cambridge.

Aveni, A. F. 2006. Evidence and Intentionality: On Evidence in Archaeoastronomy, in T.W. Bostwick and B. Bates (eds) *Viewing the Sky Through Past and Present Cultures: Selected Papers from the Oxford VII International Conference on Archaeoastronomy*: 57–70. Phoenix Arizona: Pueblo Grande Museum Anthropological Papers n° 15.

Awienagua, G. J. 2017. Appropriating Land, Worldviews, and Spiritual Navigation: The Dynamics and Praxis of Everyday Life in the Alavanyo-Nkonya Land Dispute in Ghana. *Anthropos* 112 (2): 583–96.

Azéma, M., J. Clottes and B.Tavernier 2015. *La prehistoire du cinema: Origines paleolithiques de la narration graphique et du cinematographe.* Paris: Edition Errance.

Bakhtin *et al.* 1982. The dialogic imagination. Four essays. University of Texas Press Slavic series. Austin: University of Texas Press.

Bartoletti, T. 2019 Greek divination from an Amerindian perspective. *HAU: Journal of Ethnographic Theory* 9 (2): 334–358.

Bialas, V. 1988. *Astronomie und Glaubensvorstellungen in der Megalithkultur: Zur Kritik der Archäoastronomie.* Treatise 166, Munich.

Bialas, V. 1989. Archäoastronomie - Eine kritische Auseinandersetzung mit Gegenstand und Methoden. *Der Vermessungsingenieur* (3): 77–80.

Becker, U. 1981. *Lexikon der Astrologie. Astrologie, Astronomie, Kosmologie.* Basel, Wien: Herder.

Biemann, U. 2015. The Cosmo-Political Forest: A Theoretical and Aesthetic Discussion of the Video Forest Law. *GeoHumanities* 1 (1): 157–70.

Bogdanovic, J. 2018. Perceptions of the Body and Sacred Space in Late Antiquity and Byzantium. Milton: Taylor and Francis.

Bollnow O.F. 2010. Mensch und Raum. Stuttgart: Verlag. W. Kohlhammer.

BonJour, L. 1985. *The Structure of Empirical Knowledge.* Cambridge, Mass: Harvard Univ. Press.

Butz, S.D. 2004. *Science of Earth Systems.* Australia, Clifton Park, NY: Delmar Learning.

Campell, T. 1987. 19 · Portolan Charts from the Late Thirteenth Century to 1500, in J.B. Harley and D. Woodward *The History of Cartography: Volume One: Cartography in Prehistoric, Ancient, and Medieval Europe and the Mediterranean.* Vol. 1: 371–463 Chicago: The University of Chicago Press.

Campion, N. 2012. *Astrology and cosmology in the world's religions.* New York: New York University Press.

Chabris, C. F., and D. Simons 2011. *The Invisible Gorilla and Other Ways Our Intuition Deceives Us.* Paperback ed. London: Harper.

Coates, C. F. 2018. Cosmic Democracy or Cosmic Monarchy? Empedocles in Plato's Statesman. *Polis: The Journal for Ancient Greek Political Thought* 35: 418-446.

Comba, E. 2014. Amerindian Cosmologies and European Prehistoric Cave Art: Reasons for and Usefulness of a Comparison. *Arts* 3 (1): 1–14.

De Munter, K. 2016. Ontología relacional y cosmopraxis, desde los Andes. Visitar y conmemorar entre familias Aymara. Relational ontology and cosmopraxis, seen from the Andes. Visiting and Commemorating among the Aymara families. *Chungará (Arica)* 48 (4): 629-644.

De Munter K. and N. Note 2009 Cosmopraxis and Contextualising Among the Contemporary Aymara, in N. Note, R. Fornet-Betancourt R, J. Estermann and D Aerts, *Worldviews and Cultures. Einstein Meets Magritte: An Interdisciplinary Reflection on Science, Nature, Art, Human Action and Society*, vol. 10: 87-102. Dordrecht: Springer.

Dilthey, W. 1991. *Introduction to the Human Sciences,* in R. A. Makkreel and F.Rodi (eds) *Selected writings*, Princeton, N.J. Princeton University Press.

Doda Doffana, Z. 2019. Sacred Sites and Ancestor Veneration in Sidama, Southwest Ethiopia: A Socio-Ecological Perspective. *Cogent Social Sciences* 5 (1): 1704600.

Douny, L. 2014. *Living in a Landscape of Scarcity: Materiality and Cosmology in West Africa. The Institute of Archaeology, University College London* vol.63. Walnut Creek: Left Coast Press.

Duli, A. 2018. Reflections on the Social and Cultural Aspects of the Megalithic Site of Onto, Bantaeng, South Sulawesi, in S. O'Connor, D. Bulbeck, and J. Meyer, *The Archaeology of Sulawesi: Current Research on the Pleistocene to the Historic Period*: 313–26. Acton: ANU Press.

Fischer, J. 2000. Exzentrische Positionalität. *Deutsche Zeitschrift für Philosophie* 48 (2): 265–88.

Frank, M.C. 2015. Chronotopoi, in J. Dünne and A. Mahler, *Handbuch Literatur Raum*: 160-169. Berlin and Boston: De Gruyter.

Gadamer, H.G. 1972. *Hermeneutik I. Wahrheit und Methode. Grundzüge einer philosophischen Hermeneutik.* Tübingen: J. C. B. Mohr (Paul Siebeck).

Galotti, K.M. 2018. *Cognitive Psychology in and Out of the Laboratory.* Los Angeles, London, New Delhi, Singapore, Washington DC, Melbourne: SAGE.

Gardenier, J. S. and D.B. Resnik 2002. The Misuse of Statistics: Concepts, Tools, and a Research Agenda. *Accountability in Research* 9 (2): 65–74.

Geertz, A.W. 2003. Ethnohermeneutics and Worldview Analysis in the Study of Hopi Indian Religion. *Numen* 50: 309–48.

Gehlen, A. and C. McMillan 1988. *Man, His Nature and Place in the World.* New York: Columbia University Press.

Gibson, J. J. 2015. *The Ecological Approach to Visual Perception.* New York, London: Psychology Press.

Girardot, N.J., J. Miller, and X. Liu (eds) 2001. *Daoism and Ecology: Ways Within a Cosmic Landscape.* Cambridge, Mass. Harvard University Press.

Gonzales, T. and M.Gonzalez 2010. From Colonial Encounter to Decolonizing Encounters. Culture and Nature Seen from the Andean Cosmovision of Ever: The Nurturance of Life as a Whole, in S. Pilgrim and J. Pretty (eds) *Nature and Culture: Rebuilding Lost Connections*: 1–20. Oxford: Routledge.

González-García, A.C. 2013. Profiting from Models of Astronomical Alignments to Unveil Ancient Cosmologies in Europe and the Mediterranean, in I. Šprajc and Peter Pehani (eds)

Ancient Cosmologies and Modern Prophets: Proceedings of the 20th Conference of the European Society for Astronomy in Culture: 49-66. Ljubljana: Slovene Anthropological Society.

Guenther, M.G. 2015. Therefore Their Parts Resemble Humans, for They Feel That They Are People. *Hunter-Gatherer Research* 1 (3): 277–315. https://doi.org/10.3828/hgr.2015.16.

Guenther, M.G. 2020. *Human-Animal Relationships in San and Hunter-Gatherer Cosmology.* Cham: Palgrave Macmillan.

Gummerman, G. J. and M. Warburton. 2005. The Universe in Cultural Context: An Essay, in J.W. Fountain and R.M. Sinclair (eds), *Current Studies in Archaeoastronomy: Conversations Across Time and Space: Selected Papers from the Fifth Oxford International Conference at Santa Fe, 1996.* Durham, N.C.: Carolina Academic Press.

Günzel, S. 2010. *Raum: Ein interdisziplinäres Handbuch.* J. B. Metzeler/Springer-Verlag: Berlin Heidelberg.

Habermas, J. 1989. *The Theory of Communicative Action Vol. 2. Lifeworld and System: A Critique of Functionalist Reason.* Boston: Beacon.

Hamel, F. 2020. *Human Animals.* Kiel: Alpha Editions. Reprint.

Haverkort, B. and W. Hiemstra (eds) 1999. *Food for Thought: Ancient Visions and New Experiments of Rural* People. ETC/COMPAS in association with Books for Change and Zed Books.

Held, K. 2012. *Phänomenologie der natürlichen Lebenswelt.* New studies in phenomenology 9. Frankfurt am Main: Lang.

Henty, L., B. Brady, D. Gunzburg, F. Prendergast and F. Silva (eds) 2017. *The Marriage of Astronomy and Culture: Theory and Method in the Study of Cultural Astronomy, Culture and Cosmos 21: 1 and 2.* Bristol: Culture and Cosmos and Sophia Centre Press.

Henty, L. and D. Brown (eds) 2020. *Visualising Skyscapes: Material Forms of Cultural Engagement with the Heavens.* London and New York: Routledge. https://doi.org/10.4324/9780203730935.

Hergovich, A. 2018. *Allgemeine Psychologie: Wahrnehmung und Emotion.* 2., aktualisierte und überarbeitete Auflage. Wien: Facultas.

Hill, E. 2013. Archaeology and Animal Persons: Toward a Prehistory of Human-Animal Relations. *Environment and Society* 4: 117–36.

Hogrebe, A. 2005. *Profile prognostischen Wissens in Wissenschaft und Kultur.* Würzburg: Königshausen & Neumann.

Holenstein, E. 1972. Der Nullpunkt Der Orientierung: Eine Auseinandersetzung Mit Der Herkömmlichen Phänomenologischen These Der Egozentrischen Raumwahrnehmung. *Tijdschrift voor Filosofie* 34 (1): 28–78.

Husserl, E. 2008. *Die Lebenswelt: Auslegungen der vorgegebenen Welt und ihrer Konstitution; Texte aus dem Nachlass (1916 - 1937).* Edited by Rochus Sowa. Dordrecht: Kluwer.

Husserl, E. and K. Held (eds) 2007. *Phänomenologie der Lebenswelt.* Universal-Bibliothek 8085. Stuttgart: Reclam.

Ingold, T. 2011a. *The Perception of the Environment: Essays on Livelihood, Dwelling, and Skill.* London: Routledge.

Ingold, T. 2011b. *Being Alive: Essays on Movement, Knowledge, and Description.* London: Routledge.

Iwaniszewski, S. 1995. Archaeoastronomy and Cultural Astronomy: Methodological Issues, in Accademia Nazionale Dei Lincei (ed.) *Archeologia E Astronomia: Esperienze E Prospettive Future: Atti Dei Convegni Lincei No. 121*: 17–26. Roma: Accademia Nazionale dei Lincei.

Iwaniszewski, S. 2003. The Erratic Ways of Studying Astronomy in Culture, in M. Blomberg (ed.) *Calendars, Symbols, and Orientations: Legacies of Astronomy in Culture: Proceedings of the 9th Annual Meeting of the European Society for Astronomy in Culture (SEAC): The Old Observatory, Stockholm, 27-30 August 2001*: 27–30. Uppsala: Uppsala University.

Iwaniszewski, S. 2010. Ancient Cosmologies Understanding Ancient Skywatchers and Their Worldviews. *Journal of Cosmology* 9: 2121–29.

Jackson, M. and A. Piette (eds) 2017. *What Is Existential Anthropology?* New York and Oxford: Berghahn.

Jacobson, M.C. (ed.) 2011. *Earth System Science: From Biogeochemical Cycles to Global Change.* San Diego: Academic Press.

Janowski, M. 2020. Stones Alive! *Bijdragen tot de Taal, Land en Volkenkunde* 176 (1): 105–146.

Jodry, M.A. and C.M. Santoro 2017. Walking Closer to the Sky: High-Altitude Landscapes and the Peopling of the New World. *Quaternary International* 461: 102–107. https://doi.org/10.1016/j.quaint.2017.10.007.

Jones, W.T. 1972. World Views: Their Nature and Their Function. *Current Anthropology* 13 (1): 79–109. https://doi.org/10.1086/201252.

Kearney, M. 1988. *World View.* Novato: Chandler & Sharp Publishers, Inc.

Kohn, E. 2013. *How Forests Think: Toward an Anthropology Beyond the Human.* Berkeley: University of California Press. https://doi.org/10.1525/j.ctt7zw36z.

Kraus, B. 2015. The Life We Live and the Life We Experience: Introducing the Epistemological Difference Between "Lifeworld" (Lebenswelt) and "Life Conditions" (Lebenslage). *Social Work and Society. International Online Journal* 13 (2).

Kumar Sarma, U. 2011. Eco-Cosmologies and Biodiversity Conservation: Continuity and Change Among the Karbis of Assam. *The International Indigenous Policy Journal* 10 (4: Art. 10): 1–10.

Lawrence, D.L. 1990. The Built Environment and Spatial Form. *Annual Review of Anthropology* 19: 453–505.

Leder, D. 2012. Embodying Otherness. *Environmental Philosophy* 9 (2): 123–142.

Lewin, K. 1934. Der Richtungsbegriff in der Psychologie. Der spezielle und der hodologische Raum. *Psychologische Forschung* 19: 249–251.

Mackenzie, K., W. Siabato, F. Reitsma, and C. Claramunt 2017. Spatio-Temporal Visualisation and Data Exploration of Traditional Ecological Knowledge/Indigenous Knowledge. *Conservation & Society* 15 (1): 41–58.

Magli, G. 2020. *Archaeoastronomy: Introduction to the Science of Stars and Stones.* Cham, Heidelberg, New York, Dordrecht, London: Springer.

Magowan, F. 1997. Waves of Knowing: Polymorphism and Co-Substantive Essences in Yolngu Sea Cosmology. *Australian Journal of Indigenous Education* 29 (1): 22-35.

Makkreel, R. A. 1982. "Husserl, Dilthey and the Relation of the Life-World to History." *Research in Phenomenology* 12: 39–58.

Malecka, A. 1999. Solar Symbolism of the Mughal Thrones A Preliminary Note. Arts Asiatiques 54: 24–32.

Maul, S.M. 2013. *Die Wahrsagekunst im Alten Orient. Zeichen des Himmels und der Erde.* München: C.H. Beck.

Mazard, M. 2016. The Algebra of Souls: Ontological Multiplicity and the Transformation of Animism in Southwest China. *Social Analysis: The International Journal of Anthropology* 60 (1): 18–36.

McBride, D M. and J.C. Cutting, 2019. *Cognitive Psychology: Theory, Process, and Methodology.* Thousand Oaks, California: SAGE Publications, Inc.

McCluskey, S. C. 2004. The Study of Astronomies in Cultures as Reflected in Dissertations and Theses. *Archaeoastronomy: The Journal of Astronomy in Culture* 16: 20–25.

Melo, M. M. de and C.H. Saito 2013. The Practice of Burning Savannas for Hunting by the Xavante Indians Based on the Stars and Constellations. *Society & Natural Resources* 26 (4): 478–487. https://doi.org/10.1080/08941920.2012.713087.

Merleau-Ponty, M. and D.A. Landes 2012. *Phenomenology of Perception.* Abingdon England, New York: Routledge.

Ong, W. J. 1969. World as View and World as Event. *American Anthropologist* 71 (4): 634–647. https://doi.org/10.1525/AA.1969.71.4.02A00030.

Pankenier, D.W. 1995. The Cosmo-Political Background of Heaven's Mandate. *Early China* 20: 121–176.

Patočka, J. 2016. *The Natural World as a Philosophical Problem*, in I. Chvatík and L. Učník (eds). Evanston, Illinois: Northwestern University Press.

Patomäki, H. 2010. Cosmological sources of critical cosmopolitanism. *Review of International Studies* 36: 181–200.

Pauketat, T.R. 2012. *An Archaeology of the Cosmos: Rethinking Agency and Religion in Ancient America.* Hoboken: Taylor and Francis.

Pedersen, O. 1982. The Present Position of Archaeo-Astronomy, in D.C. Heggie,*Archaeoastronomy in the Old World*: 265–74, Cambridge: Cambridge University Press.

Plessner, H. 1975. *Die Stufen des Organischen und der Mensch: Einleitung in die philosophische Anthropologie.* Berlin: De Gruyter. https://doi.org/10.1515/9783110845341.

Praet, I. 2009. Shamanism and Ritual in South America: An Inquiry into Amerindian Shape-Shifting. *The Journal of the Royal Anthropological Institute* 15 (4): 737–54.

Rappenglück, B. 2013. Myths and Motifs as Reflections of Prehistoric Cosmic Events: Some Methodological Considerations, in I. Šprajc and Peter Pehani (eds) *Ancient Cosmologies and Modern Prophets: Proceedings of the 20th Conference of the European Society for Astronomy in* Culture: 67-83. Ljubljana: Slovene Anthropological Society.

Rappenglück, M.A. 1999. *Eine Himmelskarte aus der Eiszeit? Ein Beitrag zur Urgeschichte der Himmelskunde und zur paläoastronomischen Methodik, aufgezeigt am Beispiel der Szene in „Le Puits", Grotte de Lascaux (Com. Montignac, Dép. Dordogne, Rég. Aquitaine, France).* Frankfurt am Main: Lang.

Rappenglück, M.A. 2007. Copying the Cosmos: The Archaic Concepts of the Sacred Cave across Cultures, in H. Jung and M.A. Rappenglück (eds) *Signaturen des Lebens: Bilder und Zeichen von Kosmos und Bios und Symbole des Alltags - Alltag der Symbole*: 63–84, Frankfurt am Main: Lang.

Rappenglück, M.A. 2009. Constructing Worlds: Cosmovisions as Integral Parts of Human Ecosystems, in J. A. Rubiño-Martín (ed.) *Cosmology Across Cultures: Proceedings of a Workshop Held at Parque De Las Ciencias, Granada, Spain, 8 - 12 September 2008*: 108–15. San Francisco: Astronomical Society of the Pacific.

Rappenglück, M.A. 2013a. Astro Maniacs - Methodological Concepts of Cultural Astronomy Focused on Case Studies of Earlier Prehistory, in I. Šprajc and Peter Pehani (eds) *Ancient Cosmologies and Modern Prophets: Proceedings of the 20th Conference of the European Society for Astronomy in* Culture: 83-100. Ljubljana: Slovene Anthropological Society.

Rappenglück, M.A. 2013b. The Housing of the World: The Significance of Cosmographic Concepts for Habitation. *Nexus Network Journal* 15 (3): 387–422.

Rappenglück, M. A. 2014a. The Cosmic Deep Blue: The Significance of the Celestial Water Sphere Across Cultures. *Mediterranean Archaeology and Archaeometry* 14 (3): 293–305.

Rappenglück, M.A. 2014b. Weltgehäuse: Zur kosmographischen Symbolik von Höhle, Heiligtum und Haus, in H. Jung (ed.) *Symbolon: Gesellschaft für wissenschaftliche Symbolforschung e. V.* 19 Neue Folge: 237–62. Symbolon 19. Frankfurt am Maine: Lang.

Rappenglück, M.A. 2015a. Possible Calendrical Inscriptions on Paleolithic Artifacts, in C. Ruggles (ed.), *Handbook of Archaeoastronomy and Ethnoastronomy*, Ch. 102: 1197-1204. New York: Springer Science+Business Media New York.

Rappenglück, M.A. 2015b. Possible Astronomical Depictions in Franco-Cantabrian Paleolithic Rock Art, in C. Ruggles (ed.),*Handbook of Archaeoastronomy and Ethnoastronomy*, Ch. 103: 1205-1212. New York: Springer Science+Business Media New York.

Rappenglück, M. A. 2016. "Keepers of Time and Guardians of Space. Some Basic Concepts of Astronomy and Power." In: *Astronomy and Power. How worlds are structured: Proceedings of the SEAC 2010 conference*, edited by M. Rappenglück, B. Rappenglück, N. Campion and F.P. Silva, BAR international series 2794. Oxford: British Archaeological Reports Ltd.

Rappenglück, M.A. 2018a. The World as a Living Entity: Essentials of a Cosmic Metaphor. *Mediterranean Archaeology and Archaeometry* 18 (4): 335–43.

Rappenglück, M.A. 2018b. The World Tree: Categorisation and Reading of an Archaic Cosmographic Concept. *Journal of Skyscape Archaeology* 3 (2): 253–67.

Rappenglück, M.A. 2019a. Himmlische Reiseführer: Wie sich die alten Kulturen in Raum und Zeit orientierten, in G. Wolfschmidt (ed.) *Orientierung, Navigation und Zeitbestimmung - Wie der Himmel den Lebensraum des Menschen prägt: Proceedings der Tagung der Gesellschaft für Archäoastronomie in Hamburg 2017*: 221–67. Hamburg: tredition.

Rappenglück, M. A. 2019b.Die Urgeschichte des Zählens, des Rechnens und der Rechenhilfen in der Steinzeit, in G. Wolfschmidt (ed.) *Vom Abakus zum Computer. Geschichte der Rechentechnik, Teil 1*:17-55. Hamburg: tredition.

Rappenglück, M.A. 2020a. Der Himmel Im Leben Der Menschen – Was eigentlich ist Kulturelle Kosmologie? In G. Wolfschmidt (ed.) *Maß Und Mythos, Zahl Und Zauber - Die Vermessung Von Himmel Und Erde: Tagung Der Gesellschaft Für Archäoastronomie in Dortmund 2018.* Hamburg: tredition.

Rappenglück, M. A. 2020b, Catchy World Model: The Concept(s) of Cosmic Mountains(s) Used by Ancient cultures, in: S. Draxler, M.E. Lippitsch, and G. Wolfschmidt (eds) *Harmony and Symmetry. Celestial regularities shaping human culture: Proceedings of the SEAC 2018 Conference in Graz.* SEAC Publications; Vol. 01: 135-145. Hamburg: tredition.

Rappenglück, M.A. 2021, How Do We Know What They Were Thinking? Archaeoastronomy Between Science and Speculation – Palaeolithic Case Studies, in González-García, César; Frank, Roslyn M.; Sims, Lionel D.; Rappenglück, Michael A.; Zotti, G. (eds) *Beyond Paradigms in Cultural Astronomy, Proceedings of the 27th SEAC.* Meeting Held Together with the 25th EAA. BAR international series 3033: 65-72. Oxford: BAR.

Rescher, N. 1973. *The Coherence Theory of Truth.* Oxford: Oxford University Press.

Rousseau, D., J. Wilby, J.Billingham and S. Blachfellner 2018. *General Systemology: Transdisciplinarity for Discovery, Insight, and Innovation.* Singapore: Springer Singapore. https://doi.org/10.1007/978-981-10-0892-4.

Ruggles, C.L.N. 1993a. The Study of Cultural Astronomy, in C.L.N. Ruggles and N.J. Saunders (eds) *Astronomies and Cultures: Papers Derived from the Third Oxford International Symposium on Archaeoastronomy, St. Andrews, U.K., September 1990*: 1–31. Niwot: University Press of Colorado.

Ruggles, C.L.N., ed. 1993b. *Archaeoastronomy in the 1990s: Papers Derived from the Third "Oxford" International Symposium on Archaeoastronomy, St. Andrews, UK, September 1990.* Loughborough: Group D Publ.

Ruggles, C.L.N. 2005. *Ancient Astronomy: An Encyclopedia of Cosmologies and Myth.* Santa Barbara, California: ABC-CLIO.

Ruggles, C.L.N. 2011a. Pushing Back the Frontiers or Still Running Around the Same Circles? 'Interpreting Archaeoastronomy' Thirty Years on, in C.L.N. Ruggles (ed,) *Archaeoastronomy and Ethnoastronomy: Building Bridges Between Cultures: Proceedings of the 278th Symposium of the International Astronomical Union and "Oxford IX" International Symposium on Archaeoastronomy Held in Lima, Peru, January 5 - 14, 2011*:1–18. Cambridge: Cambridge Univ. Press.

Ruggles, Clive L. N. (ed.) 2011b. *Archaeoastronomy and Ethnoastronomy: Building Bridges Between Cultures: Proceedings of the 278th Symposium of the International Astronomical Union and "Oxford IX" International Symposium on Archaeoastronomy Held in Lima, Peru, January 5 - 14, 2011.* IAU symposium proceedings series 278. Cambridge: Cambridge Univ. Press.

Ruggles, C.L.N. (ed.) 2015. *Handbook of Archaeoastronomy and Ethnoastronomy.* New York: Springer. https://doi.org/10.1007/978-1-4614-6141-8.

Saniotis, A. 2019. Becoming Animals: Neurobiology of Shamanic Shapeshifting. *Neuroquantology* 17 (5). https://doi.org/10.14704/nq.2019.17.5.2258.

Schäfer, M. 2004. World View Theory and the Conceptualisation of Space in Mathematics Education. *Pythagoras* 0 (59). https://doi.org/10.4102/pythagoras.v0i59.127.

Schütz, A. and T. Luckmann 1974. *The Structures of the Life-World.* Evanston, IL: Northwestern University Press.

Sims, L.D. 2002. Comment on C. Tilley, S. Hamilton and B. Bender. 2000. Art and the Re-Presentation of the Past. *Journal of the Royal Anthropological Institute* (N.S.) 6, 35-62. *Journal of the Royal Anthropological Institute* 7 (1): 154–55.

Sims, L.D. 2006a. The Solarization of the Moon Manipulated Knowledge at Stonehenge. *Cambridge Archaeological Journal* 16 (2): 191–207.

Sims, L.D. 2007. Lighting up Dark Moon: Ethnographic Templates for Testing Paired Alignments on the Sun and the Moon, in M.P. Zedda and J.A. Belmonte (eds) *Lights and Shadows in Cultural Astronomy*: 309-318. Isili: Associazone Archeofila Sarda.

Sims, L.D. 2009. Entering, and Returning From, the Underworld: Reconstituting Silbury Hill by Combining a Quantified Landscape Phenomenology with Archaeoastronomy. *The Journal of the Royal Anthropological Institute* 15 (2): 386–408.

Sims, L.D. 2010. Which Way Forward for Archaeoastronomy? West Kennet Avenue as a Test Case. *Journal of Cosmology* 9: 2060–2071.

Sims, L.D. 2013. Monuments as Myth or Myths of Monuments?, in I. Šprajc and Peter Pehani (eds) *Ancient Cosmologies and Modern Prophets: Proceedings of the 20th Conference of the European Society for Astronomy in* Culture: 237-254. Ljubljana: Slovene Anthropological Society.

Sims, L.D. 2016. Where Is Cultural Astronomy Going?, in F. Pimenta, N. Ribeiro, F. Silva, N. Campion, A. Joaquinito and L. Tirapicos (eds) *SEAC 2011 Stars and Stones: Voyages in Archaeoastronomy and Cultural Astronomy: Proceedings of the SEAC 2011 Conference*: 336–40. BAR international series 2720. Oxford: Archaeopress.

Sims, L.D. 2017. SEAC Educational Strategy for Cultural Astronomy, viewed March 2021, <http://www.archeoastronomy.org/content/education/>.

Sims, L.D. 2020a. Anthropology at UEL, 1990-2019, in M. Rustin and G. Poynter (eds) *Building a Radical University: A History of the University of East London*: 21–35. London: Lawrence Wishart.

Sims, L.D. 2020b. Bootstrapping our Breakout. *Journal of Skyscape Archaeology* 6 (1): 114-117.

Sims, L.D. 2020c. Toads Turning Time Verifying Visualisations of the Sanctuary (Avebury, Wiltshire) by Interdisciplinary Method, Chapter 6 in L. Henty and D. Brown (eds) *Visualising Skyscapes: Material Forms of Cultural Engagement with the Heavens.* London and New York: Routledge.

Sims, L. D. 2021. Snared Suns and Liberated Moons: Decoding Cryptic 'Astronomies' in Indigenous Cultures, viewed March 2021, <https://www.academia.edu/8544206/Snared_Suns_and_Liberated_Moons>.

Sims, L.D. and D. Fisher 2020. Through the Dark Vale: Interpreting the Stonehenge Palisade Through Interdisciplinary Convergence. *Journal of Skyscape Archaeology* 6 (1): 5-29.

Sims, L.D. and J.C.Holbrook, 2014. Magic - Another Method for Archaeoastronomers, viewed March 2020, <https://www.academia.edu/10339752/Magic_-_another_method_for_archaeoastronomers>.

Sinclair, R.M. 2005. The Nature of Archaeoastronomy, in J.W. Fountain and R.M. Sinclair (eds), *Current Studies in Archaeoastronomy: Conversations Across Time and Space: Selected Papers from the Fifth Oxford International Conference at Santa Fe, 1996*: 3-13.Durham, N.C.: Carolina Academic Press.

Singh, R.P.B. 2009. *Cosmic Order and Cultural Astronomy: Sacred Cities of India.* Newcastle upon Tyne: Cambridge Scholars.

Sinha, V.S. 2019. Event-Based Time in Three Indigenous Amazonian and Xinguan Cultures and Languages. *Frontiers in Psychology* 10 (454): 1–21.

Stegmüller, W. 1973. *Probleme und Resultate der Wissenschaftstheorie und analytischen Philosophie: Zweiter Halbband: Statistisches Schließen, Statistische Begründung, Statistische Analyse.* Berlin, Heidelberg, New York: Springer-Verlag.

Stegmüller, W. 1986. *Das Problem der Induktion: Humes Herausforderung und moderne Antworten. Der sogenannte Zirkel des Verstehens.* Darmstadt: Wissenschaftliche Buchgesellschaft.

Strang, V. 2004. "Close Encounters of the Third World Kind: Indigenous Knowledge and Relations to Land." In Bicker, Sillitoe, and Pottier 2004, 93–117.

Strang, V. 2005. Water Works: Agency and Creativity in the Mitchell River Catchment. *The Australian Journal of Anthropology* 16: 366-381.

Sweatman, M.B. and D.Tsikritsis 2017. Decoding Göbekli Tepe with Archaeoastronomy: What Does the Fox Say? *Mediterranean Archaeology and Archaeometry* 17 (1): 233–50.

Tamisari, F. 1998. Body, Vision, and Movement: In the Footprints of the Ancestors. *Oceania* 68 (4): 249–70.

Tatlow, D.K. 2018. China's Cosmological Communism: A Challenge to Liberal Democracies. Imperial philosophy meets Marxist orthodoxy in Beijing's global ambition. MERICS (Mercator Institute for China Studies) CHINA MONITOR July 18, 2018: 1-9.

Thagard, P. 2000. *Coherence in Thought and Action.* Cambridge, Mass: MIT Press.

Tickner, A.B. and A. Querejazu 2021. Weaving Worlds: Cosmopraxis as Relational Sensibility. *International Studies Review 2021,* viaa100.

Treadwell, J. 2017. Cosmology and Structure: The "Tāhuhu" in the 19th-Century Whare Māori. *The Journal of the Polynesian Society* 126 (1): 93–122.

Thuillard, M., J. Le Quellec, J. d'Huy, Y. Berezkin 2018. A Large-scale Study of Word Myths. *TRAMES* 22 (72/67) 4: 407–424.

Tymieniecka, A.T. (ed.) 2013. *Phenomenology and the Human Positioning in the Cosmos: The Life-World, Nature, Earth: Book Two.* Dordrecht: Springer. https://doi.org/10.1007/978-94-007-4795-1.

Underhill, J.W. 2009. *Humboldt, Worldview, and Language.* Edinburgh: Edinburgh University Press. https://doi.org/10.3366/j.ctt1r29b9.

Van Manen, M. 2016. *Phenomenology of Practice: Meaning-Giving Methods in Phenomenological Research and Writing.* London and New York: Routledge.

Viveiros de Castro, E. 1998. Cosmological Deixis and Amerindian Perspectivism. *The Journal of the Royal Anthropological Institute* 4 (3): 469–88.

Waldenfels, B. 2005. *In den Netzen der Lebenswelt.* Frankfurt am Main: Suhrkamp.

Watzlawick, P., J. Beavin Bavelas and D.D. Jackson 2014. *Pragmatics of Human Communication: A Study of Interactional Patterns, Pathologies, and Paradoxes.* New York: W.W. Norton & Company.

Wearden, J. 2016. *The Psychology of Time Perception.* London: Palgrave Macmillan UK.

Webb, H.S. 2012. *Yanantin and Masintin in the Andean World: Complementary Dualism in Modern Peru.* Albuquerque: University of New Mexico Press.

Wilcock, D., G.Brierley and R. Howitt 2013. Ethnogeomorphology. *Progress in Physical Geography: Earth and Environment* 37 (5): 573–600. https://doi.org/10.1177/0309133313483164.

Willerslev, R. 2004a. Not Animal, Not Not-Animal: Hunting, Imitation and Empathetic Knowledge Among the Siberian Yukaghir. *The Journal of the Royal Anthropological Institute* 10 (3): 629–52.

Willerslev, R. 2004b. Spirits as 'Ready to Hand'. *Anthropological Theory* 4 (4): 395–418. https://doi.org/10.1177/1463499604047918.

Exploring Theory in Skyscape Archaeology: Symbols, Materiality, Relationality and Rhizomes

Nicholas Campion

Introduction

The current move towards a requirement for theory in the understanding of the human relationship with the sky and celestial objects, is bringing the study of archaeoastronomy in line with other academic disciplines. This move is marked by the suggested shift towards the use of the term skyscape archaeology (Silva and Henty 2015), representing an interdisciplinary approach to what has often been archaeoastronomy's narrow focus on astronomical alignments regardless of wider contexts. Lionel Sims has promoted this shift for over two decades: this chapter will explore in particular the use of the word 'symbol' by Lionel Sims and David Fisher in their analysis of monuments in the Avebury and Stonehenge complexes, from their paper presented at the 2016 conference of the European Society for Astronomy in Culture (SEAC), published in *Culture and Cosmos* (Sims and Fisher 2017: 11–30). My interest is in how concepts of symbol and ideas associated with the word, may illuminate our appreciation of ancient sites, and how the concept links up with other current conversations on relationality, phenomenology, material religion, the new materiality and rhizome theory.

In their paper in *Culture and Cosmos*, Sims and Fisher refer to Mike Parker Pearson's (2012) interpretation of monuments in the Stonehenge complex. Parker Pearson had argued that, in the Neolithic, stone, as at Stonehenge, represented death while, wood, as at the neighbouring monument, Woodhenge, represented life. Wood and stone were then separate but paired, as rituals for the living and the dead are paired. Sims and Fisher, observing that stone occurs at Woodhenge and wood is present at Stonehenge, set out a more complex and nuanced set of possibilities in what they call their 'Integrated Model', in which all parts of the Neolithic environment, person and planet, wood, stone and water, landscape and skyscape, would have been seen to operate together as part of a single whole. As part of their discussion, Sims and Fisher use the words 'symbol', 'symbolic' and 'symbolism'. Using their paper as a starting point I am concerned with how these words may be understood and how such understanding may enrich our appreciation of Neolithic culture. Sims and Fisher refer to symbols and symbolism in several passages. For example, in one section they refer to the 'symbolic loadings' placed on wood and timber:

> In sum, the monuments' designs, excavated archaeology and landscape positioning all suggest that timber and stone structures were contemporary and in dualistic mirroring dialogue with each other. Instead of a categorical distinction between these two building materials then whatever symbolic loadings were placed on each of them by the monument builders *in combination* they were probably utilised for some fused *diacritical* level of meaning (Sims and Fisher 2017: 16).

They continue:

> Anthropology accepts that all rituals are characterised by a multi-media redundancy and amplification of symbols, and that structures that we find in one dimension of symbolism will be rehearsed and repeated in other associated dimensions (Sims and Fisher 2017: 17).

Discussing the contrasting combinations of topography and astronomy, as well as the distinctive phenomena evident at the sites, which include horizon markers, expanses of water and the movements of the Sun and Moon, Sims and Fisher challenge the notion of binary opposites, arguing that different substances (such as wood and stone) are not separate but complementary. They add that:

> the symbolic structure emerging from these... models suggests we need to consider rituals simulating a journey *between* worlds that include an underworld. This exercise in paring cognate models to the point that they can be integrated therefore suggests that other relevant models should be consistent with diacritical materialities, landscapes and astronomies that extend beyond this world (Sims and Fisher 2017: 21).

Lastly, Sims and Fisher (2017: 23) talk about the Moon's complex cycles, including its reappearance following a period of invisibility at Dark Moon, which they interpret as a 'resurrection' which, in turn, comprises part of a 'symbolic repertoire [which] is more suitable for a cosmology that requires contradiction and complexity rather than the one-dimensional Sun'. Altogether Sims and Fisher speak of symbolic loading, symbolic structure and symbolic repertoire, but they do not define 'symbol'. Yet Ruggles (1999: 155) argued that, if we could only understand the astronomical symbolism at Neolithic monuments we would understand the cosmology of the period on its own terms, free from modern preconceptions.

The nature of symbols

The Greek verb *ballo* means 'throw'. The Greek preposition 'sun' (sometimes Romanised as 'syn') means with, or together with, so literally 'throw together', but also to 'collect' and 'compare' (Ladner 1979: 223). As Peter Struck (2004: 78) writes, in its earliest meaning 'a symbol is one half of an object – usually a piece of cloth, wood, or pottery – that is deliberately split into two and then allocated to the parties to an agreement. It is reassembled at a later time to verify the deal'. Behind the symbol, he continues, is the notion of agreement, and therefore a symbol was originally social. Dorian Greenbaum adds further detail:

> The basic meaning of *sumbolon* is a tally or token, broken in half and given to two contracting parties, so that they may identify each other when the pieces are fitted together. Early *symbola* were often halved *astragaloi*, or knucklebones, used as dice, themselves a form of divination where each throw corresponded to a given verse; put together, the verses predicted outcomes. *Sumbolon*, of course, comes from *sumballw*, throw together (the same as Latin *conjicio*). The interpreter and the sign are "thrown together" and realize the meaning (identity) only when both are involved (Greenbaum 2007: 12).

Significantly, as Ladner (1979: 223) points out, a symbol therefore requires a partner. Wherever we find a symbol it is therefore one part of a larger whole. It is an 'authenticating token' (Struck 2004: 79).

However, the word then achieved a secondary meaning which Ladner (1979: 224) characterised as 'deeply spiritual and even mystical'. According to Struck, in his study of the classical world, a symbol was then:

> ... a form of representation that has an intimate, ontological connection with its referent and is no mere mechanical replication of the world, that is transformative and opens up a realm beyond rational experience, that exists simultaneously as a concrete thing and as an abstract and perhaps transcendent truth, and that conveys a unique density of meaning (Struck 2004: 5).

A symbol might therefore possess powers such as the ability to heal, a property evident in Neoplatonic theory. For example, according to Iamblichus:

> It is the power of ineffable symbols comprehended by the gods alone that establishes theurgical union. Thus, we don't perform these acts intellectually... In fact, these very symbols, by themselves, perform their own work, and the ineffable power of the Gods with which these symbols are charged, itself, recognizes, by itself, its own images. It is not awakened to this by our thinking (Iamblichus, *De mysteriis* 96:13–97.9).

Ladner (1979: 224) argues that this secondary meaning appeared 'fully fledged' in the Christian world around 500 AD, the symbol then functioning as a bridge between the worlds of the senses and the visible on the one hand, and of the numinous and the invisible on the other, in the soul-matter binary of the Christian cosmos. The symbol therefore has power through being infused or empowered by divinity in a world given meaning by God. In this sense, a symbol is connected to the thing it symbolises by a level of reality known in classical discourse as an essence or substance; concepts present in Platonic (Cornford 1937) and Aristotelian cosmologies (Irwin 1988) as Ideas, Forms, or Archetypes. In that an essence is the structure of a thing, atomic structure can also be an essence (Averill 1982): for example, the atomic structure of gold gives the metal its particular qualities.

The cosmos, as Cleomedes wrote, is a single system, and for the Stoics, by whom Cleomedes appears to have been influenced (Todd 2001), it was a single living system (Diogenes Laertius 1925: 139,142). A symbol, whether made of wood or stone, is therefore alive and, if it is alive, to follow this logic, it must have agency – the ability to engage with and affect other objects with which it has a relationship (Latour 2007: 63-86). For Iamblichus, the symbol has real power derived not from any human action, but from divinity. However, the *source* of the power is not pertinent to the fact that a symbol has its own power. Symbols, in Newell's (2018) view, are 'affective': that is, they affect the world around them. It may be that they affect the emotions, as might an image of Buddha, or Christ, or a flower, but it might be that they also exert a chemical effect by entering the body, as would incense in a temple or church, or would the scent of a blossom. As Kathleen Stewart (2007: 21) wrote, 'The potential stored in ordinary things is a network of transfers and relays'. Things themselves can 'store up affect', as Newell puts it, until it is released with 'physiological, psychological and social repercussions' (Newell

2018: 6). In an affective cosmos, human beings are a fully integrated part of the affective system, so they can make symbols that then, in turn, affect them. As Clement of Alexandria (c. 150–215 AD) reported, talking of the Egyptians:

> When they want to indicate the sun, for example, they make a circle, and the moon a crescent shape, according to the literal form... Other things they engrave figuratively... and they transpose and alter their character; they change some things, others they recast entirely (Clement of Alexandria, *Stromateis* 5.4.20–21).

This is the principle of magic: relying on the divine power of the universe it is possible to construct a talisman, an object which can then act on individuals and collectives, both human and other-than-human, a practice which survives into the present day in various forms of religious practice, such as Orthodox Christian icon-making. 'Most material symbols', Ian Hodder writes, 'tend to be iconic' (2012: 97). A symbol may indeed be an object, such as a piece of stone or wood, but it might also be a ritual, gesture, word, or sound, acting as, Victor Turner argued, a container for meaning:

> By "ritual" I mean prescribed formal behaviour for occasions not given over to technological routine, having reference to beliefs in mystical beings or powers. The symbol is the smallest unit of ritual which still retains all the properties of ritual behaviour; it is the ultimate unit of specific structure in a ritual context (Turner 1967: 19).

'The symbols I observed in the field', Turner adds, 'were empirically objects, activities, relationships, events, gestures and spatial units in a ritual situation' (1967: 19). If a symbol is ontologically real, then a precise movement or special sound has the capacity to act on its environment in particular ways, as does a piece of stone or wood, or a planet. Hence, the objects present at, and rituals that occurred at Avebury and Stonehenge were themselves symbols, acting on the environment.

A symbol may be an active agent but it may also be a signifier as, for example, in Christian theology, an image of the crucified Christ might be a sign of suffering and redemption. In Christian theology (Ladner 1979: 225-7) and in modern theory (Parmenter 2015: 7) there is no necessary difference of meaning between a symbol and a sign: if a symbol has power, so must a sign. A symbol is, for Deleuze and Guattari, (1988: 130), actually a kind of sign, in a chain of signification, of the endless connections between multiple signs: 'every sign', they write 'refers to another sign, and only to another sign, ad infinitum' and 'all signs are signs of signs' while a symbol exists 'in a constant movement of referral from sign to sign'. In this formulation both the symbol and the sign are deprived of essential meaning. Ferdinand de Saussure, significant in this respect, distinguished the sign from the symbol in terms of their relative arbitrariness:

> The word *symbol* is sometimes used to designate the linguistic sign, or more exactly that part of the linguistic sign which we are calling the signal. The use of the word *symbol* is awkward, for reasons connected with our first principle. For it is characteristic of symbols that they are never entirely arbitrary. They are not empty configurations. They show at least a vestige of natural connection between the signal and its significations.

> For instance, our symbol of justice, the scales, could hardly be replaced by a chariot (Saussure 2013: 78).

Hence, even if there is no deep essence connection between a symbol and the symbolised, there must still be *something*. And arbitrary itself does not mean random. As Saussure adds:

> The word arbitrary also calls for comment. It must not be taken to imply that a signal depends on the free choice of the speaker... The term implies simply that the signal is unmotivated: that is to say arbitrary in relation to its significations, with which it has no natural connection in reality (Saussure 2017: 78).

As Parmentier (2015: 4) commented, 'for Saussure, symbolic codes are socially shared and historically transmitted, and every attempt to dislocate them from their socio-historical grounding is a methodological derailment'. Not even a sign, then, is unconstrained by its relationships. There are still some limiting factors, but they are external and rooted in cultural, social and linguistic convention. In modern English a symbol is now generally understood as an object which represents something else without having any essential, ontological relationship with it. This is the sense in which Ruggles (1999: 147) uses the term: he argues that there would only be consistent relationships between words and symbols if such things were governed by general laws. Benjamin (2015: 162-3) attributes the arbitrariness of the symbol to Kant while Ladner (1979: 228) argues that the symbol was redefined as a matter of arbitrary assignation by the late 19th century, by which time western intellectuals had generally concluded that the universe was meaningless, rather than meaningful as it had been in the Christian and Neoplatonic worlds. As Turner (1967: 19) wrote, 'following the *Concise Oxford Dictionary*... a "symbol" is a thing regarded by general consent as naturally typifying or representing or recalling something by possession of analogous qualities or by association in fact or thought'. The connection between the symbol and the thing symbolised is therefore a cultural one: for one thing to represent another does not require an essential connection between the two. The modern understanding of the word is not necessarily inconsistent with the original Greek *symbolon*, as one thing thrown together with another and which does not require an ontological connection.

According to this view, the belief that such connections exist is therefore a fundamental error. As Mary LeCron Foster (1994: 370) wrote, 'Symbolism arose and evolved into human culture because of a growing appreciation and social utilization of abstract likenesses between objects and events separated in time and space' (see also Foster and Botscharow 1990). Having been identified, symbols then acquire collective power. And as Foster (1994: 366) continues, a symbol 'is any entity that has socially participative meaning'. Meaning is given to a symbol, but the symbol does not, itself, contain meaning. For Foster, symbolism is, then, central to the functioning of human society: 'Without symbolism', she writes, 'there could be no culture... Culture is not itself formed of symbols, but of the meaning that lies behind and unites symbols (Foster 1994: 366). Clifford Geertz (1973: 99) takes a similar view: culture is 'an historically transmitted pattern of meanings embodied in symbols, a system of inherited conceptions expressed in symbolic form' (see also Geertz 1966: 3). But, as Foster wrote, 'This meaning only exists in the minds of participants in culture, but it is acted out through the manipulation of symbols, which objectify meaning' (Foster 1994: 366). When a symbol represents something, the representation is arbitrary: in this conception, symbols may be socially shared in the Greek sense, but lack the real power ascribed to them by Neoplatonism and Christianity.

Modern anthropology has therefore bought into the notion of the meaningless cosmos; a position which places the anthropologist in an awkward position, for they are forced to attribute any concept that the symbol has intrinsic power to either social construction (everyone agrees that the symbol has power) or subjective consciousness (the idea that a symbol has power only exists in people's minds) (Newell 2018: 7). Newell adds that the postmodern position, according to which everything is reduced to a 'text' is no longer sustainable.

However, the assumption that any supernatural ontology must be considered automatically false has been challenged in recent decades. It was criticized by Peter Berger (1969, 1974) as being what he called 'methodological atheism', and has been heavily critiqued by scholars within the study of religions. David Hufford (1987) attacked the adoption of disbelief as the default position in sociology, as having no more credibility than does an automatic assumption of belief, while Ninian Smart (1973: 94, 108) then posed 'methodological neutralism' or 'agnosticism' as the only credible academic positions. As Douglas Porpora (2006) has argued, methodological atheism is increasingly difficult to sustain as a viable academic position and only methodological agnosticism, a deliberate withdrawal from the imposition of truth claims on anthropological data, can generate credible research. And Linda Tuhiwai Smith (1999) has called for a wholesale decolonisation of academic studies of indigenous people and a rejection of the view that the anthropologist knows best. Anthropologists such as Jack Hunter (2019) argue that if an individual reports a paranormal experience then the reality of that experience has to be accepted not just as a matter of subjective consciousness but in terms of ontological reality.

The question then becomes how we understand not just modern indigenous ontologies, but Neolithic ones. Sims and Fisher artfully avoid an explicit discussion of this difficulty. They do, though, argue that the environment around Avebury and Stonehenge was envisioned as a single unified whole, within which Neolithic people engaged through monument construction and ritual movement. As they concluded:

> The locally available landscape at Avebury allowed the building of two avenues' prescribed routes and Silbury Hill to symbolically represent a Moon that enters, travels through and emerges from the underworld. At Stonehenge the Avenue and the discontinuous Palisade served a similar function to construct prescribed views of Robin Hood's Ball as a facsimile of the Moon entering and returning through 'the dark and gloomy vale' (Psalms 23:4) of the underworld (Sims and Fisher 2017: 30).

But what does it mean when the avenues' processional routes represent the Moon's journey? The word 'represent' itself has a range of meanings: as Parmenter (2015: 2) noted, one thing can re-present another with which it is therefore linked, just as a Greek symbol could consist of two parts of an original object. And methodological agnosticism means that we cannot assume that such a link is either arbitrary in the modern sense, or meaningful in the Neoplatonic and Christian sense. Robin Hood's Ball, a causewayed enclosure within the Stonehenge complex, may have been constructed, as Sims and Fisher conclude, as a facsimile, or exact copy, of the Moon's entry to and return from the underworld, but that says nothing about whether, as a symbol, it possessed its own essential power or was just representational, in the OED sense, and lacking essential power. Sims and Fisher's text may point to both definitions. The difference between the two meanings of symbol – as either possessing or lacking ontological reality – is central, though, to archaeoastronomical assumptions. For example, if a standing stone at Avebury is purely a representational symbol in the modern sense, it is just a lump of stone and any meaning attributed to it by Neolithic people existed entirely within their own minds. However, if a standing stone as a symbol is alive, possessing power and agency, then it becomes a participant in whatever rituals rook place at Avebury or Stonehenge. It watches the Sun or the Moon, just as a person watches them, and it receives their life-giving light, just as a person receives it. A direct comparison is offered by the Andean *huacas*, distinctive natural features, sometimes carved and decorated, which, as symbols, are both representational *and* alive (Malville 2016).

Material religion and the new materiality

A wider epistemological framework for the concept of the symbol as being alive is provided by parallel developments: on the one hand material religion and, on the other, the 'new materiality'. Material religion examines the religious significance of material objects, including human beings as embodied beings (as in performance and ritual), as opposed to a traditional theological study of dogma and ideas. As the editors of the newly formed journal, *Material Religion*, put it:

> Material Religion [is] a new project in the study of religious images, objects, spaces, and material practices. The study of religion may be conducted through any number of lenses. One may regard religion through the lens of narratives, or documents such as sermons and doctrinal statements... Material Religion sets out to consider religion through the lens of its material forms and their use in religious practice (The Editors 2005: 4).

Material religion does not claim that the study of the range of phenomena found at Neolithic sites, including earth monuments and standing stones, is new, but it does bring them into a revised framework in which they exist in the same theoretical context as material objects in modern religion. As David Morgan argued:

> If culture is the full range of thoughts, feelings, objects, words, and practices that human beings use to construct and maintain the life-worlds in which they exist, material culture is any aspect of that world-making activity that happens in material form. That means things, but also includes the feelings, values, fears, and obsessions that inform one's understanding and use of things (Morgan 2008: 228).

Material religion deals with practice and behaviour and includes both 'things' – icons, images, statues, incense, mass produced artefacts, sacred spaces, temples, stone circles, art, liturgical objects, music, relics, ceremonial dress – and actions - practices such as display, ceremony, ritual, magic, performance and pilgrimage, along with anything that relates directly to the senses, all of which are considered symbols by Victor Turner. It is apparent that the material remains that are the sole evidence for Neolithic thought are well encompassed within the general rubric of material religion.

However, parallel with material religion, and easily regarded as a conceptual expansion of it, is the 'new materiality'. New materiality rejects two previous models of matter, but owes a debt to a third (DeLanda 2015: 16–21). It rejects both the Platonic and Aristotelian schemes, in which matter is animated by Ideas or Forms which have a separate existence, as well as the Newtonian, in which inert matter is subject to general laws. However, it falls within a general Stoic lineage in which the entire world is a single, living organism in which, as Long (1996) makes clear, all things are related and there is no boundary between matter and consciousness. Material objects may therefore be active or affective agents, changing the world around them. A classic example, developed by Luci Attala (2009), is water, which continually shapes the geology, geography, biology and climate of the Earth and without which human beings would not exist. To apply this model to the stones at Avebury and Stonehenge, as individual entities they were installed by humans but, once installed, they shape human experience, framing the space in which ritual actions take place. And, like water, they themselves move and change. Like individual puddles of water, individual stones carved from the same quarry were originally part of the same mass and, in the future, after they have been completely eroded, will become part of another mass. The new materiality does not ascribe intentionality to stones or water, but it does ascribe agency to them, and they therefore participate with humanity in shaping the environment. Attala, as an exponent of this new materiality, relies on a number of metaphors, including entanglement (borrowed from quantum mechanics (Attala 2009: 14)) and Bruno Latour's Actor Network Theory, in which all things both have agency and are linked: they both act in themselves and do so as part of myriad networks (Latour 2007). Thus, the thing can exist in itself, as a stone is a stone, a word is a word and water is water, and all relate to each other.

Relationality

It is central to Sims and Fisher's 'Integrated Model', that all parts relate to each other, adding up to a greater whole. 'We argue', they write (2017: 23), 'that each monument is in a relation of reversible dualism with its doppelganger but in a unity which, while split, is consistent within this dualism'. Each object and each monument therefore exists in relation to itself and every other object in each monument. This is somewhat consistent with classical notions of cosmology as relational. As Cleomedes wrote:

> "Cosmos" is used in many senses, but our present discussion concerns it with reference to its final arrangement, which is defined as follows: a cosmos is a construct formed from the heavens, the Earth, and the natural substances within them. This [cosmos] encompasses all bodies, since, as is demonstrated elsewhere, there is, without qualification, no body existing outside the cosmos... And that the cosmos has Nature as that which administers it is evident from the following: the ordering of the parts within it; the orderly succession of what comes into existence, the sympathy of the parts in it for one another; the fact that all individual entities are created in relation to something else... (Cleomedes, *On the Heavens* 1.3.3, 1.3.11).

The classical cosmos, then, contains everything and everything must therefore exist in relation to everything else: nothing exists as an independent, discrete entity. Thus, all tangible, visible and intangible and invisible phenomena are connected – including wood and stones as well as the dreams, hopes and emotions of people who gather at monuments constructed from them.

In Cleomedian cosmology all relationships are qualified by sympathy, itself both a physical quality and an attractive force (as opposed to tension, the repulsive force) (Diogenes Laertius 1925: VII.140). Cleomedes' relational ontology – his theory of being in which all things are related – is therefore rooted in the essential characteristics of things: for example, 'wood' has the character, or sympathetic nature, of 'woodness', stone of 'stoneness' and water of 'waterness'. But because wood, stone and water are all connected by relationships, there is no clear boundary between one thing and another. The same problem of distinguishing between a single thing and the many things to which it is related occurs in recent conversations around relationality. For example, Benjamin wrote:

> The truth of relationality inheres in what is always at work within relations, namely, the effective presence of a founding and irreducible plurality. Within the structure of this general argument, singular relations, which can be more accurately described as pragmatic occurrences within relationality, can only ever be secondary (and this is the case despite the possibility of attributing a form of originality to them). Such occurrences always depend upon the presence of an original form of multiplicity or plurality (Benjamin 2015: 2).

Benjamin's argument (2015: 2) is that relationality is 'primary' and possesses 'an original presence'. Nothing, he argues, can exist except in a relationship and pluralities must therefore precede singularities: somewhat counter-intuitively, two things must exist before one thing. Therefore, in respect of Avebury and Stonehenge, nothing exists without everything else and no stone exists without other stones, or without the earth in which it stands, or the air which surrounds it. Or, if this claim is too large, nothing can be understood aside from its relationships with everything else. The distinction between a classical perspective, as outlined by Cleomedes, and a modern one, as set out by Benjamin, is whether the substances of which things in a relationship are made are significant. For Cleomedes they are but for Benjamin they are not.

Sims and Fisher themselves do not define cosmology, except by inference. The cosmology of the southern British Neolithic is described by them in terms of the total symbiosis of land, sky and waterscapes: sky, earth, water, people, wood, stones, Sun, Moon and world are part of a single system:

> For a culture that believes in a stationary flat earth one interpretation stands out: if the Moon is below the horizon then it must be travelling through the underworld. Since such a cosmology would also understand that when the Moon has disappeared from the sky at dark Moon it must be travelling through the underworld, then the purposeful choosing of sites with interrupted horizon views of the southern standstill moons is consistent with lunar-solar alignments that conflates the Sun's solstice settings with the standstill dark Moon (Sims and Fisher 2017: 20).

Sims and Fisher's total environmental view is framed within their own use of landscape phenomenology (Sims and Fisher 2017: 13, 28) which, for them, means actually witnessing celestial events in relation to the landscape rather than working from maps or measuring instruments alone. Clive Ruggles (1999: 151–152), also advocates a phenomenological view, citing Ed Krupp's experience of the solstice at Stonehenge:

> One should make a point of being there. Celestial events take place in context. When you see what actually happens in the landscape, you learn a great deal more about it. It is, of course, possible to determine the alignment of a building with instruments, but nuances of light and shadow details of the horizon, difficulties in practical observation, and many more subjective aspects of a site can only be appreciated in person (Krupp 1995, cited by Ruggles 1999: 151).

As Dermot Moran wrote:

> Phenomenology is best understood as a radical, anti-traditional way of philosophising, which emphasises the attempt to get to the truth of matters, to describe *phenomena*, in the broadest sense as whatever appears, in the manner in which it appears, that is as it manifests itself to consciousness, to the experiencer (Moran 1999: 4).

Drawing on Wylie (1989: 94) Ruggles and Saunders discuss the paradoxical importance of recognising both the value of the insights that one might gain from phenomenological experience, as well as the limitations of such insights:

> Analogical inference is of considerable importance because the multidisciplinary nature of cultural astronomy, like post-positivist archaeology, is increasingly concerned with the epistemic limits of enquiry, in other words, with the status of what can be understood of the past. It is important to note that what can be known of the past is seen to depend on the theoretical and ideological presuppositions that are brought to the enquiry. Thus "facts" about what constitutes the past are themselves neither stable nor self-evident but are paradigm-dependent and consequently open to continuing revision in the light of empirical and theoretical developments (Ruggles and Saunders 1993: 19).

When phenomenologists observe and engage with phenomena, how can they know whether they are observing or engaging as people five thousand years ago? One can conduct a simple observation exercise and see the Sun rise in relation to a certain horizon feature on a particular date, a piece of information one might not notice from a map. But for the anthropologist phenomenology requires total participation in the subject, of object, or study, to the extent that the difference between subject and object disappear. The stone, earth, water and wind must be experienced as alive, and that means genuinely alive, not just alive in the modern academic imagination. Sims and Fisher observe the environment but they also go beyond strict observation. For example, when the Moon sets all we see is its disappearance. Sims and Fisher's specific statement that when the Moon sets below the horizon it enters the underworld, lacks direct testimony, and there can be none from an oral culture of four to five thousand years ago. However, it is a reasonable position given the comparison with cultures which have left written records, such as Egypt, in which the setting Sun embarks on a journey through the underworld (Schweizer: 1994).

Sims and Fisher employ landscape phenomenology to revise assumptions about the layout, context, design and function of Avebury and Stonehenge. They present both sites in their broader environments as what Victor Turner calls a 'ritual field' (1974: 179). However, when they invite us to experience the Moon's entry to and return from the underworld, what are they asking? How should we respond? Is the underworld a dark place, as imagined by the Mesopotamians who mourned Inanna's (Venus's) descent to the underworld (Kramer and Wolkstein 1983), or as envisaged by Christians who mourned Christ's death and experience of Hell following the vernal equinox? Should we allow ourselves to weep with grief as the Moon descends below the horizon? Does phenomenological experience require psychological participation? As Freya Mathews (1991: 109) wrote, 'Cosmologies are not of course pulled out of the air to suit the convenience of the communities to which they are attached. They are conditioned by many and various historical, environmental, technological, psychological and social factors'.

We may then ask what psychological factors characterised Neolithic monument builders, even if any conclusions can only ever be provisional. One speculation on Neolithic psychology was that of David Lewis-Williams and David Pearce (2009: 61), who argued that 'a tension is present between one form of cosmology which arises "spiritually" from within human beings... and another that derives from people's observations of what they see and measure'. It is fair enough, then, to reach conclusions concerning the inner world of the Neolithic monument builders. However, the way that Lewis-Williams and Pearce frame the question is a modern one, born of a binary distinction between inner and outer worlds, spirituality on the one hand and measurement on the other. There is a hint here of the Cartesian split between mind and body, between notions of subjectivity and objectivity, of real knowledge on the one hand and imagination on the other. Yet, contrary to Lewis-Williams and Pearce, there is no evidence that Neolithic people thought like this; instead, there is circumstantial evidence that they didn't, by drawing on research into premodern and non-western cultures. There is, for example, substantial evidence from indigenous studies indicating that what are regarded as inanimate objects in modern scientific materialism are sentient, beginning with Irving Hallowell's seminal report (1975: 141–78) on Ojibwe ontology, originally published in 1960 and many resulting conversations down to Graham Harvey's examination of animism in indigenous teachings (Harvey 2017: 481–97). Even the standard cosmology of pre-seventeenth century Europe depended on classical notions of the correspondence, or sympathy, between all things, codified in the so-called Great Chain of Being, according to which every single thing, including people, planets, stars, stones and wood, is linked in multiple series of vertical and horizontal connections (Lovejoy 1936). Symbols were themselves a central concept within this scheme.

For Ian Hodder, meanwhile, entanglement requires materiality as a starting point for analysis and understanding, emphasising a need to consider the relationship between things (Hodder 2012: 97; Der and Fernandini 2020). 'My aim here', Hodder writes (2012: 97), 'has been to say that the webs and networks in which humans live are as much symbolic, meaningful, spiritual, religious, conceptual, as they are practical, technical, economic and social'. And as he writes of entanglement in relation to the terrorist attacks of 9/11, 'a system of emotions and values was part of the human-thing entanglement that linked planes and bombs and postboxes' (Hodder 2012: 97). To return to Stonehenge and Avebury, wind, stones, earth, water, Sun, Moon and people are all entangled.

Rhizome theory

Hodder's discussion of symbols is deeply indebted to Gilles Deleuze and Félix Guattari's influential work, *A Thousand, Plateaus,* first published in English in 1987. Deleuze and Guattari's key metaphor is the rhizome: biologically, a rhizome grows through sending out horizontal roots which can produce new shoots, by contrast with a plant which has a single stem or trunk with one set of leaves or branches above and one set of roots below (Deleuze and Guattari 1988: 5–6). They applied this biological metaphor to social structures, rejecting hierarchical models and instead reimagining societies as connected by nodes of energy and activity, any one of which might send out cultural shoots to develop a new focus of change and innovation. 'A rhizome', they write, 'ceaselessly establishes connections between semiotic chains, organizations of power, and circumstances relative to the arts, sciences, and social struggles' (Deleuze and Guattari 1988: 6). Expanding the metaphor, they add:

> A semiotic chain is like a tuba, agglomerating very diverse acts, not only linguistic, but also perceptive, mimetic, gestural, and cognitive: there is no language in itself, nor are there any linguistic universals, only a throng of dialects, patois, slangs, and specialised languages. There is no ideal speaker-listener, any more than there is a homogenous linguistic community... There is no mother tongue, only a power takeover by a dominant language within a political multiplicity. Language stabilises around a parish, a bishopric, the capital. It forms a ball. It evolves by subterranean stems and flows, along river valleys or train tracks; it spreads like a patch of oil (Deleuze and Guattari 1988: 6).

A semiotic chain is a series of meanings linked by signs and symbols and Deleuze and Guattari (1988: 5–6) argue, 'Any point of a rhizome can be connected to anything other, and must be'. To apply their model to Avebury and Stonehenge, stone rows and circles, earth works, causeways, palisades, barrows, hills, rivers, sky, planets, plants, animals and people comprise chains of meaning. And to apply rhizome theory to Sims and Fisher's integrated model, the semiotic chain incorporates not only the Moon's entry to and exit from the underworld, along with every other single and interconnected thing, tangible or not: including the people who celebrated, commemorated and memorialised their lives at Neolithic monuments, along with their emotions and feelings, including hope, fear, longing, excitement, awe, love, anger, boredom, desire, jealousy – the totality of embodied phenomena which might be encompassed by material religion.

Deleuze and Guattari (1988: 5) go on to develop the concept of the assemblage, using a book as their example: 'There is no difference', they write, 'between what a book talks about and how it is made. Therefore a book also has no object. As an assemblage, a book has only itself, in connection with other assemblages and in relation to other bodies without organs'. A single book is the product of an entire cosmos of creation, from the author as a biological being with thousands of ancestors and millions of years of evolution, dreams, thoughts and an entire culture which lies behind them, together with the tree that makes the paper, the seed the tree grew from, the processes which manufactured the book, and so on:

> In a book, as in all things, there are lines of articulation or segmentarity, strata and territories; but also lines of flight, movements of deterritorialization and destratification.

> Comparative rates of flow on these lines produce phenomena of relative slowness and viscosity, or, on the contrary, of acceleration and rupture. All this, lines and measurable speeds constitutes an *assemblage*. A book is an assemblage of this kind, and as such is unattributable. It is a multiplicity (Deleuze and Guattari 1988: 5).

Deleuze and Guattari (1988, 2) resist any singular definition of an assemblage. As a book an assemblage is a multiplicity, they claim, only then to then to state that 'we don't yet know what the multiple entails'. One answer is that an assemblage is characterised by 'relations of exteriority' (Delanda 2006, 2) as opposed to interiority. That is, there is no necessary internal similarity between the parts of an assemblage. All that matters is that they exist in relation to each other: in the case of a book, author to idea to ink, paper, publisher and printer. Yet, still Deleuze and Parnet (2002, 69, cited in DeLanda 2016, 1) describe assemblages as connected by what they call a 'co-functioning' or a 'sympathy'.

From this perspective, the southern British Neolithic monuments and their environments are therefore constantly shifting, co-functioning, with sympathetic patterns and interactions over time, extending from the Neolithic and perhaps earlier, down to the present day. They are indeed, as Chris Fowler (2013, 2) put it, assemblages. D.H. Lawrence, anticipating the notion of the assemblage, argued that:

> We should ask for no absolutes, or absolute. Once and for all and for ever, let us have done with the ugly imperialism of any absolute. There is no absolute good, there is nothing absolutely right. All things flow and change, and even change is not absolute. The whole is a strange assembly of apparently incongruous parts, slipping past one another'. (Lawrence 1971: 186; see also Childs 2005: 73).

In an assemblage there are no absolutes: all parts are equal and there are no hierarchies, just the constant movement of one thing into another. There is, as Deleuze and Guattari put it, no 'mother tongue' (1988: 6). The priest, priestess or shaman may preside over a ritual at a Neolithic site, but they are nothing without a chorus or congregation, stones, grass, air, wind and water. But there are no interior relations, no essential nature, no 'stoneness' in stone, no 'woodness' in wood, and so on. Moreover, that any point of a rhizome can be connected to anything other, 'is very different from the tree or root, which plots a point, fixed in order' (Deleuze and Guattari 1988: 5–6); 'There are no points or positions in a rhizome, such as those found in the structure tree or root. There are only lines' (Deleuze and Guattari 1988: 7). And this, in turn, is the metaphor adopted by Timothy Ingold:

> Thus rephrased, my contention is that wayfaring is the fundamental mode by which living beings inhabit the earth. Every such being has, accordingly, to be imagined as the line of its own movement or – more realistically – as a bundle of lines. In reaching this conclusion I had – without realising it at the time – stumbled upon a key insight of one of the late twentieth century's most influential, if idiosyncratic philosophers, Gilles Deleuze (Ingold 2011: 12–13).

Ingold is well known for his development of the concept of lines through what he calls wayfaring, a contrast with the concept of purposeful, linear travelling through time. In wayfaring a journey is comprised of multiple turns through unexpected encounters, and where lines cross we encounter 'knots' (Ingold 2011: 148), while maps of multiple knots point to 'meshworks' (Ingold 2016: 82, 104) which may be interwoven (rather than interconnected) and serve as indicators of the complexity of lived experience. The entire confluence of lines across the biological and cultural world is then described as biosocial (Ingold and Palsson 2013). 'The scale of the rethinking', Ingold writes,' we are calling for can scarcely be overestimated... It is to rebuild our understanding of life and its evolution, and of our human selves, on entirely different ontological foundations... akin to the replacement of classical mechanics by the general theory of relativity' (Ingold and Palsson 2013: 9–10).

If everything is connected, then 'A landscape', as Christopher Tilley writes 'is a series of named locales, a set of relational places linked by paths, movements and narratives. It is a "natural" topography perspectivally linked to the existential Being of the body in societal space' (Tilley 1994: 34). This is exactly the integrated model applied by Sims and Fisher. Like Ingold and Hodder, Tilley is also indebted to Deleuze and Guattari: Chapter 2 in *The Materiality of Stone* includes the words 'Shooting Rhizomes' (Tilley 2004: 33). The consequence, he argues, is that metaphors should be understood as indicating real connections. He concludes that:

> To be human is to think through metaphors and express these thoughts through linguistic utterances and objectify them in material forms. The essence of metaphor is to work from the known to the unknown, to make connections between things so as to understand them. A Metaphorical logic is an analogical logic serving to map one domain in terms of another. This is precisely what we do in all interpretative work in the social sciences. Metaphors are thus the medium and outcome of any phenomenological analysis (Tilley 2004: 23).

Ingold adds:

> This is to acknowledge, however, that cultural forms arise within the weave of life, in conjoined activity. And evolution? This can only be understood topologically, as the unfolding of the entire tapestry – of the all-embracing matrix of relationships wherein the manifold forms of life that we call 'cultural' emerge and are held in place (Ingold and Palsson 2013: 8).

In view of such interconnection, Ingold emphasises the importance of interpreting human experience in a multidimensional and sensuous way, rather than through an abstract analytical gaze. 'Perception', as Tilley writes, 'is not amenable to a clear cut subject-object dualism. If I touch my hands together, which hand touches which hand? If I touch a stone, I also feel its touch on my hands' (Tilley 2004: 23). But, the attempt to understand the Neolithic mind is held back at the last step by a modern sensibility: Tilley (2004: 17) adds 'the stone is not sentient'. As Jonathan Culler (2001: 207) observed, the distinction between literal, real connections between symbol and object on the one hand, and representational and figurative connections, on the other, is 'unstable' and 'unanswerable'. Sims and Fisher's goal is precision in the sense that they aim to show how significant, visible celestial events really do relate to landscape features, including artificial ones. And yet it is in the nature of the attempt to recover cosmologies from five thousand years ago that the rationale for any decisions taken by Neolithic people must remain unanswerable. Sims and Fisher's reasonable certainty is therefore constrained by an overarching uncertainty.

Conclusion

The question I have addressed is how we understand the word symbol, which is used by Sims and Fisher, but not explained. The proposition that a symbol can only exist in relation to something else fits well with the shift from an archaeoastronomical concern with single objects or alignments to a recognition of plurality. As Parker Pearson (2012: 49) noted, a transition in our understanding of the astronomy of Stonehenge occurred when Clive Ruggles (1997) shifted attention from individual alignments (as in the notion of the prehistoric observatory) to a focus on the monument as a whole. Sims and Fisher's use of the word symbol is broad and incorporates the wide range of symbols which occur within Turner's ritual field and the total landscape phenomenology of Ingold and Tilley. We can discern a range of meanings from the discussions about, and uses of, symbol. We can start with the fundamental proposition that all symbols represent something else, or may be partnered with it. To be in relationship with something else, or a multiplicity of other things, is therefore a necessary precondition of the definition of a thing as a symbol. However, beyond this, the question is whether symbols possess power, and we can discern the following variations:

1. Symbols have power ascribed to them and agreed by social convention or psychological error. They may be extraordinarily potent but only because they carry collective expectations through organised religion or politics. This may well be the case with currently contested symbols such as the confederate flag in the USA. Their power is therefore entirely a matter of external relations.
2. Symbols have power as a consequence of participation in a world in which relationships are the primary condition of an entangled universe, as expressed through relational ontologies, rhizome theory and its offshoots, such as knots and meshworks.
3. Symbols have power as a result of their ability to create affects or have agency (to create change) as through their participation in networks of relationships.
4. Symbols possess power which is essential in the sense that it is interior, existing within the nature or structure of a thing, whether its basis is perceived as natural, divine or both.

In this multiplicity of views we have to note Fowler's warning (2013: 2) that the 'concepts, terms, series, typologies, and techniques that we deploy are as much part of the reality we are studying, and studying within, as the material remains of the past'. We can never entirely reproduce the Neolithic experience. That said, and to return finally to Sims and Fisher's use of the word 'symbol', we have a choice as to whether to regard symbols as solely representational and containing no essential power, or as representatives of real mutual connections between subject and object, and object and subject. If we pursue the latter then there are two ways to experience Sims and Fisher's Neolithic integrated land, water, wind and skyscapes, with all their human and other-than-human participants. It may be alive, infused with divine and transformational power, and it may be composed of networks, meshworks, interwoven lines and complex connections of rhizomes and assemblages. Whatever the case, Sims and Fisher (and Sims himself with his entire body of work) have helped move our understanding of Neolithic astronomy away from the limited concept of prehistoric observatories and decontextualised single celestial alignments, towards an appreciation of the total, living, ritual field characteristic of skyscape archaeology.

References

Attala, L. 2009. *How Water Makes Us Human: Engagements with the Materiality of Water*. Cardiff: University of Wales Press.

Averill, E. 1982. Essence and Scientific Discovery in Kripke and Putnam. *Philosophy and Phenomenological Research, 43*(2): 253-257.

Benjamin, A. 2015. *Towards a Relational Ontology: Philosophy's Other Possibility.* Albany: SUNY Press.

Berger, P. 1969. *The Sacred Canopy: Elements of a Sociological Theory of Religion*. New York: Anchor Books.

Berger, P. 1974. Some Second Thoughts on Substantive versus Functional Definitions of Religion. *Journal for the Scientific Study of Religion* 13: 125–33.

Childs, P. 2005. *Modernism*. London: Routledge.

Clement of Alexandria. 2004. *Stromateis* 5.4.20–21, in P. Struck, *The Birth of the Symbol: Ancient Readers at the Limits of Their Texts*: 199. Princeton (NJ): Princeton University Press.

Cleomedes 2004. On the Heavens, 1.3.3, 1.3.11, in A.C. Bowen and R. B. Todd (trans) *Cleomedes' Lectures on Astronomy*. Los Angeles (CA): University of California Press.

Cornford, F.M. [1937] 2001. *Plato's Cosmology: The Timaeus*. London: Routledge.

Culler, J. 2001, *The Pursuit of Signs*. London: Routledge.

DeLanda, M. 2006. *A New Philosophy of Society: Assemblage Theory and Social Complexity*. London: Bloomsbury.

DeLanda, M. 2015. The New Materiality. *Architectural Design* 85 (5): 16–21.

DeLanda, M. 2019. *Assemblage Theory*. Edinburgh: Edinburgh University Press.

Deleuze, G. and F. Guattari [1988] 1999. *A Thousand Plateaus*. London: Bloomsbury.

Deleuze, G. and C. Parnet 2002. *Dialogues II*. New York: Columbia University Press.

Der, L. and F. Fernandini (eds) 2020. *Archaeology of Entanglement*. London: Routledge.

Diogenes Laertius 1925. 'Zeno' in *Lives of Eminent Philosophers*, trans R.D. Hicks. London: William Heinemann.

Foster, M. LC. 1994. Symbolism: The Foundation of Culture, in Tim Ingold (ed.) *The Companion Encyclopedia of Anthropology*: 366-9. London: Routledge.

Foster, M. L.C. and L. Botscharow (eds) 1990. *The Life of Symbols*. Abingdon, Oxford: Routledge.

Fowler, C. 2013. *The Emergent past: a relational realist archaeology of early Bronze Age mortuary practices.* Oxford: Oxford University Press.

Geertz, C. 1966. Religion as a Cultural System, in M.P. Banton (ed.) *Anthropological approaches to the study of religion*: 3: 1-46. London: Tavistock; New York: Frederick A. Praeger Press.

Geertz, C. 1973. *The Interpretation of Cultures*. New York: Basic Books.

Greenbaum, D. 2007. Rising to the Occasion: Appearance, Emergence, Light and Divination in Hellenistic Astrology, in A. Voss and J. H. Lall, (eds), *The Imaginal Cosmos: Astrology, divination and the sacred*, 9-14. Canterbury: University of Kent.

Hallowell, A. I. 1975. Ojibwa Ontology, in D. Tedlock and B. Tedlock (eds) *Teachings from the American Earth: Indian Religion and Philosophy*: 141–78. New York: Liveright.

Harvey, G. 2017. If Not all Stones Are Alive…: Radical Relationality in Animism Studies. *Journal for the Study of Religion, Nature and Culture* 11 (4): 481–97.

Hodder, I. 2012. *Entangled: An Archaeology of the Relationships between Humans and Things.* Oxford: Wiley-Blackwell.

Hufford, D. 1987. Traditions of Disbelief. *Talking Folklore* 1 (3): 19–29.

Hunter, J. (ed.) 2019. *Greening the Paranormal: Exploring the Ecology of Extraordinary Experience.* Milton Keynes: August Night Press.

Iamblichus, 1995. *De mysteriis*, 96:13–97.9, in Gregory Shaw *Theurgy and the Soul: The Neoplatonism of Iamblichus*: 84. University Park (PA): Pennsylvania State University Press.

Ingold, T. 2011. *Being Alive: Essays on Movement, Knowledge and Description.* London: Routledge.

Ingold, T. 2016. *Lines: A Brief History.* London: Routledge.

Ingold, T. and G. Palsson (eds) 2013. *Biosocial Becomings: Integrating Social and Biological Anthropology.* Cambridge: Cambridge University Press.

Irwin, T. 1988. *Aristotle's First Principles.* Oxford: Clarendon Press.

Kramer, S.N. and D. Wolkstein 1983. *Inanna, Queen of Heaven and Earth: Her Stories and Hymns from Sumer.* New York: Harper and Rowe.

Krupp, E. 1995. Message in HASTRO-1 internet mail list 8 August, cited in C. Ruggles 1999. *Astronomy in Prehistoric Britain and Ireland*: 151. New Haven (CT) and London: Yale University Press.

Ladner, G. B. 1979. Medieval and Modern Understanding of Symbolism: A Comparison. *Speculum,* 54 (2): 223-256.

Latour, B. 2007. *Resembling the Social: An Introduction to Actor-Network Theory.* Oxford: Oxford University Press.

Lawrence, D.H. 1971. *A Selection from Phoenix.* Harmondsworth: Peregrine.

Lewis-Williams, D. and D. Pearce 2009. *Inside the Neolithic Mind: Consciousness, Cosmos and the Realm of the Gods.* London: Thames & Hudson.

Long, A.A. 1996. *Stoic Studies.* Cambridge: Cambridge University Press.

Lovejoy, A.O. 1936. *The Great Chain of Being.* Cambridge (MA) and London: Harvard University Press.

Malville, K. 2016. Passages between Worlds: Heaven, Earth, and the Underworld in the Andean Cosmos. *Culture and Cosmos* 20, 1 and 2.

Mathews, F. 1991. *The Ecological Self.* Savage (MD): Barnes and Noble.

Moran, D. 1999. *Introduction to Phenomenology.* Routledge: London.

Morgan, D. 2008. The materiality of cultural construction. *Material Religion* 4 (2): 228–29 .

Newell, S. 2018. The Affectiveness of Symbols: Materiality, Magicality, and the Limits of the Antisemiotic Turn. *Current Anthropology*, 49 (1): 1-22.

Parker Pearson, M. 2012. *Stonehenge: exploring the greatest Stone Age mystery.* London: Simon and Schuster.

Parmentier, R.J. 2015. Representation, Symbol, and Semiosis: Signs of a Scholarly Collaboration. *Signs and Society*, 3 (1): 1–7.

Porpora, D. 2006. Methodological Atheism, Methodological Agnosticism and Religious Experience. *Journal for the Theory of Social Behaviour* 1: 57–75.

Ruggles, C. 1997. Astronomy and Stonehenge in B. Cunliffe and C. Renfrew (eds) *Science and Stonehenge.*: 203-229. Oxford: Oxford University Press

Ruggles, C. 1999. *Astronomy in Prehistoric Britain and Ireland.* New Haven & London: Yale University Press.

Ruggles, C. and N. Saunders 1993. The Study of Cultural Astronomy, in C. Ruggles and N. Saunders (eds) *Astronomies and Cultures*: 1–31. Niwot (CO): University of Colorado Press.

Suassure, F. de. 2013, *Course in General Linguistics.* London: Bloomsbury.

Schweizer, A. 1994. *The Sun God's Journey through the Netherworld.* Ithaca: Cornell University Press.

Silva, F. and L. Henty 2015. Editorial. *Journal of Skyscape Archaeology*, 1 (1): 1-7.

Sims, L. and D. Fisher 2017. Through the Gloomy Vale: Underworld Alignments at Stonehenge. *Culture and Cosmos* 21: 1 and 2: 11–30.
Smart, N. 1973. *The Science Of Religion And The Sociology Of Knowledge: Some Methodological Questions*. Princeton (NJ): Princeton University Press.
Smith, L.T. 1999. *Decolonizing Methodologies: Research and Indigenous Peoples*, 2nd edn, London: Zed Books.
Stewart, K. 2007. *Ordinary Affects*. Durham, NC: Duke University Press.
Struck, P. 2004. *The Birth of the Symbol*. Princeton: Princeton University Press.
The Editors 2005. Editorial Statement. *Material Religion*, 1: 4–8.
Tilley, C. 1994. *A Phenomenology of Landscape*. Oxford: Berg.
Tilley, C. 2004. *The Materiality of Stone: Explorations in Landscape Phenomenology*. Oxford: Berg.
Todd, R.B. 2001. Cleomedes and the Problems of Stoic Astrophysics. *Hermes*, 129 (1): 75–78.
Turner, V. [1967] 1970. *The Forest of Symbols: Aspects of Ndembu Ritual*. Ithaca (NY) and London: Cornell University Press.
Turner, V. 1974. *Dramas, Fields, and Metaphors: Symbolic Action in Human Society*. Ithaca (NY): Cornell University Press.
Wylie, A. 1989. Matters of facts and matters of interest, in S.J. Sherman (ed.), *Anthroplogical Approaches to Cultural Identity*. London: Unwin Hyman.

Skyscape Archaeology as Ontological Turn: Towards an Archaeoastronomy Rooted in Modern Archaeological Theory

Fabio Silva

Introduction

That there has been a divide between archaeoastronomy and archaeology is not new (e.g. Campion 2015; Henty 2015, 2020; Hutton 2013). The reasons for this divide, centred as they often are on the debates surrounding British megalithic monuments in the 1960s and 1970s, may very well be historical; but what is less debated is why the divide still exists today. Archaeology has certainly moved on and, with the inception of post-processualist, hermeneutic or interpretative theoretical approaches in the late 1980s, archaeologists began to be interested in, among other things, belief systems, worldviews and cosmology (e.g. Johnson 2010). One would have expected that the work of archaeoastronomers would have been ripe for consumption and collaboration, filled as it is with claims of cosmological alignments. However, especially in Britain and wider Europe, this has not occurred except for rare instances of cross-disciplinary collaboration (e.g. Ruggles 2006; Kirch and Ruggles 2019). Archaeoastronomy's sister fields of ethnoastronomy and history of astronomy/astrology are considerably more embedded within the disciplines that engage with their respective primary sources, namely anthropology and history, actively engaging with wider debates (e.g. Campion 2012, 2016; Lopez 2020; Lopez and Altman 2017). Archaeoastronomy too needs to make a similar leap.

Over the past decade or so, a vocal minority of archaeoastronomers have expressed concerns that it is archaeoastronomy that needs to step up to this challenge. Clive Ruggles, one of the key scholars in the field for the past forty years, argued that archaeoastronomy needs to reflect 'the fundamental shift that has taken place in the archaeological paradigm during the past thirty years' (2011: 2). Lionel Sims, another key figure in British archaeoastronomy, wrote that 'a discipline that stands still waiting for others to accept it is a discipline in danger' (2010a: 11). At the time of writing, it could be argued that very little has changed. Archaeoastronomy, especially in Europe and as judged by the vast majority of papers in recently published edited volumes (e.g. Draxler *et al.* 2020; Hernandez *et al.* 2016; Prendergast *et al.* 2018; Silva *et al.* 2016), is stuck in the same rut with the critiques raised by Ruggles and Sims being still valid today. Against this backdrop of stagnation and resistance to change, only a few scholars have been trying to break new ground by engaging with anthropological insights (e.g. Iwaniszewski 1989; 2003; 2011), alternative frameworks (e.g. Malville 2015, this volume; Rappenglück this volume) or methodological advancements (e.g. Silva 2020a, 2020b).

Most archaeoastronomers, however, prefer to remain in the safe space of the 'no man's land' of an interdiscipline, as advocated by Anthony Aveni (see Belmonte 2016), rather than follow Ruggles' suggestion to explicitly bridge the gap between archaeoastronomy and archaeology

(2011: 6-7). The latter is what Henty and myself called for when we came up with the term *skyscape archaeology* – a realignment of archaeoastronomy within wider archaeology and a deepening of their ties (Silva and Henty 2015, 2018). To achieve this, as Tim Darvill, a leading British archaeologist, put it, will require 'integration through shared ontological perspectives, compatible epistemologies and the investigation of common themes' (2016: 264). In other words, archaeoastronomy needs to engage with archaeological theory – a view expressed by a number of archaeologists (Brophy 2020; Darvill 2015, 2016; Pauketat 2016), despite having been largely ignored by archaeoastronomers.

Within archaeology, theory is a set of 'structured concepts, statements, or models that are intended to make understandable in some way a specified set of phenomena' (Darvill 2008, 456). Archaeological theory is recognised as one of the cornerstones of the discipline, its history and developments always represented in graduate textbooks as well as being the subject of many volumes and articles (e.g. Bintliff and Pearce 2011; Crellin *et al.* 2021; Harris and Cippola 2017; Renfrew and Bahn 2020; Thomas 2015). At present, it is a very multivocal arena, with various currents placing emphasis on different perspectives and research questions. Nevertheless, there is a general consensus towards the anthropological and philosophical currents of posthumanism, relationality, indigenous paradigms and the ontological turn (e.g. Thomas 2015; Crellin *et al.* 2021a).

This chapter will explore one of these currents – the ontological turn – which, like so many others, originated from anthropology before crossing over into archaeology where it is already a quite recognisable theoretical framework (Alberti 2016; Cipolla 2021). After an introduction to this important paradigm, the specific implementation systematised by Holbraad and Pedersen (2017) is explored in more detail. It is then shown how the foundational pillars of the latter have been foreshadowed within the works of some archaeoastronomers, including Lionel Sims, before more clearly taking shape in the works where the term skyscape archaeology was first introduced. Finally, how Holbraad and Pedersen's ontological turn can be implemented in future skyscape archaeology projects is explored. Fully aligned with the theoretical premises presented, this chapter does not attempt to be a manifesto for what skyscape archaeology *should* be, but rather an experiment with what skyscape archaeology *may* be. Its aim is to show that new questions can be asked, new approaches taken and, in the process, inspire scholars to seek out their own pathway of engagement with archaeological theory.

Turning Ontological

Western scholars interested in the ethnographic or material records have routinely taken one of two approaches: either attempt to explain it or try to interpret it. The former focuses on *explaining* why something happens, for example why people behave in a certain way or why they built such-and-such a structure. Explanation is the purview of the scientific method and, within the humanities, it is found at the core of structural-functionalism in anthropology and processualism in archaeology (Barnard 2000: 70-76; Johnson 2010: 12-88). Although it could be argued that processualism is still alive within archaeology, under the guise of archaeological science, this approach is virtually non-existent within anthropology today, where it has been replaced by the postmodernist turn (Barnard 2000: 158-177). Postmodernists' disillusionment with positivism opened up the way for relativism, the belief that knowledge and truth are not absolute (as in positivism) but relative to the cultural or socio-historic context in which they are produced (e.g. Lyotard [1979] 2015). This led to the proposal of approaches that took inspiration from textual analysis by emphasising the need to *interpret* or translate the verbal and material records of different cultures and shed light on the role of the researcher, and their own cultural and personal biases, in the production of knowledge. This influential approach also found a home within archaeology where it materialised in the form of post-processualism, now more commonly referred to as interpretivism (Johnson 2010: 102-121).

As an example, consider a certain group of people that states that ghosts exist (Holbraad and Pedersen 2017, 16). A given anthropologist might approach this by being interested in explaining why such a group believes in ghosts. The research process might involve exploring what social institutions exist (such as religion) that nurture and sustain such a belief. A different anthropologist, more inclined to approach this problem hermeneutically, may attempt to interpret this group's statements as evidence of a wider belief system that informs everything they say or do. However, whether this is done consciously or not, by cataloguing the problem as one of *belief*, both anthropologists have automatically been taking western views of reality for granted: ghosts don't *really* exist, so why does this group *believe* in them?

Some anthropologists have noticed that, despite decades of postmodernist effort to cast a light on the biases and hidden subjectivities of scholarship, there are layers of western ethnocentrism that have hardly been scratched. Argyrou argued that anthropology's questions are consistently treated epistemologically, which is to say they are treated as the clash between two different *kinds* of representations of reality – that of the researcher and that of the researched (Argyrou 1999: S31). The reality underlying the clashing representations is presupposed to be that of the researcher, often of western descent. To return to the example above, the issue of why people *believe* in ghosts can only be raised because the question of what might ghosts *be* has not been properly explored. In other words, anthropology's problems may be *ontological* – i.e. about the *nature* of things – rather than *epistemological* – about the *meaning* of things (Argyrou 1999). Had the problem of belief in ghosts been explored ontologically, the question of *why* people believe in ghosts would stop being necessary, just as it is not a question to the people being studied. Similarly, 'the reason why the things people say or do might require interpretation at all may be that they go beyond what the anthropologist is able to understand from his conceptual repertoire' (Holbraad and Pedersen 2017: 17).

This is not to say that indigenous people don't have epistemological concerns, but rather to emphasise how scholars have been almost exclusively approaching the data in this way, whilst leaving ontological questions untouched. The fact is that when a scholar encounters *otherness*, that difference between western and indigenous modes of thought, the default approach is to treat it as a matter of epistemological difference, i.e. to assume that the scholar and the native are talking about the *same thing*, but have different knowledge, views, understandings or attach *different meanings* to it. Another option, the one advocated by Viveiros de Castro (2015), is to treat it as ontological difference, that is to recognise that the western scholar and the native we are talking about *different things* altogether.

Cartesianism vs Perpectivism

It can be argued that what lies at the root of western scholars 'wholesale conversion of ontological questions into epistemological ones' (Jones and Alberti 2016: 25) is the Cartesian split between mind and matter that is at the core of western philosophy. Descartes theorised that reality was divided in two distinct and mutually exclusive substances: *res cogitans* (a thinking thing) and *res extensa* (an extended thing) or, in other words, *mind* and *matter* (Nelson 2014: 279-280). This ontological rift can be said to ultimately lie behind the object/subject and nature/culture dualities that have been so fundamental to the western scholarly endeavour (Viveiros de Castro 2015: 293). Nature, being composed of matter and being physical, can be approached objectively. Culture, on the other hand, being composed of thoughts is intangible and subjective. Postmodernism added an extra layer to this, by accepting that there is but one reality (one world or nature) whose study is the purview of the natural sciences, while positing a plurality of representations (many cultures) that need to be studied by the humanities. By treating indigenous discourses and material culture as 'elaborate metaphorical accounts of a "reality" that is already given' (Henare et al 2007: 1), one is automatically cataloguing them into this dualistic, and inherently western, ontology that necessarily undermines any claim that they may have over their own reality. In other words, if they claim to be talking about reality, rather than about a representation of reality (they say ghosts are *real*, not that they *believe* in ghosts) why not treat their statements as such? To do anything less is an act of colonialism not dissimilar from the many others identified by scholars (Gosden 2004).

The differing attitudes of westerners and Amazonians towards mind and body feature heavily in Viveiros de Castro's early ethnographic works and are undoubtedly the inspiration behind his revisionist approach to anthropology (e.g. 1992, 1998, [1992] 2011). One of his first observations was that, whether westerners posit that there is a single *world* (composed of Cartesian matter) but multiple world*views* (Cartesian mind), Amazonians turn this upside down by theorising that it is matter, not mind, that distinguishes different orders of beings (Viveiros de Castro 1998, 2015: 191-324). According to Viveiros de Castro's cosmological perspectivism, different orders of beings (e.g. pigs, humans, jaguars, spirits) all see their world in the same way (same mind), but the worlds they embody (matter) are uniquely different. A jaguar would see himself and other jaguars as humans with which to establish the same social relations that exist between humans. The humans that are killed by jaguars would appear to the jaguar as pigs do to humans. The blood they drink would appear like beer. And, when humans hunt them, the jaguar sees them as spirits preying upon the living. In other words, the mind of human and jaguar (and any other being) are the same; what distinguishes them is the body they inhabit, that is matter. Viveiros de Castro sees this as turning the Cartesian model on its head by positing a single culture (human culture is projected to all orders of beings) but with a plurality of natures. Perspectivism, when fully apprehended, induces a certain amount of discombobulation in the western scholar. The reason for this is that it is not merely another interpretation of a reality that we are already familiar with (for that would merely lead to cognitive dissonance), it theorises a reality that is completely alien to westerners. It therefore needs to be catalogued completely differently, not just as another representation or world*view* but as describing very different *worlds*.

The Ontological Turn as Philosophy

In Viveiros de Castro's hands, perspectivism became much more than a conceptual model that may or may not have ethnographic validity (which is still the object of debate, e.g. Apter 2017; Hornborg 2015; Lenclud 2014; López 2019), it became the springboard to a whole new philosophy. This philosophical theory is at odds with western ontology – or at least with most narratives on western ontology – but this is what empowers it to be deployed as anthropological theory. The core of Viveiros de Castro's work is not so much Amazonian perspectivism itself, but that a *perspectival anthropology* is possible (2015: 55-74). He conceives an anthropology that rejects the centrality of western ontology, posits a plurality of worlds and, by doing so, starts asking ontological questions about the nature and reality of things, including the nature of the anthropological exercise and the anthropologist. These observations led to something of a revolution within anthropology, usually referred to as *the ontological turn* and described as a 'bomb with the potential to explode the whole implicit philosophy so dominant in most ethnographers' interpretations of their material' (Latour 2009: 2).

Having identified what for him was a core issue for anthropology, Viveiros de Castro went on to suggest a way forward. Ontologies are conceptual frameworks or, perhaps more accurately, frameworks of *concepts* – those concepts that form the reality, the world, that one thinks with. Viveiros de Castro first suggested this when he wrote that we must start by treating indigenous ideas as concepts and follow through 'on the consequences of such a decision: to determine the preconceptual ground or plane of immanence that such concepts presuppose, the conceptual personae that they deploy, and the material realities that they create' (Viveiros de Castro 2015: 17). Concept is here being used in the sense of an 'ontological assumption' or an assumption about the reality of things (Holbraad and Pedersen 2017, 15), rather than as representations, categories or cognitive processes – to treat them as the latter would be to fall prey to the Cartesian mind/body split. As Viveiros de Castro (2015: 17, emphasis mine) put it:

> Thus, the type of work for which I am advocating is neither a study of "primitive mentality" [...], nor an analysis of the natives' "cognitive processes" [...]. My object is less the indigenous manner of thinking than *its objects, the possible world that its concepts project*. Nor is it a matter of reducing anthropology to a series of ethnosociological essays about worldviews.

Concepts are not evidence that non-western societies think differently, but that the content of their thinking – the objects in the above quote – is different, and that, therefore, the worlds they describe are different from that of the scholar. Because concepts are intellectual they can only be tapped by *conceiving them*, that is by thinking them into being. The ontological turn's mission therefore is not 'trying to determine how other people think about the world [... but] how *we* must think in order to conceive a world the way they do' (Henare et al 2007: 15). This is an important, though subtle and often ignored, aspect of Viveiros de Castro's work: the onus is on researchers to change *their* concepts and not just the concepts they have about the societies they study. This is what Holbraad (2012: 46) called *recursivity*, the willingness to allow one's analytical concepts to be transformed in relation to indigenous ones.

For Viveiros de Castro and those that followed him, the ontological is not merely another strata to be added to the many already considered by anthropologists, such as the social, cultural, political, aesthetic, economic, ecological or psychological spheres. Nor does it somehow lie deeper than the ones just mentioned. The ontological turn cannot be simply reduced to a form of relativism because, as discussed above, relativism itself is based on a Cartesian ontology. What it is, as Henare et al (2007: 7) put it, is 'a methodology where the "things" themselves may dictate a plurality of ontologies [...] a methodology that might generate a multiplicity of theories'.

Ontologising material culture

Viveiros de Castro's approach was developed exclusively with the ethnographic record in mind. However, it has been extended to material culture and, therefore, is primed for application to the archaeological record. The primary sources for archaeologists are the things left behind by a society – their structures, their material culture and their rubbish. Such things can have the 'same kinds of reflexive effects on anthropological conceptualization' as the statements given by people (Holbraad and Pedersen 2017: 200). By treating the *things themselves* seriously, one is allowing them to make a difference to the way we think about them, in a manner not dissimilar to what Viveiros de Castro has argued for with respect to indigenous statements. This approach also provides a natural link to the posthuman and new materialist approaches that have also taken a hold within archaeological theory (e.g. Crellin *et al.* 2021a, Thomas 2005).

Henare *et al.* (2007), who first took this leap, suggested that the way to achieve this is to take *things* as concepts. Their approach, later extended by Holbraad and Pedersen (2017: 209-220), is based on the realisation that things are as much concepts as they appear to us as material objects – they don't disclose themselves as perceptions but as conceptions and, therefore, our experience of them is conceptual (Henare et al 2007: 14). We must therefore discard the assumption 'that concepts are ontologically distinct from the things to which they are ordinarily said to "refer"' (Henare et al 2007: 13). Because things are concepts they, first of all, are concepts *to us*, which is to say that when scholars are looking at some material object such as a ceramic pot or megalithic site, they are already operating from the basis of a predefined conceptual and hence ontological framework. How can one decide *a priori*, before engaging with it, that 'the cloak worn by a Mongolian shaman is best conceived as a "material object"' (Holbraad and Pedersen 2017: 210)? The first step to overcome this is to remove the classificatory power that things have over us and treat them heuristically, i.e. treat them in a way that helps define a field of study without allowing them to limit, constrain or influence the analysis (Henare *et al.* 2007: 5-7; Holbraad and Pedersen 2017: 210-212). The second step is 'to realise that "different worlds" are to be found in "things"' (Henare *et al.*2007: 15) and allowing those worlds to be conceived, that is disclosed, by the things themselves.

The ontological turn's injunction for dealing with material culture, therefore, is to 'instead of treating all the things that your informants say or do to and with things as modes of "representing" the things in question, *treat them as modes of defining what those things are*' (Holbraad and Pedersen 2017: 213, emphasis original). This approach further fleshes out the fact that to be ontological is to use *the other's* statements and material culture to reconstruct *our* concepts, rather than try to interpret those things. Therefore, 'to be ontological does imply [...] that the entirety of the analytical apparatus and what is being studied should be included in the analysis' (Alberti 2016: 174), thereby further highlighting the recursivity mentioned above.

Like many other scholars, some archaeologists have taken a leaf from the ontological turn's book and started to consider both ontologies and ontological questions in their works to the point that it is now a widely acknowledged and cutting edge framework (Alberti and Marshall 2009; Alberti 2016; Crellin *et al.* 2021b; Cipolla 2021). However, archaeologists have largely mirrored other scholars and focused on either the reconstruction of alternate ontologies from ethnographic or archaeological data, or the construction of new ontologies to be deployed in scholarly work, i.e. new ways of conceiving data and how it fits together (Alberti 2016; Crellin *et al.* 2021b: 8; Cipolla 2021: 154-161; Holbraad and Pedersen 2017; 30-65). Such attempts, rewarding as they may be, fall short of Viveiros de Castro's injunctions because, in their pursuit for alternate ontologies, they either promulgate the western Cartesian 'ontology of one ontology' (Henare *et al.* 2007: 10) – the notion that there should be *one* ontology out there that is better than the current western one – or they fall into the trap of reducing ontology to just another synonym for culture (Henare *et al.* 2007: 10). What made Viveiros de Castro's work a theoretical explosive was precisely his unwillingness to seek refuge in the safe space of a disguised Cartesianism. Strictly speaking, the ontological turn should focus on asking '*ontological* questions without taking *ontology* as an answer' (Holbraad and Pedersen 2017: 11). Within archaeology, and despite some early solid work (Alberti and Marshall 2009, Alberti 2016), this is still a largely untapped arena that nevertheless may benefit from a recent systematisation of the methodology of the ontological turn (Holbraad and Pedersen 2017).

The three pillars

Taking the works of Viveiros de Castro (2015) and Henare et al (2007) forward, Holbraad and Pedersen's seminal volume (2017) not only streamlines their approach but also tracks the roots of the ontological turn by also acknowledging the significant influence of Roy Wagner's concept of invention (2016) and Marilyn Strathern's rethinking of the role of relations, comparisons and scales (e.g. 2020). As described by Holbraad and Pedersen, the implementation of the ontological turn rests on three pillars – *reflexivity*, *conceptualisation* and *experimentation* – which will now be explored in more detail.

Reflexivity

Reflexivity is not a new concept in either anthropology or archaeology, where it is often defined as 'the capacity for self-reference and/or critical self-reflection' (Vivanco 2018). Essentially this means that the scholar should not only pay attention to his data, but also to the manner in which the research is done – to reflect upon the scholarly process, paying particular attention to any biases that may have a bearing on data gathering and subsequent analyses. Reflexivity is the mandate to cast a magnifying lens over the often-unacknowledged influences of the researcher's society, gender, political outlook or religious views on the societies they study. The ontological turn, however, deepens the humanities' commitment to reflexivity by extending the domains which one might be reflexive about, to also include the ontological domain. According to Holbraad and Pedersen, the ontological turn demands one to be reflexive about one's own ontological assumptions, which is to say, assumptions about what 'kinds of things there are, [while being ...] open to new kinds of things' (Holbraad and Pedersen 2017: 10).

Postmodern applications of reflexivity, especially early ones, used it as a critical tool to expose and deconstruct interpretations and representations that were silently influenced by the circumstances of their production. Holbraad and Pedersen, however, emphasise reflexivity's potential for generating new ways of thinking (2017: 11-12). Prior ontological assumptions about what things are stop scholars from seeing new things in their data. The first step towards overcoming that obstacle is to cast a light on those assumptions, make them explicit, and then change them. As Holbraad and Pedersen put it (2017: 12): 'It is in this sense that the ethnography becomes the ground of new concepts, providing the lever with which anthropological perception can be transformed.'

Being reflexive in this way can raise instances of otherness or *alterity*, not at the level of meaning but at the conceptual, and hence ontological, level. Alterity, ontological difference or ontological tension, is here understood as 'a function of the divergence between ethnographic materials and the assumptions the analyst brings to them' (Holbraad 2012: 54). It is that which westerners find most strange or alien in ethnographic accounts and is the staple of good anthropological writing. The ontological turn elevates alterity to the role of anthropological pivot, the point of inflexion in the research process.

Conceptualisation

In the same way that explanation and interpretation are the ultimate goals of positivist (processual) and hermeneutic (post-processual) approaches, respectively, conceptualisation is the ultimate goal of the ontological turn. However, the latter has much deeper roots than explanation and interpretation. Before scholars can attempt to *explain why* people do what they do, they must presuppose to understand *what* it is that people are doing. To be ontological is to show that such *why* questions are often based on a misapprehension of *what* (Holbraad and Pedersen 2017, 16), as seen above in the example about belief in ghosts. Post-modern hermeneutics is equally founded upon conceptual assumptions which the ontological turn would see questioned. Prior to the cultural translation which underlies the task of interpretation, the scholar must assume that they are equipped with the necessary concepts that can help the translation process – as anyone who frequently speaks two languages understands very well. To pick one example given by Holbraad and Pedersen (2017: 17-18), it is not uncommon to find hermeneutic insights such as 'for peasants, time is circular, with the past ever returning to the present' in the literature (e.g. Eliade 1991; Gell 1992: 30-6). However, such statements are, as they put it, 'ambiguous in the very least, and often deeply incongruous and confusing' (Holbraad and Pedersen 2017: 17). The idea of an ever-returning past is woolly since if the past is ever-returning to become present, what exactly is past about it? What characterises these forms of relativism is that they *abuse* familiar western concepts by placing them in otherwise illogical statements – they blur the definitions of those concepts rather than replace them with truly alternative variants. Such statements are therefore, more often than not, declarations of the conceptual (and hence ontological) limitations of the researcher rather than being the declarations of the actual, alternative ways of thinking of the researched that they purport to be – thereby adding fuel to the ontological colonialism mentioned above.

To be ontological is to start the research process from the premise that alternative ontologies are *alternative*, that they imply completely different conceptual toolboxes that go beyond the researcher's capacity to use, or abuse, familiar concepts (Holbraad and Pedersen 2017: 18). Using the previous interpretative statement as a starting point, the ontological endeavour would proceed by asking of oneself and of the data how might time be conceptualised as circular and what might past, present and future mean in such circumstances? It is through similar conceptual experimentations – experimenting with concepts of time, past, etc. –

that the ontological turn is 'an attempt to take the challenge of relativism to its ultimate conclusion' (Holbraad and Pedersen 2017: 18).

Much as with reflexivity, conceptualisation is not a new endeavour for anthropology, which has a long history of questioning assumptions that are taken for granted and highlighting diversity across different societies, including different ways of thinking and seeing the world. Holbraad and Pedersen (2017: 15) go so far as to say that one of the most basic concerns of anthropology, which could be extended to the humanities in general, is to address how to conceptualise things. The ontological turn, however, changes these concerns in two ways: firstly, it moves conceptualisation from the side lines into the centre stage of the anthropological endeavour; and secondly, it deepens it and intensifies it (Holbraad and Pedersen 2017: 17). In fairness, Holbraad and Pedersen explicitly state that there is a degree of continuity between the hermeneutical enterprise and that of their own. The ontological task, much like the hermeneutic one, can still be seen as an act of translation. Nevertheless, as the Italian adage *traduttore, traditore* (translator, traitor) poetically summarises, every translation is an act of betrayal. A good translation, however, is one that betrays not the source but the target language, or as Viveiros de Castro put it, it is 'one that allows the alien concepts to deform and subvert the translator's conceptual toolbox so that the *intention* of the original language can be expressed within the new one' (2015: 58, emphasis original). It is this that lies at the heart of conceptualisation.

Experimentation

At surface value, this last pillar might be easily misunderstood to align the ontological turn with a more positivist agenda. However, Latour has already crumbled the wall that divides experiment from observation when he noted that an observation 'is an experiment where the body of the scientist is used as instrument, complete with its writing device, the hand' (Latour 1990: 57). Holbraad and Pedersen further highlight how anthropological research already is experimental: firstly, due to it emphasising participant observation which is but a form of self-experiment, and secondly, because of the 'more of less controlled *intervention* in the lives of the people studied' as well as the ethnographer' (2017: 19-20).

The ontological turn exposes and revels in the self-experimental impulse of anthropology by extending it, much like as described for the other two pillars, to a meta level wherein researchers are encouraged to experiment with what fieldwork, fieldworker and even data may be. Holbraad and Pedersen summarised it when they wrote that 'the ontological turn amounts to a sustained experiment with what a concept, and indeed an experiment, could be' (2017, 20). It also allows, and even encourages, anthropologists to extend their self-experimental habitus to encompass not only the fieldwork dimension but also the analytical dimension: data gathering and analysis should not be treated separately, but as elements of a single undifferentiated procedure (Holbraad and Pedersen 2017: 24). To be ontological is to pass one's own thoughts and concepts through the same self-experimental machine as the people whose lives we study – i.e. to apply recursivity to one's research.

Finally, how can success be measured when such an experimental approach appears to exponentially raise the bar of variance and relativism? Holbraad and Pedersen indicate that success should be measured not by arriving at an explanatory framework that seems to apply to the data (as it would be measured by positivist approaches), nor by constructing an interpretation that blurs our conceptual toolbox while betraying the original (as is so often the case with hermeneutic approaches) but by 'the degree to which potentially useful concepts have been generated... [and] the extent to which this ontological experiment has explicated, problematized and improved existing ways of thinking (2017: 23). Holbraad and Pedersen's systematisation of the ontological turn, following on from Viveiros de Castro's insights, is indeed a whole new way of doing anthropology.

Foreshadowings

In alignment with the pillars of the ontological turn just mentioned, this chapter aims to experiment with what skyscape archaeology may be, especially with what a skyscape archaeology that engages with Holbraad and Pedersen's systematisation of the ontological turn may look like. Having laid the foundations above, it is useful to look at whether they have been foreshadowed in past archaeoastronomical studies, thereby providing useful hooks upon which to develop an ontological approach to skyscape archaeology.

A certain degree of reflexivity has been present within some archaeoastronomical studies. A popular example is that of Clive Ruggles' questioning of whether equinoxes should be part of the conceptual repertoire of archaeoastronomers, considering how they are based on a 'a highly questionable implicit assumption that our Western concept of the equinox is a universal one' ([1997] 2017: 130). However, as this volume is in honour of Lionel Sims, it makes sense to look at how he has deployed reflexivity and conceptualisation, especially in questioning the definition of the so-called lunar standstills (e.g. Sims 2016a, 2016b).

If one observes and tracks sunrise (or set) from the same location for a period of a year one would notice that its position changes in a regular way. Like the swing of a pendulum, sunrise has two extreme positions where its movement from dawn to dawn slows down to a halt

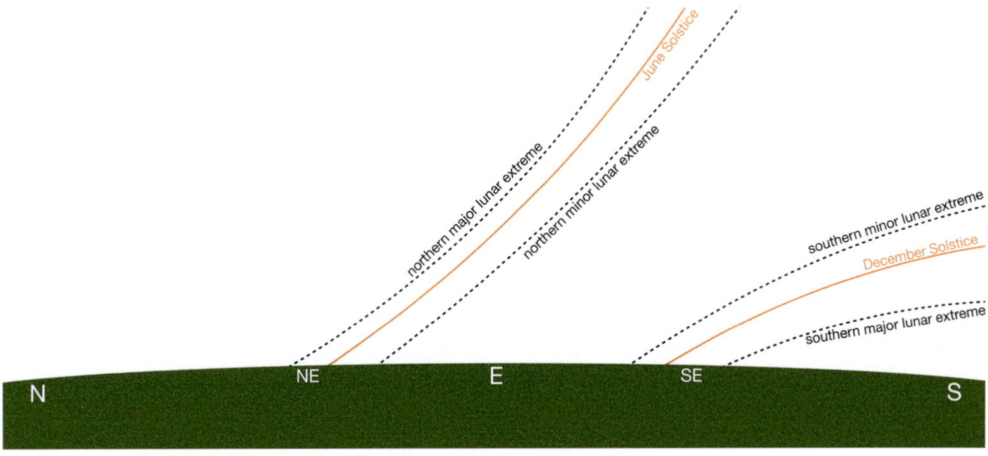

Figure 1. Rising position and paths taken by sun at the solstices (orange solid lines) and by the moon at the major and minor lunar extremes (black dotted lines), as seen from a location at the latitude of London and with a flat horizon.

before it starts moving in the opposite direction. These extreme positions occur at and around the solstices and therefore, from a fixed location and on any given day, sunrise will always occur in-between the solstitial extremes (Figure 1). If one instead observes moonrise every day, one would notice a similar movement over the course of a lunar month. Unlike the Sun, however, if the extreme points of the Moon's swing are tracked over several years, one would notice that they themselves also move between a minimum and a maximum value (Figure 1; Ruggles 1999: 36-37). These are usually referred to as *lunar standstills* although, *lunar extremes* or *lunar limits* are better monikers since the Moon's rising position, unlike the Sun's at the solstices, doesn't actually stand still (Fisher and Sims 2017).

This definition of a lunar extreme is entirely based on the horizontal motion of the Moon and ignores its other properties, like its phasing. Just as the Sun has no phases, and its annual cycle across the skies can be reduced to its horizontal motion, this definition puts greater emphasis on the maximum lunar extreme (more commonly referred to as the major lunar standstill) when the Moon rises and sets beyond the reach of the Sun. Sims has criticised this conceptualisation as one where 'the Moon behaves as if it were a "super-Sun"' (2016a: 69) and therefore ignores the minimum lunar extreme (the minor lunar standstill).

Sims' work, especially his early study of Stonehenge (2006), developed a different conceptualisation that focused on a property of lunar extremes that, according to him, would make them more attractive to societies in the late Neolithic of northwest Europe (e.g. Sims 2016a, 2016b). This property is that both maximum and minimum lunar extremes combine with the solstice Sun to display a reversed lunar phase cycle (Sims 2016a, 74). If one focuses on the extreme positions of the Moon, every 9 or so years when these extremes are either at their minimum and maximum breadth, the position of moonrise or set displays 'a reversed set of 13 lunar phases spread over the course of one year every 27.3 days' (Sims 2016a: 75), which synchronises the peaks of the lunar phase cycle (Dark and Full Moon) with the extremes of the solar cycle (the solstices). Looking at the most common lunar alignments identified at prehistoric British monuments, Sims notes that the spotlight is being shone over those sequences of thirteen reversed lunar phases that synchronise winter solstice with Dark Moon and summer solstice with Full Moon. Sims calls this the only model that does not 'fail the tests (...) to explain the properties of prehistoric monument alignments on the Moon' (Sims 2016b: 477).

In this and other works Sims routinely deployed reflexivity and conceptualisation in order to test and deconstruct specific interpretative models (e.g. 2009a, 2010b; Sims and Fisher 2020). He never explicitly referred to these anthropological concepts – for example, he called his conceptualisation an interpretative model – but, as an anthropologist himself (see introduction to this volume) they would no doubt be in the back of his mind. One thing he did do was rely on the identification of anomalies such as the presence of a wooden structure where only stone structures would be expected by a given model (e.g. Sims and Fisher 2020). Such evidence is usually disregarded as anomalous but, as Sims put it: 'perhaps it is the model, rather than the evidence, which is anomalous' (2009a: 340). He never explicitly pursued these anomalies as instances of ontological tension but, in his writings, taking such anomalies seriously have almost always led to new conceptualisations of megalithic monuments.

Examples such as those of Ruggles and Sims are actually rare in archaeoastronomy, likely due to the fact that hermeneutics and interpretation are yet to become ubiquitous within the field (e.g. Ruggles 2011). Rarer still is the archaeoastronomer that casts a reflexive eye on the epistemic process behind a claim of alignment. As discussed above, before one can interpret *something* one must know what that *something* is. Scholars like Sims have pushed the envelope by being sharply focused on the no-less important task of questioning what alignments *mean* – but what *are* alignments?

Two studies that touched upon this question happened to be the ones where the term *skyscape archaeology* first appeared (Henty 2014; Silva 2014). In the first of these, Henty set herself to use Tomnaverie Recumbent Stone Circle as a vehicle to compare and contrast the methodologies, results and interpretation of archaeologists and archaeoastronomers (Henty 2014). Tomnaverie being one of the few recumbent stone circles to have been recently excavated (Bradley 2005), it provided a good testbed to expand on previous archaeoastronomical work, which largely focused on the orientation to the midpoint of the recumbent (e.g. Ruggles 1999). Henty decided to take a phenomenological approach that, instead of relying on simple numerical correlation between measurement and celestial object, used astronomical software to visualise and experience the setting of Sun, Moon and stars against the entire recumbent

Figure 2. The recumbent arrangement at Tomnaverie recumbent stone circle, Aberdeenshire. Photo by Liz Henty, with permission.

arrangement (Henty 2014: 15). This embodied but time-consuming approach allowed Henty to witness the choreography of the skyscape on a stage set by the recumbent (Figure 2), in a way not dissimilar to how a prehistoric individual could have experienced it at Tomnaverie.

One of Henty's key conclusions was that 'the sunsets at Tomnaverie did not appear as a static event at a fixed point (the solstices) but as a gradual movement from first to last graze along the horizon' (Henty 2014: 8). This realisation, at first sight, may not appear to be particularly innovative – after all, others have made similar observations in the past. Thom, for example, included several observations of the grazing of both Sun and Moon at several British monuments (Thom 1967). What set Henty apart, and what more closely aligned her with the ontological turn, was that the above reflection led her to question the modern definition (and hence conceptualisation) of alignment: 'the term alignment and all that implies *to archaeoastronomers and archaeologists alike*, may be misleading' (Henty 2014: 8, emphasis mine). She thereby opened up room for alternatives that may be closer to the conceptual framework of the prehistoric builders of these Scottish stone circles. The ontological nature of her questioning was not further pursued, but the paper does conclude with Henty proposing an alternative definition which she called 'conceptual alignment, the expression of a religious and cosmological idea, not a precise observation' (2014: 13).

In similar fashion, the present author took a reflexive look at previous archaeoastronomical attempts to study the orientation of passage graves, or dolmens, in Iberia (Silva 2014). These structures are far from presenting straight lines in the architecture of their passages, whether by design or the passage of time, and this casts many doubts over archaeoastronomers' reliance on measurements of orientation of *axes of symmetry* (Silva 2014: 26). This led the author to question the idea that one can even capture the orientation of these structures in a single measurement (see Figure 3, left). After all, it is possible that the passage 'was intended only to indicate a general [as opposed to a precise] direction, and that a topographic or other feature, visible from within the chamber would mark the precise point of the alignment' (Silva 2014: 26).

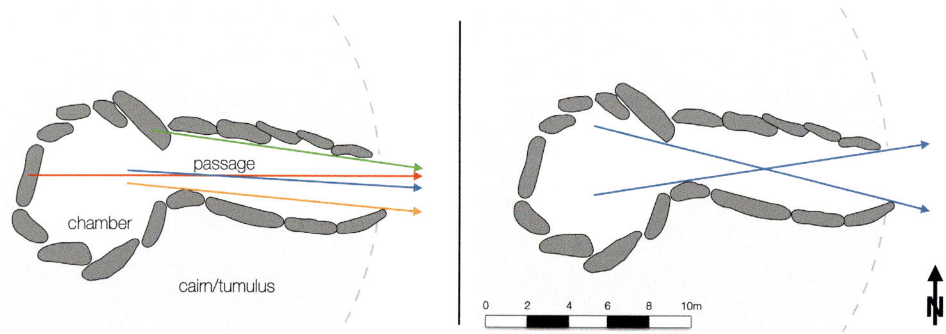

Figure 3. Plan of a typical Iberian passage grave showing different ways of capturing the orientation of the passage by measuring the orientation of a single line (left), along with the two measurements for the *window of visibility* (right). Adapted from Silva (2020a).

What then is a sensible measure for the orientation of these structures? To answer this question the concept of *window of visibility* emerged, defined as 'the region of the horizon that, given the structure's corridor and entrance geometry, can be seen from within its chamber' (Silva 2014: 27). This defines the entire range of orientations that are afforded by the architecture of each individual site (see Figure 3, right). Such windows can be considerably wide – the average width of west Iberian passage graves being about 40° (Silva 2020a: 69) – but with this increased uncertainty came an improved confidence that if an object, celestial or topographic, was being targeted by the prehistoric Iberians it would definitely have to appear within this window; something that could not be said for the 2-3° margins of error considered by previous scholars.

The idea of a window of visibility, as a new concept underpinning the data gathering process, required a completely new epistemic pathway for the assessment of potential celestial alignments. This experimental development had started in a previous publication (Silva 2012) and resulted from what was then a very intuitive series of steps: 'If a celestial event was meant to be observed, the dolmen users needed only to make sure that the event was visible within the window formed by the corridor and chamber entrance' (Silva 2014: 26). Therefore, as was elaborated upon elsewhere, 'If one of the many directions in this range was of astronomical importance to the dolmen builders then one would expect this direction to be visible from within all dolmen chambers' in a certain geographical region (Silva 2015a: 130). In other words, if prehistoric structures belonging to the same megalithic cluster were intentionally aligned to the same celestial object, then looking at their visibility windows should reveal a pattern. This approach presents itself as obvious once the scholar has ontologically shifted from a concept of orientation that is predicated on precision and discrete point measurements, to one that is more akin to the concept of *view* than to that of *direction* (see Table 1).

As with Henty, the above was not, at the time, consciously recognised as an application of the ontological turn. Reflexivity was sufficient to realise that there was an issue of uncertainty with respect to the orientation of these structures, but that problem can be conceived as either methodological (and hence epistemological) or ontological in nature. The former involves conceiving the window of visibility as a measurement uncertainty, but without ever questioning the reality (i.e. the ontology) of the concept of orientation employed. This is the approach that the present author has popularised and further developed as he strove to justify the validity, applicability and usefulness of his methodology through recourse to robust statistical frameworks hitherto unused within archaeoastronomy (Silva 2015a, 2017a, 2020a, 2020b). Alternatively, however, the problem can be conceived as ontological in nature, by recognising that it is not just the measurement of orientation but its very definition that is uncertain. The distinction may appear subtle at first sight, but it is exactly the line that

Orientation	a position with relation to something else
Direction	*a point* to or from which a person or thing moves or faces
View	*something seen* from a particular position, especially beautiful scenery

Table 1. Three definitions according to the Oxford English Dictionary (O.E.D. 2012). Author's emphasis.

divides epistemology from ontology, the line which the ontological turn demands that we move past as we strive to think like the people we are studying.

As can be seen from the above, both Henty and the present author skirted the ontological turn, asking the right questions but without recognising their ontological nature. Both scholars encountered alterity in the archaeological record, which led them to, quite independently, question the definitions of orientation and alignment, two of the core concepts of archaeoastronomy. Rather than allow this reflexivity to stop at the level of deconstruction, they pushed through by proposing new concepts and, particularly Silva, by experimenting with new analytical approaches. All pillars of the ontological turn were, therefore, found in these early works which were seminal to their views of where archaeoastronomy should go next (Silva and Henty 2015, 2018). It must be highlighted that what set these works apart from others where reflexivity and conceptualisation have been employed (e.g. Sims 2016a; Ruggles [1997] 2017; López 2016) was the extent to which Henty and the present author were willing to be ontological not just about the societies whose structures we were studying but about how we were doing archaeoastronomy. As discussed above, this recursivity is also a key ingredient of the ontological turn that, one could argue, has been absent from archaeoastronomy.

Towards an ontological skyscape archaeology

Far from being perfect exemplars, the common thread and unique selling point of the two papers just discussed was the authors' willingness to use the archaeological record in order to ask ontological questions about how archaeoastronomy is done – in the process raising doubts over concepts that have been unquestioned for well over a century. From this perspective one could argue that to be ontological, in the sense of Holbraad and Pedersen (2017), was part and parcel of skyscape archaeology from the very first time this term was used. Having noted how the pillars of the ontological turn were surreptitiously present in those early works, one could now experiment with what a skyscape archaeology that consciously implements the ontological turn might look like. To realise this requires more than a couple of imperfect case studies that unconsciously, and rather loosely, deployed the ontological turn. What future scholars need are some guidelines on how to approach a skyscape research project from an ontological perspective, i.e. an approach that has been systematised in a way that can be deployed at will, just like any other theory and method. To be an ontological skyscape archaeologist one must ask what concepts one must change in order to see the worlds of the societies we study in a way that explains, first and foremost, what (and not just why) they did by encoding alignments into their architecture. Inspired by Holbraad and Pedersen's work, four steps can be suggested as forming the heart of the recipe for such a skyscape archaeology.

Step 1. Recognising alterity

The ontological turn asks us to subvert our ontological expectations. We must acknowledge, recognise and come to terms with the fact that unless one is studying a society that is conceptually close to the modern west, there is a conceptual (and not only cultural) chasm between the researcher and the researched. The job of the ontological researcher is to bridge that chasm through application of reflexivity, conceptualisation and experimentation, but these tools should be pinned on something so as to avoid a complete conceptual breakdown. Therefore, the prime methodological prescription should be to actively search for things we could not have anticipated because they are inconceivable, nonsensical or anomalous to us. It is precisely the *otherness* with which they present themselves to us that can help pinpoint our own conceptual limitations thereby shedding light on the worlds of the researched. As Holbraad (2012: 45-46) put it: 'to think about difference, on this view, is to think differently: to transform one's most basic assumptions in light of the differences that trump them'. Observed anomalies and incongruences should neither be ignored nor dismissed but considered in light of the ontological tension that may be behind them.

Anomalies may appear for a number of reasons, but they always present themselves as anomalous relative to something, such as a pattern, an assumption or a model. It is when they have the potential to raise questions over the nature of what is being studied that they can be looked at from an ontological perspective. They may appear anomalous only in so much as we have approached them using concepts that are at odds with those of the people we are studying (e.g. Silva 2021: 163-164). Anomalies should therefore be considered prime suspects to unpack ontological difference, and hence to identify alterity. Alterity describes those things that do not make sense to us, but that otherwise would have made perfect sense to the researched. When studying the past, especially prehistory, we do not have the luxury of knowing what made sense to people back then, but we can certainly identify things that don't make sense to us and, reflexively and experimentally, play with whether they may have made sense to past people. Recognising alterity, therefore, should be a key step in the process of skyscape archaeology.

Step 2. Being reflexive

Alterity may not result in obvious anomalies but rather manifest in subtler ways. It is therefore essential to deploy reflexivity to ensure that our conceptual frameworks are continuously questioned since it is in them that alterity tends to hide in plain sight. The second methodological injunction is therefore to standardise reflexivity as a core component of research in skyscape archaeology.

Although not systematised in any way, within archaeoastronomy reflexivity has most often been directed at interpretations – such as the meaning of a particular structural alignment – or at the approaches of previous scholars – such as what is seen in critiques of Thom's paradigm (e.g. Ruggles 1999). It could be argued, however, that the choice of methodology and its implementation, the acquisition of measurements and estimation of their uncertainty, the employed techniques for data visualisation and analysis, as well as explanatory or interpretative frameworks are all domains where more reflexivity is needed in archaeoastronomy.

To be ontologically reflexive, however, one must also step beyond those domains to reflect upon 'what kinds of things there are' (Holbraad and Pedersen 2017: 10), meaning to be reflexive about the very things that comprise the subject of our study: the structures, orientations, alignments, celestial objects, iconography, etc. What kinds of things are there to study? What concepts of orientation, alignment or monument are disclosed by the archaeological record? In the absence of any writings, can evidence be found, independent of any identified alignments, that the society would have conceived of alignment in such-and-such a way? Every concept employed, every methodological choice, of both prior researchers and one's own, should be questioned and reflected upon. Equally importantly, this act of reflexivity should be done explicitly and transparently included in publications, rather than merely paid lip service to.

In addition, reflexivity would go a long way into stymieing the apparition of fresh archaeoastronomical narratives that reflect more the conceptual and cultural biases of the researcher than the past societies that they are supposed to be about. This is somewhat of a necessity since skyscape research, by its very nature, is prone to attract all kinds of speculation, colonialist thinking and logical fallacies. Requiring reflexivity to be a central and explicit part of skyscape research projects would not only help curtail the researcher from falling into the traps that have beset many an archaeoastronomer in the past but would also further differentiate scholarly research from non-academic speculations.

Step 3. (Re)conceptualising

Holbraad and Pedersen's ontological turn demands that the reflexive analysis does not stop at the point of nullification of a particular bias but is used as the springboard to look for alternative thought-processes – new concepts or methodologies – that would be better suited for the problem at hand. The task of this third step is therefore to rethink the problematic concepts that have been highlighted by the previous steps. This is to be done by bringing those concepts to bear on the differences which one seeks to make sense (Holbraad 2012: 45).

It is difficult to be prescriptive for this, precisely because any conceptualisation will be contextual and, hence, relative to the situation being studied and the data being employed. Let it however be said that it is a process of translation between two ontological frameworks: that of the scholar and that of the society they are studying. Translation here can be read in both of its modern dictionary definitions because it is as much a process of conversion as it is a movement from one ontological reality to another. As Iwaniszewski put it: 'in order to adequately evaluate non-western celestial lore we need to describe it in terms that are understandable to us' (2011: 30-1). In fact, archaeoastronomers routinely employ concepts stemming from modern astronomy such as solstices, lunar standstills and heliacal risings. But, as Iwaniszewski continued, 'why should the astronomical knowledge of non-western people be exclusively evaluated in terms of modern astronomical theory?' (2011: 31). One is reminded of Viveiros de Castro's definition of good translation, mentioned above, as one that 'allows the alien concepts to deform and subvert the translator's conceptual toolbox' (2015: 58) rather than the other way around.

As an example, Belmonte has considered whether the concept of 'ancient observatory' is relevant for archaeoastronomy (2015). Taking as his starting point the Oxford English Dictionary definition of observatory as 'a building equipped with a *telescope* or other *scientific* equipment for the study of *natural* phenomena' (OED 2012, 495, emphasis mine), Belmonte makes the case that some ancient buildings, such as the Ming Dynasty Beijing observatory or the site of Chankillo in Peru, do indeed fit this definition since 'it can be demonstrated that the astronomical components on site had "a practical purpose for the living"' (Belmonte 2015: 142). Many others, such as Newgrange or the temples of Egypt, Belmonte believes should not fit into this category since they were sites for the dead or for the gods rather than for the living (2015: 142). What he does, therefore, is not to deconstruct the modern concept but rather to tighten its applicability which should be based on the site's functionality and intended recipients. However, in doing so, Belmonte abuses the concept by claiming that said function 'does not need to be a purely scientific one' (2015: 142) despite the clear references to science and the nature/culture Cartesian split in the modern definition. Belmonte, therefore, has not allowed the archaeological evidence to deform and subvert his own conceptual toolbox, as the ontological turn demands one does.

A valid ontological question to ask is whether archaeoastronomers' unwillingness to let go of the modern concept of observatory is not allowing them to see different worlds and, equally importantly, different ways of doing archaeoastronomy. It is interesting to note that archaeoastronomers, consciously or not, have been treating archaeological sites as if they were observatories: sites where there is something to be measured to some degree of precision (like a *telescope*), using *scientific equipment* (compasses and theodolites), and where the research focuses on the *natural* phenomena they may align with, rather than on the social dimensions of the sites. Descriptions of fieldwork methodologies in archaeoastronomy are still single-mindedly built upon a conceptualisation of orientation as direction, rather than as view (e.g. Ruggles 1999; Prendergast 2015; Magli 2016). Why does one go to sites solely to observe and measure (i.e. exactly what a astronomer does at a modern observatory) and not to experience, feel, etc? Where are the qualitative methodologies in archaeoastronomy? Even phenomenology, *passé* as it may be within archaeology, is not routinely mentioned nor described in the reference works in archaeoastronomy and, more broadly, has only been applied by a small number of scholars in this field (most notably Cristofaro 2017; Henty 2014; Sims 2009b). Perhaps a new approach to fieldwork (see below) can lead into (re)conceptualisations of what these sites were.

Similar thinking around how modern astronomical concepts, including astronomy itself, may be behind archaeoastronomy's stagnation have been expressed elsewhere and were behind the (re)introduction of the concept of skyscape into the field (Silva 2015b, 2017b). The purpose of this was not to simply replace one label by another. Rather, its purpose was for the label skyscape to be an *aide-memoire* alerting the researcher not to make any conceptual assumptions, not even about the very object of their study. That's why skyscape archaeology can't be just another name for archaeoastronomy, it needs to become something where the reconceptualization of astronomy as skyscape recursively applies also to the research questions and methodologies chosen by the researcher.

Step 4. Experimenting

Alterity and reflexivity are great tools to get to the stage where one doubts what things *are*, but once preconceptions have been deconstructed, how can one ensure that a newly minted concept is a better alternative? This fourth step is about giving oneself the freedom to be playful, to both wander and wonder at the possibilities of what *might be*. Precisely because of its playfulness it is impossible to be prescriptive about experimentation, except to say that this stage is part of a feedback loop with the previous stage of conceptualisation. Experimentation is part of the process of conceptualisation and vice-versa, in so much as one must experimentally test new conceptualisations by embracing them and letting them play their course. This may lead nowhere, in which case the concept can be discarded and maybe replaced by a different alternative; but it may equally lead somewhere new and unexpected. The route to this may itself be experimental but the destination should be as unmistakeable as those 'moments of ethnographic "revelation" – in which unanticipated, previously inconceivable things become apparent' (Henare *et al.* 2007: 1).

The present author's experimentation with data gathering and analytical techniques based on the window of visibility concept has already been mentioned above (Silva 2012, 2014, 2020a, 2020b). Different research projects will require pathways entirely dependent on the nature of the alternative concepts and the breadth of experimentation one is willing to put them through. One option that can be highlighted involves the reconceptualisation of fieldwork as a laboratory for experimentation.

Fieldwork in archaeoastronomy is thought of solely as a device for the acquisition of data (e.g. Prendergast 2015), the implication being that the data has an ontological reality that precedes, predates and pre-exists the fieldwork exercise. However, one could say that the act of surveying an orientation is built upon interpretation: the decision of what orientations to measure is entirely based on interpreting which orientations are worth measuring. This point, famously made by Hodder (1997) for excavation in archaeology, has been missed by many archaeoastronomers who often omit details of fieldwork, including methodological protocol, as if they should be obvious to anyone.

To be ontological one must go deeper than this. Like Freud's famous iceberg metaphor (Green 2019), the choice of which orientations are worth measuring rests on largely unconscious conceptual frameworks which are comprised of, among others, two core ontological assumptions: the nature of the structure being studied and the nature of orientation (Figure 4). To decide on which orientations to measure one needs to have a preconceived notion of what an orientation is, as well as a pretty good idea of what the structure being surveyed might have been in order to decide (i.e. interpret) which of the many orientations afforded by it may have been meaningful. This is true regardless of whether one is collecting quantitative or qualitative data. The ontological underpinnings of fieldwork are thus laid bare, and they go much deeper than Hodder's 'interpretation at the trowel's edge' (1997: 693).

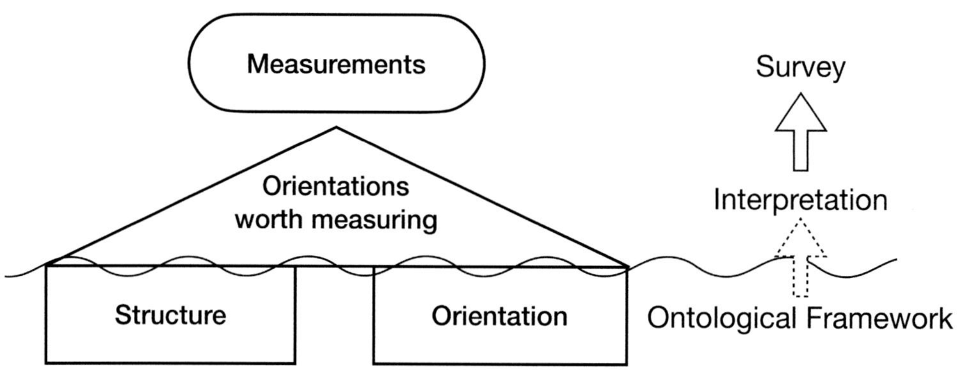

Figure 4. The iceberg model of fieldwork in skyscape archaeology. The wavy line, mirroring the iceberg analogy, divides the unconscious conceptual assumptions that underlie fieldwork, from the more conscious interpretive and methodological decisions that are routinely made.

Under the ontological turn, fieldwork itself should be reconceptualised as an opportunity to experiment with conceptualisation *in situ*. Experiencing the site in its geographical context, armed with the details of the excavation report(s), under the light of Sun, Moon or stars, and with alterity and reflexivity in mind can be a laboratory for the development of fresh ways of thinking. This way, fieldwork would no longer be just surveying or experiencing the site but rather becomes an experiment in alterity, an active attempt to continuously undermine one's (pre)conceptions and identify alternates worth considering. To put a spin on Holbraad and Pedersen's sentence about ethnography (2017: 12): it is in this sense that *fieldwork* becomes the ground of new concepts, providing the lever with which *archaeological* perception can be transformed.

Rather than the fast measure-and-go approach, or the somewhat passive immersion of the phenomenologist, this is an active form of immersion where one constantly attempts to use the site to undermine the very nature of what one takes for granted, such as the reality of the structure (Is it really a tomb? Could it have been used in a different way? If so which other ways?), the reality of orientation (Is this line I am about to measure really the only possible definition of orientation at this site?), and even the reality of the research project (Would the questions I am asking of this site make sense to the people who built it? Are these questions the only ones possible to ask?). The experimentation that is a core tenet of the ontological turn, effected through a fieldwork exercise, should be published as a reflexive report. Routine publication of such details would go a long way towards adding the transparency and openness that archaeoastronomy has lacked with its conceptual, interpretive and methodological assumptions hidden underneath a veneer of (in this author's opinion, false) positivism.

Having argued for the above, fieldwork should not be the only such laboratory. There are plenty of other opportunities for this degree of conceptual experimentation both prior to and post fieldwork: alterity, for example, is not necessarily found when in the field, but can crop up later when analysing the data, as it did for Henty (2014). In fact, Holbraad and Pedersen explicitly extend experimentation to both the data-gathering and data-analysis stages (2017: 24). There is therefore an opportunity here to recognise experimentation, applied to both fieldwork and analysis, as forming another core pillar of future skyscape research.

How then should success be measured in skyscape archaeology? As gleaned from Holbraad and Pedersen (2017: 23), one could say that success should not be measured by identifying an explanation for the orientation of such-and-such a structure, nor by crafting a meaning or interpretation for said orientation that blurs western concepts while likely betraying the ontology of the society being studied. Rather, success in skyscape archaeology should be measured by the level to which fresh concepts that explicate, problematise or improve existing ways of thinking about the societies being studied have been generated. In other words, for the ontological skyscaper a new concept is worth more than a thousand alignments.

Concluding remarks

For archaeoastronomy to become of interest to archaeologists, it needs to renew and update itself. One way of doing that is through engagement with archaeological, and by extension anthropological, theory. This chapter has suggested one possible route based on a paradigm shift that is still reverberating through the halls of academia. After introducing the basis for the ontological turn, the specific way in which it was used by anthropologists like Viveiros de Castro, Holbraad, Pedersen and Henare was presented in more detail, paying special attention to the role of reflexivity, conceptualisation and experimentation as well as the recursive nature of the ontological enterprise. Some of these aspects had also been appearing in archaeoastronomical works, such as those by Sims, before coming more strongly to the fore in the publications where skyscape archaeology was first mentioned. It was then suggested that one way for archaeoastronomy to bolster its theoretical premises would be to become a skyscape archaeology that embraces this and more consciously turns ontological.

What this might look like was discussed at length, both by looking at those early publications and by providing new recommendations of how to deploy the three pillars systematised by Holbraad and Pedersen (2017) to skyscape studies. In the way of a summary, it is suggested that ontologically-minded skyscape archaeologists seek not to explain or interpret a particular site or celestial alignment, but to produce new concepts that restructure their own conceptual frameworks in light of the evidence, thereby improving existing ways of thinking about the societies being studied. To achieve this, they will need to learn to recognise ontological tension for what it is and approach fieldwork and data analysis as laboratories to reflect and experiment with conceptualisation. None of this is at odds with previous descriptions of skyscape archaeology, it merely deepens, intensifies and reifies those calls for reflexivity, socio-historic contextualisation and a stronger engagement with the humanities (Silva and Henty 2018).

How would adopting these recommendations help archaeoastronomy overcome its current stagnation? Firstly, engaging with the ontological turn, in either the variant elaborated upon here, or others, is a gateway into the wider theoretical frameworks that inform archaeological and anthropological research at present. On its own, this would not only be a step in the right direction, but a significant leap towards overcoming the gaps between the fields. Secondly, because the skyscape archaeology argued for in this chapter deploys an approach that aims to 'generate a multiplicity of theories' (Henare et al 2007, 7), the new concepts and methodologies that will be generated will ensure the continued renewal and revitalisation of the field. Skyscape archaeology, therefore, represents a strong drive for innovation. This is not of the passive kind wherein one patiently waits for developments in related fields to seep through, but an active determination to innovate at every turn. Every new research project, new society or structure one studies, new publication and even new field season and data analysis run should be conceived as an opportunity to rethink our assumptions and presumptions, not only about the people we are interested in but, importantly, also about what skyscape archaeology is and how it is done. This is what it means to be ontological, and it is one way to breathe new life into an otherwise stagnant field.

Acknowledgments

The author would like to thank Ingrid O'Donnell, Pamela Armstrong, Anna Estaroth, Gerald Bennett and André Henriques for comments made on earlier drafts of this chapter. I would also like to express my gratitude to the anonymous reviewer and to Liz Henty whose comments considerably strengthened my arguments and their presentation. Remaining opinions and mistakes are my own.

References

Alberti, B. 2016. Archaeologies of Ontology. *Annual Review of Anthropology* 45: 163-179. DOI: 10.1146/annurev-anthro-102215-095858

Alberti, B. and Y. Marshall 2009. Animating Archaeology: Local Theories and Conceptually Open-ended Methodologies. *Cambridge Archaeological Journal* 19(3): 344-56. DOI: 10.1017/S0959774309000535

Apter, A. 2017. Ethnographic X-files and Holbraad's double-bind: Reflections on an ontological turn of events. *HAU: Journal of Ethnographic Theory* 7(1): 287-302. DOI: 10.14318/hau7.1.021

Argyrou, V. 1999. Sameness and the Ethnological Will to Meaning. *Current Anthropology* 40(supplement): S29-S41.

Barnard, A. 2000. *History and Theory in Anthropology*. Cambridge: Cambridge University Press.

Belmonte, J.A. 2015. Ancient "Observatories": A Relevant Concept?, in C.L.N. Ruggles (ed) *Handbook of Archaeoastronomy and Ethnoastronomy*, 133-146. New York: Springer.

Belmonte, J.A. 2016. Is There a Conflict between Archaeology and Archaeoastronomy? An Astronomer's View. *Journal of Skyscape Archaeology* 2(2): 255-260. DOI: 10.1558/jsa.31902

Bintliff, J. and M. Pearce (eds) 2011. *The Death of Archaeological Theory?* Oxford: Oxbow Books.

Bradley, R. 2005. *The Moon and the Bonfire: An Investigation of Three Stone Circles in Aberdeenshire.* Edinburgh: Society of Antiquaries of Scotland.

Brophy, K. 2020. Teaching Skyscapes: Keeping our Feet on the Ground. *Journal of Skyscape Archaeology* 6(2): 268-272. DOI: 10.1558/jsa.19638

Campion, N. 2012. *Astrology and Cosmology in the World's Religions.* New York: New York University Press.

Campion, N. 2015. Skyscapes: Locating Archaeoastronomy within Academia, in F. Silva and N. Campion (eds) *Skyscapes: The Role and Importance of the Sky in Archaeology*, 8-19. Oxford: Oxbow Books.

Campion, N. 2016. *Astrology and Popular Religion in the Modern West: Prophecy, Cosmology and the New Age Movement*. London and New York: Routledge.

Crellin, R.J., C.N. Cipolla, L.M. Montgomery, O.J.T. Harris and S.V. Moore (eds) 2021. *Archaeological Theory in Dialogue: Situating Relationality, Ontology, Posthumanism, and Indigenous Paradigms.* London and New York: Routledge.

Crellin, R.J., C.N. Cipolla, L.M. Montgomery, O.J.T. Harris and S.V. Moore 2021b. Introduction: locating the book, in R.J. Crellin, C.N. Cipolla, L.M. Montgomery, O.J.T. Harris and S.V. Moore (eds) *Archaeological Theory in Dialogue: Situating Relationality, Ontology, Posthumanism, and Indigenous Paradigms*: 1-14. London and New York: Routledge.

Cipolla, C.N. 2021. In search of different pasts, in R.J. Crellin, C.N. Cipolla, L.M. Montgomery, O.J.T. Harris and S.V. Moore (eds) *Archaeological Theory in Dialogue: Situating Relationality, Ontology, Posthumanism, and Indigenous Paradigms*: 151-167. London and New York: Routledge.

Cristofaro, I. 2017. Reflecting the Sky in Water: A Phenomenological Exploration of Water-skyscapes. *Journal of Skyscape Archaeology* 3(1): 112-126. DOI: 10.1558/jsa.32170

Darvill, T. 2008. *Oxford Concise Dictionary of Archaeology*. 2nd edition. Oxford: University Press.

Darvill, T. 2015. Afterword: Dances Beneath a Diamond Sky, in F. Silva and N. Campion (eds) *Skyscapes: The Role and Importance of the Sky in Archaeology*, 140-148. Oxford: Oxbow Books.

Darvill, T. 2016. Spirits in the Sky. *Journal of Skyscape Archaeology* 2(2): 261-264. DOI: 10.1558/jsa.31866

Draxler, S., M.E. Lippitsch and G. Wolfschmidt 2020. *Harmony and Symetry: Celestial regularities shaping human culture.* Hamburg: Tredition.

Eliade, M. 1991. *The myth of Eternal Return, or Cosmos and History*. London: Arkana.

Fisher, D. and L. Sims 2017. Modelling Lunar Extremes. *Journal of Skyscape Archaeology* 3(2): 207-16. DOI: 10.1558/jsa.34686

Gell, A. 1992. *The Anthropology of Time*. Oxford and Washington, DC: Berg.

Green, C.D. 2019. Where Did Freud's Iceberg Metaphor of Mind Come From? *History of Psychology* 22(4): 369-372. DOI: 10.1037/hop0000135

Gosden, C. 2004. The Past and Foreign Countries: Colonial and Post-Colonial Archaeology and Anthropology, in L. Meskell and R.W. Preucel (eds) *A Companion to Social Archaeology*: 161-178. Oxford: Blackwell Publishing.

Harris, O.J.T. and C.N. Cippola 2017. *Archaeological Theory in the New Millennium: Introducing Current Perspectives*. London and New York: Routledge.

Henare, A., M. Holbraad and S. Wastell (eds) 2007. *Thinking Through Things: Theorising Artefacts Ethnographically*. London and New York: Routledge.

Henty, L. 2014. The Archaeoastronomy of Tomnaverie Recumbent Stone Circle: A Comparison of Methodologies. *Papers from the Institute of Archaeology* 22: art. 15. DOI: 10.5334/pia.464

Henty, L. 2015. An Examination of the Divide Between Archaeoastronomy and Archaeology, in F. Silva and N. Campion (eds) *Skyscapes: The Role and Importance of the Sky in Archaeology*, 20-31. Oxford: Oxbow Books.

Henty, L. 2020. Skyscape archaeology: the place of the sky in the academy, in L. Henty and D. Brown (eds) *Visualising Skyscapes: Material Forms of Cultural Engagement with the Heavens*. Oxon: Routledge.

Hernandez, J.P., C. Gonzalez Garcia, G. Magli, D. Nadali, A.Polcaro and D. Verderame 2016. Astronomy in Past and Present Cultures (Special Issue) *Mediterranean Archaeology and Archaeometry* 16(4).

Hodder, I. 1997. 'Always momentary, fluid and flexible': towards a reflexive excavation methodology. *Antiquity* 71: 691-700.

Hornborg, A. 2015. The political economy of technofetishism: Agency, Amazonian ontologies, and global magic. *HAU: Journal of Ethnographic Theory* 5(1): 35-57. DOI: 10.14318/hau5.1.003

Holbraad, M. 2012. *Truth in Motion: The Recursive Anthropology of Cuban Divination*. Chicago and London: The University of Chicago Press

Holbraad, M. and M.A. Pedersen 2017. *The Ontological Turn: An Anthropological Exposition*. Cambridge: Cambridge University Press.

Hutton, R. 2013. The Strange History of British Archaeoastronomy. *Journal for the Study of Religion, Nature & Culture* 7(4): 376-396. DOI: 10.1558/jsrnc.v7i4.376

Iwaniszewski, S. 1989. Exploring some anthropological theoretical foundations for archaeoastronomy, in A.F. Aveni (ed) *World Archaeoastronomy*: 27-37. Cambridge: Cambridge University Press.

Iwaniszewski, S. 2003. The erratic ways of studying astronomy in culture, in M. Blomberg, P.E. Blomberg and G. Henriksson (eds) *Calendars, Symbols, and Orientations: Legacies of Astronomy in Culture*: 7-10. Uppsala: Uppsala University.

Iwaniszewski, S. 2011. The sky as Social Field, in C.L.N. Ruggles (ed) *"Oxford IX" International Symposium on* Archaeoastronomy. *Proceedings IAU Symposium No. 278*: 30-37. DOI: 10.1017/S1743921311012440

Johnson, M. 2010. *Archaeological Theory: An Introduction*. 2nd edition. Chichester:Wiley-Blackwell.

Jones, A.M. and B. Alberti 2016. Archaeology after Interpretation, in B. Alberti, A.M. Jones and J. Pollard (eds), *Archaeology After Interpretation: Returning Materials to Archaeological Theory*. Oxon: Routledge.

Kirch, P.V. and C. Ruggles 2019. *Heiau, `Aina, Lani: The Hawaiian Temple System in Ancient Kahikinui and Kaupo, Maui*. Honolulu: University of Hawai'I Press.

Latour, B. 1990. The force and the reason of experiment, in H.E. Le Grand (ed.), *Experimental Inquiries*: 49–80. Dordrecht, Netherlands: Kluwer Academic Publishers.

Latour, B. 2009. Perspectivism: 'type' or 'bomb'? *Anthropology Today* 25(2): 1–2.

Lenclud, G. 2014. From one ontology to (an)other. *HAU: Journal of Ethnographic Theory* 4(3): 363-372. DOI: 10.14318/hau4.3.023

López, A.M. 2016. A Topology of Power: Sky and Social-Space in the Argentinean Chaco, in M. Rappenglück, B. Rappenglück, N. Campion and F. Silva (eds) *Astronomy and Power: How Worlds are Structured*: 217-221. Oxford: Archaeopress.

López, A.M. 2019. Review: Martin Holbraad and Morten Axel Pedersen, The Ontological Turn: An Anthropological Exposition. *Journal of Skyscape Archaeology* 5 (1):108-115. doi: https://doi.org/10.1558/jsa.38835.

López, A.M. 2020. Problematizando el concepto de 'observación astronómica'. Reflexiones metodológicas a partir de la experiencia etnográfica entre los moqoit del Chaco. *Cosmovisiones/Cosmovisões* 1 (1).

López, A.M. and A. Altman 2017. The Chaco Skies: A Socio-Cultural History of Power Relations. *Religion and Society* 8(1): 62-78. DOI: 10.3167/arrs.2017.080104

Lyotard, J-F. [1979] 2015. *The Postmodern Condition: A Report on Knowledge*. Manchester: Manchester University Press.

Malville, K. 2015. Meaning and Intent in Ancient Skyscapes – An Andean Perspective, in F. Silva and N. Campion (eds) *Skyscapes: The Role and Importance of the Sky in Archaeology*: ix-xvi. Oxford: Oxbow Books.

Magli, G. 2016. *Archaeoastronomy: Introduction to the Science of Stars and Stones*. New York and London: Springer.

Nelson, A. 2014. Descartes' dualism and its relation to Spinoza's metaphysics, in D. Cunning (ed.) *The Cambridge Companion to Descartes' Meditations*: 277-298. Cambridge: Cambridge University Press.

O.E.D. 2012. *Paperback Oxford English Dictionary*. Oxford: Oxford University Press.

Pauketat, T. 2016. A Ray of Theoretical Sunshine. *Journal of Skyscape Archaeology* 2(2): 251-254. DOI: 10.1558/jsa.31901

Prendergast, F. 2015. Techniques of Field Survey. In C.L.N. Ruggles (ed.) *Handbook of Archaeoastronomy and Ethnoastronomy*: 389-410. New York: Springer.

Prendergast, F., A.C. Gonzalez Garcia, G. Wells, G. and J.A. Belmonte 2018. Road to the Stars (Special Issue) *Mediterranean Archaeology and Archaeometry* 18(4).

Renfrew, C. and P. Bahn 2020. *Archaeology: Theories, Methods and Practice*. 8th edition. London: Thames & Hudson.

Ruggles, C. 1999. *Astronomy in Prehistoric Britain and Ireland*. New Haven and London: Yale University Press.

Ruggles, C. 2006. Interpreting Solstitial Alignments in Late Neolithic Wessex. *Archaeoastronomy* 20: 1-27.

Ruggles, C.L.N. 2011. Pushing back the frontiers or still running around the same circles? 'Interpretative archaeoastronomy' thirty years on, in C.L.N. Ruggles (ed.) *"Oxford IX"*

International Symposium on Archaeoastronomy. Proceedings IAU Symposium No. 278: 1-18. DOI: 10.1017/S1743921311012427

Ruggles, C.L.N. [1997] 2017. Whose Equinox? *Journal of Skyscape Archaeology* 3(1): 127-131. DOI: 10.1558/jsa.33312

Silva, F. 2012. Landscape and Astronomy in Megalithic Portugal: the Carregal do Sal Nucleus and Star Mountain Range. *Papers from the Institute of Archaeology* 22: 99-114. DOI: 10.5334/pia.405

Silva, F. 2014. A Tomb with a View: New Methods for Bridging the Gap Between Land and Sky in Megalithic Archaeology. *Advances in Archaeological Practice* 2(1): 24-37. DOI: 10.7183/2326-3768.2.1.24

Silva, F. 2015a. The View from Within: a 'Time-Space-Action' Approach to Megalithism in Central Portugal, in F. Silva and N. Campion (eds) *Skyscapes: The Role and Importance of the Sky in Archaeology*: 120-139. Oxford: Oxbow Books.

Silva, F. 2015b The Role and Importance of the Sky in Archaeology: An Introduction, in F. Silva and N. Campion (eds) *Skyscapes: The Role and Importance of the Sky in Archaeology*: 1-7. Oxford: Oxbow Books.

Silva, F. 2017a. Inferring Alignments I: Exploring the Accuracy and Precision of Two Statistical Approaches. *Journal of Skyscape Archaeology* 3(1): 93-111. DOI: 10.1558/jsa.31958

Silva, F. 2017b. Defining Skyscape, Sophia Centre Press Blog, viewed 16 August 2021, < https://sophiacentrepress.com/defining-skyscape/>

Silva, F. 2020a. On measurement, uncertainty and maximum likelihood in skyscape archaeology, in L. Henty and D. Brown (eds) *Visualising Skyscapes: Material Forms of Cultural Engagement with the Heavens*: 55-74. London and New York: Routledge.

Silva, F. 2020b. A probabilistic framework and significance test for the analysis of structural orientations in skyscape archaeology. *Journal of Archaeological Science* 118: 105138. DOI: 10.1016/j.jas.2020.105138

Silva, F. 2021. Review of Chris Scarre and Luiz Oosterbeek, 'Megalithic Tombs in Western Iberia: Excavations at the Anta da Lajinha'. *Journal of Skyscape Archaeology* 7(1): 160-165.

Silva, F. and Henty, L. 2015. Editorial. *Journal of Skyscape Archaeology* 1(1): 1-7. DOI: 10.1558/jsa.v1i1.26951

Silva, F. and Henty, L. 2018. Editorial. *Journal of Skyscape Archaeology* 4(1): 1-5. DOI: 10.1558/jsa.36090

Silva, F., K. Malville, T. Lomsdalen and F. Ventura 2016. *The Materiality of the Sky*. Lampeter: Sophia Centre Press.

Sims, L. 2006. The 'Solarization' of the Moon: Manipulated Knowledge at Stonehenge. *Cambridge Archaeological Journal* 16(2): 191-207. DOI: 10.1017/S0959774306000114

Sims, L. 2009a. The Logic of Empirical Proof: A Note on the Course of the Beckhampton Avenue. *Time & Mind* 2(3): 333-345. DOI: 10.2752/175169609X12464529903218

Sims, L. 2009b. Entering, and returning from, the underworld: reconstituting Silbury Hill by combining a quantified landscape phenomenology with archaeoastronomy. *Journal of the Royal Anthropological Institute* 15: 386-408.

Sims, L. 2010a Which Way Forward for Archaeoastronomy? West Kennet Avenue as a Test Case *Journal of Cosmology* 9: 2160-2171. URL: http://journalofcosmology.com/AncientAstronomy107.html

Sims, L. 2010b. Coves, Cosmology and Cultural Astronomy, in N Campion (ed.) *Cosmologies*: 4-28. Ceredigion: Sophia Centre Press.

Sims, L. 2016a. What is the Minor Standstill of the Moon? *Journal of Skyscape Archaeology* 2(1): 67-76. DOI: 10.1558/jsa.v2i1.30212

Sims, L. 2016b. What is a lunar standstill III? *Documenta Praehistorica* 43: 467-478. DOI: 10.4312\dp.43.24

Sims, L. and D. Fisher 2020. Through the Dark Vale: Interpreting the Stonehenge Palisade through Interdisciplinary Convergence. *Journal of Skyscape Archaeology* 6(1): 5-29. DOI: 10.1558/jsa.38690

Strathern, M. 2020. *Relations: An Anthropological* Account. Durham and London: Duke University Press.

Thom, A. 1967. *Megalithic Sites in Britain*. Oxford: Oxford University Press.

Thomas, J. 2015. The future of archaeological theory. *Antiquity* 89: 1287–1296. DOI: 10.15184/aqy.2015.183

Vivanco, L.A. 2018. *Oxford Dictionary of Cultural Anthropology*. Oxford: Oxford University Press. DOI: 10.1093/acref/9780191836688.001.0001

Viveiros de Castro, E. 1992. *From the Enemy's Point of View: Humanity and Divinity in an Amazonian Society*. Chicago and London: The University of Chicago Press.

Viveiros de Castro, E. 1998. Cosmological Deixis and Amerindian Perspectivism. *The Journal of the Royal Anthropological Institute* 4(3): 469-488.

Viveiros de Castro, E. [1992] 2011. *The Inconstancy of the Indian Soul: The Encounter of Catholics and Cannibals in 16th-century Brazil*. Chicago: Prickly Paradigm Press.

Viveiros de Castro, E. 2015. *The Relative Native: Essays on Indigenous Conceptual Worlds*. Chicago: HAU Books.

Wagner, R. 2016. *The Invention of Culture*. 2nd edition. Chicago and London: University of Chicago Press.

Breaking the Mould: Space, Place and Phenomenology

Liz Henty

Introduction

While archaeology focuses on what can be gleaned from the ground, archaeoastronomy looks to the sky to find evidence of astronomy on culture that is incorporated in sites of archaeological interest by precision alignment, orientation, or symbolism. They have developed quite separately from their early beginnings in antiquarianism, despite both being concerned with extant material remains in the landscape. During the 1980s, indications of a shift in archaeological theory came with the publication of Ian Hodder's edited volume, *Symbolic and Structural Archaeology* in 1982. This was not an abandonment of archaeology's useful scientific methods of processing data, but rather indicated a new way of approaching the findings in a complementary way; a reformulation in which interpretation took centre stage rather than the processual attempts to achieve 'an apparent rigour and the veneer of a natural science' (Hodder 1982: viii). Postprocessualism broadened the range of questions asked to include elements of sociology, anthropology and behavioural psychology. It was augmented by a number of philosophical strands such as phenomenology and reflexivity, which were mined for their insights to help develop new ways of interpreting the material record. The use of such theories has changed the way some British archaeologists, especially prehistorians, view space, place and entire landscapes.

Archaeoastronomers are also concerned with these concepts and more recently have examined the notion of a culture's skyscape, in addition to their habitual focus on celestial rising and setting events at the horizon. This has moved the field on from the strict rules that Clive Ruggles initiated in the 1980s (see for example Ruggles 1983; 1999), which favoured the statistical testing of alignments, discovered through the use of a specific methodology involving surveying and astronomical calculations, to assess probability and intentionality. This methodology was only possible for large groups of similar sites, such as stone rows or recumbent stone circles, and left little room to explore unique sites situated within their own distinguishing landscapes and skyscapes. In hindsight, Ruggles went on to favour 'more contextual studies of the possible patterns of thought and symbolism' that determined the location of sites (Ruggles 1996: S69). To implement his ideas would have required thinking out of the box and employing concepts that the archaeoastronomers were not familiar with. So, the resulting hiatus in a rather stultified field remained until recently when, from outside the field of archaeoastronomy, two new researchers, employing phenomenology rather than statistics, made discoveries which had a lasting impact and broke the mould. Firstly in 2006, the archaeologist Jan Harding and his colleagues studied the Thornborough monument complex in Yorkshire to understand how Neolithic beliefs and practices were linked to observation of the sky or as they termed it, '[the] people's skyscape' (Harding *et al.* 2006: 26). In their paper, they showed how they placed themselves 'in an environment whereby the phenomenology of experience could be considered' (Harding *et al.* 2006: 28). The second outsider to explicitly use phenomenology as a method was Lionel Sims, an anthropologist who, in 2009, combined 'the

Solarizing the Moon (Archaeopress 2022): 226–240

phenomenology of a particular monument [Silbury Hill] with another robust method, in this case archaeoastronomy (Sims 2009a: 389).

In this chapter, ideas about space and place will be explored to show their influence on subsequent phenomenological research relating to archaeoastronomy. It will look specifically at the body of work created by Harding and Sims to show how they combined these philosophical strands to produce influential and ground-breaking work on the margins of mainstream archaeology and archaeoastronomy methodology. This will lead on to a consideration of landscapes and skyscapes and how these have been interpreted differently by archaeologists and archaeoastronomers. Finally, I hope to demonstrate how the founding of a new sub-field, that of *skyscape archaeology*, owed much to the catalytic influence of Harding and Sims who broke the mould and progressed the field.

Space and place

Lionel Sims' work has always been grounded in his appreciation of space and place, as gleaned from Yi-Fu Tuan's seminal volume *Space and Place: The Perspective of Experience* ([1977] 2001; Sims 2013: 27). Tuan wrote that to understand his surroundings, he narrowed his focus 'to the closely related "space" and "place" components of the environment', adding 'More importantly I try to develop my material from a single perspective – namely that of experience' (Tuan 2001: v). He argued that 'space and place are basic components of the lived world' (Tuan 2001: 3). Our appreciation or imagination of space and place can change through our experience of it which allows a single place to have a multitude of different meanings. While maps and plans are useful in themselves, 'they need to be complemented by experiential data that we can collect and interpret' so that 'What begins as undifferentiated space becomes place as we get to know it better and endow it with value (Tuan 2001: 5-6). As Durkheim ([1912] 2008: 13) pointed out, space loses its neutrality when cultures make distinctions within it.

Tuan added some grounding to the philosophical ideas about space and place and there is some connection with the earlier thoughts of Ernst Cassirer, though this is not acknowledged. Cassirer ([1955] 1971: 84-85) examined the difference between the 'mythical' intuition of space or 'perceptive' space and the abstract space of pure cognition; the 'logical' space of empirical scientific astronomy. Tilley (1994: 16) also drew on Tuan and others and expanded this idea of perceptual place by saying that 'the centre of such a [perceptual] space is grounded in individual perception of distances and directions, natural objects and cultural creations. This space is always relative and qualitative'. As Brown argued, place is not an objective location but is more akin to Heidegger's dwelling places (Brown 2013: 8). It is this engagement with place that makes it an experience. But of course experience cannot be pinned down because it is subjective and therefore fluid: a place experienced at different times of the day or during different seasons can engender a variety of feelings. These may be totally unrelated to the ways in which prehistoric communities dwelled in these places, despite Brown's contention that 'their voices still echo in the landscape', waiting to reveal their meanings (Brown 2013: 24). Yet, in the specific context of archaeoastronomy, as Iwaniszewski (2015: 4) pointed out, 'despite the growing interest in ancient epistemologies and indigenous ontological views, archaeoastronomers rarely deal with spatial and temporal representations of cultures and peoples'. Nevertheless, as Brown concluded, using astronomy in the context of a 'real place within a landscape has been the first step to understanding place', and this allows a possible 'solution to some typical dilemmas faced in modern archaeoastronomy' (Brown 2013: 6). In this context he argued that by exploring 'the place experience', which he termed as 'watching', helps not only to understand the meaning of it, but overcomes some of the limitations of scientific archaeoastronomical techniques (Brown 2013: 7; Brown 2015a: 33).

The cardinal directions define our maps and imbue these with an objective sense of location where the terms north or south indicate objective geocentric directions, but it is by no means self-evident that prehistoric monument builders defined their space in this way. More subjectively north can be described as cold and dark, a place where the sun never appears, while the south is sunny and warm. We need, as Massey (1994: 6) suggested, to 'rethink the unity of space and place in different terms'. In the context of an archaeological site, for example, a monument in its landscape, we can consider two types of experience noted by Tuan (2001: 6); 'direct and intimate' or 'indirect and conceptual, mediated by symbols'. He added that experience is the mode through which we know and construct a reality and it is 'compounded of feeling and thought' Tuan (2001: 8-10). When visiting the past and in particular any period's material remains, we create our version of them through the lens of our own imagination, skills, interests and experience: the prescription is a mixture of our own individuality tempered by what we have learnt as students along the way. In this way we not only reorganise them and create patterns and relationships but also imbue them with meaning and significance, which may be far from their original purpose because of our own constraints. Indeed, Thomas (1993: 25) stated that the way we represent pictures of past landscapes, 'the inhabitant would hardly recognise', adding that 'clearly, no set of concepts or ideas developed in the present will ever grasp the whole essence of the past' (Thomas, 1999: 5). Similarly, Trubshaw (2005: 1) argued, 'Places mean different things to different people, and perhaps even different things at different times'.

Never was this so true as in the way archaeologists and archaeoastronomers look for different patterns within these spaces, through simply wearing different glasses. These problems have been acknowledged by Del Favero (2015), when she observed that not only are disciplines speaking different languages but they also see things differently 'when they look at the same phenomena'. Indeed, Krishnan (2009: 5) noted that because academic work generally happens within narrow or artificial boundaries this sometimes prevents academics from seeing 'the close connections of different phenomena'.

Phenomenology

Phenomenology in archaeology

The philosophical origins of phenomenology can be found in Edmund Husserl's seminal text, *Ideas: General Introduction to Pure Phenomenology* ([1913] 1972), which was first published in German in 1913. To understand social expression it is not enough to deal with facts so he suggested phenomenology as an alternative method, describing it as 'turning inwards in pure reflexion, (following exclusively "inner experience" and "empathy" to be more precise), ... [to] obtain an original and pure descriptive knowledge of the psychical life as it is in itself' (Husserl 1972: 7). This could only be achieved by 'bracketing' the prejudicial assumptions that surround any particular experience to expose the core of pure consciousness and the phenomena immanent within it, according to Thomas (2006: 44). Moran (2002: 1) described

Husserl's pioneering work on phenomenology as 'the unprejudiced, descriptive study of whatever appears to consciousness', in other words 'embedded consciousness', while Johnson (2010: 118) suggested that phenomenology helps understand subjective human experience. Another key influence was Heidegger, mentioned above, whose phrase 'being-in-the-world' encapsulates the idea that humans cannot be separated from the world in which they live (Hodder 2012: 28). Hodder expressed this as entanglement; that materialism is 'embedded within the social, the historical, the contingent' (Hodder 2012: 96).

As postprocessual ideas permeated archaeology from the mid 1980s onwards, science, the building block of processualism, was looked at with new eyes, especially with the realisation that scientific knowledge was not purely objective but socially constructed, according to Johnson (2010: 44-46). Postprocessualism broadened the range of questions asked to include elements of sociology, anthropology and behavioural psychology and it was augmented by a number of philosophical strands such as reflexivity and phenomenology. This was a development of Husserl's critique of scientific empiricism which argued that experience and data are very different. Phenomenology's usefulness in archaeology is evident because 'the material world is a complex thing that is not easily understood in its own right' (Johnson 2010: 117). Phenomenology was first introduced into archaeology by Christopher Tilley in *A Phenomenology of Landscape* (1994) as an additional tool for understanding space, place and landscape. He argued that you could only learn about a particular landscape by visiting it in person and experiencing it through all one's senses. He later explained, 'A phenomenological perspective provides a general philosophical background for understanding material forms: an attitude, an orientation, a disposition, a mode of understanding' (Tilley 2013: 202). The picture drawn from verifiable data, measurement, size, location and so on 'can never even approximate an understanding derived from the nuances of being in the field, of experiencing place' (Tilley 2013: 204). In other words, as Johnson pointed out (2010: 117), 'the physical experience of the monument affects its perception'. Tilley concluded that the overriding purpose of phenomenology was to form a relationship with the past through our senses, though he pointed out that phenomenological narratives, written from individual perspectives are 'in principle, endless' (Tilley 1994: 32).

For Thomas (2006: 57), the keystone of the phenomenological approach was that 'the subjective aspects of experience are not superficial elements...but are the means through which the material world reveals itself to us'. He (Thomas 2006, 54) also argued that it was Tilley who was the 'principal inspiration' behind the phenomenological approach. However that turning point could be identified earlier with Timothy Ingold's work on taskscapes and Richard Bradley's perceptions of monumental culture, both predating Tilley's book. For example, Ingold (1993: 159) drew on Merleau-Ponty's idea that in the act of observing the world we participate in it, to find a more meaningful narrative about the past from the present, while Bradley (1993: 47-49) examined the built-in experiential nature of monuments. The premise for these authors was that landscapes are not places devoid of meaning but are part of a cultural lifeworld for the people who inhabit them and phenomenology helps recover this. There are no rules when using a phenomenological approach so each researcher is allowed to make his/her own observations; observations which are as valid as any others. Of course, there have been many criticisms and questions asked of an approach which relies on sensory experiences: does the experience differ from person to person or change with gender, age or occupation and so on? Similarly Brück (2005: 54, 59) questioned whether contemporary experience in the field 'can ever approximate the actual experience of the past', concluding that phenomenological archaeology projects 'modern Western concepts of the person into the past'. Nevertheless these experiential experiments often provide important new insights while allowing a creativity which is not completely unfettered but which springs from a sense of being or belonging in the space under consideration.

Springing from phenomenology, reflexivity is expressed as the 'need to be *aware* of our personal responses and to be able to make choices about how to use them ..... [and] also be aware of the personal, social and cultural contexts in which we live and work and to understand how these impact on the ways we interpret our world', according to Etherington (2005:19). To this end, Bourdieu and Wacquant (1992: 256) had earlier suggested reflexivity as a way to overcome the partiality of the 'hidden reality' which exists because of the gap between 'objective truth' and 'lived truth'. This methodological approach, where we not only try to bracket out our bias and preconceptions but continuously reflect on and acknowledge them, involves taking a fresh, impartial and objective look at the material under consideration. Hodder introduced reflexive methods into archaeology with the aim of doing it 'differently.....at all levels', from the initial research design to the final writing up (Hodder 2000; 2008: 196). As he explained, 'By reflexivity here, I mean initially the recognition and incorporation of multiple stakeholder groups, and the self-critical awareness of one's archaeological truth claims as historical and contingent' (Hodder 2003: 56). Practically speaking, this leads to a two-pronged methodological approach where we not only try to bracket out our bias and preconceptions but continuously reflect on and acknowledge them. Indeed reflexive phenomenology requires Foucault's 'blank, indifferent' space (Foucault 2002: 43) before we venture forth to experience space in the present and imagine it in the past. However, adding all these checks and balances when seeking a reflexive phenomenological experience, can severely limit what is after all a very personal understanding of space and place. So, despite these strictures, phenomenology is in reality the subjective way in which we experience and describe phenomena from our own standpoint.

Phenomenology in archaeoastronomy

While phenomenological methods were late in coming to archaeology, Sir Norman Lockyer (1906: 4-5) suggested that astronomy might help to understand humankind's 'first attempts to grasp the meaning and phenomena of the universe'. He advocated that 'to get at the bottom of the matter', a thorough investigation should be carried out at the sites, not just looking at their archaeological or astronomical features, but to find out 'whether there are any concomitant phenomena, and, if there be any, to classify them and study the combined results' (Lockyer 1906: 179). To this end, influenced by the late nineteenth century anthropological literature of Edward Burnett Tylor and J. G. Frazer, he recommended the examination of folklore, traditions, holy trees, sacred wells and fires. Lockyer's work was all but forgotten in the later decades of the 20th century as archaeoastronomy dealt with controversies promoted by Alfred Watkins' leylines theory, Gerald Hawkins' computer survey of Stonehenge and Alexander Thom's megalithic science. In Clive Ruggles' statistical approach, designed to be palatable to archaeologists, there was no room for philosophical reflections and at that time, from the 1980s onwards, archaeoastronomy was dominated by alignment-seeking astronomers. Recently though, phenomenology has been reintroduced into archaeoastronomy, following Jan Harding's seminal work on Thornborough (Harding *et al.* 2006) and through the body of

Lionel Sims' work. Not only did these influencers break the mould by coming from disciplines outside archaeoastronomy, archaeology and anthropology respectively, they considered the entire skyscape, not just horizon events.

Archaeoastronomers have of course always been concerned with the sky but by focusing on rising and setting events at the horizon, the dynamism, movement and sheer spectacle of the sky got lost, along with its possible meaning (See also, Henty 2020: 25). If there was less focus on horizon events, the entire skyscape could come under consideration. This had been made clear by the archaeologists Jan Harding and his colleagues in their ground-breaking research relating to Neolithic beliefs and practices at the Thornborough henge monument complex in Yorkshire. They had studied this complex in order to understand how Neolithic beliefs and practices were linked to their observation of the sky or as they termed it, '[the] people's skyscape' (Harding *et al.* 2006: 26). Describing their methodology, they showed how they placed themselves 'in an environment whereby the phenomenology of experience could be considered' (Harding *et al.* 2006: 28). Rather than looking for the traditional solar and lunar horizon events, they wanted to collate as much information about the sky as possible, including the movement of stars (Harding *et al.* 2006: 27). Their research, which included the use of a three-dimensional virtual reality model, suggested that the henges at Thornborough might have deliberately referenced the midwinter sunrise, Orion's Belt and other celestial phenomena as replicating earthly seasonal movement; therefore suggesting that there was a close relationship between the 'people's skyscape and life cycles' (Harding *et al.* 2006: 26).

Of course it is difficult to assess whether these orientations were intentional but Harding suggested other evidence in favour of this idea (Harding 2013). Firstly, Orion's Belt would have risen in the direction of the Yorkshire Wolds, the final destination for the movement of numerous polished stone axes and possibly the homeworld from where many of the pilgrims came. Secondly, the periods of first visibility for Orion's Belt would have coincided with harvest time and it would have continued to appear through autumn until spring before disappearing; both times marking a distinct difference in the seasonal landscape (Harding 2013: 211). Also the extensive use of gypsum, a brilliant white substance metaphorical of bone, was, he argued, 'a profound act of commemoration, creating a strong bond between people, their ancestors, and their earthworks' (Harding 2013: 200). His findings demonstrate 'the close relationship between skyscape and life-cycles, a connection anchored by the monuments themselves' (Harding 2013: 214). In other words the people would have been aware of the seasons but the ritual observation of celestial phenomena would have ensured harmony between land and sky. Overall it was these works by Harding which helped pave the way for phenomenological archaeoastronomy in Britain (see for example, Grigsby 2018; Henty 2014; Nowakowski *et. al.* 2020).

The second outsider to use the phenomenological method explicitly in archaeoastronomy was Lionel Sims, an anthropologist who, in 2009, combined 'the phenomenology of a particular monument with another robust method, in this case archaeoastronomy', to 'address different properties of the same monument', that of Silbury Hill (Sims 2009a: 389). Sims began by evaluating how archaeoastronomy survey methods could be allied to Tilley's (1994) postprocessual landscape phenomenology, which he interpreted as being the rejection of abstract models in favour of seeing cultural meaning as constantly being created and negotiated (Sims 2013: 27). So for Sims, the individual sensation of walking monumental landscapes allows us to 're-experience' some of the prehistoric builders' experience, thereby allowing plausible interpretations as to purpose (Sims 2013: 27). Acknowledging Tuan's influence, phenomenology allowed him to appreciate 'the changing experience of up/down, wet/dry, left/right and within each monument the variable sense of open/closed, high/low, wood/stone' and colour (Sims 2013: 27). Through his unique phenomenological understanding of the monuments he has explored, walked through and observed, Sims created innovative interpretations of how they functioned in the past. His approach was driven by his opinion that 'Thinking from things alone is unable to attain the thick description required to interpret prehistoric culture' (Sims 2015a: 42). For example, in order to come closer to prehistoric culture, he looked for azimuths not declinations and uses a quadrant system to differentiate directions. This he explained (Sims 2020), is because declination is a modern concept which bears no relation to prehistoric cosmology which, in his view, was based on the idea of a flat earth with the underworld below it and the other world above. This is not dissimilar to Willis and Curry's own phenomenological perception of the world: 'an absolutely stable, fixed earth beneath our feet, the still centre round which sun and moon and the whole starry firmament revolve' (Willis and Curry 2004: 128). From examples of pre-scientific cultures around the world, they found a similar tripartite worldview; an upper world identified with the sky, a middle world in which we reside and the invisible lower world (Willis and Curry 2004: 135). Science alone cannot help us recover these insights.

According to Thomas (2006: 57), phenomenology has an invaluable contribution to make to the investigation of material culture and Sims drove the phenomenological approach in archaeoastronomy and used it to inform his work. For example, at Avebury, the stone circle was connected to the Sanctuary, a pillar and post circle, by a double row (a and b) of about 100 standing stones known as the West Kennett Avenue (Sims 2015a). No stone was erected at position 30b and despite numerous archaeological studies there had not been a satisfactory explanation for this phenomenon. Nevertheless Sims found that the surviving stones fluctuated in height to be level with their background horizons; a finding that could not have been made without repeated observational processions along the avenue. Therefore, from his physical experience of the avenue, Sims concluded that 'position 30b is shown to combine a lunar-solar paired alignment on dark moon at the winter solstice' (Sims 2015a: 56).

Other important findings, informed by this phenomenological approach, come from his work on Silbury Hill, an artificial chalk mound, deliberately truncated, near Avebury. Sims was always innovative, not only in his theories but in his methods of testing them. For example, over the years he developed tests to compare numerous logically possible alternative arrangements of the sites within their local landscape, to discover the reasons why they had been precisely placed in the configuration needed for the builders' cosmological purposes. He used these methods to particular advantage in his examination of the Avebury monument complex (Sims 2009a). There Sims systematically explored all thirty of the possible avenues to and from Avebury to account for Silbury Hill's positioning in the complex. Built into Silbury Hill's terrace is a short arc of white chalk which suggested to him that it was a simulacrum of the moonset when viewed from a certain position from the southern inner stone circle centre (Sims 2009a: 403). Continuing along five of the different paths afforded, he found that the arc of chalk, 'is a representation of the first or last glint of crescent moon in its waning crescent, dark, and waxing crescent phases on the horizon when rising or setting', so that Silbury Hill acts as a 'lunar facsimile' (Sims 2009a: 404-405). This appealing lunar explanation is in contrast to how other investigators have interpreted the use of white materials, gypsum in the case of Harding above, or the concentration of quartz scatters at recumbent stone circles, where Bradley admitted that colour might have been important and that moonlight would have created a special effect by picking out the pieces of quartz (Bradley 2005: 20, 112).

Sims did not restrict himself to single sites but also suggested that only through landscape phenomenology could he link sites, such as Stonehenge, Avebury and Silbury Hill, together in a three-dimensional monumental complex, which on the face of their two-dimensional plan views have different properties. He explained, 'Landscape phenomenology places the embodied active individual within the landscape context of the locally related monuments considered as a single complex' (Sims 2013: 28). That is not to say that Sims was uncritical of a phenomenological approach, being aware that any view is 'embedded in a political and cultural context', adding that 'We do not directly observe reality – we construct it to make it intelligible' (Sims 2010a: 8). His rider was that while phenomenology was a useful method to find what is individually observed, it would not be able to uncover the collective experience of that culture (Sims 2013: 28). He uses it as one method in his multidisciplinary approach, which also combines anthropology, archaeology, linguistics, folk-lore and myth, arguing that the statistical method is not the only method available to archaeoastronomy (Sims 2010a: 10, 25). Rather than relying on a singular approach, he argued that the combination of these enabled emergent properties 'exponentially reduce the number of testable interpretations' (Sims 2010a: 26). To this extent he suggested that 'monument design and landscape context as a terrain of choices... together with the skyscape' could be studied as coupled systems (Sims 2010b: 85). These factors and their astronomical dimensions can be modelled using computer technology to provide a test-bed for alternative hypotheses (Sims 2010c. 2015b: 337): this helps reduce the subjectivity which is associated with phenomenology. Additionally, he has never allied himself to any camps and spent a considerable amount of effort disproving Gillings' 2008 interpretation of Avebury which suggested that the Beckhampton Avenue did not stretch as far as Fox's Covert when, according to Sims, it did (Gillings *et al.* 2008; Sims 2009b). Similarly he contested Ruggles' view that the cove at the northern end of the Avebury circle had no 'discernible commonality' with the others (Sims 2010a: 24).

Sims agreed that Ruggles' statistical methods left little room for researching individual monuments which is why he is so rigorous in explaining his methods, as they had never been combined in this way before in archaeoastronomy. In his words he developed a 'methodology which considers prehistoric monuments, skyscape and landscape as coupled systems amenable to a multi-disciplinary interpretive method integrated by the concept of re-emergence' and consequently 'decoded' both Stonehenge and the Avebury monument complex (Sims 2013: 32-33). His vision for archaeoastronomy was that it is the 'keystone discipline that can unlock impediments in each discipline [archaeology and anthropology] to raise our power to understand the past' (Sims 2013: 33). For an archaeoastronomy, as evidenced by the majority of papers presented at the European Society for Astronomy in Culture (SEAC) conferences, entrenched in surveying for precision alignments to the exclusion of cultural context, Sims' research was and is certainly a departure. However, in the greater part of archaeoastronomical studies, his innovative ideas have been largely unrecognised and this was evident in Ruggles' 'running around in circles' address (Ruggles 2011) which critiqued the lack of progress in archaeoastronomy.

While the take up of phenomenology in archaeoastronomy is limited to date, there have been some attempts to incorporate it along with other interdisciplinary approaches in more comprehensive archaeoastronomical studies. Examples include Silva's (2014) examination of Portuguese dolmens, the results of which were also corroborated by folklore; Ilaria Cristofaro's (2017) exploration of the reflection of the sky in water which was an auto-ethnographic project using reflexive phenomenology and my own research at Tomnaverie recumbent stone circle (Henty 2014).

Landscapes and Skyscapes

In archaeology and archaeoastronomy the dichotomy between landscape and skyscape, which has been created because of differing viewpoints, is less than helpful when interpreting prehistoric culture. Whatever happens seasonally on the land is the result of the cyclical movements of the Sun in terms of determining the times of planting, growing and harvesting. This is attested to by the many examples of monuments that have been found to be aligned either to the Sun, the Moon or the Stars. While contemporary societies may have modified this land-sky relationship so we can have strawberries on the table at Christmas for example and no longer need to navigate by the stars or synchronise other rituals with the Moon's phases, prehistoric life, lived on the land, mirrored the all important cycles in the sky.

The dichotomy is played out by archaeologists who generally ignore the sky and archaeoastronomers who generally neglect the landscape which lies between monument and horizon. Like space and place, landscape cannot be an objectified location; you do not see landscapes denoted on maps, they are not fenced in by neat borders; rather they exist in the mind. They cannot be neutral as they reflect cultural experience, expression and even desirability or displeasure: Blake's 'green and pleasant land' (1810); Hockney's 'A Bigger Green Valley' (2008); Wordsworth's 'daffodils' (1807) or T.S. Elliot's 'The Waste Land' (1922) are some examples of subjective views of landscape. As Bender (2006: 303) argued, because they are open to many understandings they are both volatile and contested, with endless permutations. Tilley and Cameron-Daum's observation (2017: 5) that 'A landscape is certainly a complex kind of thing' could not be more apt. Nevertheless and before these problems were really understood or debated, landscape archaeology came into its own in the 1970s, following the 1974 publication of *Landscape Archaeology* by Aston and Rowley. These early studies were limited in scope and failed to recognise historical, gender, age, class and religious differences, according to Bender (1992: 735).

The current archaeological view of landscape owes much to the preparatory work of Ingold (1993) and Tilley (1994), referenced earlier. While prehistoric monuments had traditionally been thought of and excavated as sites, after their insights they became considered within and as part of their landscapes with other nearby monuments forming part of a monumental complex, (see for example Darvill 1997, 2006; Harding *et al.* 2006). However as Schofield pointed out, we should not be misled by thinking that prehistoric architecture is of paramount significance within these landscapes as ethnography has shown the critical importance of natural features such as hills, rivers and so on in 'the mythic and cosmological worlds' of hunter-gatherers and early farmers (Schofield *et al.* 2011: 52). They point to a growing trend within archaeology to study the 'archaeology of past landscape' to find out how societies viewed and shaped their landscapes (Schofield *et al.* 2011: 75). Cooney agreed, saying that landscape 'is the relationship constructed between people and the places they inhabit' (Cooney 2012: 6), adding that while today we might see it as the background for economic and social activity, in the past 'it would have been seen as alive' (Cooney 2012: 20).

It is an irony that these mythic and cosmological worlds must also include the skyscape; a term that did not appear in either the archaeological or the archaeoastronomical literature until Harding in 2006 and Sims in 2010c respectively. More attention should be paid to Sims' idea of 'coupled systems', mentioned earlier. Independently, though perhaps unconsciously informed by these ideas, the notion of skyscapes gained traction through a series of sessions at the Theoretical Archaeology Group annual conferences between 2012 and 2016 and the publication of *Skyscapes: The Role and Importance of the Sky in Archaeology*, edited by Fabio Silva and Nicholas Campion (2015). Skyscape(s), both as a term and a concept, was developed to explore the cultural engagement that societies had/have with the sky and why skyscapes are important, as well as the suggestion that its use would distance it from old archaeoastronomical assumptions so that 'new connections can be crafted' (Silva 2015: 3). Harding and his colleagues did not explicitly explain their use of skyscape but it can be inferred from a close reading of their paper. This shows how they made a distinction between the sky as being part of the natural world which could be reproduced with the use of planetarium software and the people's skyscape which is imbued with meaning. Drawing on Cumming's use of landscape, Silva (2015: 2) expressed this idea by saying 'the sky is a natural phenomenon that is turned into a cultural skyscape through human agency'. As yet the usage of the term skyscape varies: for example, Sims spoke of 'a less restricted definition of landscape which includes skyscape' (Sims 2009a: 389) and Brown has recognised skyscape as the sky 'set in scene by people, landscape and monument' (Brown 2015b: 95).

Perhaps the inevitable next step was to create a new methodology or even a subfield to advance the study of the skyscape to find out its integration in or impact on cultures throughout the world. After much discussion, Fabio Silva and I thought *skyscape archaeology* would be appropriate and we independently trialled it individual papers in 2014 in order to propose its usefulness (Silva 2014; Henty 2014). I specifically aimed for subsequent studies to incorporate 'the awareness of location and landscape and the integration of the sky with all its associated events' (Henty 2014: 57). To a certain extent we too were outsiders to archaeoastronomy, having come from different academic backgrounds so we were able as relative newcomers to view archaeoastronomy with fresh and critical eyes. Together we founded the *Journal of Skyscape Archaeology* in 2015 as a venue for 'cross-fertilization' between archaeoastronomy, archaeology, cultural astronomy, anthropology and history (Silva and Henty 2015: 1). Harding and Sims were also from different disciplines but, in retrospect, they were both practising skyscape archaeology before it had even acquired a name and from my perspective, their influence helped shape its later form.

Conclusion

When we view space, place, landscape and skyscape through a phenomenological lens we obviously describe our experience in a very personal way. Yet literature and art show that our subjective responses are very similar to what might be called a collective experience. For example, who has not metaphorically relaxed in Blake's 'green and pleasant land', felt joy at Wordsworth's 'golden daffodils; beside the lake, beneath the trees', or been exhilarated by T. S. Eliot's suggestion that 'in the mountains, there you feel free'. The large number of visitors to prehistoric sites or the almost obligatory stopping off at predesignated 'viewing points', seems to underline how we respond collectively to places which have been judged at some point to be remarkable in some way. In relation to archaeological sites, they remind us that those monuments created in prehistory were also areas of collective social activity, chosen mutually in the past for reasons that may no longer be clear. Phenomenology seems to imply that we can use our present-day experience to shed light on experiences in the past. While this may be possible, as seen from the phenomenological studies outlined here, phenomenology has to proceed on the basis of it being combined with detailed archaeological and archaeoastronomical methodology and data, as Sims advocated.

Jan Harding and his colleagues looked at the Thornborough complex with archaeologists' eyes and Lionel Sims continued to examine prehistoric sites in the south of Britain from an anthropological perspective. In their separate ways, and from different disciplines, they broke the mould of the alignment-hunting and statistic-verifying archaeoastronomy that preceded them. They acted as catalysts for a change that was long overdue and which was welcomed by a fresh input of archaeoastronomy researchers such as Fabio Silva and myself. In the humanities, change proceeds slowly and is often hampered by past traditions and blinkered methodology so it sometimes needs outsiders to show the way forward. The very notion of skyscape archaeology was predicated on cross-fertilisation and interdisciplinary collaboration and has been built of the shoulders of those who had the courage to break the mould.

References

Aston, M. and T. Rowley 1974. *Landscape archaeology: an introduction to fieldwork techniques on post-Roman landscapes*. Exeter: David & Charles.

Bender, B. 1992. Theorising Landscapes, and the Prehistoric Landscapes of Stonehenge. Man, New Series, 27 (4): 735-755.

Bender, B. 2006. Place and Landscape, in C. Tilley, W. Keane, S. Kuechler, M. Rowlands and P. Spyer (eds) *Handbook of Material Culture*. London: Sage Publications Ltd.

Blake, W. [1810] 2015. Jerusalem, viewed August, 2015, <www.poetryfoundation.org/poem/241908>.

Bourdieu, P. and L.J.D. Wacquant 1992. *An Invitation to Reflexive Sociology*. Chicago: Chicago University Press.

Bradley, R. 1993. *Altering the Earth*. The Rhind Lectures 1991-92, Monograph Series No. 8. Edinburgh: Society of Antiquaries of Scotland.

Bradley, R. 2005. *The Moon and the Bonfire*. Edinburgh: Society of Antiquaries of Scotland.

Brown, D. 2013. The Experience of Watching: Place Defined by the Trinity of Land-, See-, and Skyscape. *Culture and Cosmos*, Special Issue on Landscape-Seascape-Skyscape, Fabio Silva (ed.) 17 (2): 5-24.

Brown, D. 2015a. 'Skyscapes: Present and Past – From Sustainability to Interpreting Ancient Remains', in F. Silva and N. Campion (eds) *Skyscapes: The Role and Importance of the Sky in Archaeology*, Oxford: Oxbow Books.

Brown, D. 2015b. Exploring skyscape in Stellarium. *Journal of Skyscape Archaeology* 1 (1): 93-112.

Brück, J. 2005. Experiencing the past? The development of a phenomenological archaeology in British prehistory. *Archaeological Dialogues* 12 (1): 45-72.

Cassirer, E. [1955] 1971. *The Philosophy of Symbolic Forms, Vol. 2, Mythical Thought.* Connecticut, USA: Yale University Press.

Cooney, G. 2012. *Landscapes of Neolithic Ireland.* Oxford: Routledge.

Cristofaro, I. 2017. Reflecting the Sky in Water: A Phenomenological Exploration of Water-skyscapes. *Journal of Skyscape* Archaeology, 3 (1): 112-126.

Darvill, T. 1997. Ever increasing circles: The sacred geographies of Stonehenge and its landscape. In B. Cunliffe and C. Renfrew (eds) *Science and Stonehenge.* Oxford: Oxford University Press.

Darvill, T. 2006. *Stonehenge: The Biography of a Landscape.* Stroud: Tempus.

Del Favero, M. 2015. Academic Disciplines - Disciplines and the Structure of Higher Education, Discipline Classification Systems, Discipline Differences, viewed October 2015, <education.stateuniversity.com/pages/1723/Academic-Disciplines.html>.

Durkheim, È. [1912] 2008. *The Elementary Forms of Religious Life.* Trans, C. Cosman, abridged with an Introduction and Notes by M. S. Cladis. Oxford: Oxford University Press.

Elliot, T.S. 1922. The Waste Land, viewed August 2020, <https://www.bl.uk/works/the-waste-land>.

Etherington, K. 2005. *Becoming a Reflexive Researcher: Using Ourselves in Research.* London: Jessica Kingsley Publishers.

Foucault, M. 2002. *Archaeology of Knowledge.* Oxford: Routledge.

Gillings, M., J. Pollard, D. Wheatley and R. Peterson 2008. *Landscapes of the Megaliths: Excavation and Fieldwork on the Avebury Monuments, 1997-2003.* Oxford: Oxbow.

Grigsby, J. 2018. Skyscapes, landscapes, and the drama of Proto-Indo-European myth. PhD thesis, Bournemouth University.

Harding, J. 2013. *Cult, Religion and Pilgrimage: Archaeological Investigations at the Neolithic and Bronze Age Monument Complex of Thornborough, North Yorkshire.* York: Council for British Archaeology Research Report 174.

Harding, J., B. Johnston and G. Goodrick 2006. Neolithic Cosmology and the Monument Complex of Thornborough, North Yorkshire. *Archaeoastronomy: The Journal of archaeoastronomy in Culture,* 20: 26-51.

Henty, L. 2014. The Archaeoastronomy of Tomnaverie Recumbent Stone Circle: A Comparison of Methodologies. *Papers from the Institute of Archaeology* 24: 45-59.

Henty, L. 2020. Skyscape archaeology: the place of the sky in the academy, in L. Henty and D. Brown (eds) *Visualising Skyscapes: Material Forms of Cultural Engagement with the Heavens.* London and New York: Routledge.

Hockney, D. 2008. A Bigger Green Valley, viewed August 2020, <https://www.artsy.net/artwork/david-hockney-a-bigger-green-valley>.

Hodder, I. 2003. Archaeological Reflexivity and the "Local" Voice. *Anthropological Quarterly* 76: (1) 55-69.

Hodder, I. 2008. Multivocality and Social Archaeology, Ch.13 in J. Habu, C. Fawcett and J, Matsunaga (eds) *Evaluating Multiple Narratives: Beyond Nationalist, Colonialist, Imperialist Archaeologies.* USA: Springer Science+Business Media.

Hodder, I. 2012. *Entangled: An Archaeology of the Relationships between Humans and Things.* Chichester, UK: John Wiley and Sons.

Hodder, I. (ed.) 1982. *Symbolic and Structural Archaeology.* Cambridge: Cambridge University Press.

Hodder, I. (ed.) 2000. *Towards Reflexive Method in Archaeology: The Example at Çatalhöyü.* Cambridge: McDonald Institute for Archaeological Research.

Husserl, E. [1913 Eng. trns. 1931] 1972. *Ideas: General Introduction to Pure Phenomenology*. Trans. W. R. Boyce Gibson. New York: Collier Books.

Ingold, T. 1993. The temporality of landscape. *World Archaeology* 25:125-174.

Iwaniszewski, S. 2015. Concepts of Space, Time, and the Cosmos, in C.L.N. Ruggles, (ed.) *Handbook of Archaeoastronomy and Ethnoastronomy*. New York and London: Springer Science+Business Media.

Johnson, M. 2010. *Archaeological Theory: An Introduction*. UK: Wiley-Blackwell.

Journal of Skyscape Archaeology, Equinox. Journal of Skyscape Archaeology, viewed August 2020, <https://journal.equinoxpub.com/JSA/index>.

Krishnan, A. 2009. What are Academic Disciplines? Some observations on the Disciplinarity vs. Interdisciplinarity debate. ESRC National Centre for Research Methods, NCRM Working Paper Series, 03/09: 1-59.

Lockyer, Sir N. 1906. *Stonehenge and Other British Documents Considered*. London: Macmillan and Co. Limited.

Massey, D.B. 1994. *Space, Place and Gender*. USA: University of Minnesota Press.

Moran, D. 2002. Editor's Introduction, in D. Moran and T. Mooney (eds) *The Phenomenology Reader*. London: Routledge, 2002.

Nowakowski, J. A., C. Kennett, J. Gossip and B. Sheen, 2020. Investigating Archaeology and Astronomy at The Hurlers, Cornwall 2013 – 2019. *Journal of Skyscape Archaeology* 6 (1): 53-85.

Ruggles, C.L.N. 1983. A Reassessment of the High Precision Megalithic Lunar Sightlines, 2: Foresights and the Problem of Selection. *Archaeoastronomy, Supplement to the Journal for the History of Astronomy* 5: S1-S36.

Ruggles, C. 1996. New approaches to the investigation of astronomical symbolism within the ritual landscapes of the prehistoric British Isles, in V. Koleva and D. Kolev (eds) *Astronomical Traditions in Past Cultures*, Proceedings of the First Annual General Meeting of the European Society for Astronomy in Culture, Smolyan, Bulgaria, 31 August - 2 September, 1993. Sofia: Institute of Astronomy, Bulgarian Academy of Sciences, National Astronomical Observatory, Rozhen.

Ruggles, C. 1999. *Astronomy in Prehistoric Britain and Ireland*. New Haven and London: Yale University Press.

Ruggles, C.L.N. 2011. Pushing back the frontiers or still running around in the same circles? 'Interpretative archaeoastronomy' thirty years on, in C.L.N. Ruggles (ed.) *Archaeoastronomy and Ethnoastronomy: Building Bridges between Cultures*: proceedings of the 278th Symposium of the International Astronomical Union and 'Oxford IX' International Symposium on Archaeoastronomy, held in Lima, Peru, January 5-14, 2011. Cambridge: Cambridge University Press.

Schofield, J., J. Carmen and P. Belford 2011. *Archaeological Practice in Great Britain*. USA: Springer.

Silva, F. 2014. 'A Tomb with a View': New Methods for Bridging the Gap Between Land and Sky in Megalithic Archaeology. *Advances in Archaeological Practice: A Journal of the Society for American Archaeology* 1(2): 24-37.

Silva, F. 2015. The Role and Importance of the Sky in Archaeology: An Introduction, Ch. 1 in F. Silva and N. Campion (eds) *Skyscapes: The Role and Importance of the Sky in Archaeology*. Oxford: Oxbow Books.

Silva, F. and N. Campion (eds) 2015. *Skyscapes: The Role and Importance of the Sky in Archaeology*. Oxford: Oxbow Books, 2015.

Silva, F. and L. Henty 2015. Editorial. *Journal of Skyscape Archaeology* 1 (1): 1-7.

Sims, L. 2009a. Entering, and returning from, the underworld: reconstituting Silbury Hill by combining a quantified landscape phenomenology with archaeoastronomy. *Journal of the Royal Anthropological Institute (N.S.)* 15: 386-408.

Sims, L. 2009b. The Logic of Empirical Proof: A note on the course of the Beckhampton Avenue. *Time and Mind* 2 (3): 333-345.

Sims, L. 2010a. Coves, Cosmology and Cultural Astronomy, in N. Campion *Cosmologies: The proceedings of the seventh annual conference of the Sophia Centre for the Study of Cosmology in Culture, University of Wales, Trinity Saint David, 6-7 June 2009*. Ceredigion, Wales: Sophia Centre Press.

Sims, L. 2010b. Theoretical sampling of simulated populations at West Kennet Avenue: transcending the individualistic fallacy in cultural astronomy by considering monument design and landscape phenomenology as coupled systems. In *From Alexandria to Al-Iskandariya: astronomy and culture in the ancient Mediterranean and beyond*, Proceedings of SEAC17. Privately published on Academia.edu, viewed August 2020 <www.academia.edu/22251902>.

Sims, L. 2010c. Which Way Forward for Archaeoastronomy? West Kennett Avenue as a Test Case. *Journal of Cosmology*, 9: 2160-2171.

Sims, L.D. 2013. Interpretation through emergence: reconstituting the lost complexity of the Late Neolithic/Early Bronze Age cosmovision by multi-disciplinary method. PhD Thesis, University of East London.

Sims, L. 2015a. 30b – the West Kennet Avenue Stone that Never Was: Interpretation by Multidisciplinary Triangulation and Emergence through Four Field Anthropology, in F. Silva and N. Campion (eds) *Skyscapes: The Role and Importance of the Sky in Archaeology*. Oxford: Oxbow Books.

Sims, L. 2015b. Where is Cultural Astronomy Going?, in F. Pimenta, N. Ribeiro, F. Silva, N. Campion, A. Joaquinito and L. Tirapicos (eds) *SEAC 2011 Stars and Stones: Voyages in Archaeoastronomy and Cultural Astronomy, Proceedings of the SEAC 2011 conference*. Oxford: Archaeopress/British Archaeological Reports.

Sims, L. 2020. Through the dark vale: interpreting the Stonehenge Palisade through inter-disciplinary convergence. Presentation at the Sophia Centre, Skyscape Archaeology Lecture Series, Zoom, 9th June, 2020.

Thomas, J. 1993. The politics of vision and the archaeologies of landscape, in B. Bender (ed.) *Landscape: Politics and perspectives*. Oxford: Berg.

Thomas, J. 1999. *Understanding the Neolithic*. Oxford: Routledge.

Thomas, J. 2006. Phenomenology and Material Culture, in C. Tilley, W. Keane, S. Küchler, M. Rowlands and P. Spyer (eds) *Handbook of Material Culture*. London: Sage Publications.

Tilley, C. 1994. *A Phenomenology of* Landscape. Oxford: Berg.

Tilley, C. 2013. Phenomenological Archaeology, in C. Renfrew and P. Bahn, *Archaeology: The Key* Concepts: 201-207. Oxford: Routledge.

Tilley, C. and K. Cameron-Daum 2017. *An Anthropology of Landscape*. London: UCL Press.

Trubshaw, B. 2005. *Sacred Places: prehistory and Popular Imagination*. Loughborough: Heart of Albion Press.

Tuan, Yi-Fu [1977] 2001. *Space and Place: The Perspective of Experience*. Minneapolis: University of Minneapolis.

Willis, R. and P. Curry 2004. *Astrology, Science and Culture: Pulling Down the Moon*. Oxford: Berg.

Wordsworth, W. 1807. Daffodils, viewed August 2020. <http://www.bbc.co.uk/poetryseason/poems/daffodils.shtml>.